Nathan Cook Meeker

Life in the West

Stories of the Mississippi Valley

Nathan Cook Meeker

Life in the West

Stories of the Mississippi Valley

ISBN/EAN: 9783744661881

Printed in Europe, USA, Canada, Australia, Japan

Cover: Foto ©ninafisch / pixelio.de

More available books at **www.hansebooks.com**

LIFE IN THE WEST;

OR,

Stories

OF THE

MISSISSIPPI VALLEY.

BY

N. C. MEEKER,
AGRICULTURAL EDITOR OF THE NEW YORK TRIBUNE.

New York:
SAMUEL R. WELLS, PUBLISHER,
No. 389 BROADWAY.
1868.

PREFACE.

A LONG residence in the Mississippi Valley, frequent journeys through its whole extent, and years of service as the Illinois correspondent of the New York TRIBUNE, have furnished the materials for the following stories. Within forty years a country has been developed equal to the whole of Western Europe; new habits and customs prevail, families about to be extinguished have received new vigor, and the lowly have been exalted. Innumerable cities, towns and villages have arisen, and more than a million of highly productive farms have been brought into cultivation. Results must follow which will be different from any the world has yet seen, because wealth, having ceased to descend to the oldest son, is divided among many. In no other country have the producers been able to keep so much wealth from the grasp of the idle and the wicked, and devote it to the education of their children and to making home comfortable.

One language is spoken, knowledge and industrious habits are universal, and the religious sentiment guides. A soil of remarkable fertility, a climate rich in sunshine and showers, give abundance of food; and orchards and vineyards abound. Thousands of families, by their own industry, have created beautiful homes, and they sit at tables spread with as good, with as varied food, as any king can command with his slaves and gold. Did the shadow of a king stretch across that region, the red man and his game would linger still. No sentiment is stronger than a love for the Union founded on Freedom. Were it possible for the nations of Europe or of Asia to unite, they could not become as wealthy, as intelligent and as powerful as ours is destined to become with its centre in the Mississippi Valley.

From our new conditions we have new ideas, and they will impress themselves on the society of the whole of the two American Continents. What this impress shall be, may, in some degree, be gathered from an account of the labors and hopes, from the disappointments and triumphs, and from the sorrows and joys in families.

In the Eastern States educated persons look on the comic and burlesque exhibited in the Western character as an evidence of a want of culture. Difficulties and labors which appal the refined, in the West have been overcome. During the hours of darkness and doubt relaxation was a necessity; free from restraint, and unfettered by rules, a cultivated cheerfulness ran into the comic. These things had their origin in the Atlantic States, and they are new as one's children are new.

N. C. M.

CONTENTS.

	Page
THE OLD AND THE NEW; or, the Settlement of Michigan	7
GOING TO DIE; the Effects of being too Successful	20
SERVING TWO MASTERS; or, an Ohio River Story	27
THE STEAMBOAT CAPTAIN; or, Life on the Lower Mississippi	48
THE MISSISSIPPI RIVER, and Plantation Life	79
MARCHING ON; or, Change of Opinion during the War	115
THE WAY AND THE WILL; or, Missouri and Wisconsin Life	128
THE NORTHERN REFUGEE; or, a Refined Family in a Rough Settlement	150
PRAIRIE LIFE IN EARLY DAYS; or, How Settlements Progress	169
RUNNING A MACHINE; or, Results of Extensive Farming	222
A FORTUNATE CALAMITY; or, Saved from Ruin by going West	231
TAKING AN APPRENTICE; or, Modern Ideas of Family Government	243
GOING TO BE A MORMON; or, Life on the Ohio Western Reserve	252
THE SHOEMAKER'S STRIKE; or, the Fortune of a City Mechanic	263
HENRIETTA; or, from Pennsylvania to the West	274
THE LITTLE TURNPIKE AND THE SEVEN GARDENS	287
FARMING AND LAW: or, a Lawyer goes West	295
THE LANGUAGE OF CATTLE — How to Read it	306
THE EGYPTIAN PREACHER; or, North Carolina Ideas	315
THE SHEPHERD OF SALISBURY PLAIN; or, Hope of the Poor	327
A DESCRIPTION OF THE MISSISSIPPI VALLEY	339
Western Pennsylvania — West Virginia — Ohio — Indiana — Illinois — Wisconsin — Minnesota — Iowa — Missouri — Kansas — Nebraska — Arkansas — Kentucky — Tennessee — Mississippi — Louisiana.	
LAND OFFICES — Where Located	360

THE OLD AND THE NEW.

A FEW years before steamboats began to run on Lake Erie, there was a great emigration from New York and other Eastern States to Michigan. The first boat which did much was the Enterprise, next the Superior, and then the Henry Clay. They ran only to Detroit. Chicago was a village somewhere across the country, but was supposed to be too far away ever to amount to much. Now and then emigrants ventured on sailing vessels, but the great body went by land. The ridge roads along the south shore of the lake were crowded with moving wagons. Ten or twenty could be seen at a time; over a hundred, sometimes two hundred, passed in a day. Besides these were two-horse carriages, in which rich families rode. To almost every wagon a cow was tied, and flocks of sheep were driven. A part of every family walked, for the wagons were well loaded with household goods. Some were on horseback; then there were men on foot not belonging to any of the teams; they had packs on their backs, and were going to look at the country. Those now going with teams had been out the same way. Many were single men.

Among these was a young man of the name of Dean. He was scarcely eighteen; tall, rather awkward; his pantaloons were too short, his face was fresh, somewhat freckled; he had an intelligent look and a quick way. He carried an ax, and a pack made of tow cloth; there were places through which he put his arms, a strap crossed his breast and made all fast. He, too, was going to Michigan—going to stay.

He had money enough to take him through if he bought lunch for dinner, which was half price. All he was worth was with him. In some way he expected to get land. Every day he walked as many as thirty miles; when he came to a shady brook he would wash his feet and put beach leaves on the blisters, and then hobble on. Those riding on horses and in carriages, and who were in a hurry, kept up with him; the rest, gradually, were left behind.

In due time he reached the part of the State he was going to, and, after resting a little, he took a job of clearing ten acres of land. He was to chop every stick, log, burn, fence and fit for the plow, for ten dollars an acre. How he did work! Then was his time, if ever. He was deciding whether he would be poor or rich. The timber was tall and heavy, but he stood it well. Youth bears some kinds of grief better than the hardened laborer. Sometimes he had a little fun. He would spend the best part of a day in chopping trees almost down, and so that one would fall on another. He would get up a couple of hours before day, and chop off the last tree. Then there was the awfulest crashing you ever heard. It was thickly settled, though it was in the woods. The people wondered what was going to take place. His last caper was to cut a tree here and there, so that it was likely to hang an hour or so; at late bed-time he would go out and cut one tree, when a crash would break out, and then stop; by the time folks fairly were asleep it would break out again. In this way he kept it up all night long. When a man grows old and looks back on his youth, if he sees nothing worse than this, he does not wince much. Often he will shut his eyes and hasten to think of something else. In the summer Mr. Dean hired out to work on a farm. He got ten dollars a month and his board. In those days money was everything and board nothing; in these, board is everything and money nothing.

Meantime, when he got leisure, he studied arithmetic, grammar, and the like. The next winter he made out to get a certificate, and taught school. It was almost like clearing land. He was at the school-house every morning before sunrise, studying to keep out of the way of his best scholars. Once or twice he got fast with a sum, and said he was so hurried he had not time to do it then; he would look it over after school. He struggled desperately with such difficulties. At last he got ahead, and kept ahead. Afterwards, this discipline enabled him to do many things.

The time came when he bought land. He looked around a good deal first. He selected the first quality, and in a neighborhood where the people were intelligent and enterprising. A part of his farm was on very high ground; the rest was low and bordered on a lake. He commenced clearing on the high ground; here he would build; here wheat and corn would grow, and fruit would always be sure. Grass would be heavy on the low ground, and in dry seasons corn and potatoes would be heavy. Between the high and low, was a sheltered valley of seven or eight acres of large hard-maples; this would be his sugar camp.

Then he married a pretty girl. The girls always are pretty. They should be so good that their husbands will take no notice of their growing old. They had a good log-house to live in; there was a log-barn, a yoke of cattle, a few hogs, and a plenty of hens. A young married woman tries her hand on raising chickens. Hens like to lay in a log-barn. You will hear their uproar early in the morning.

Money was very scarce; neither grain, tallow, sugar nor honey would bring it. Potash was the only article that would fetch money. Mr. Dean built an ashery, and from the ashes of his clearing, and from what he could buy of his neighbors, he made potash; it was called black salts. In this way he got a good start.

When children began to grow in Mr. Dean's house he became more serious, for he was a gay young man. He liked to dance; he could drink a dram; he was the life at all log-rollings, raisings and huskings. Near by was a flourishing church; he attended a revival-meeting and experienced religion. A man who has a family, and can think, will see the necessity for morality and for order. He will consider how wonderfully man is made; he sees an Intelligent First Cause. To every one the grave and the future are near, and he will ask what it is to be wise. He sees, too, that every one is sinful and weak, and that sickness and pain beset our pathway.

Mr. Dean became a worthy member of the church. Frequently at evening meetings he would give short exhortations. He spoke rapidly and in a high key; often he said some things quite sensible. He could make a warm prayer. After awhile, people began to like to hear him. It seemed certain that when he should get more age he would become a deacon.

He was saving and industrious. He had fair crops; his stock increased. People had to confess he was a good farmer. He had set out a large orchard. The rows were so long one scarcely saw the end. He had apples almost as soon as those who planted earlier. This was because he cultivated his trees, and kept off insects. He said a fruit tree is worth as much care as a hill of corn. This given, it will thrive. Who would think of raising corn in a meadow? He kept up his ashery; either he or a hired man was running a team to buy ashes. Twice a year he took two or three tons of black salts to Detroit.

Almost every day he would read more or less. If dinner was not quite ready he would take up a book. In his exhortations he showed he was a reading man. He became instructive. At last, folks understood he intended to be a minister. One might have known this from the books he bought. These were Clark's Commentaries—I do not say what edition; Calmet's Dictionary, Mosheim, and like large works. This was quite an undertaking for a man thirty-five years old, with a family growing around him and a large farm to attend to. But he was not in the least hurry. His farm work and ashery went on the same, and he himself labored as before. But he diligently improved all spare time; a farm life gives more leisure than an any other occupation, and when he was at work it was plain he was thinking of something. Still he talked as freely as ever, and he told stories which made people laugh.

In ten or twelve years Mr. Dean had plenty of fruit, and he sold much. When fruit was cut off on low grounds, people came from a distance to buy, and they would bring corn; for good fruit, it was bushel for bushel. Then he had a cider mill. One going by heard it complaining far down in the orchard. All around was the clear sky; below, lay woods and farms.

Mr. Dean was one of the first to build a nice house; it was a large and very high two-story building, with kitchen and wood-house attached. It stood on the highest ground, and was in plain sight from many distant points—three, five, and even ten miles.

His boys grew up to be strong fellows. They worked faithfully. They were well behaved, and when abroad, were so sober as to seem like young deacons. Of course, they had their play and fun, but they were under strict control. Their father had made them ambitious to get property and learning. When boys are of this inclination there is little else one can wish them to be. Such boys will have rough hands, full faces and broad shoulders. They do not feel easy in genteel parties. If it is important to be genteel, it will not take long to learn to be so. It takes longer to be honest, sincere and loveable. The sisters were much like them. They, too, were brought up to work; they made their own clothes; but for Sunday they had calico dresses. In these days, we think it hard to pay twenty cents a yard for calico. It was higher then, and money so scarce that they thought as much of a sixpence as we do of a dollar. The girls enjoyed themselves much. The oldest ones had beaux, those next them expected soon to have. They could sing some songs beside religious ones; you could hear them while they were spinning, and all about love. They had apple-parings, sleigh-rides and singing-schools. On the whole, theirs was a highly prosperous and respectable family. There was no haughtiness; all things were plain. Of their plenty they bestowed, on the poor first, to foreign missions next.

At last the time came when Mr. Dean was licensed to preach, and he filled appointments in neighboring townships, speaking on cold winter days in school houses, or in some farmer's large kitchen. When meeting was over he would start for home, that he might go to work in the morning. When he spoke in the evening, and he had ten or fifteen miles to go, he was late; frequently on the way he saw a light from his house; his wife was up, with a good fire burning, and something on the hearth to eat. There were few homes so pleasant and comfortable, though all the neighbors were well off.

Mr. Dean did not promise to be a great preacher; his voice was too high and shrill. He was liked better by older than by young persons, for his views were too practical, and he used too many homely arguments. He had good congregations, but there was not the least excitement. Some laughed a little that a good farmer should turn to be a poor preacher; but they had to confess he knew what he was talking about, and that they had heard those they liked less. After a year or so it was noticed that he improved; his sermons became more lively, for he mingled anecdote; and the young folks got interested. It was a proud day for Mr. Dean, for his family and all his friends, when several persons, having become converted under his preaching, united with the church.

Upon this event he was ordained as a regular minister, and he took a stand among the clergy as their equal. He had been tried and found to be a useful servant of the cause. Some said if he had been a poor man he would not have met with this honor. They did not think that the ability he had exhibited in getting property enabled him to be an instructive and useful minister.

All this time he worked on the farm. He usually took most of Saturday to prepare his discourse; but he abated nothing in agricultural enterprise, and with each year his farm improved. He was one of the first to take a paper on farming, and when an agricultural society was started in the county he lent it his hearty support. There were some views advocated by scientific men which he ridiculed, and he was not forward in adopting new methods except on a limited scale. He valued his experience more than a scholar's theory. He said agricultural societies ought to be encouraged for the healthful influence they exert on young men.

Up to this time the condition of society had not changed. In many respects it was the same as had prevailed in all civilized countries from the time the Roman Empire was in its grandeur. Our generation has seen more important changes than any other generation since the dawn of civilization. For thirty years we have been dazzled with a constant overturn of old methods and ways. In the midst of the whole, we have been, and we are, guided by the principles which produced the Protestant Reformation.

Ministers of much pretension or learning had worn broadcloth clothes, and now it was becoming common for the many to dress almost as well; goods were getting cheap, and the women dressed fine. Mr. Dean would make but few changes. In winter his outer garments were full-cloth, his underclothes red flannel, all made in the house. Sometimes he wore heavy calfskin boots; generally he had cowhide shoes, tied with leather strings. The most he would consent to adopt was a silk hat, a dickey—which is a shirt-bosom and collar with strings to tie it around the neck and waist,—a black silk cravat, and a red bandanna handkerchief with white spots. While his appearance was plain, it was neat and respectable.

In the third year of his ministry he was settled as the pastor of the church to which he belonged. This was the height of his ambition, and for this he had labored. Thus to have the esteem of the members of his own church was an applause he valued most among earthly honors. He would live and die among his own people. Seldom did a man more meekly fill the pulpit; still he maintained the dignity of his calling. The young folks had his esteem; even the children lingered around him. Through his influence a new and handsome church was built, and the rocks heard the sound of the church-going bell. It stood on another hill, a mile and a half from his house, and was seen even from the county seat. The farms all around were well tilled, the farm buildings of the first class; and orchards were everywhere. At the feet, even on the tops of the hills, burst springs of the purest water. No region in the State is more thrifty or romantic.

For some time the different churches of this denomination had wanted a seminary of learning conducted in their interest, and now they felt able to build and endow it. Several places strove for the location, but it was to be secured by the one which could give most. Mr. Dean was urged by his church to use his influence for them; but he hesitated long, for he doubted whether it would be for their good. At last he was persuaded, and he himself subscribed $500. After much solicitation from men of all classes, he succeeded; the school was to be in their midst.

Immediately work commenced. Over fifty men were constantly employed. In about a year a large and noble building was completed. It was built of the fine stone found in the hills. It stood not far from the church; and so grand was its situation, that for many miles the people on farms and in villages could see its windows blaze in the morning sun. Meanwhile, several houses for the accommodation of boarders and the professors were built, mechanics came in, stores were established, and a pleasant new village arose.

Then the students appeared, the president and professors opened their classes, and the school was in operation. For the first year there were difficulties,—things were new, there was not room; but more houses were built, and the second year opened more prosperously. Clearly the plan was successful, and members of the denomination, far and near, were willing and proud to patronize their institution.

It made them strong; it was an honor to the county and to the State.

Mr. Dean's oldest son was married and lived in the house. His wife was a smart and intelligent woman. They were an exception to the rule that two families cannot live under one roof. Perhaps the best reason was they had a plenty of everything. But the young folks thought it their duty to appear and dress as well as their neighbors. The Seminary had brought in the fashions; everybody had to follow them. Mr. Dean and his family had always gone to meeting in the two-horse wagon;—I mistake; when the country was new they went with oxen. Now the son and his wife, and all the children, and even the old lady, said they ought to have a plain carriage, or at least a nice buggy. He said they might do as they pleased, but he would not ride in it; he would have no hand in such vanity and extravagance. A nice, shining two-horse buggy was bought;—true, he went along, when it was bought, to see that they had a good bargain; but he would not put his foot in it. Then the family would come to meeting as grand as could be. After a while he would appear in his cow-hide shoes, with the Bible and hymn-book in his hands. If the roads were muddy, he would ride the old mare. There was no hard feeling; no one heard of any dispute, although there were hired folks in the house.

The church was large, and all the students could get in, but it was full. Sometimes one of the professors would preach, but usually Mr. Dean officiated. He did his best to deliver practical and interesting sermons. He contrived generally to be new; his illustrations were drawn from every-day life, from common occurrences in families, frequently from newly settled countries. He delighted to dwell on the days when the forest was all around, when game was plentiful, and when all the neighbors, being upon one level, were much like a family. He seemed to regret that the old days were gone. But, rising from these thoughts, he would speak of the duties which belong to all conditions of society, and how the virtues everywhere may flourish, and lead us to the love of divine things and to immortal life.

For a year or so this went on very well. But at last there was dissatisfaction. A party rose up wanting a more stylish preacher. They said it was a damage to the Institution that the scholars should be forced to listen to such an oldfashioned preacher. Mr. Dean thought there was some justice in this complaint. He would preach in the forenoon, one of the professors should preach in the afternoon; in this way the church and the school would be represented. But this did not satisfy long. Some of the church-members, seeking to be genteel, said it was scandalous to allow a man so plainly dressed to go into the pulpit; it was not showing proper respect for the house of worship. They wondered how Mr. Dean had the assurance to go up into the pulpit, and sit down by the well-dressed professors, in his cow-hide shoes and full-cloth coat; he was as big as any of them. Once, when he was preaching, his dickey got loose, and they had a peep at his faded red flannel shirt. They wished he would get a new pocket handkerchief; he had used that one full ten years, and they were tired of it. In short, they were tired of him. They wanted a preacher who would dress in shining clothes, and not bid defiance to custom; such a one could be more useful. Did Mr. Dean mean to condemn the professors by shaving so close when they wore such comely whiskers? They knew if they got another preacher they would have to pay, but they were willing, they did not care. It seems that Mr. Dean would take only $52 a year: he said a dollar a day was enough; if they felt like paying more, they might give it to the poor.

Mr. Dean had nothing to say. If the church did not want him she must say so; he would not resign. He had one great advantage,—perhaps no one knew why it was, except himself: his sermons were more satisfactory to many than the professors'. He had taken great pains in forming a clear and simple style. It was clear English. The professors used high-sounding words; their sentences, sometimes, were confused, and the thoughts were separated much as they are in Latin. People had seen Mr. Dean, as he sat behind them when they were preaching, faintly and shrewdly smile. But this was of no consequence to those who favored new things. Perhaps Mr. Dean preached well enough; but one must keep up with the changes in society,—not to do so, is to fight against progress and light. They wanted no preacher who would tell them about burning log-heaps, and that the perfume of the fields and woods is more pleasant than the choicest extracts. He had been useful in his day; that day was past. There were places where he was needed; it was in the back townships. They would give something to sustain those weak churches if he would preach for them.

Mr. Dean's family saw the storm coming. They were proud of him. They were not certain he was wrong, but they urged him for their sake to conform to the wishes of the church; the Old was pleasant, but he could not keep back the New. His only reply was by whistling an old psalm-tune in a sort of whisper, which was his way when he would not contend.

At such times he would go off to work by himself at clearing land. Every year he cleared half an acre of land for turnips. He was not able to work as well as formerly; but here he would work,— chopping, piling brush, and burning log-heaps. He said he took more comfort in his clearing than in the most refined society.

Every spring he made sugar. He had everything prepared: there was a house where he boiled; the sap ran into sheet-iron pans through a pipe from large troughs, he had pine buckets for catching the sap,—these were stored in the boiling-house through the rest of the year; and here he had wood prepared, dry and fine. It was a pleasure to him to have the young folks come and see him when he was boiling; he would always take some syrup and sugar off.

The students of the Seminary were invited, and they came

in crowds, every lady with her beau. They would not eat much; for the girls thought they ought not to — there were so many of them,— and the young men mostly desired another kind of sweet. He would tell them laughable stories, often with a deep meaning which they did not understand till years were passed. Then they had to stop at the house and get apples. The girls looked on him with a sort of wonder; some even wished they could get such a husband.

Mr. Dean's second son was studying to be a minister. Every winter forty or fifty students would teach school. This young man went with the rest to the county seat to be examined. Almost all got certificates; he failed. Really, he was the best scholar of them all, but he was embarrassed by some unusual question, and by a bluff manner. There were girls in ribbons and flaring dresses who knew little, but succeeded; they were supposed competent and but few questions were asked. This mortified the family. The father could see now what it was to keep children in the background. He said it would come all right, for everything everywhere will find its true level. This proved true, to tell how requires another narrative.

At last the storm which long had threatened, broke out. The deacons came to talk with him; there was great dissatisfaction; a meeting of the church was demanded. Such and such ones were determined to have a new minister; they wanted one of the Professors. He said he would not talk on the subject; let the church meet and decide, it was the only way. On this they departed. His family could see that he felt bad; his wife could tell much. Old times and old manners were changed and gone, and a stranger was ready to fill the throne.

On Sunday he preached from this text—" Finally, brethren, farewell; be perfect, be of good comfort, be of one mind, live in peace, and the God of love and peace shall be with you." His sermon interested all. It was the last time they were likely to hear him. He spoke of the early days of the church, of her trials and rejoicings. He referred to old members who started with them—their bodies were in the churchyard, their souls with the saints. New families had been established and had grown up in their midst, they had prospered in all their undertakings. There was no bitterness in his sermon, and no reference to his situation except in his text, and this he repeated as he closed.

The next day the church met; the whole township was in a ferment. The friends of the new order were certain of success. It was not known who Mr. Dean's friends were. There were two or three to be sure, but they were abrupt and hasty old men who had little influence. The truth was, most of the members had not expressed an opinion, they were afraid of offending Mr. Dean or the Seminary. It was not known that any, except the few, had said a single word in his favor. This made his case look very dark. At last they put to vote this question: whether it was advisable to change their pastor? There were about three hundred votes, and fifty of them were advanced scholars, young gentlemen and ladies who had united with the church. There was profound silence and great anxiety. When the votes were counted it was found that about seven-eighths were opposed to a change.

Of course the old-fashioned folks had to rejoice a little. Then they were asked why they voted as they did. They were ready with an answer. They wanted a minister they could understand. The affair ended in good humor. The Seminary continues to prosper. Great attention is paid to the study of the English language. I would advise you, if you go into those parts, to stop over Sunday and hear Mr. Dean preach.

GOING TO DIE.

JAMES CARR was a most promising young man. He had a good common-school education. When seventeen years old he taught school; he was liked, he taught every winter; the rest of the year he helped his father on the farm. All the money he got he put out at interest. When twenty-one he had several hundred dollars. With this he bought a farm of a man who had settled it, but made little headway. At once, James cleared more land, planted an orchard, built good fences, and made things shine. The reason why he got along so well was, he did not expect to do great things. To get a farm was his highest ambition. His father could not help him. One winter he had taught school in an English neighbourhood, and he learned how profitable it is to keep sheep, and that the best way to keep them is to raise ruta baga turnips and other roots. He built a large barn, with a stone basement, in which was a cellar where he kept his turnips.

All this was done before he had a wife, but while he was looking for one. The girls watched him. Almost every one was ready to step out should he ask her. At last it was seen that Rhoda Miller was the happy girl. Her parents were good farmers; the rest of her sisters were married off. She lingered, enjoying herself, dressing neatly, engaged a part of the time in making clothing for the heathen, and part of the time making clothing for the family she expected to have. Another part of the time she visited and went to great doings with her beaux. She had flannel and linen sheets, towels, tablecloths, and the like. Her father furnished the flax and the wool; she took her own way and time. Of course this was at an early day. The country was new. The only kind of sugar was maple sugar. The whole settlement, for miles around, was composed of pious families, and one who did not belong to the church was little esteemed.

When James got Rhoda's consent, he consulted with her about the house, and they united upon a plan. It was not large, it was convenient, and so arranged that an addition could be put to it. They did not know, but thought it not improbable, they might want considerable room. The size of the parlor was fixed by the length of the carpet she had in the loom. When the house was finished they were married, and moved into it.

Mr. Carr proved to be a good husband. He seldom scolded, or spoke in any other than a low, it was a decided, tone. He was not much given to talking at all. He had one bad habit. At night, when all work was done, he smoked his pipe. Sometimes his wife asked him why he did not talk more. He asked her what he should say. Often, on looking up from her work, she saw him gazing on her with a smile. He was a smiling, industrious, persevering man. Morning and evening they had family worship. No matter what the weather was they went to meeting on Sunday. Mrs. Carr was a good housekeeper. Everything was neat, no one had better bread, better sweet-cake, or richer minced pies. Her parlor was almost elegant; in the bed-room adjoining was the nice spare bed. She cultivated some flowers, and her roses and grass pinks were very fine.

Of course they prospered. They had a good start. How different is the lot of the many who spend the greater part of their lives in attaining what this couple at first possessed. Mr. Carr was respected. Almost without opposition he was elected to fill important township offices. He was known by many ten and twenty miles distant. He was on Grand Juries; he settled estates. He had run some in debt for more land, he paid for it in wool. If wool was cheap so was land. It was a good place to go visiting. Book agents and pedlars always put up with them. If anybody had apples some could be found in his cellar; they were not seedlings, but choice fruit, Rhode Island Greenings, Northern Spys, and Golden Russets. When they went to meeting no one had better horses. Their clothes were rich, still were plain. All the women and girls had to come and look at Mrs. Carr's baby. No baby ever was so pretty; how nice was its hood, its mantle, and all its clothes, and the rest of her children looked so good and smart. It was a wonder too that she held her own so well; she was as fresh as when she was married. But she had such a nice home, and her husband was so kind.

When there is a large farm, and when new children frequently come into a family, there is much work to do; it cannot be avoided. The cooking alone may occupy the most of one's time. Often the style of cooking is such as to lay the foundation of disease in every member of the family. Some of us are apt to talk on this subject quite as much as we know. There is little difference in all families. Care, labor, and decay come to all.

About fifteen years after their marriage people noticed that Mrs. Carr grew feeble. She became pale, and had a pinched, small look. Scarcely a bloom was left on her cheek. Several Sundays passed and she did not come to meeting. At last she came only when the weather was very fine; but her husband and the children would come. The women noticed that though their clothes were clean, they looked less neat; his shirt bosom was frayed, his black neck handkerchief was carelessly tied, and his hair was too long.

Mrs. Carr seemed to be breaking down, and yet she was in the prime of life. She had a constant pain in her side; she thought the liver was affected, and at times, on rising from her chair, she almost stumbled she had so little strength in her feet. After this she began to cough, and she spit up so much that it seemed clear she was going into consumption. The doctor was called, but the medicine he gave was so harsh, and it so much distressed her, she could not take it. Still she was around and kept doing. She said it seemed to her she would die if she stopped working. She coul dnot do much, and though there was hired help her active labors were missed.

She grew worse. Her cough so increased that during the latter part of the night she could get no sleep. Her eyes sank and grew lustrous; her cheeks fell in and she wasted away. She often enquired of herself if her mortal frame must decay, if her limbs, then able to move, must moulder in the ground.

Every one saw that she was *Going to Die.* But a celebrated doctor was sent for. On attempting to take his medicine she was thrown into spasms and they thought her dying. She rallied a little. The doctor said she was past help, and he prescribed palliatives to smooth her passage to the better world. Thus she lingered, not expecting to live a week, certainly not a month, and yet several months passed. Her cough remained the same, but she grew weaker and poorer, and her husband easily lifted her in his arms.

During this time Mr. Carr thought much of the future, and he considered what could be done for the small children soon to be motherless. Other things were presented; how could he keep house, how maintain his standing in society, and how preserve his property from waste. Clearly he must marry again; but whom should he marry? He was well off, he ought to have a woman both well-informed and rich. He tried to throw off such thoughts, but he suffered them to return. He knew one or two women in particular, but he wished them richer. He had some friends in a city, certainly, they would recommend him to a rich wife. But would she be willing to live on a farm? O, but he would use her well. She need not work, he would build a fine house, they would visit in the best families, his children would not trouble her much, but she would be so good that she would gladly take care of the little ones for the sake of the dear one gone. The older ones should have land or go away to school, for there would be money enough. Being rich, this new wife would be handsome, very handsome. She would have earrings, bright finger-rings, her hands would be white and her step light. He confessed to himself this was foolish and wicked thinking; but, did he not deserve so much? He was some body.

Once he asked the doctor how long he thought Mrs. Carr would live. He had it in his mind to get saw logs while there was snow, that he might build a new house for the new rich wife. Sometimes he looked at her, considering she would soon pass away, and he said to himself: she had been a most faithful, loving wife, through many labors and trials she had been true as steel; her memory always should be held dear, and when she died there would be no tombstone in the churchyard so beautiful and costly as the one he would place over her grave. He would teach all the children to cherish her memory. The girls should have all her things. Should he get a rich wife she should not have a towel.

At this time there was an epidemic, or plague, in the country; it had come up from the interior. Few recovered. If they did, they were long in getting well, for a complication of disorders ensued. After being heard of in various townships it came into the one where Mr. Carr lived. It was as fatal as the cholera, and it traveled from place to place. It was so new, or so malignant, that the doctors were unprepared with any remedy. In this State it was so fatal that to this day gaps in families show its ravages.

One Sunday morning Mr. Carr came in from feeding the cattle. The weather was very cold, even for that cold country. He felt strangely, and he wondered whether he was not going to have the plague. In less than an hour he had it.

The doctor who was having most success, if it was success, was sent for. The case was a bad one. The sores which broke out under the arm were uncommonly red, but two things were favorable: he did not froth at the mouth quite so much as some, and instead of seven carbuncles on his back, only five came. The fits of cramping were as violent as in other cases.

A part of the time he knew what was going on, but when his senses left him the doctor and the nurses kept out every member of the family. The plague lasted exactly seven days, when the patient usually died. When this time was up Mr. Carr came to. He was aroused by the tolling of the bell. Sometimes there were six funerals in a day, and it was hard work to dig the graves, the ground was frozen so deep.

When the doctor came he saw Mr. Carr was likely to get well, for all the carbuncles were running. The truth was, the violence of the plague was abating. His was one of the best cases. None of his family took it. It is not known that the doctors cured a single one.

Still, Mr. Carr was likely to die. The disease assumed a typhoid character of the most malignant type. There were symptoms of other diseases. Above all, his lungs were disordered. There was danger of his dying of suffocation. Trusty nurses and the utmost care were required.

When he was taken sick Mrs. Carr first thought of what would become of the children, for they would soon be made orphans. When she was told how much her husband suffered she was anxious to help him. She could walk a little; those having the consumption walk almost to the last. She could do some little things—prepare gruel and tea, and select and warm his underclothing when a change was required. These efforts, instead of weakening, seemed to strengthen her. When it was proper the doctor permitted her to see him, and she smoothed his brow and encouraged him. Then he would gaze upon her with a sorrowful look and burst into tears. The distress of his mind seemed greater than that of his body, and frequently, with wild exclamations, he would enquire if he could be forgiven.

When he was out of immediate danger she was so encouraged that a slight color came to her cheek, and when the doctor urged the importance of good nursing, she insisted on doing something. He was astonished at her improvement, when he called to mind, from his books, the statement that the virus of plagues, and even of epidemics, has been known to effect the cure of certain chronic diseases. This led him to conclude that her disease was not the true phthisis, but one of general debility, arising from over-doing, united with a loss of mental energy, so common with people who, being well off, have no fear of the future and no prize to gain. In such cases, regular and prolonged horseback exercise is most beneficial.

For many long weeks did Mr. Carr lie, as if every day *Going to Die*. Finally, he got well. He often repeats that he owes his life to his wife's tenderness and care. She was much restored. The doctor advised him to take her on a journey. He also gave him some other advice, which was very good. Mr. Carr followed it, and she became a hearty woman.

Several years have passed; Mr. Carr and his wife still live. Before he was taken sick he treated her very well; it is impossible to describe how tenderly he regards her now. Her cheeks have that intense, healthful red so common among many English people.

SERVING TWO MASTERS.

SOME think the scenery on the Hudson the finest in America; others that it is too wild, and that the views on the Ohio River between Cincinnati and Louisville are grander. The prospect is wider. The same may be said of another part of this river, between Evansville and Paducah. In one place the hills gradually rise above each other to a great height, while the land is level enough to make good farms. These farms adjoin, and rise above the ones fronting them, and make, either from them, or from the river, a beautiful prospect.

Here so many families have come from Ohio that it is called the Ohio Settlement. The neatness and order of the buildings, the numerous orchards, and the conspicuous school-houses, remind one of many scenes in that great Central State. The useful and the domestic, when united with the lofty and the wide, makes the finest scenery.

Twenty-five years ago Mr. Welch came hither, and located a farm, which, when the timber was cut away, proved to be most sightly and desirable. The river, three miles distant, seems on the side of an inclined valley; and yet it is so far below that eagles and other birds of prey, when coming up with fish in their mouths, have a weary flight. The limestone soil is of such fertility that to-day it yields fair crops of corn without manuring; while for some kinds of apples, such as the New-York Pippin or the North-Carolina Red, it has proved exceedingly valuable. The kind of white winter wheat, so justly esteemed in the Boston market, grows here as if on its native soil; when pains are taken with the seed, and other conditions are observed, it is seen as thick as wheat can grow in this climate, while nothing else, except young clover, springs through the small pieces of decaying limestone.

Mr. Welch was an intelligent and industrious farmer. Having only two children, a son and a daughter, he educated them, built a good house, and in the decline of his life enjoyed the fruit of his labors. He had only one trouble,—his son Alfred did not like to live at home, and he became a pilot on the river. To fill this station with credit, he applied himself for several years with such diligence that he became expert. Very few Northern people are aware of the great length of time, the study, the reflection, and the memory, required to become a pilot on these waters. To learn the rocks, chains and channels in the Ohio is not difficult; but when sand-bars are forming, one must watch their course and progress. The Mississippi is quite different. Here, for hundreds of miles, the shores are so similar to each other, and the natural landmarks are so few, that frequently the pilots are puzzled to tell a pupil what they know. For instance,—they steer for a certain tree with a limb pointing east or west, then for a cabin, a house, an old chimney, or a black stub; then, such a distance from the bank, till they come within so many rods of the head of an island. Meanwhile the current is so strong, and the soil so loose, that the channel is constantly shifting, when the pilot is to be guided by the color of the water and the throwing of the lead. When it is considered that such are all the guides, even when the night is stormy and dark, it will be seen how much is required to fill this responsible post.

The wages a pilot receives is large. Formerly it was from $150 to $200 a month; recently, during the war, on first-class boats it was often as much as $500 a month.

Alfred used to run on the river about nine months in a year; during the hot months he would stay at home, enjoying himself on the farm. He would work in the cool of the day, and for the rest of the time would loiter about, dressed in thin clothes of the finest material. But in harvest he worked long and late. He would allow no one else to put a cradle into the wheat, and in this he took especial pride. Then he would spend long hours in trying to read, or in sleeping, in a cool place—oftenest under trees by the spring-house, where the air is fully 20 deg. cooler than elsewhere, and so cool that neither flies nor mosquitoes can live in it. Of course he had to ride every day in his buggy or on a horse down to the landing, to get a paper and to chat with the officers of the packet.

He was a man of the fewest words. Once he used to talk; but the girl he was going to marry died,—afterwards he seldom smiled. He mixed but little in society, and he was passing through life as if he took little interest in it. His father and mother kept the house and the farm in order, while their daughter Ellen went and came as she pleased; but never was a girl more dutiful or careful, or more interested in her family.

The landing is a very small village, for the rocks so encroach upon the river that there is not room for many houses. There are two stores, a grist-mill, and several machine-shops. The native black-walnut, butternut, and ash,—having been left standing, while the tops have been cut out so that there may be no danger by their falling,— hide most of the houses from the passing steamers. An abundance of springs burst out of the rocks. For a place of the size, there is much business done; for the two roads coming hither are good, and the adjoining settlements are composed of thrifty farmers. The chief articles exported are wheat, fruit, lime, and flour.

Aleck Campbell, who used to go to school with Alfred, was his friend. He kept a store and the post-office. Aleck was a young man about twenty-four, tolerably well off, anxious to be rich; and he had a happy faculty of pleasing all classes, by which means he drew much custom from the other store, particularly as he had the post-office to help him, which he attended to faithfully.

It was a high ambition with Aleck Campbell to get Alfred's sister Ellen for a wife. She was about twenty, with sharp, snapping, yet most modest eyes. She was good-looking; had she not been, her good behavior and correct taste in dressing would have made her look well. He showed her the greatest attention, and always conducted himself in the most proper manner. He led in singing in the church, and he was a zealous professor of religion.

But, after all his care, he was pained to see that she had some regard for another young man, named Howard Willis, whose parents would have been better off if they had not paid out so much money in sending Howard and the other children away to school. However, they were by no means poor, and their standing was as good as the best. The reason why there are not schools here, to which young people can be sent, is because the greater part of the settlers came from the Slave States, who, though being able to support schools, care not enough for education to do so.

The other storekeeper wondered why Aleck got so many customers of the class that naturally should trade with him; for he sold no cheaper, while, being from Ohio, he thought only the Ohio people should buy of him. The real reason was, that Aleck made it his business to sell goods. He scarcely ever spoke or thought except with this object in view. He would talk in a friendly manner with every body; he was never tired of taking down and putting up his goods; if a thing bought did not suit, he would exchange it or pay back the money; if a mistake was made, he was willing to correct it. He was always ready, and unless he was away to Cincinnati after goods, a customer did not need to enquire for him. He had an excellent clerk, and yet people preferred to trade with him. He had been brought up a farmer, and he could talk with farmers, and to all others he could say something interesting. To church-members he could address his language according to their piety, knowledge, and taste; and to men of the world, who had no principle, he would slily tell smutty stories, and laugh with them, as if they were the greatest friends. This, as the world goes, is not considered a defect; for one may safely introduce subjects of this kind to most men, often to church-members, and be thought more of; for he is supposed to be witty; good-naturedly to tell a dirty story, if it is a little personal it is just as well, and to give the hearer a punch with the finger, will go far in doing a country business. How many good qualities are necessary to compensate for this habit, and to make a life-long business a success, is another question. Aside from this, so much study and art are required, that perhaps the time bestowed on other objects would be more profitable. In no respect do merchants of this kind make such awful mistakes as in supposing that because one is not a church-member he has a relish for vulgar stories. Such listen with all the indifference that a well-bred lady passes by a nude statue, while at the same time they hold the speaker in the utmost scorn. Still, they maintain good characters.

Aleck was tall and really good-looking. He dressed well, and in young company had no superior. By studying individuals, he had came so to understand them that he knew what would please them best. With Alfred he was particularly intimate, both because he respected him and because he loved his sister.

Howard Willis mingled little in society, because all the time he could spare was to be devoted to his studies. He had graduated, and was preparing to go to a theological seminary. He had kept company with Ellen and they harmonized in many things. He loved her with great devotion, and once he told her so, but she put him off, neither accepting nor refusing. It was known that she had treated Aleck the same way. The truth was, she wished to wait two or three years before she married, for she had learned from Fowler's, and like works, that this would be best for her. Then she would be two or three-and-twenty. Of the two young men she thought she saw more good qualities in Howard, but it was clear that Aleck would be able to make her a more pleasant home. The principal and only real objection she had to Howard was, he did not belong to the same church that she did. She was afraid they might not be harmonious. Still, and on the whole, she was unable to say which of the two, finally, she might choose, but it would be one of them.

Such was the condition of things when the war broke out. Of course the Ohio Settlement went in a solid body for the Government, and the other settlements against it. Parts of several regiments were raised in this region, such as the 30th, 31st, 18th, infantry, and the 6th cavalry, and several young men around the landing volunteered. Among them was Howard. There were young men, too, of Southern birth and prejudices, who also volunteered, such was the influence of Logan, Lawler, and others, while there were not a few old settlers who took sides with the Union, and cheerfully and joyfully gave up their boys. Still, a large portion of those who came to the landing to do business were opposed to the cause. Some even had sons in the rebel army.

This suited the other storekeeper, for the lines were drawn, and all at once his business increased, while Aleck's decreased. The post office, however, they could not get, and it did much to sustain him. Aleck boldly came out, and said he was going to have this government sustained; he did not care if it took all the property he was worth, if required, to help to do it. His store was the head-quarters of the Union men; they were proud of him and he was proud of them. Ellen, in particular, looked on him more kindly, and he saw that when the war should be over, and the rebels be put down, he would enter upon a high road to prosperity. What did he care for the loss of a little trade for a year or so; it would all come back and five times more with it.

When the Ohio Settlement boys went off, they were made much of. The day they departed there was a gathering of all their friends and acquaintances, and they were supplied with a great variety of food and delicacies, such as they were not likely to get in camp. To Howard, Aleck was particularly generous, for when he selected some things he needed, and among them a pair of fine boots, Aleck said he would not take a cent. He deserved them, and more too, since he was going to fight for his country. He told Howard he really envied him, for instead of seeking a commission, as so many did, and which he would honor so much, he was contented to be a private. But he would rise. He could not help it.

The blockade of the Mississippi threw many pilots out of employment. To a great extent those who had been running in the lower trade looked on the war with disfavor, and the first thought with them was, that if they should go against the South they would be remembered when they should go down, and they would be a fine mark, in their pilot houses, from the shore. They wanted peace. The South ought to have her rights. It was a shame to go to war with our best and only customers. None of the people of this region had the least interest in the war; they had every reason to be opposed to it. There was some truth in this.

When Commodore Foote began to form a navy there was a difficulty. Some of the pilots would not go, others had a diarrhœa, many hesitated. A few, however, were glad of a place. When Alfred heard of this, he took the first boat for Cairo and reported himself. The commodore gladly accepted him. Here was a first-class pilot, not afraid to serve his country, and one too who was contented with moderate wages. From that time there was a change; others followed, and there has been no trouble since. Some one was needed to lead the way. The pilots have done well. They have stood by the wheel through showers of cannon and musket-balls. Their boats have been boarded, set on fire, wrecked. There is scarcely an instance where they failed to do their duty.

Alfred was often employed where danger and difficulties were greatest. In that vast and wonderful work of General

Pope's, by which Island 10 was captured, where thousands worked to open a channel for the boats through a flooded country, sawing off huge sycamores, standing and fallen from ten to fifteen feet under water, he steered his boat where boat never was seen before, while the chimneys and the pilot-house were switched by the upper limbs of trees, and with blazing fires he steered past cabin doors, miles from the Mississippi. Then, at Fort Henry and Donelson, he and his companions brought their boats into the converging fires of batteries of heavy guns. Then, in Yazoo Pass, in the Sun Flower and other narrow and secluded courses, where, saying nothing of steamboats, man himself, except as a fugitive, seldom had ventured, they, by night and by day, struggled with the tree-tops and flood-wood, ringing their sharp, tingling bells to stop, to go forward, to back again, to go ahead, and all at the bidding of the determined Grant. In these enterprising scenes Alfred found great enjoyment. For years he had seemed to wear a weed on his hat, and to wear it well. Now, he acted as if in a world requiring men alive to duty. Who shall tell how many souls, sunk in grief and despondency, joyfully awaked by that war, did deeds of valor and renown?

It was not long before the adjutant of Howard's regiment was found incompetent. Another, who professed that everything was regular, was soon found to have the accounts perfectly confused. They were at a loss. The colonel had been watching Howard, though he was nobody. He had seen that he differed from the many. He did not swear, drink, or play cards. He kept with the sober and the old. What time was his own he read and wrote. At last the colonel asked him if he knew anything about accounts. Not much, but he might learn. Well, look over these papers and see what can be done with them.

The colonel was right. Howard was made for an adjutant. He did the duties so well that a graduate of West Point said they could not be done better. He had help. No one may tell how faithfully he labored to learn quickly.

The men were pleased. There would be no mistakes in their pay rolls, clothing accounts, or anything else.

When they came to make long marches Howard walked most of the way, that some foot-sore soldier might ride his horse. It did a soldier as much good to ride on the adjutant's horse as if he had been promoted. One would tell another, to see him laugh. The colonel took the hint, and let the weary ride. They had no chaplain. A better one could not be found. He could not hold two offices, still he was chaplain.

Howard went through many battles and not once was wounded. At last, when the regiment come to re-enlist as veterans, his name was sent to General Thomas as worthy of a good position in a colored regiment. Of course he got it. Time passed. The family had been hearing from him all along. The last heard from him was this: he went out from Memphis with General Sturgiss; a shameful, dreadful defeat followed. It was probable that Howard was taken prisoner and killed, for he was wounded in the leg. Two of his soldiers were helping him on a horse, Forrest's men rushed in. That was the last heard from him, and the regiment had returned.

The truth was, they had to flee across the country. He was hid in various places. The blacks everywhere assisted and brought provisions. Finally, he and his two soldiers were brought into Memphis, where his leg was taken off and his other wounds dressed. Then he was sent to the Mound City Hospital.

The war was lasting much longer than Aleck supposed it would last. Trade was going to the other store. He doubted whether it was his duty to let an enemy to the government get all the money. By degrees, as his old customers came after letters, he enticed them back. He knew how to do it. To keep them was another thing. The other store set counter currents in motion. It is impossible to know all, but Aleck certainly had a talk with the leading copperheads. This was about the time of the Congressional election. Aleck's clerk, who was supposed a good Union man, said he would like to vote for McClellan, for President. Aleck himself said that McClellan had not had justice done him. When he undertook to show his Union friends why, he had to confess he was not as well posted as he ought to be. Well, McClellan wouldn't do. He was for having somebody take hold and put the rebels through. It was unaccountable how things dragged along. He thought if he only had charge of things he could close up in six months. Yes, if it was the best way, make the negroes fight, make every man that could leave his business go. Raise a million, two millions of men, and sweep the board. If they didn't do it he was afraid the country would go to ruin. Gold was 140, calico $22\tfrac{1}{2}$ to $23\tfrac{3}{4}$, and Spragues 24, domestic 46, sugar $16\tfrac{1}{2}$ to $16\tfrac{3}{4}$, by the hogshead, and cotton yarn 55 cents a dozen. People couldn't stand any such prices; they were not going to do it. Then he stretched himself out on the counter, and rested his hand on a pile of calico, as if he were the man.

We happen to know that the question was asked why there was no Union League at the landing. We happen to know that Aleck was given to understand that if a Union League was not started he could not hold the post-office. Certainly we ought to have a Union League. It was singular nobody had started one. If nobody else would move, he would. He was not much used to public business, but he could set the thing a-going. It was impossible to do without it. "Tell your folks to come down here to-morrow night; we are going to have a little talk on national affairs, —all in a quiet way. Don't fail to get out the old man. No, no women; —just a little matter of business."

Then the Union League was started. There were good Union men in it; and soon there were many whom nobody ever expected to become Union men; while some names were proposed, but dropped—it was too bad. The object was to bring everybody into the Union—to sweep the board. Look, now: nobody can object to the oath, nothing said against anybody, except the enemies of the government; surely that is a very bad man who is an enemy to the government. In the end it became important, when any particular business was to be transacted, that a little Union League was got together; and the first thing discussed was—What kind of a Union League have we got?

The other storekeeper confessed that Aleck was too smart for him. At sun-down the steps in front of Aleck's store were crowded with men who watched others pitching quoits, while only a few, sometimes none, were on his steps; all day teams and horses would crowd around his store,—a spell ago he thought he would have some more hitching-posts made, but he concluded he had enough. He wondered what kind of a place it would be for trade further west. What splendid colors dazzle the eye of the beholder when he views the successful man! When these colors are true gold, they are worthy of admiration; but if they are only gilded copper, they fade, and we wonder again.

Three years of the war had passed, and Ellen was twenty-three. It was time she should seriously consider; for, if she delayed much longer, she did not know what might happen. No unmarried woman looks upon the passage of years without emotion. Aleck was still attentive; he had said he would wait, he was waiting. She knew she need only smile a little more sweetly to get him to ask her to marry him. The immense business he was doing no doubt helped her to decide in his favor; and after long reflection she concluded to have him.

When he saw the sweet smile, and his eyes caught her eyes modestly gazing upon him, he knew the time had come; he proposed, and was accepted. The prize he so long and patiently had sought was his at last. Well could he say to himself that there were no obstacles he could not overcome; and he prided himself in his business, in his wife that was to be, and in everything that was his own.

The wedding-day was fixed; for why should either longer delay? Alfred was at home, and father and mother were in good health: they could have no better time. She would come down to the store and pick out her dress.

Her father drove the buggy for her, and she went in. The store was filled with folks, and there was great news. The rebels, 50,000 strong, had crossed the Potomac, the telegraph was cut, two passenger-trains between Baltimore and Philadelphia were robbed and burned, Gen. Franklin taken prisoner; important bridges burned, Gen. Wallace defeated in a pitched battle at Monocacy bridge; Maryland overrun, farmers and everybody fleeing; and, by last accounts, heavy fighting was going on in the suburbs of Washington.

Aleck was busy, but he could talk. Calico was 50 cts. a yard, domestic 80 cts., and gold 2.80; by latest advices from Cincinnati goods were rising every hour, nobody knew what to ask for leading staples, and even the single article of bacon had gone up 5 cts. at a jump.

"Now I'll wait on you, Ellen. You see how busy we are. Jaconette, you say."

He showed her a piece which cost 50 cts. before the war. Such goods do not go off fast.

"How much a yard?"

"Well, we shan't think of charging you anything, you know. How much will you have? We sell it at $2.00 a yard; it is worth $1.75 in Cincinnati."

"Well, but I am going to pay for it."

"No, you shan't."

"I tell you I am going to pay for it. Alfred gave me the money, and a plenty more beside. He told me to pay for all I got."

"Well, $1.75 is as low as we can afford it. How many yards do you say?"

"Let me see."

She stood by the counter, holding the cambric at arm's length, considering the width and how many breadths were needed in the skirt. Aleck stood with the yard-stick in his hand, looking at her, and feeling happy enough. Just then a farmer came to the counter, shook hands with Aleck, and asked him the news. He repeated what he had said before, which was discouraging enough, and added a little; when a young soldier standing near, with one empty sleeve, said—

"Mind, I tell ye, Gen. Grant 'll knock this business higher nor a kite, fust thing ye know."

"Why don't he do it?" said Aleck; "now is his time. But I've heard this too often; I don't see any of the good things coming I've heard of so much."

"Nor I, either," said the farmer.

The young soldier spoke up short, and did not mind an oath that was personal.

"—— The trouble is you don't want to see."

"Yes, I do. If you 'll only show it to me, no man will be more glad of it than I. But, so far as I can see, the country is ruined; and I don't see how we shall help it."

"That's my fix," said the farmer.

Ellen turned towards him, and seeing who he was, she gave a heavy sigh, and the cambric dropped from her hands like a signal-flag.

"Now, Ellen, how many yards?"

"Did I understand you to say that the country is ruined?"

"Yes, I did, and it's plain enough."

"Then I don't want any white dresses."

"Why, what's this? What's the matter now?"

"Nothing, only I want no white dresses—I might get a black one, perhaps. I'll not take anything to-day. I wonder where father is?"

Aleck is as spry as can be. Before she got to the door, he came round the end of the counter and said:

"What's this nonsense? Come back, now. You shan't go off without this dress. I wonder if you thought I was going to charge you for it? I shan't charge you a cent, and I'll throw in all the trimmings and everything. You want some other things. Come now, this won't do."

"No, no, I say. When I said it I meant it. Ah, here's father. Come, father, I'm ready."

Ellen was putting some biscuit in the stove oven when

Aleck came into the porch, shaded by Concord grape vines, from which hung hundreds of clusters, already large and heavy. The river was spread out below, the Evansville packet was going around the upper bend, and the sun, shining on the water, made it blaze. Just as soon as the customers began to thin out, he had got on his horse and come up, determined to have an explanation. The packet had brought the latest papers, one of which he handed to Alfred. The news was not quite so discouraging, but nothing seemed clear.

As Ellen came out of the cook-room she took off her apron and hung it up behind the door, then sitting down, not far from Aleck, said she supposed he had come up to talk to her. She would listen to what he had to say. Her mother sat near the doorway, knitting; her father was at work at some hoop poles on a shaving horse under the trees, and Alfred sat in the porch looking over the paper. He had gay carpet slippers on his feet, and his clothes were as white as the driven snow.

Aleck thought she must have taken some offence to leave so suddenly.

"No offence in particular."

"Well, why didn't you take the dress? Shan't I send it up to you?"

"I might as well tell you first as last that I am not going to marry you."

"Well, now, I'd like to know what I've done?"

"You are not the man I took you to be—not the man you pretended to be. You are not a Union man."

"What! I not a Union man! That's good, now. What makes you think I am not a Union man? You must be sharper than anybody else. Haven't I suffered in business on account of my Union sentiments? Haven't the copperheads hooted me and abused me past telling, because I have stuck by the Union first, last, and every time?"

"You may think you are a Union man, but it seems to me that you don't know what it means to be a Union man.

According to my weak apprehension there is no merit in being for the Union when prospects are bright and everything goes well. Everybody is for the Union then. But when clouds darken, and things are uncertain, that is the time for a Union man to show himself. That is the very time for him to be bold, to waver not, and to show his faith by works. What is he good for if he fail in darkness and in the hour of peril?"

"Very well; but are you not willing that facts should speak for themselves?"

"Yes, facts. But when you say the country is ruined you are assuming a fact. How do you know the country is ruined? I'll tell you when the country is ruined. It is when men say it is ruined. It is their saying so that ruins it. From copperheads we expect nothing. From children, women, and many men we expect little. From leading business men, who pretend to be for the Union, we do expect something. I had just as lief talk plainly to you as not. You deserve it. There are so many copperheads around you, who are continually talking against the government and saying the Constitution is destroyed, and you are so weak, or something else, that you see with their eyes and hear with their ears, and, to tell my opinion, I don't believe you have the substance of a Union man in you. I should think that a man with half an idea, when the enemies of the government echo every word he says, at least would look around to see where he is standing."

"Well, you know it wouldn't do for me to come out harsh and hurt the feelings of my customers. I hope I may be a Union man without hurting one's feelings."

"That is the trouble with you, sir. You are trying *to serve two masters.* Let me tell you, you can't do any such thing. The nature of the case is such that you will serve the worse one, for if you serve the good one you will have nothing to do with the bad one. In a war like this, what business have you to be looking after the feelings of your enemies, only you don't know it, and the enemies of every human being on the face of the earth, themselves not excepted—the enemies of all light, all science, all knowledge, all religion. I care no more for their feelings, when in sympathy with the rebellion, than I do for the feelings of the fallen angels. You are trying to deceive yourself. Can't you respect their feelings in any way besides giving them comfort? You make no distinctions between treating them well and taking up their hollow-hearted cries. Now, look how you get along in trying to serve two masters. The feelings of the enemies of the government are very tender. What respect, what regard, what provision, are you making for my feelings? Or do none have feelings but traitors?"

"Now, Ellen, I see that plainly enough. You are right; I am wrong. I want you to look over it. I have so much on my mind that I don't make distinctions as I ought to. There's no mistake but what you are in the right, entirely in the right. I hope, upon my soul, I will get over this little difficulty. Suppose, now, you tell me how much a Union man should be willing to do, and see if we agree."

"I am not surprised that you want to know. A Union man is determined to restore this Union, because no future peace is possible if it be not restored. If the rebels, in temporary success, should throw Sherman's army across the Ohio, and there be fighting in the streets of Cincinnati; if Grant's army should hasten to the defences of Washington, and the rebels should drive it into the Blue Mountains or the Catskills, and run military trains through Baltimore into Philadelphia,—nay, should they feed their horses from the curbstones of Wall street; if our money should become as worthless as brown paper; if we dare not send a ship to sea, and commerce be dead, still he will be determined to restore the Union. For, so long as we have nineteen millions, and they not seven, so long as the sun shines and the rain falls over fertile fields, where grass, corn, wheat and oats grow, where flax, and hemp, and wool grow, and the hands to spin are ready, he will carry on this war.

Every furnace, forge, and foundry, every machine shop, every machinist establishment, shall be organized to carry on this war. Every blacksmith shop shall make shoes for cavalry horses, or put them on; every spare bushel of grain or bale of hay shall go to the army, and all muscles, willing or unwilling, shall be strained to help to overthrow the rebellion. He will count no days, no months, no years, till this is accomplished."

"I confess," said Aleck, "I am not quite prepared to go this length."

"I know you are not, and that is the reason you can't have me. I'll tell you another thing: when we count the advantages and blessings which will follow the restoration of this Union,—when out of the heart of this nation we tear the foul cancer of slavery, which has corrupted every walk of life, from the highest to the lowest; there will be room, time, opportunity, and will to build a pure structure on our Constitution,—and then, sir, we will begin to see what a true Union man of these days is worth. It is a poor, beggarly estimate, to say he is worth his weight in gold. If the world itself were a solid globe of gold, it would not be worth his little finger; if all the stars of heaven — no matter how vast or how many they may be—were gold, they would not be worth the hand that holds the musket that brings a rebel to the dust. Gold? Are you thinking of gold? There are things in this world, and here, where we live and move, millions of times more precious than gold."

"Well, this is a thing I never expected. I confess it is a great disappointment. I think I shall live it through."

"Aleck, there is one thing I forgot. Do you want to hear it?"

"O, yes; I'll listen all day, all night."

"I think you do not understand the first principles on which this war is waged; nor do I believe that you care. I'll tell you the reason why. Never in my life did I hear you say a single word against slavery and its awful crimes —of selling one church-member to another,— or conveying the least idea that it is a sin, or has anything to do, one way or another, with this war."

"Maybe I haven't. I've had enough to do besides filling my head with politics. But I think the country has got to a fine pass, if everybody has got to do just as Abe Lincoln says, and one can't be a Union man unless he votes for him."

Ellen saw through this in a moment, and said,

"Ah, I see you are for Fremont."

"Certainly I am. Here is your brother Alfred, now, who always was a great Fremont man;—he can't complain if I come over to his side at last."

"I thought, Aleck," said her brother, "that you knew more than this. Let me show you the difference. If the copperheads had gone to Fremont, I would have nothing to say,—they would be converted; but, since he has gone to them, he is converted; and I am not such a fool as to follow him."

"Well, fix it up as you please among you. I see I'm out, somehow. But it's news to me that I am not a Union man,—quite news."

"Aleck," said Alfred, "there's a thing that's been on my mind a good deal, and, since you're for Fremont, I want to ask you a question. When Jim Allen and Bartlett ran for Congress, the Union ticket in this precinct was short just two votes. We know all who pretended to vote for the Union. Now, didn't you and your clerk vote for Jim Allen? I remember you said Bartlett wasn't fit; but I had no idea you bolted the ticket. What do you say?"

Aleck started, but said,

"Do you consider yourself authorized to demand how I cast my vote?"

"Not at all, not at all. You needn't say any more, because if you had voted against Allen you would say so."

This was so unexpected to Ellen that she fired high.

"That ever I should have dreamed of marrying a man who voted for Jim Allen! Why, he never pretended to be for the Union; and in Congress, whenever in any possible manner he could oppose the government he has done so. Oh, dear, this is too bad! Here it is again,—trying to serve two masters. And now you call yourself a Union man! Boo! I know that's not pretty, but I declare I've no patience on finding out what a traitor you are."

"I must confess you're pretty hard on me; and, as things stand, I think I'd better leave." Aleck got up and walked around, quite important. Then he turned to Ellen, and said, "By the way, I suppose you will be looking around for somebody else. But I'm sorry to tell you that Howard has had his left leg cut off, and he's shot in the arm; maybe that will have to come off too."

"Howard? Howard? Have they heard from him? Where is he? Did you get a letter?"

"No, but just as I came away his folks did; and he's in the Mound-City Hospital. You seem mightily interested. I hope you won't think of marrying a man crippled up as he is,—besides, you know he doesn't belong to your church."

"Who said anything about marrying him? I didn't. But I'll tell you, Mr. Aleck Campbell, that if they should cut off Howard's left leg, as they have, and should cut off his right leg,—and I won't stop here,—if they should cut off both arms, and there were nothing left but his body for me to put my arms around, I would marry him, I—I can't tell how much sooner I would marry him than I would you! You throw it up that he does not belong to my church. Bless your innocent soul! you do not seem to know, that, as he is a true Christian and a true Union man, we can walk hand-in-hand through the doors of all true churches."

"Stop, Aleck," said Alfred; "don't be in a pet because my sister has taken another shute. Supper will be ready soon."

"No, I thank you; I won't stay."

The next morning Howard's parents were at the landing, waiting for the packet. They had not been there long when down came Alfred and Ellen. She said it was no time for ceremonies; she was going down to see Howard. The boat came along; they got aboard, and Alfred went into the pilot-house,—in no other part of the boat could he be contented to stay.

They found Howard with his leg cut off, it is true, and a flesh-wound in his arm; but he was doing well, and the surgeons had said he could go home in a few days. He was pale when they came in; but you never saw a man so color up as he did when he saw Ellen. He had given her up entirely, and he knew not what to make of it.

When all got quiet, and the old folks were busy at something else, Ellen went and sat by him.

"Now, Ellen, this is very kind in you."

"Oh, not at all."

"But it is, now. Tell me, does it mean anything—anything in particular?"

"Why, certainly; I came down to help take care of you."

"Yes, I know that; but would you have come if you had never known that I loved you?"

"No, I don't think I should."

"Well, then, you love me a little, don't you,—but not so much as you would if I had another leg?"

"Oh, more; a thousand times more."

"Thank you for those words, my dearest life and love! They pay me for all I have suffered. 'The Lord bless thee, and keep thee. The Lord lift up His countenance upon thee, and give thee peace.'"

In a few days they got him home. They had to be quite particular, but the journey was made without difficulty.

Then the folks began to talk. You know what was naturally said by the illnatured. Howard was getting well so fast, that Ellen consented to have the talking stopped. It would give her a good chance to take care of him. She went down to pick out a dress. She had traded so long in one store, she thought she would see what they had in the other. She bought what she wanted, but she required a yard and a half of bleached drilling, and she went into Aleck's to get it. He saw in at once how the case stood.

At first he was rather sullen; but soon, in a careless way, he asked her why she did not get her dress of him. She said she would as lief trade with one copperhead as another.

Then they had a wedding. Everything was nice and good, and crowds of folks were there. It is not often that a man gets married just after he has a leg cut off. They told him it would do just as well to sit down. No, he was going to stand up. Ellen got his crutch, and steadied him a little till the minister was ready; then she took his hand. There is no doubt that they were full as happy when he got well.

There was another revolution in commercial affairs at the landing. At sundown, the steps in front of the other store were filled with men watching others pitching quoits; during the day, it looked as if Aleck had more hitching-posts than he needed. Having time on his hands, he took to reading Fremont's travels. He frequently remarked that there must be a good country out west. If he should go thither, we can tell him, as well as any other like him, that whoever undertakes to serve two masters will fail.

THE STEAMBOAT CAPTAIN.

ON the Illinois shore of the Ohio River lives the Rev. Mr. Moss. He went thither a few years after his marriage. He seldom preaches, because he has weak lungs, and it was on this account that he went to this warm country. He is a farmer. It is necessary to go back and relate some matters, that I may describe the character of his son, who is a steamboat captain. Mr. Moss resided in Vermont, near Lake George. In the place where he was attending college he fell in love with a girl who lived with her parents near the town, and it was agreed that when he should finish his studies and see how they were to get a living, they would be married. They had only one trouble, which arose from his requesting her not to receive any attentions from any other young man, which she agreed to; but she insisted that he should pay no attentions to any other young lady. She was determined on this, and he had to submit, for she was not going to wait several years and run the risk of some artful girl picking him up, and leaving her to do the best she could. She kept good watch of him. He was faithful; he pursued his studies with diligence; finally, he graduated and was ordained. Immediately after this he received a call to take charge of a church near where he was brought up. Nothing was to be done, then, but to marry the lady of his choice, which he did, and brought her from the level country, across the Green Mountains, to the pretty home that was provided on the shore of Lake George.

At that time the writings of Graham, Alcott and the

Fowlers were first introduced. They taught the importance of a vegetable diet, of dressing loose, of frequent bathing, and other things. These Delia carefully studied and laid to heart. Naturally, her husband was of her way of thinking—indeed he was fully as strict—and they kept house with no means for making tea or coffee; they had no salt-cellar, and their diet was composed of Graham bread, vegetables, eggs, milk, and all the varieties of fruit. They would not eat butter because it was fat, but in a short time Delia brought a plate of butter on the table, smiling as she did so, and saying she did not believe it would hurt them. The young minister smiled too, for he thought as she did. Of course they had salt in it, and afterwards they used salt in their food, quite forgetting that it is a mineral. With this change in their diet they were contented for many years, and enjoyed excellent health. After a long time a chicken was killed; it seemed good, and tasted as of old. As children came on they found it necessary to have lard; hams were good too; and they had meat, but they eat very little, often it was not on the table for months. They never have tea or coffee, except when there are visitors, and to this day their bread is made of unbolted flour.

They were married in May, and Mr. Moss was very desirous that his wife should pay attention to some studies which she had neglected, and he marked lessons for her which she was to commit to memory. His object was to make her better fitted to hear him converse, and to engage in conversation with intelligent people who should visit them. This she undertook to do, and she made some progress; but she had work which she wished to attend to, and she thought, too, that at the age of twenty-four it was too late to go to school. After several months' trial with her the minister gave up the plan, simply saying it was too hard work. To tell the truth she was thinking of something else.

But in the meantime, if he proposed that they should walk or ride among the mountains, she was ready, and nothing pleased her more than a sail on the water through the many islands. Most persons consider that for water scenery of this kind Lake George is as fine as any found in America. Sometimes, if he was quite busy writing his sermons, she would take the boat herself, and getting in the shade of an island, would sit reading, or watch the shadows of the clouds flying across the mountains; or she would look down into the water, past the fish, to the bottom, or would wave her hands to and fro in the water so long that the flesh would be drawn up. As they were rambling among the mountains she would urge him to stop by the waterfalls and the fountains, and she would gaze upon them so long that when he pulled her by the hand, or gave her a kiss, she seemed to awake from a dream.

Frequently, when the weather was warm, they would take their bathing dresses to the lake, where shelters were prepared, when they would go into the water, and this pleased her so much that she almost learned to swim, and she would have learned if she had not been afraid to dive, for she would only duck her head a little. The summer, being spent this way, was quite a merry one; and though she thought she had much work on hand, she now looks back and sees how idle she was, and how little she could have had to do, for they could not always keep the food she cooked from spoiling. The only thing disagreeable arose from her being averse to study, but this soon was forgotten by her getting on hand a job of work.

The baby was a boy. The first thing she did, on looking at it, was to feel its head, and then to endeavor to decide what temperament he had. He was a pretty fellow. His body was white as milk, his hair was white, but it would grow dark, and he was as plump as a ripe apple. Every morning he had to be washed all over in a tub, and as he seemed to like to have the water drop over him, while he would splash in it, she thought that if it was deep and wide enough he might swim; for she had heard that every young baby, if put into water not so cold as to shock it, will swim away like a duck.

They gave him the name of Charles. The next child was a girl, and named Alice, the next Mary, the next Arthur, and there were others.

After preaching seven or eight years Mr. Moss found his health failing. To write two sermons every week was more than he felt he could continue to do; and though the people liked him much, he decided to quit preaching and remove to a warmer country. He would buy some land and become a farmer, an occupation which he had followed in his youth. He thought that no part of our country would suit him so well as on the Ohio River, and having saved money enough for this purpose he went thither.

At that time, much was said about the beautiful and desirable locations easy to be obtained on the banks of this river, and many gentlemen of taste and leisure selected them. Mr. Wirt's picture of Blennerhasset's Island was fresh in many minds, and they thought it not difficult to create homes equally beautiful. But some important matters were not foreseen. Nowhere, except in towns and in a few settlements, was there anything like refined society, and schools were rare. Often the country is broken by hills, or divided by creeks, which, in high water, can be crossed only in boats, for they have few bridges, and all bottoms overflow; but the greatest objection lay in the class of people, who were from the Slave States.

Mr. Moss was fortunate in getting a farm on the borders of the Ohio Settlement. The land was partly cleared and was good, but hard work was required. His health improved, and he labored with fair prospects of making himself well off. He had great advantages in being able to turn to his books when weary, and of restoring his strength through a new supply of nervous energy. He wisely labored, and wisely studied.

Delia did not miss much. She was busy in her household, and she took delight in teaching her children to assist her and to read. Still she found her labors too constant and exacting, the many children occupied all her time, and for several years she scarcely had a day she could call her own. No woman ever was more joyful at the sight of her first child than she, for she had wondered and waited, but the constant care it required wearied her; then, when others came, she felt overwhelmed with the demands made upon her. Still she lived through it all; her husband was kind, frequently there were glimmers of beautiful light, and at last, when no more children came, she was nearly as glad as she was at the sight of the first, and her spirits sprang up elastic. No tongue ever shall describe the great riches which belong to a family where study is united with industry, temperance with plenty, and where cheerful piety is the rule and guide.

Charles proved to be a good boy, and apt to learn. When two or three years old he was in the habit of coming to his mother and asking her what such a letter was called; and when she thought she would teach him the letters, she was surprised that he knew them. In almost the same way he learned to read, and when he was six years old he could write.

As he grew older, his father took him in charge, and bestowed upon him a knowledge of common branches and some Latin and Greek. It was intended to give him an education and fit him for a profession—it was hoped the ministry; but as he grew older he showed an important defect, which neither of his parents at first were willing to see. He was extremely careless; he had no order, and he depended upon seeing quickly more than upon care. He placed no true value on his books or clothes; when he was set about any work he would perform it, perhaps, in a new or surprising way, but he was likely to do some damage that made his labor unprofitable. His father had tools of various kinds, as every good farmer will have, and Charles handled them with great ingenuity, showing himself to be a natural mechanic; but he would waste timber, he would use many more nails than were required, and he left the nails and tools scattered around. His father was saving and careful, and it pained him to see his son so much to the contrary. He talked to him continually, threatened him, and punished him mildly, but nothing would work a cure.

On one occasion he became so vexed that he got a good whip and laid it over his shoulders heavy and long. Delia and all the children came running to see what was the matter. How could he? What had the poor boy been doing to deserve such a beating? The girls stood round wiping their eyes with the corners of their aprons, and looking reproachfully at their father. At first, he told Delia not to interfere, for, if she did, he could not tell what would happen; then, throwing away the whip, he showed them a piece of writing which he had told him to do, which was little more than a scrawl. He was getting worse and worse. He wrote better five years before. More than this, he was defacing all his books; he had even dared to write in the library books, and he was scrawling on the door, the window-casing, on the fence and everywhere. If it was good writing there might be some excuse, but it was the merest scribble. He had whipped him soundly, and he would whip him every day if he did not stop such work or learn to write a decent hand. Certainly, how could Charles be so careless and not pay attention to his father! He must be whipped if he would not mind.

So far as this was concerned, it was one of the best things that could happen to the young man, for ever afterward he took pains with his writing, and he learned to write a most beautiful hand, which, when it became settled, his father could not equal. In fact, it was the foundation of his success in life.

When Charles was about sixteen, his father sent him to Louisville with the products of their labors on the farm for the year, and it was thought an opportunity to teach him how to do business, while, at least, the charges of the commission merchants would be saved. He was told to keep full and exact accounts of expenses and receipts, and to be careful in everything besides. This was his first trip on the river by himself, and he was highly pleased with the undertaking.

He returned safely, and handed his father a sum of money, but no accounts of any kind. Why did he not do as he was bid? Well, he had forgotten it! but there was the money, every cent, and it was all right. It was counted. It would do. But more was expected. What were the expenses? Is there no account at all? Nothing? Charles felt in his pockets and pulled out some letters and crumpled papers. Yes, here is the account of passage money. Where was the little book he took? It was there. His father took it and saw nothing but a description of the Ohio Falls, with some bad spelling. He said he could remember. He made a verbal statement. A balance was struck; it might be right: could he tell? He said he could tell nothing more about it. Then, what did he mean by doing business in this style? What prevented him from doing as he was told? How did he expect to go through life in this way? He was sorry. He would never do so again. The matter was overlooked.

About this time he was sent away to school. It was necessary, at least, that he should know the world. After long and faithful trials his father became satisfied that he was doing no good. It is true he learned some, and he thought he was learning much. He spent money without giving accounts, notwithstanding the strictest orders. He seemed to have a mental one-sidedness. The child seemed to mingle with the youth. It was clear he would neither make a scholar nor a man of business. When he came home, a terrible time followed. The father, mother and all, were discouraged and out of patience. Mr. Moss said he regretted the loss of the money more than anything else, for it would have done the other children so much good.

In other respects, Charles was a fine young man. He had read much; his memory was good; he had a way uncommonly attractive, while he was good-looking; and, from what he related, it was evident he had made many friends. So far as his father ever could see or learn, he was pure in his morals; his tastes, for the most part, were correct, and though he had not then professed religion, he was not the least inclined to scepticism. Such cases are not so rare as many might think, though the defects may be different and less glaring. With them, twenty-one is a very tender age; that they shave is nothing.

From what has been said, it may seem strange that Charles should get it into his head that a business life would suit him better than any other. His father laughed at him, and his mother asked him how long he would keep a situation, for he need not expect his father would intrust him with money. Oh! he was going to learn; he knew he could learn. He could make so much money. He thought he would like to be a clerk on a steamboat. His father smiled.

About this time Alfred Welch, who became a pilot, visited in the family, and he fell in love with the oldest daughter Alice. In every respect she was amiable; she improved in her studies, and, when sent away to school, she made great progress; but her health declined. She had to come home, and then Alfred first saw her. He and Charles became good friends, and both agreed they would like to follow the river. Alfred soon got the situation of pilot's apprentice, but Mr. Moss would not let Charles go, and told him he must stay at home till he was of age, for not only did he need him, but it would be unwise to let him go into the world with the careless habits he had acquired. He should learn by experience how to place a value on property, and what it is to earn one's living by the sweat of the brow.

Charles did not complain a word. He went to work earnestly. He was always cheerful; even when night came, and he was tired, he was gay. He was the life of their society. To go out into the fields and breathe the air of the hills enlivened him; to sing and talk in young company made others happy. To swim in the river, even when the water was chilly, was almost a necessity. Often after a hard day's work he would swim to the old Kentucky shore.

He had a boat with a sail, and he was pleased if he could get out all the family and run around the island; but he was more pleased to take his mother alone; he would prepare her the nicest and softest seat, and away they would go. At such times she would gaze fondly upon him and remember. To his sisters he was almost as attentive as a lover, and they always attended to his remarks on their dress or behaviour. He taught them to stand and sit straight. In such things he was precise. He would never go to the post-office at the landing, or to mill, unless he blackened his boots and made himself look nice.

At last Mr. Moss thought he would intrust him with another shipment of produce. The season had been favorable, they had worked hard, and much profit was expected. Seven full wagon-loads were hauled to the landing. Charles bade them good-by, promising to come back with a plenty of money.

When he returned, the boat landed at the front of the door,—which was a surprise, as the landing was so near,—and he came in with good spirits; still his father saw that something was the matter. Was he well? Yes, but he was tired. How did he make out? First-rate; there was the money, every cent, it was all right. It was counted. "Is this all?" "Yes." "Well, let us have the accounts." He had none. "None?" He was not told to keep any this time; but it was all right,—he had sold at the top of the market, and he had lost none. "If ever—". There was blank astonishment through the whole family; no one could speak. The father was the first to break out. It need not be repeated. After the storm died a little, Charles and his father spent several hours in making an account. There were several hundred dollars; so much was saved. They figured long, added, substracted, remembered, corrected; it might be right, it might be wrong,—who knew?

The father lost all confidence in him. What was he good for? nothing, nothing. He should go to work. A pretty business-man he would make! He said he felt bad enough;

when he should go for himself he would pay it all back; nobody should lose anything by him. The father said he would be glad if he could take care of himself; he doubted not that he would have to help him.

After a little, Mr. Moss learned through Delia that he was offered the situation of second clerk on a steamboat. Not while he was responsible for his conduct should he stir a step. But he did not know how much they wanted him, nor how much they thought of him.

This was true. Business men really did take a fancy to Charles. They saw in him the rare qualities of patience and a desire to please; he had every appearance of being honest. Such a one could not fail to attract. When he should get experience he ought to command great wages.

At last, Charles talked with his father about it. He said he told them he was not fit to do business, but they said he could learn; if he would only agree to come, they would be to the expense of sending him to a commercial college; that would prepare him. Did his father not see what a chance this was,—and one not likely to come again? There did seem something in it; but only look, for one moment,—reflect. True, true;—well, he would be twenty-one by-and-by. Still, if his father would let him go he would give all the money he got. The father reflected; he was afraid of being made responsible for some careless act; better work for ten cents a day, than fail in such a station. Delia helped Charles; of course she could not say much, but she leaned on his side a little. At last, he might go, on the condition that he got a writing from his employers that the father should not be responsible. No, that would not do;—it would disgrace the family; and he did not wish to avoid responsibility. He was his son, and he would take care of him; he would neglect his duty if he did not decide as it seemed best. He should not go at all; he should keep at work. There was time enough; why should young men hasten to plunge into the troubles of the world? Charles worked on as before; he did not take it to heart. Then letters arrived inviting him to come. The offer was tempting. It was hard. Finally, he might go, — but, for the sake of the girls, for the sake of father and mother growing old, he must not act so as to bring wretchedness and disgrace. He could not have a moment's peace in this life if he should bring them to poverty. If this was likely, he would not go, he would stay—he ought to stay; it was all right.

At this time Alfred came home to spend the summer months, and he visited Alice daily. Alas! she had the consumption. Every one could see that she must die. She lingered till autumn, when she died. The very moment she passed away, she made a remark that she was dying. Alfred held one hand, her mother the other. For years Alfred mourned. The family had to console each other; separation was not to be thought of.

In the spring, Alfred got the place and wages of a first-class pilot. He was known by all, and his influence was great. He told the company why they could not get Charles. Immediately the trouble was overcome, and Charles went to a commercial college. He studied faithfully, and made himself master of bookkeeping, copartnership, and everything relating to steamboat business.

During the first season he was entry clerk. The next season he was first clerk. He succeeded well. There was no other such clerk on the rivers. Whoever knew him wanted to ride on his boat; they would often wait days, or a week. No one ever was more guarded or careful in doing business; and yet he was rapid. Often he would lie awake thinking of figures and books, or jump up to examine them and count over the money. He would rather lose a thousand dollars of his own money than a dime belonging to the boat. He felt that his life was at stake; and with this was connected the hopes, the fears and the interests of the family. He was going to show them that he could do business. What was past was past; the present and the future he could control.

Formerly, steamboat clerks, captains, and almost all hands, had united to rob the owners. This was so common, that it was said a clerk could not hold his place unless he would steal half. A change had taken place. Owners themselves had been obliged to go as clerks. The whole business was reorganized. Men of greater moral principle run the boats; rough and profane officers began to disappear; elegance of furniture, and decorations and sumptuous tables, were united with gentlemanly, and often high-toned Christian clerks and commanders. Charles had found his place.

On the coast, above Baton Rouge, Charles became acquainted with a planter's daughter named Lillie Gibson, and fell in love with her. She could speak French and Spanish as well as English. She dressed beautifully, and was a handsome and good girl. She didn't know about marrying a steamboat clerk; if he was an owner he might do; but papa had money and he could buy her a boat. She would wait and see. While she was waiting she fell deeper in love with him. This was in the winter. The boat was carrying cotton all the season from the neighboring plantations, for, with Charles aboard, they would get all they could carry.

Mr. Moss and his family rejoiced in his success. Charles was something after all. Meanwhile, terrible blows threatened the family. The rest of the girls were likely to have the consumption, and go the way of Alice. Some had scrofulous swellings in their necks, others had runnings from their ears. This was the way with Alice. It was a hereditary taint. The close rooms and indoor employment of the New England women have planted this disease in the veins of many, if not all, of their people. The minister saw that the women from the South had little of this. They had a plenty of exercise, for there are few who did not work out doors, at least in their gardens. He saw it after long reflection. His wife saw but faintly. She had brought up her girls in the New England fashion. She thought that reform in diet should save them from the scourge. That was not enough. It was their fathers who should have reformed, or, they should not have abandoned old customs.

Sweet rye and Indian bread had ceased to be good enough.

The minister made up his mind. Here is a new sidesaddle. This horse is gentle. You puny thing, get on him, and go to the post-office. Why, father, can she ride a horse? Let her try, let her try. Come, get on. No more buggy rides. One of these sucker women, as you call them, is worth a shipload of such stitching, embroidering, little-fingered, flat-breasted creatures. So far as the Southern women go, they are right. We want no nerves that are nervous, no muscles that are nerves. We want nervous nerves and muscular muscles. It is surprising, mother, how much better I feel; perhaps father is right. So it was the next day, and every day. Two more side-saddles were bought. How much better Mary does look—the black is almost gone from under her eyes, and the swelling on her neck is most out of sight. Emily's ears are getting better fast. True enough. They have more blood. In riding, they catch breath, with every step of the horse their lungs expand; to fill them, more blood is required. To make more blood, they must eat more then, must ride more, or stir around. Your school exercises of slapping hands and the like amount to nothing; they never can help. God never intended, or made the human body to be healthful by any such means. To undertake it is to climb over the wall like a thief and a robber. Come, girls, every one of you, help me rake up this hay, then you shall help load and mow it away. Isn't that too bad, father? Likely enough; but Charles is gone, Arthur is over-worked, and there is no other way. They must take hold and work. By-and-by the corn must be gathered, they must get their hands ready. Mother need not say much or she will get a call. If they want amusement let them ride. The consumption must be taken out of them, and it shall be. If the New England people go on in the present way they will be exterminated. The reason why society progresses so slowly is because the human race has to be kept up by ignorant laboring people. Get your rakes.

Charles prospered. He had high wages. He sent his money home for his father to keep. In addition, he speculated. He bought produce in Cincinnati and St. Louis and sold it in the lower country. At first he made; next he lost. It was very uncertain business. At last, he would agree to deliver nothing, except on a written contract, to fill which he had optional ones at the North. In this way he was safe. In one year he made nearly five thousand dollars.

In his love affair he could get no decision. Lillie's father liked him; he never saw a man he liked better. But he must stand higher, he must be part or principal owner in a steamboat. Then he could have his daughter. Of course it would take money—a big pile of it; he wouldn't mind going in as one of three himself. Had he no friend who would take a share? Yes, Alfred had talked of such a matter. Alfred was seen, he was willing. The matter was arranged. Of course Charles was to be the captain. From the first it was agreed that the boat should be called the LILLIE GIBSON. There was no higher ambition among the Southern belles than to have a steamboat bear their names. How extremely fortunate did Charles consider himself. The contract was signed in New Orleans. The father and daughter came up in the boat. Before they landed, Charles found Lillie in her state room; he kissed her, and O, the joy of it—she kissed him. The plantation extended for miles along the river. Their house was grand, and surrounded by trees, shrubberies, and flowers. There were hundreds of slaves. The cotton they raised some years loaded a boat. Such a splendid home; such magnificent people seldom are seen on the American continent.

The boat was to be built at Cincinnati. Charles wanted to build a first-class boat, but he saw they could not do it; they would have to borrow some as they stood. They might build one of the second class, but it should be fast; it must be finished without a fault. Men were set to work. They hoped to make the first trip early the next spring.

Charles came to visit the old folks and get his money. He wanted his father to be paid for what he had lost on the produce. His father would not think of it. He was building a boat. He confessed they would have to borrow; that they could do. He would learn something by the time he got through.

Charles had to tell his mother and girls all about his wife that was to be. Would she ever come to see them? Charles looked around the room—perhaps. Oh, no, she never would come hither; she would be frightened to sleep in our poor home. Well, they were glad he was so fortunate, and that he was going to be so happy. Of course she would be happy, Charles was so good. If they should have children it might be different: then perhaps she might come.

Charles wrote every week. The boat was launched; they were getting in the boilers and engines. But it cost much money. They thought they would work it through. She would pay for herself the first season.

In February a steamboat stopped, and Charles came up to the house. He looked thin and care-worn. After shaking hands and kissing round, he wanted to know where father was. They must have more money, no matter at what interest. Had father got any? Rather blank answer, that he had. Did they know how much? Not exactly. Whither did he go, when was he coming back? He went after wood, he was coming down the hill.

A pale, anxious son, shaking hands with a mild, hearty father. Mr. Moss had the peculiar Vermont smile on his face, which is both good-natured and shrewd. He had believed that, sooner or later, his son would come for money. There was not much visiting. Charles was hard run. The boat was nearly finished. Their own means had run out. They had got as much accommodation as they wished to ask for. Mr. Gibson had done something—they would not apply again. Now, if father and Alfred's father would undersign, they could get along. Had Alfred's father, Mr. Welch, been seen? Alfred wrote to him and he referred the matter to father. How much was wanted? The sum was named. There was a long silence. At last, why this was what a good farm was worth. But they would not have it to pay. Very true; but if——. It was no use. But had he no money? O yes, a little. The fact was, steamboat men must help each other. It is no place to go to farmers, who have labored their whole lives to get a home. Merchants and bankers have got rich out of the farmers; they were the men to make commercial ventures. There was no wisdom in a farmer investing in matters of which he could have no knowledge. He could not do it. The home must not be put in jeopardy; he might want to come to it himself some day. Some of them always would want it, so he could do nothing; how could he? It was a pity that at this point they should fail. Ah! that was the Baltic coming up; he must get aboard. Couldn't father come up and see the boat—see what they had done? Charles was surprised to hear him say that he would come up. He would start the next day. Farewells and kisses were exchanged. Our son's face seemed to lighten as if with hope.

Mr. Moss went to Mr. Welch, and they talked long together. They thought they might do something. They put what they had together; it was from the sales of wheat for several years. It should be ready cash or nothing. By no means would they risk anything else. If this were lost, it would matter little; they could live on the old farm the same as when the money was lying idle. The time to help boys most was not when they were starting, and could do well, but after they had started, after they had done well, and were come to a tight pinch. They knew this before; they had prepared for it.

Mr. Moss went to Cincinnati. He was dressed in a neat black suit, with a minister's white handkerchief around his neck. He went into the boat-yard and was walking around. The workmen thought he belonged to the Bethel church. Charles saw him at a distance, but did not know him; besides, he was busy picking up spikes and nails. His father thought this a good sign. At last he had come to attach a value to things. They met; Charles was proud to take his father all around,—but not quite so proud as he used to be to show how he could swim, or to fix his mother's seat and sail away with her. The engines were ready, they had taken the boat out on a trial trip. They were fixing some things; in the cabin workmen were busy painting and gilding. The state-rooms needed spring-mattresses and furniture. They could get time on a part, but the workmen needed their pay; they could get money by a mortgage, but they dreaded to give it. Alfred came in. The minister had great confidence in him.

Then he wanted to see accounts. Everything was ready for inspection, and in that fair round hand which cost something. He enquired cautiously of others, and with fair business tact; he took time; in two days he sifted their affairs. Finally he was satisfied, and he paid them a good sum. It was more than they expected. Heavy though it was, it made their hearts light.

The health of the girls had so improved and their appearance was so changed that they looked like new creatures. They could eat anything, and when farm-work hurried, they would go out and labor well. Their beaux learned not to come on a visit in a buggy, for if they did they would get on their horses; they must come on horseback,—and with good horses too, or they would run away from them, for they preferred to ride the highest-spirited horses on the farm. O that Alice could come back! Many good things resulted. When they read, wrote, sang, or played, they did so with pleasure and profit. They were healthful and strong; thin, small shoes would not do for them. They themselves made many things which others buy; for some things they had no use. They lacked neither politeness nor grace. Similar is the result when the farmer carefully cleans the wheat he is to sow. It was a frequent remark of the minister, that, naturally, all things seek a worse condition.

The Lillie Gibson did not come down so soon as was

expected; there had been delays. At last a letter stated what day they might be expected, though they could not tell how she would run; they could be ready by 10 o'clock. The girls were going to New-Orleans on this first trip; their dresses were made in time, and nothing remained but fifty or sixty little things, which they thought they could finish aboard. They had got up early and put on their traveling-dresses, and were eating breakfast, when there was a disappointment — a heavy fog hid the sun and settled down on the river.

A calliope is a steam-organ; and it is generally placed on the hurricane deck, in front of one of the chimneys. The keys are similar to those of the organ, and the whole is of iron and steel; the music is made by steam running through a pipe from the boilers. The airs usually played are of a popular, lively kind; the music is piping and grand, and can be heard a long distance. Breakfast was scarcely over, when all were startled by music on the river. The north door was opened. A boat was coming down past the landing, but the fog hid everything. The wonder was if this could be the boys' boat; it is not customary for boats to run in a heavy fog,—it must be Charles's boat, and Alfred was the pilot, he knew the river so well. When past the landing, the music ceased, and they could hear the heavy, guttural puffing. It was coming down on them very fast. Just above them the music burst out again. They listened, but nothing could be seen. The father asked what tune it was. Didn't he know? it was — "Out of the Wilderness." Then he knew whose boat it was.

The Lillie Gibson passed swiftly by; at the same time she was rounding to. The sounds of the music receded, and the echoes of the hills of Illinois answered those of the wooded Kentucky shore. Then the music came nearer. They could not mistake. Hastily the girls' trunks were carried down to the river, and they followed with their satchels crammed with unfinished work.

There is good landing anywhere on this shore; but the

pilot needed to understand it well to run in that thick fog. The family stood waiting. All at once they saw high in the air the tops of two tall chimneys, their red and green lamps still burning; then on a sudden the whole boat came out of the fog. Even when the sun shines there is no work of art which makes a more magnificent sight than one of these steamers. The Lillie Gibson seemed like an apparition. Her upper decks were crowded with newly painted wagons, ploughs and farming machinery for the cotton and sugar plantations, and below were barrels of pork and flour and boxes of dry-goods, while, by the sound, there was a drove of mules aboard. A crowd of folks were out on the guards.

While the family was beholding these things, and while the steam-whistle was screeching in the most awful manner, a man jumped ashore with a rope and took a turn around a tree, where he stood, and a crowd of men were shoving out the staging, when Charles ran along it, and coming to the end jumped to the land. The passengers smiled to see him kiss so many girls, and when they saw him kiss one who was not a girl, they knew it must be his mother. There was no time for much speaking. The fog was breaking away, the girls and their trunks were hurried aboard, while Charles lingered to talk with his father. He was happy to receive his approbation. The pilot tapped the bell, and yet the captain lingered. He was listening to these words: "He that walketh righteously and speaketh uprightly, he that despiseth the gain of the oppressor, that shaketh his hand from holding bribes, that stoppeth his ears from hearing of blood, and shutteth his eyes from seeing evil, he shall dwell on high, his place of defence shall be munitions of rocks, bread shall be given him, his waters shall be sure."

The Lillie Gibson having a full and through cargo, did not delay, and she only landed to take or leave passengers. Being a new boat, she attracted great attention, and the captain and pilot were greeted by many friends. Some urged that, for once, they ought to break the rule, good though it was, and take a social glass. The reply was, that if in observing the rule they had been prosperous, they ought not now to disregard it for fear of what might happen—or, did they not see there was no bar aboard?

It was important for the reputation of the boat that she should make the trip as soon as possible. It was evident that she was making good time, and, as they drew near Mr. Gibson's plantation, they could boast that the Lillie was nearly as fast as any on the Western waters.

Lillie and her father had been advised by telegraph, both from Memphis and Vicksburg, at what time the boat would arrive, and she drew near at the expected hour. It was a great day on the plantation. All the slaves were paraded on the bank, dressed in their best clothes. The calliope sounded as grandly here as on the Ohio; but, the river being wider, Alfred gave a more grand flourish in rounding to. Lillie, and her father, mother, and two brothers, were waiting, and they felt proud of the captain as they saw him on the lofty deck; nor did they tire in spelling the large letters of the name of Lillie Gibson. Charles, seeing from his station the evidences of vast wealth, was struck with the contrast when he compared the scene to his father's limited farm on the Ohio hills. But he felt a joyous pride in being able, at last, to bring before their door his boat, fresh and new, and named after the dear lady who was the daughter of the man who was so rich and grand.

The family were going to New Orleans, and as speed was what all required, they hurried aboard. When Charles's sisters first came into the cabin they were received with marked attention, and by their polite behavior and intelligence won the esteem of all. But the great sensation of the passage was when Mr. Gibson and his family came through the cabin doors, and Lillie was pointed out as the lady after whom this fine boat of ours is named. Whomsoever she addressed or looked upon was honored, and it was thought something to be brushed by her clothes. At the table, nothing was too good for her—whatever she requested was handed with delight; smiles, bows, and the kindest wishes met her on every hand. Her father was scarcely less observed, and her brothers were looked upon with admiration and respect.

After a little, the Northern passengers were surprised to find the family both sociable and amiable. They had no haughty, ill-bred airs; they treated none as superiors, and they engaged as freely in conversation as if all were equals, and had been acquainted long. The truth is, they knew how to behave, and none better than they could afford to condescend.

Lillie, in particular, was charming. When the captain's sisters were introduced to her, she shook each by both hands and kissed them, and in every way expressed her delight in seeing them. Perhaps she felt that she stooped; she did not stoop. Lillie's father and mother paid them great attention, and the girls confessed to each other that they had been deceived with regard to the Southern people. In no society had they seen folks whom they liked so well.

Charles was busy in attending to his duties; he would see that nothing was left undone, and the minutes were few in which Lillie could see him. She complained, and once caught him by the ear, as if he was a bad boy.

The Lillie Gibson reached New Orleans in a time so short as to secure most favorable notice in the daily papers. As a consequence, freight for a return trip, as well as a good passenger list, was offered. She was quickly unloaded and reloaded, and in a few days, with colors flying and music playing, she started for the North.

Charles expected Lillie would fix upon a day when they would be married; but Mr. Gibson plainly told him that he must wait till he should earn enough to pay all the debts, and to purchase from the pilot his share; then he could have his daughter. Charles thought this was hard; but he consented, and told them it would not be long before he should claim her, and he fixed the time on New Year's day. The boat had entered upon a business which one of the first class seldom reached, and it would increase rather than diminish. The parting of the lovers was very tender, and the hearts of all were filled with generous emotions.

Charles was a little too sanguine in his calculations. During the hot months business was dull; the time was improved in making alterations and repairs, and it was not until March that he attained his object.

But unexpected changes had marked the New Year. Mr. Lincoln had been elected President; the South threatened to secede, and business and other arrangements were likely to be interrupted. Alfred had been willing to sell; but Charles wished to wait till they could see what Mr. Gibson would do, and he feared the worst. Business had been enormous during the winter. The South had been buying provisions in the largest quantities; agents were ordered to buy without limit as to quantity or price, and sugar and cotton were shipped direct by Cairo to make the payments. Every boat was urged to take freight till it could carry no more. Charles had improved the chance, and he had a plenty of money.

The boat, going down, stopped at the plantation, and Mr. Gibson and Lillie came aboard; but as there was no place for conversation, they waited till they reached New Orleans. Charles could not fail to notice that they looked on him with more tenderness and regard than ever before, and in her state-room she gave him kisses so sweet that he wondered why he had not dreamed of so much happiness being in store. To Alfred, also, they paid particular attention, and, though he was not easily flattered, he showed that he was gratified.

The four were together in the room of the hotel. Charles stated that for his share he had money enough to permit him to become a two-thirds owner of the boat. Mr. Gibson said that this was nicely done; certainly, few river men had ever before been so successful. But he wanted to talk with them a little about political affairs. Both said that they did not meddle in such matters, and it was for their interest to say little. All very proper and judicious in days past and gone, but now, new lines are drawn; every one must take sides. The question he wanted to ask was this: in case of a separation, which side would they take, the North or the South?

They started. A separation! They had heard such a thing talked of, but did not conceive any one in earnest. Earnest! It was a fixed fact, and no future event could be more certain. If this were so, it would be Southern, not Northern men, who would strike the blow. Most true, and soon they would be ready to strike it, nor would they be alone; the great Democratic party of the North would go with them hand in hand. Lillie had been watching Charles intently; at this, she saw him flush, and she expected he would be rash. He collected himself, and said that a part might, but nothing was more certain than that the great body of the Northern people were opposed to disunion. Why, they had not even discussed the subject. Well, this did not answer the question: grant a secession, which side would they take? Alfred said that question need not be asked. Charles said he was about to say the same thing. Mr. Gibson said, that in that case he did not longer wish to have an interest in the boat. Very well, they could pay him what was due him.

But they should not be hasty. The breaking of the ties of affection is hard. In some cases it must be done. In this it was wholly unnecessary. Then he went on to show how much better they would do to run the boat on the lower Mississippi. Boats would be in great demand. Intelligent business men could command the wealth of the country, they might control it. The water he would have to run on would be an empire in itself. To this effect he talked long. The sweat stood on Charles's face, and when Mr. Gibson spoke of controlling the Mississippi he clinched his fist. In his reply, he said the Lord of the Heavens and the Earth had decreed the Mississippi to run through an undivided country, and no inferior power could decree otherwise. When he said this he looked at Lillie, she was ghastly pale, he saw he had lost her—he gasped for air, and his heart almost ceased to beat. After some silence, Mr. Gibson said that at their earliest leisure they would close the copartnership, and as he had nothing more to say, he and his friend, the pilot, would leave the young gentleman to bid his daughter adieu.

When their footsteps died away she sprang around his neck. She implored him not to desert her, not to go away,—not to break her heart. Why, why, why, should they part? Between almost every word she kissed him and her eyes flowed with tears. Most wretched man! He was choked, he was blinded, but he could feel her lips, her arms, her sobbing. At last he told her not to hate him for what he should say; he confessed he was surprised, it was a subject he had scarcely thought of, but she need not dream that he would lift the weight of his little finger against the government—rather, he would use all the ability God had given him to help sustain it. What, would he do nothing for her? Yes, much; he had not time to tell how much. He would do any thing a man ought, or dare do. But what was she, what were her parents, what was the whole country without the government? She was asking him to help bring ruin upon her, and her people.

Oh, no! She should not leave her parents. What could prevent him from running the boat bearing her name past the house that was her house and his home? Oh! how happily they could live together. He must not tear himself away.

He was sorry to tell her that rather than agree to do what she required, dearly as he loved the boat, dear as it was for the name it bore, and dear as it was for the hopes it contained of his future life, he would set it on fire and in the midst of the conflagration plunge where he would fall on the hissing, red-hot boilers and be scorched and twisted like a leaf.

She started back in defiance, and, without a warning, spat on him. In a proud voice she ordered him to leave the room. He bowed to her cold beauty and obeyed. When without, he did not weep, he smiled. The smile arose from the depth of his being, where dwells a superior love—the love of country, of society, on which all blessings depend.

As they started for the North they concluded, from the temper of the people, that this would be their last trip.

They had an overflowing list of passengers, and yet at every landing more came aboard. They were told there was no room, and that even the cots were all taken, but they would come. One man said that he was fleeing from the wrath to come. At Vicksburg there were threats from the crowd, and they backed out so soon that some passengers could not get on their trunks. At Napoleon the boat was fired on, and a hand was wounded. The shot spattered against the cabin and the fright among the families was extreme.

At Memphis there were more passengers, and while the clerk was on shore collecting the freight bills, a party of armed men rushed aboard, ordered the fires dampened, and the chain cables to be got out fore and aft. The boat should not leave. They were not going to have all the boats taken out of the river. They crowded around the captain so that he could scarcely stir, and when he gave orders they threatened to shoot him. He asked them if they did not know that this was piracy. Piracy might be —, etc. He could do nothing. Alfred saw what was going on, he found the first-mate, they went to the engineers and formed their plan. Then he went up into the pilot-house. The first-mate had run the river for many years, he was from Pittsburg, and if he was not rough, his voice was. He came around carrying a six-shooter in his hand. Haul in this staging and be lively, every man, heave away; you don't half lift—back with it. At the same time the engineer's bell rang to fire up. The pilot's bell rang to back one wheel. The boat moved, the staging dragged. The pirates ordered the boat to stop. The harsh voice resounded like a speaking trumpet. Heave ahead, the last man of you, heave! All who are going ashore had better be lively. The ruffians saw they were likely to take a ride. They ran down the staging and jumped off, and waded. Both wheels started ahead, the staging rose dripping from the water. The boat was saved. There were shakings of hands and exulting shouts. Then the calliope played in shrill pipings, "The Star Spangled Banner," "O say, Can you see by the Dawn's early Light?" The clerk took the cars for Columbus, and when the boat reached Cairo he came aboard. Charles afterwards learned that the rebel leaders at New Orleans had sent despatches to seize the Lillie Gibson.

War followed. The lower Mississippi was closed. During the summer most of the steamboats were laid up. In the fall there was a move. At times, government took every boat to transport troops and supplies. The Lillie Gibson was chartered and continually employed. In the attempt to penetrate the bayous in rear of Vicksburg she was damaged. The limbs of trees and cannon balls carried away one chimney, and ripped open the wheel-houses. There were musket balls through her cabin windows, and blood stains on her decks. She had given a good fight herself, for a battery of artillery was aboard. Her captain and pilot went through these terrible scenes with undaunted courage, and when they could do no more, they returned to the upper country for repairs. The minister and his family saw a sad sight when the Lillie Gibson was towed past their house, no steam, no music.

Still the boat was sound; at New Albany crowds of workmen thronged around her, and soon she was as good as new. One bright day in June she came back shining, and playing "Dixie." "In Dixie's Land I take my Stand."

She was at the surrender of Vicksburg, and beheld the rebels' last grasp on the Mississippi relax at Port Hudson. Then the river was opened. Some of us remember how a first-class steamer, anxious to be the first, came through from New Orleans to Cairo, a thousand miles, with no other freight than one box of oranges.

Charles left the Lillie Gibson, and went down the river in an iron-clad, which was to patrol the river, driving out guerrillas or looking after torpedoes. When opposite Mr. Gibson's house they anchored, and Charles was put ashore, with a guard of marines. The walks had grown up to grass and weeds, but there were signs of tramplings. All was silent, and no one could be seen. It was a dangerous neighborhood; the guerrillas swarmed the country. A week before they had fired on a transport from a field near the house. A gunboat had come up from Baton Rouge; there was a little fight, during which a shell had gone through the upper story. He knocked; there was no answer. He turned the knob; the door opened, and he went through the wide hall. His footsteps sounded hollow. The carpet had been taken up for rebel blankets. Evergreens were seen through the back door. On stepping forth, he saw Lillie come out of the basement; as she did so, she wiped her lips with the back of her hand. When she saw Charles, she sprang up the steps, and said she was glad he had come. They had seen such times, such fightings, and such sights! She was in black.

They were seated in the hall. The marines were on the verandah. How was it she was quite alone; where were her folks—her father, mother, and brothers? She could hardly answer. After the fall of New Orleans her father took it so to heart that he gradually sank away, and last August he died. He had no disease. Her mother, long declining, followed in September. One of her brothers fell in the battle of Champion Hill; the other died in the hospital at Mobile. Not one of the family was left. Her relatives in New Orleans had been sent, by Lake Ponchatrain, across the Confederate lines.

This, indeed, was sad. What was she going to do? She did not know. What troubled her most was the constant going to and fro of bad men, and the fighting. By the way, where were the negroes? Gone, all gone, except a few too old to move. These had been sick; she had watched and nursed them. For a long time she had cooked, washed, and baked. She couldn't have things nice.

Then she wanted to ask him a question. Certainly she should ask. Did he own the boat still? Yes, it was at Port Hudson. Well, had he—had he changed the name? No; still it was the Lillie Gibson. She raised his hand to her lips and kissed it. Would he pardon her? He would pardon her anything except her being an enemy to his country.

True—true; he could not pardon that. But they had been deceived, wickedly and cruelly. Father often said so before he died. Her brothers said there had been much lying going on, and that they did not have men enough. They had been told that the North would help them, and that without trouble they could hold the Mississippi. It seemed as though they could not hold anything. She did not profess to understand these matters. She had acted and believed as she was taught; he did the same, only he knew so much more. They were ruined—everybody was ruined.

The bell on the gunboat rang. The marines were stirring. He could not stay. Could he do anything for her? No, nothing, unless he could make peace. He took her hand. She looked into his eyes. Was that all? Was what all? Alas—alas! it would never return. He placed her head between his hands and kissed her forehead. Once, how tenderly, how truly he had loved her. She was the blood of his heart, the life of his life. The bell rang. The boom of a heavy gun came up the river; there was the distant sound of musketry-firing. Could he not call again? Yes, he would call. And so she did love him, after all? O, yes! she could not tell him how much. Their lips met, and the bell rang with an angry swing.

Black smoke was streaming out of the chimneys as they got aboard. Now for them. It seems that these guerrillas have artillery, and are standing up to the work well. They are after yon transport hugging the east side of the island. A tin-clad is peppering them. With this strong current, and our full head of steam, we shall soon be upon them. That tin-clad does not like a short range, and is dropping down. Here we round to, and give them a pill from our 11-inch kicker. That was too high. This salt-water lieutenant will sight; now pull. Did anybody ever see anything more beautifully done? Why, their two-gun battery is nowhere. They had better give up talking about their Mississippi.

Three days after, Charles called again. This time it was

from a tin-clad. She was going to lie there. The guerrillas were swarming. The officers told Charles to beware of pretty women; they smile to deceive.

When he went in he looked around. Have we any one here? Whom could he be talking of? Did she know that her race was treacherous, that many a poor fellow last was seen entering deceitful doors? Yes, she did know it; but if she deceived him, he should shoot her first. Hope had lighted her eye, and given color to her cheek.

Now, then, she would have the past forgotten; only a bridge should come thence, and its name should be love. Well, what would she have? she must speak plainly. She wished nothing more than to be his true, loving wife. With him strife should banish, battles cease; oh, that it could be so with all others! "Whither thou goest, I will go, where thou lodgest I will lodge; thy people shall be my people, and thy God my God."

It was enough. That same day a chaplain came from the gunboat—the officers came also—and they were married. The poor blacks sat by, and joyously saw their mistress and the captain become man and wife.

Then she had something to tell him. Not all the cotton was burned. Some had been fired when the boats first came in sight; it was to deceive. She had a map of the places where it was hid, and it could be found.

This was a surprise to Charles. He went to Vicksburg to get a permit. Of course, a loyal man like Captain Moss had a right to do with his own as he chose. On the banks of bayous, under paw-paw bushes, in corn fields, over which plows had run, under piles of cotton-seed, and in other places, was the cotton found. Much of it was dirty and torn, but it had a large, clear heart. The Lillie Gibson was so well loaded that her machinery was protected from cannon-balls, and the bales were piled up to the cabin-deck. We take all aboard. These poor people, who have grown weary and old hoeing and picking cotton, shall find a Northern home. Now, Lillie, bid the old place a good-bye; we may not see it again till gentle peace returns. Till then, the government, with its heavy, its remorseless hand, will have its way.

All aboard with Lillie and her cotton. They and others are convoyed by one of the Marine Brigade, huge transports, oak and ironclad, hiding within horses, saddled and bridled, with a battery in front. If guerrillas show themselves we land, a door opens and out rush our cavalry, they spur up the bank and dash after, with pistol and sabre.

Lillie began to forget her sorrows in the new life, and in the enjoyment of what was left. She took new interest in her boat. With her husband she would walk below through the black mazy machinery, and talk with the soiled engineers. She even felt a pride in putting her hand on the polished brass or iron, or on a heavy beam. With wonder she would walk in front of the intensely blazing fires, stepping across the never-ending stream of water and coals, and where the crowd of firemen—naked to the belt—shoveled the black coal into the dazzling furnace, or fed the fiercely roaring blazes with wood. When Alfred was on duty her husband would help her up into the lofty pilot-house, and here, where the motions are tremulous, so remote is the engine, she would sit gazing on the marvelous scenery, while the pilot, now slowly, and now swiftly, turns the polished wheel.

One day the Lillie Gibson slowly steamed up the Ohio and the calliope was playing "Come Haste to the Wedding." The boat landed and the captain led his wife ashore. To the passengers, the meeting, the shaking hands, and the kissings were as good as a theater. Then the boat went on, and the captain with it. There were watchmen. He too would watch, for one day the first-mate, smelling brimstone, was in time with a bucket of water, and the incendiary guerrilla was found, his pockets showing what he was, and in a scuffle he went overboard. The night was dark—they supposed he could swim, if he could he was fortunate, and they went on.

How quiet are these shores, how cool these shades, how

fresh the water from the spring! We never had such thick cream, nor such sweet, new butter. How did they make such light, soft bread?—it was better than any cake. She must learn if she could to make like it.

The next summer their new house was finished and they moved into it, their family three in number. One of them frequently is dissatisfied. Only one thing will please him. Often it pleases two.

In every man there is some blemish. It is a flaw which cannot be mended. At Cairo, a government contractor told me how he made a settlement with Captain Moss. He had sold him several thousand bushels of oats, and had received some money. The captain felt in all his pockets, and pulled out a great variety of papers, at last, the right ones were found in his coat-tail pocket. The contractor says that he keeps all his private accounts in this way. Every thing relating to the boat, however, is on the books in good shape. He added that he knew of one occasion where Charles had dealings with a party amounting to over ten thousand dollars, and all the papers concerning the transaction he kept in his hat. It is known that he can settle with a man any moment with papers he carries with him. But it is remarkable that every thing is complete and correct.

The causes of many of these things go back to the summer days when Delia came from her lowland home across the Green Mountains, and looked down into the waters of Lake George.

THE MISSISSIPPI RIVER.

AS civilization advances, woman is called to new and varied employments. Then only do the arts and sciences make places for her, then only is she fitted to fill them. Of all our institutions of learning which have given thorough culture and broad views, and thus prepared woman for advanced stations, none have exceeded Oberlin. In connection, it has taught reform in diet, which undoubtedly has contributed to lengthen the life of human beings.

Deacon Cowles lived in Iowa, and he sent his daughter Maria to this school, that in every respect she might fit herself for a teacher. He determined that in case she should not choose to marry, she should have an education by which she could support herself handsomely. In no station, in no country should she be helpless. Should she marry, much better would she be able to make her children, herself and her husband happy. He had not large means. The country was new, he and his family labored, saved, and did without many things to keep Maria at school. Still he prospered; with such wide views, he was also wise in worldly affairs, and he became independent.

A short time after Maria graduated, and while she was at home, her father died. She had loved him dearly, the older she grew the more she loved him, for then she began to realize how wisely and richly he had endowed her. It was a great shock, and she was reconciled only by thinking that she would meet him in the Heavenly Jerusalem.

Then she commenced the life of a teacher. There are few

girls who do not form attachments to the other sex. Oscar More was a student with her. He was going to be a minister, and they were engaged to be married when he should be ordained. He was a noble looking young man, six feet tall, a good scholar, a fine speaker, and ambitious. No one doubted but he would become distinguished.

While she was teaching, he was studying theology. He was thought much of, and the Professors considered him the most promising of all their young men. From a class-mate of his I learned his secret history of those days. It will astonish many. One evening he went to a Professor and candidly told him that he had doubts of the truth of the Christian religion, and of the immortality of the soul, and he wished to talk with him. He stated the points, and they considered them till nearly daylight. The Professor admitted that the same things had troubled him, and he could not give full satisfaction. The interview ended with the conclusion that as some things were known to be true, the others must conform and also be true. Still Oscar was not convinced. He was troubled, and at times was nearly insane.

Many scientific men become sceptical because they lead isolated lives, and have no living facts by which they can prove religion true. For the same reason have fashionable people and those living by others' industry become sceptical, or wholly indifferent. Such may be what is called educated, but it will be noted that when they read books written by great men, they understand only a part, even if the language and subject be simple. German scholars frequently are sceptical, for their ideas are confused with poverty, with beer and tobacco smoke. Finally, some practical men are sceptical, not because they do not have facts, but because they do not take pains to connect the facts in a natural and logical order.

Oscar being ambitious and yet unable to solve the problem of Christianity, grew careless and cold, and he had little religion in his heart. As a consequence, he was led away by his ambition to commit great wrongs, and he not only become one of the most wretched of mortal men, but he inflicted unspeakable anguish upon more than one faithful heart.

One time when he was in New Haven he became acquainted with a young lady whose parents were rich, who was highly accomplished, and who was distinguished for her beauty. A mutual attachment followed. Oscar could not help seeing the misery he was creating, but he thought that with his great abilities he could live through it all. He felt it to be so important to have a wife who could help him on his way that he was willing to sacrifice Maria, deeply as his heart continued to love her.

Of course Maria gradually ceased to receive letters from him, and she was alarmed. At last she wrote a letter every day for six days, determined to force a reply. He wrote, saying that he was very busy, that his affections were unchanged, but he added some reflections to the effect that this is a transient, fleeting world, and that we should always be prepared to meet disappointments. Then she wrote to a friend of hers, and who was intimate with his class-mate, to enlighten her. She made enquiries, and discovered the true state of the case. A duty was to be performed, and the New Haven lady was told every thing. Immediately she returned to Oscar all his gifts and letters, and sharply accused him. So far had preparations gone, and so great was her mortification, that she fell into a decline, and in less than a year she died.

At this very time Oscar was paying attention to another young lady in Troy. She belonged to one of the first families, she was quite young, and she fancied she loved him, at least she wrote finely about her feelings. Oscar thought he would go back to Maria, he saw retribution gathering in the future; still there was a great struggle. His class-mate has told how he labored with him almost the whole of one night, in a recitation room, and he told him if he deserted Maria, he would have no peace in this world or in the next.

Meantime, Maria had been offered the situation of a gov-

4*

erness in a planter's family near Vicksburg. Her reputation as a teacher was the very best. The invitation was pressing, the wages great. She had the matter long in suspense, for she wanted to know what Oscar would do. At last, her friend informed her that he was writing day by day to the lady of Troy, and that, as things looked, he was likely to marry her. Maria hesitated no longer. She accepted the situation, and started for the South. It was in the fall of the year. She improved the opportunity of joining a company of travelers, some of them the relatives of the planter with whom she was to live, who had been spending the warm months at St. Anthony's Falls. The water being low, they took the cars of the Illinois Central at Dunlieth, and at Cairo they waited several hours for a boat. Maria had great curiosity to visit that spot where the waters of the Mississippi and the Ohio meet. It is not always easy to approach the place where the land ends. A gentleman helped her over the marshy soil and drift-wood, and through weeds, to the place where she could see the waters mingle. The sight was grand; and, casting her thoughts backward to the many large rivers, some of them thousands of miles apart, a deep impression was made on her mind.

They landed at the planter's door. At an expense she hardly afforded, she had prepared garments of a superior quality, and she made an appearance much in her favor. By nature, she had good features and a fine form, and intercourse with the best society had given her an engaging and self-possessed air. By exercise and temperate habits, she had acquired a strong, healthful body. Beside this, she had the art of matching ribbons and the patterns of dresses to a degree a woman seldom reaches, and no one thought her anything approaching an old maid, though she was twenty-four. She understood several languages. She had a sweet, clear voice, could sing excellently, and she could play on the piano; nor did she do so simply by striking the chords, but with a practical knowledge, particularly of thorough base. She was always noted for the whiteness and regularity of her teeth. In addition, she was skilled in housewifery. She had learned much from her mother, and during three years at school, she and three other girls boarded themselves. Perhaps she had no greater qualification than that of making bread so good that every one praised it.

Such adornments can but make a superior women. In a fair degree, Maria represents the progress which has been made by Christian civilization. When we consider that it is not difficult to select almost a thousand women who, combined, do not possess her qualifications, what, we may ask, will society become when every woman shall be her equal? Clearly, when this level is reached, other things, also, will correspond, and it does not enter into the heart of me to conceive how exalted the state of society will become. At the present time, such women are missionaries; they may consider themselves fortunate if they do not become martyrs. They can only influence—it is impossible for them to control, and their chief happiness must be derived from themselves. Still, there are pleasures in this age which, during parts of one's life, are fully equal to all that the future can bestow. Nature never dies. We breathe the air, grass grows, leaves come and go, rain falls, and the sun shines.

The place where she lived afforded her every comfort. They were not elegant, but they were sensible people; they were rich, well-bred, and all strived to make her residence agreeable. A governess, on becoming one of a family, needs much skill not to derange the established order by uncommon wants, by excess of politeness, or by any singularity of speech or conduct to occasion remark. At the same time, the people must not be straightened in their means, and they must set a neat and an abundant table. It is of no consequence, it is embarrassing, if they set a fashionable table. Perhaps there is no mechanism so beautifully constructed, and yet so easily deranged, as a family. In one sense, a rich planter's family may be said to run of itself. Usually, the lady takes little part in the labor, and, at least, she realizes nothing of the constant toil; and, as most people think they always must be vexed, she magnifies trifles. She has time on her hands—she has money; she seeks how she may enjoy the one and spend the other.

The neighbors were not near, for the plantations were large, and Maria had many pleasant rides in making calls with the planter's lady. It was not long before several young men solicited the honor of her company to various places. They were respectful, some of them well-informed; she had no reason for refusing. It was seldom that she was not requested by some gentleman to accompany him to church, either at Vicksburg or to a country camp-ground. When convenient, she preferred to go with the family. She thought she never saw people better behaved, or who enjoyed more of the blessings of this world. She saw little of the horrors of slavery, for it cannot be constantly presented. It is only a fruit, and there must be seasons and influences favorable for the fruit to grow. The servants in the house were well-dressed, and were contented, while she could not see that they who labored in the fields were forced to work hard, or were poorly clad. Often was she present where they ate; their food was coarse, but sufficiently abundant, and if, by extra labor, they chose to have a greater variety, nothing prevented. They got much money of the planter even for poultry, eggs, and fish. It was true that they were ignorant, but she did not fail to notice that the poor whites were equally ignorant, and, being indolent, they were not as useful to society as the slaves. As time passed, she learned more. Instances of cruelty came to her notice; sometimes women were whipped, sometimes families were separated. She was told that they could not be trusted, and that, if opportunity offered, they would do dreadful things. She believed, because she was told that they were barbarians. She saw that they needed to be enlightened; she could see no possible prospect that the planter ever would consent that they should be enlightened. She thought that the master had some affection for the black man. She was convinced that the non-slaveholder not only hated, but feared him. He was his rival. While she did not change her views with regard to slavery, she was forced to admit, all things considered, it was an evil too great for men to remedy.

Among those who called on Maria was a gentleman of the name of Harper. He had lost his wife, and the planter and his lady were soon convinced that he was thinking of their governess to fill her place. Mr. Harper was distinguished for his wealth, for his fine taste, and for his scholarship.

To show her what a home she would have, he contrived, with some mutual friends, that she should call at his house. She did not know whither she was going, and the stop seemed accidental. She was surprised at the magnificence. The vast and solid mansion was half hidden by a grove. Long winding walks, bordered with flowers, and a garden of flowers surrounded the dwelling. The softest carpets were under her feet, huge looking glasses showed her whole figure, and fine paintings hung on the walls. A library contained the choicest literature of our own and foreign languages. A costly piano lay open, and she could not resist their united entreaties to play. From the parlor and from the library were seen long stretches both to the north and to the south of the Mississippi. The table was spread in a manner more elegant and sumptuous than she had any where seen. Vases of rare and costly flowers shed a sweet and strange perfume. There were fresh fish from the northern lakes, oysters from Baltimore, and natural and canned fruits from all parts of the world. Though the weather was warm, an abundance of ice made all things cool. The servants in attendance were dressed like gentlemen and ladies, and they took as much pains to please as if they were serving their benefactors.

When some of the company proposed to visit the rooms, she could not be excused if she did not go with them. So many large, airy, and well furnished apartments she had never seen in one house before. There were two rooms into which she stepped with a pained heart. They were the ones occupied by the wife when she was alive. She did not die here. There stood her bed, and here were many of her things as she had put them away. The dressing-room contained her articles of toilet, they were costly, and from the hands of workmen of refined taste.

Then they went to visit the servants' quarters. It was a village. Each house was of brick, there was separate apartments, well lighted, and a few, belonging to old favorites, were carpeted. The barns, and the gin-house beyond, were extensive, and showed thrift and good taste. So much was there to admire that the tongue was silent.

It was not long before Mr. Harper proposed. Though she had foreseen it, she was surprised and a blackness seemed to cover the sky. She told him she would give him an answer at a future day. She wrote to Oscar, it would be for the last time; she simply asked his intentions. Oscar replied that he loved her as much as ever, that scarcely an hour passed in which he did not think of her, still, he had doubts whether she might not be happier with some one else. She had written to her friend, the answer came at the same time and she opened it. He was still writing to the lady in Troy, and he had been to visit her.

Oscar was about to finish his course. Every tongue praised him, and already polite and refined audiences listened to him with delight. As an extempore speaker, and on occasions of public interest, few of long experience could better command attention. Calm and critical minds could perceive, however, that he was neither deep nor always correct, and that his mastery lay in a strong, full voice, in being perfectly at ease, and in paying close attention to the general rules of oratory. In addition, he was tall and well formed, his head was large and handsome, and he weighed nearly two hundred pounds. Perhaps he exerted a magnetic influence. Still such was allowed for his youth and his inexperience.

One of the Professors, an old man, who had closely watched many of the best minds of our country from their first entrance into public life, and had marked the causes of their success and their ill success, took occasion before they parted, cautiously to remark to Oscar that sometimes he had known instances where early promise had been a bar rather than a help, and that those who had become eminent had studied more after they left college than in it. The reason was, that on coming in conflict with others, they found that minds far more comprehensive than theirs had occupied the ground before them, and they had a long struggle to become their equal. To be useful, is within the reach of all. There is an eminence belonging to the young man which as much arises from what he is expected to do, as from what he does do. Another eminence is of the man of the middle and advanced age who has fullfilled the promises of his youth. It was long before Oscar fully understood these words.

With much hesitation Maria finally concluded she would become Mr. Harper's wife. There were many things which looked dark, she thought almost threatening, but she fancied she would have such forebodings were she going to marry any one else. At the best, much was uncertain. Of the awful storm which for years had been threatening, and which was about to break, she had not the faintest suspicion. I cannot believe there were any who had. She saw that her youth was nearly passed, that at least, two years would elapse before she would return North; then, others would fill her place, and that so far as worldly prospects were concerned, she could not believe she ever would be offered such again. She hoped she might be able to do something for the poor blacks, at least, much better would she be able to study slavery, and to tell the world what it was.

When Mr. Harper called on the day she had appointed, she was ready to receive him. She wore a white dress, a rose was in her hair, and she had been artful enough to make herself appear in the highest degree charming. When he entered she arose, she took his hand and smiled graciously. After a proper interval he asked her if she had decided whether she would become his wife. She answered that she would not object to his offer, and she hoped she might prove grateful for so much condescension, and capable of filling so high a station. He told her he was a happy man. Happy, indeed, should any man consider himself with a wife like Maria.

To pass through the scenes of the important day, by properly conforming to the etiquette required, was a task; but by the help of friends, by her quick perceptions, by her firmness and retentive memory she acquitted herself well. It was remarked by some who were well acquainted, that the guests collectively were worth from twelve to fifteen millions of dollars. Her appearance in bridal garments was greeted with silent or whispered admiration. She was in the prime of her beauty. Her health was excellent, and all the fruits of her parents' care in her childhood, of her studies, of her meditations, of her temperance, and of her religion, were indicated in her eyes, in her face and in her form, as before the friends she gave her hand to the man who had chosen her. When the clergyman began to speak a cloud swiftly passed over her face; as briefly she thought of Oscar, and then she listened attentively to the service.

A woman has many advantages when she marries a man who has been married before. He has reflected much of the dear one gone, and he thinks he sees how she might have been saved. In that warm climate, however hot the days, the nights are generally cool. The air passes through the green blinds, but not the light of the moon or stars, while the thin netting keeps away flying insects. Where there are trees a class of birds sing a few notes at midnight. Between two and three o'clock, great numbers begin to sing, and the chambers resound with their melody. There is an honest and a noble pride in life. To awake refreshed and to greet the one we love, to dress and to look forward with hope for the day, and for days to come, give much of all that makes life dear. As the sun arises the flowers are in their greatest glory, and it is a pleasant employment to pick and skillfully arrange them in bouquets for the table.

There are few who do not labor and strive, though with

faint hopes, that some day they may own such a house and such wealth as belonged to Maria's husband. They confess that they believe that their happiness would be complete; and some would exchange their innocence—if innocence they have—for such possessions. To every age is given a new lesson. Some may be easily and soon learned, others are more difficult. The one for our age is to show that a house which is built by unrewarded labor and whose stones are cemented with tears cannot stand.

Maria could control her husband, because he knew enough to know that she could teach him. He adopted some customs of which she showed him the importance, and often he was restrained because he wished to please her, and because she convinced him it was best.

In a short time they made an excursion to the North; they visited the principal cities and places of resort, nor did they neglect to go to her family in Iowa. He went with her to her father's grave, he dropped a sympathetic tear, and led her sorrowing away. One day, as they were riding through the streets of a city her eye met Oscar on the pavement. He raised his hat and stood still. She ventured to look back, and she saw him still standing looking towards them.

She learned from her friend whom she visited, that he had become a minister, that the lady of Troy had dismissed him, and that sometimes he was so troubled in his mind as not to be able to preach. He was still popular, and he was about to accept a call from a wealthy congregation in a large city.

Mr. Harper and his wife returned to Mississippi sooner than they intended. The country was convulsed with political discussions, and the place for him was among his people. In the middle of October the boat landed them at their pleasant mansion. In all their travels they had seen no place so much to their mind. Here they would be contented to live and to enjoy each other's society. The round globe itself contained no spot they would prefer. With music, with rides, with the duties of the day, and with the hope of a month which they could name, a few happy weeks went by.

Early in November Mr. Lincoln was elected President. Every ballot which fell on that day from the hands of the people has been answered by a death-shot or a dying groan. And because they fell the land was filled with mourning; cities and houses blazed, and thousands who knew no toil, no care went to live in exile and want beyond the seas.

Although no politician, Maria was well acquainted with the history and constitution of the country. Since her residence in the South, she had learned with amazement how generally the people advocated the doctrine of State rights taught by Calhoun. She looked upon it as an error so great as to be a folly. She saw at once that if it was true there could be no government except by general consent. There was nothing to control the bad who might wish to plunder in the midst of disorder, nor could she see how a city or a town could be held as a part of a State except by force. If it were right to compel them to remain in a State by force, it was right to compel the State to remain in the Union by force, because the relations which each bear to the other were identical. She did not see that this was a doctrine calculated for the ignorant, and that it was not a question of secession, but of the continuance of slavery.

Mr. Harper was waiting for breakfast. Where was Mrs. Harper? She was late in getting down this morning. Oh, she had been down some time and had gone out to see one of the sick women. Soon she came in, almost running, and they had breakfast. He had great news for his wife this morning. Really, she would be glad to hear it. Mr. Lincoln had been elected, and South Carolina was going to secede. In a short time all the cotton States would follow; then the planting States. That was news indeed, but could it be true? Yes, he knew it. The whole South was in a blaze. It was no spasmodic affair. It was the result of management and long calculation. He knew the whole thing through. She remarked that if it was true she thought it very wicked. Wicked! What did she mean by wicked? Why, is it not wicked—is it not a crime, to array the North and South against each other, and to cause bloodshed where all before was peace? She might call it what she pleased— it would be done. It was as good as done already. As to bloodshed, she need fear nothing of that kind. The democratic party of the North would go with them, and things would remain as before, only they would have their own country and their institutions to themselves. In that case they would have the Mississippi, when foreign capital would come in, and New Orleans would rival and ruin New York.

She asked if she was right in understanding him to say they would have the Mississippi. Yes, the Mississippi. Why not? Nothing, only she thought it was bought with the money of the whole of the people, and at the particular request of the people of the Northwest. That might be, but they were going to have it; still the North should use it the same as they always had—there might be some nominal charges and duties, for the new state, having no commerce, it must collect a revenue from some quarter. Of course they would have the permission to use the river, they wanted them to use it. She said she was of the opinion they would have it without asking permission. What, were they going to fight? That was a good one. Really now, did she think Northern men would fight, that is, stand any kind of chance with Southern men? She replied that she knew they were a peaceful people, and not at all disposed to go to war. But it must be remembered they were a commercial people. It would hardly answer for the South to forget this, or to fail to study what a commercial people demand and will have. As one had said, a man who can walk towards the east, can walk towards the west. Perhaps he mistook. Not at all, not at all. But she need not talk about war. There could be no war. Still the South was prepared. She had not been idle. Mr. Harper wished to believe there would be no war.

Such was their first conversation. Then State after State went out of the Union. The South was bitter, enthusiastic and nervous. In comparison, the North was calm. The main, and the first object of the Southern leaders was to make the people all of one mind. They fixed upon this policy early; all who would not unite with them should leave the country. If they would neither unite with them nor leave, they would fare worse. They were solemnly in earnest. Having the slaves to labor for them, they had nothing else to do but to be in earnest.

One day in February, Maria did not feel very well. Her husband thought she looked as if she had been crying, and he asked her tenderly what was the matter. She said he must pardon her, she was so foolish. Beside other things, she had been thinking of home and her father's grave. He knew how to respect her feelings. She should make some music. He led her to the piano, and raised the curtains. The sun was in the west. Before them the Mississippi lay in a long, broad, sparkling sheet. Several miles distant, a steamer was coming around the bend.

She played and sang "Sweet Home." Tears came into her eyes. He asked her for some other pieces. Then she sat silent and looked on the river. The boat was approaching, with its two black plumes of smoke thrown aloft. She thought that the people aboard had come from the far North. She put her hands to the keys, and played the "Star Spangled Banner." When she had finished, he said he had a request to make: would she be so kind as not to play that tune again, or any other national air? Certainly, if he wished it, but the notes of that tune were the symbols of the flag of our country. Yes, he knew it, and for this reason he did not wish to hear it. They would have none of these things. What, were they going to have a flag of their own? To be sure they were; they had devised the emblems already, and had mostly decided on their arrangement. They would cut loose from all associations with the Northern people; they had become hateful to them.

Maria reflected. At last, she asked him what she was to do, and what would become of her? Why, she was to be his true, loving, beautiful wife. None of these things need trouble her, and though, possibly, there might be great calamities, she would be safe; he would see that she was more secure than the bird in its nest. He approached and put his arm around her, and, with the lightest touch of his lips, kissed her forehead. She smiled; she spread her arms and clasped them around him, and rested her head on his shoulder. He smoothed her hair with his hands, then kissed her lips.

After a little, she asked him if he expected she would look at this question as he did, and, if such a thing should happen, to rejoice, and not to weep over a divided country? No, not exactly. He must make allowance for the partiality she had for her native land. After a time, he would naturally expect her to see things in a different light. Even if they could not perfectly agree, it need not disturb their happiness. The foundation of a solid happiness between married people is never laid till they see there must be some things regarding which they will differ; then they will overlook them.

She was convinced that this was true, and she was glad to hear him say it. True, they would differ, for she could not see that she ever would become reconciled to a national disunion; still, she knew that, situated as she was, she could do nothing to avert it. With him she would live—with him she would die.

Mr. Harper was highly pleased with her good sense, and he called her by many endearing names. How extremely fortunate they were that they were enabled, by their education and knowledge of the world, to talk on this exciting subject so as not to offend each other; and he gave this as an instance of true politeness. Many, under such circumstances, would become extremely unhappy.

The war gradually spread, but still gave little evidence of the proportions to which it was destined to expand. To some, however, it appeared evident that it would go on till every slave should be free. Mr. Harper still continued to receive Northern papers. The Southern leaders always have well supplied themselves with radical journals, and the

"Liberator," the "Anti-Slavery Standard," and the "Tribune" have been read attentively.

Maria saw that slavery certainly was an element of weakness, but she was convinced that to conquer a united nation of seven millions was exceedingly difficult, and the instances mentioned in history of this having been done were few. The question really was: were they a united people, and would or would not the leaders be obliged to force the people to fight? If this last were true, the rebellion would end whenever their principal armies should be destroyed; hence, their success would not depend upon the cheerful support of the people, but upon their armies. After all, her situation stopped her from looking narrowly into the subject, particularly as regards slavery; this she hardly dare speak of, although everybody else was speaking of it.

An extract from the message of Governor Yates, of Illinois, drew her thoughts into another channel. The Governor declared that before the Northwest would surrender the Mississippi, its banks would be lined with the bones of her soldiers. Then the question really was, did the Northwest take this stand? If they did, the South must submit, or there would be such a war as the world never had known. She reflected on the subject—she studied it; and, with her well-trained, logical mind, she took into view the geography of the country, the productions of the people, and the nature and necessities of commerce. Then she examined maps, and refreshed her memory by reperusing parts of the histories of the countries of the Old World. At last, she saw that the whole question of the war was divided into two distinct parts—one regarding slavery, the other regarding the Mississippi River.

One day, after the battles of Bull Run and Big Bethel had been fought, and about the time McClellan, with 150,000 men, was besieged in Washington by 50,000, and while they were eating supper, he asked her what she thought of that. She answered, that it was evident the North had very faint notions about the war, and that, unless they did better, the

South was likely to gain her independence. But she had been thinking that there was a question which neither the South nor the North seemed to understand. Ah! what was it? It was the Mississippi river. Then she mistook, at least as regards the South, for they had seized and fortified Columbus, and were going to hold the river, let what would come. She asked him if they had considered the subject, in its length and breadth, with all the attention due it. Certainly they had. By holding the Mississippi, the Northwest would be induced to unite with them, and the North would be broken into fragments. She asked him if this meant that a commercial people would become subservient, and pay tribute to an agricultural people. Well, it would amount to this. She smiled on him in her shrewd, Yankee way, and asked him if he had ever read of an instance in history where this had been the case. Ah, not perhaps an exact case of this kind; still, he thought it could be found. Yes, Carthage not only submitted to Rome—it was destroyed by her. The fact certainly was true, but at that time Rome was so much of a commercial country that she had sent colonies abroad. The Carthagenian contest was as much a war between two commercial countries as the war between England and Bonaparte. Very well, since she was such a politician and political economist, he would be glad to hear her views more at large. She said she would have no objection, but she feared he might take offence. O, no! he was determined not to be offended at anything she would think proper to say.

As she arose, he noticed that she dropped her handkerchief, and he handed it to her with as much pleasure as if he had been courting her. As he was leading her into the parlor, she said perhaps they had better sit on the piazza, as it was cooler there, and beside, the river, which was her subject, could be better seen thence.

Would he have the kindness to bring out the map of the United States? He ran and got it, and laid it on the floor at her feet. Then he procured some paper weights and placed them on the corners, for a breeze was springing up.

He sat by her side. Should he not get a rod for her to point with. No, she could point with her foot. But her wide skirts were in the way. Well, there then. Yes, that was nice. She wore satin slippers which were very clean, and her stockings were of silk.

Now, he must be quite sure he would not be offended, for she was going to try to show him that a navigable river nowhere in the world is divided by two countries—that the attempt to make such a division would result in war, and that countries so divided always would be at war. Really this was a strange proposition, but he was curious to see what she would make of it. It was for the interest of the South to look at the subject of the war from every point of view. Of course, he would take it in good part. He must kiss her then. He kissed her once, twice; many times. Once she kissed him. Unhappy couple! little did you think that you would never kiss each other again!

She told him again that he must remember. First she spoke of the Dneiper and the Don, these were large rivers. They belonged to Russia, and they were peaceful streams. The Danube is divided by Austria and Turkey, and so long as these nations have existed they have been at war. The Elbe belongs to several German States, whose united interests are similar to ours; still it has been the source of great difficulties. But it does not belong to two countries, which is the proposition. The Rhine also belongs to the German States. Sometimes a river may be a common boundary, but it is always a fruitful cause of hostilities. France claims that the Rhine is her natural boundary; she has fought many bloody battles to make it such, and never has succeeded. Waterloo was fought in the valley of the Rhine. The Seine, the Loire, the Garonne and the Rhone had always belonged to France, and the Thames to England. It is but recently they had read of the battles which wrested from Austria her hold on the lower waters of the Po. The Orinoco, undivided, belongs to Venezuela, the Amazon to Brazil, the Rio de la Plata to Buenos Ayres. Egypt has always had so much of the Nile as she wished. The Euphrates and the Tigris belong to Turkey, the Indus and the Ganges to Hindostan, and the whole of the great rivers of China to her Empire. From this it must be seen that nations never come together, or crystalize, in any other way than by including within their boundaries the whole of navigable rivers. If they do, they are constantly at war. Many of these streams, in comparison, are insignificant, and the countries which include them were established when navigation was very limited. If this condition was so indispensable in the early ages of nations, what shall we say of this commercial age, and of a river confessedly more important than any other on the globe?

Mrs. Harper continued by saying, that at Cairo, she had the opportunity to visit the point where the waters of the Ohio and the Mississippi meet; and if her husband would give her his attention she would show him what waters flowed past her feet.

There came the floods of the White Earth River out of British America and beyond Lord Selkirk's settlement; then the Marias River, interlocking with the waters of the Oregon, and within a few days' journey of Vancouver's Island and the Pacific Ocean; then the waters of Jefferson's, Madison's and Galitan's Fork, and of the Yellow Stone, made from the melted ice that flows from Fremont's Peak; then Clark's Fork and Big Horn, the Little Missouri, the Canon Ball, the Chayene and the Running Water; then the Sweet Water from the Rocky Mountains overlooking Utah, and the South Fork of the Platte from the gold mines of Pike's Peak and interlocking with the Rio Grande of Mexico; then the long sandy Platte and the Kansas, from the Spanish Peak through the great American Desert; then the Republican Fork, and Soloman's Fork and Smoky Hill Fork, the Osage and the Merrimac, past a hundred castle-rocks; then, too, are the waters of Itasca Lake, icy cool even in summer; then the Minnesota, the St. Croix, and of Lake Pepin; then the Chippewa, the Wisconsin, the Red Cedar, the Iowa, the

Des Moines, the Rock River, the Fox, the Illinois, the Sangamon, the Kankake and the Kaskaskia. Such is the multitude of rivers that flow past one's right hand.

On the other, comes the Little and the Big Wabash; then the White River, the St. Joseph's and the St. Mary's, and the Little and the Big Miamis; then the Scioto and the Muskingum, rising where Lake Erie sends down frequent showers; then the Mahoning and the Beaver, and then the Alleghany, rising almost within hearing of the great Falls of Niagara; and then the Monongahela, dashing, in its first course, among the clouds of Old Virginia. Then is the Silver Cumberland, which flows past the Hermitage and the rocks of Nashville; and then the Clinch and the Holsten, rising in the Cumberland Mountains and making the Tennessee, which flows through the gates around Chattanooga, and, bending down into Alabama, rolls north to meet the Ohio.

Here is a region larger than Europe, and so created that its waters shall meet at one place and then flow to the sea. How many hundreds of thousands of miles do they come through meadows and corn-fields, by cities and towns, past how many quiet and beautiful homes! Here the waters of North Carolina meet with those of Dacotah, those of Tennessee with Idaho, those of Alabama with New York, those of Virginia with Iowa, those of Minnesota with Kentucky, those of Missouri with Wisconsin, those of Illinois with Mississippi, those of Nebraska with Maryland, those of Georgia with Michigan, those of Colorado with Virginia. And now that these waters have run their course, and, as nature has bid, united in one, shall man, at the point where this union is complete, undertake to divide?

Many of these rivers are larger than the Rhine, the Po or the Danube. The Illinois is not great among them, but it has more commerce than the Rhine. The commerce of the Ohio River exceeds that of all the rivers of Europe; the commerce of the Missouri exceeds it; the commerce of the Upper Mississippi exceeds it. There are more commercial transactions connected with the Ohio in almost any one day than there are on the Nile in a whole year. The commerce of this region of rivers exceeds that of the Mediterranean. What would be said should this sea be cut in two?

As yet, large portions of this region are uncultivated. Then she swept with her foot from the Alleghanies to the Rocky Mountains, and said, he could not fail to see that the time was not distant when the population in this valley would exceed the whole of Europe and become nine times greater than England, and five times greater than that of England and France combined. With such a population, what must the commerce become? It would exceed the present, at least three hundred times; or, the amount that now is done in a year will then be done in a day. Had his people seen this? if they had, did they expect to offer obstructions and impose conditions? If with the limited commerce on European rivers there was hardly an instance of a river being divided, and in no case but on the condition of war, how did the South propose to cut the Mississippi in two unless on the condition of war?

She raised her eyes from the map, and she looked on the flashing waters of the river as they swept in glittering array on their journey, yet five hundred miles to the Gulf. She did not notice his darkened look, but warmed with the subject, she continued. It seemed that an agricultural people were proposing to give conditions to a commercial people; but, as she had said before, such a thing never had been done. Commerce always controls agriculture. England had fought Bonaparte twenty years at the bidding of the commercial interest. It really seemed to her that this question was kept in the back-ground, and it was likely to become the real question in the war. That regarding slavery was thought difficult; but in a few years, and in one way or another, it would be settled. In comparison, slavery was no question at all; but the question regarding the Mississippi could be settled in only one way, or there would be war—war for a thousand years.

She thought she had said too much, she turned towards him, his face was dark and strange; she remembered that she heard him say he believed she was a traitoress, she saw him prepared to strike a blow, then her senses left her, for he had felled her to the floor.

When she revived her women were around her. Her husband stood by the balustrade tearing the map to pieces. They whispered. Others came; they lifted her gently and they were bearing her through the hall when her eyes glanced upon her husband's face. It was distorted with a fearful, threatening scowl. Her lips faintly uttered "Poppœa."

It was not long before he came through the door leading from his room, and fiercely walking to her bed asked her, in a voice of thunder, who was she? She said she would be very much obliged to him if he would not distress her further, for he did not know what had happened. Again, in the same awful voice, he asked who was she? She said she hoped she would be mentioned among those "which are come out of great tribulation, and have washed their robes and made them white in the blood of the Lamb. For the Lamb which is in the midst of the throne shall lead them unto living fountains of waters, and God shall wipe away all tears from their eyes."

Maria's favorite woman, Ellen, stood in the hall door and told him she wanted to speak with him. Then she told him what was the matter. His face became haggard, his lips moved, but spoke no sound. She wanted him to answer her. Yes, yes, they should go. She ran down to the stable, their swiftest racer was saddled, brought out, a man mounted and started for Vicksburg. They told Maria the horse ran as fast as he did at the races.

At midnight there was a cry through the house. Mr. Harper was walking in the piazza. He did not ask what it was. He walked till two o'clock. The doctor came down and said she might get well, but as for the rest it was all over. She was asleep. He had never seen a woman with a stronger constitution. The doctor was going to speak further, when, near by, there was the sudden report of a heavy cannon. What was that? They had no batteries down the river. Soon they saw a small steamboat swiftly coming up the river. The channel here runs close to the shore. Both hurried down. As the boat passed they asked what cannon that was. The captain replied that Farragut's fleet was just below the bend, slowly working its way up.

In a short time every body on the plantation was dressed and stirring, though it was some time before day. The news had gone from bed to bed. The Lincoln gun-boats were coming up the river. Something was going to be done. By daybreak a crowd of people were near the river bank; they had heard the news and had come from the back country to see.

The sun was rising as the masts of the Hartford were seen across the bend. There were vast clouds of smoke across the land, and that was where the river ran. After a little the fleet came in sight. Seldom had ships from the sea come up so far. The river was filled with them. We are astonished. What can our batteries do with so many? They will give them good reception. Yes, they will shoot well. Would that our works were finished, for here at Vicksburg we make a stand. We have lost Columbus, Island Ten, Fort Pillow and Memphis. We have lost New Orleans. That was hardest of all. And Baton Rogue is theirs. We must hold Vicksburg. Once place is as good as many if we hold it. We must not give it up. Oh! that our defences were finished.

Mr. Harper went into his room to get some things. He was wanted in the city. Two messengers had come for him. He went into Maria's room and stood at the foot of the bed. He was dressed in his uniform. He glared on her with cold hard eyes. She looked at him with meek but dry eyes. He turned and departed. Neither spoke.

When the sun was well in the sky, the batteries of the town opened on the ships. Although it was quite a distance, the sound jarred the house to its foundations. Then another battery opened and they played lively. Maria bade Ellen go to the window and tell her what she saw. She said the ships were moving about. On some of the decks there were crowds of men, partly black and partly blue, while many, from top to bottom were all blue. One ship seemed first, opposite the house, and only a little smoke came out of the chimney. Ah, here were two more ships coming with great tall masts, and a tug boat was between them. There were six square black windows on the side. All the men wore caps, and had dark clothes. There! that is another battery from the town; it must be their big gun. The noise was almost too much for Maria. She shut her eyes. Suddenly, she half sprang up in her bed, for there had been a snap, a smash, and an awful crash. It seemed as though it were right in front of the window; she did not know but the roof of the house was coming down. Ellen had run back. She said the ships had commenced to shoot. She saw the flash and the smoke. What were they going to do? She believed they would all be killed. Maria listened. Another gun fired further off, then two close by. The glass and the sash shook, and the vials and tumblers danced on her stand. When she saw that this was the worst, she grew calmer, and after a little she smiled. She said they might fire, she did not care. She knew it would come to this. They were her friends; the Commodore was her friend; all the officers were her friends. The gunners, the firemen, and the humblest on board were her friends.

Towards night the ships dropped down out of range. There had been confusion all day. Smoke rose from the plantations along the coast. Cotton was burning. Many families deserted their houses. The militia men filled the country roads on their way to Vicksburg.

Mr. Harper came home long after dark. A Confederate soldier had gone ahead to let him know if any of the enemy were about. As he alighted at the stable he asked how they got along. There had been great doings. Ah, what was it? Fifteen of the best hands had left—gone on the gun-boats—

were to have fifteen dollars a month and board and clothes, but they took all their clothes. After that, forty or fifty sailors, those fellows with caps and big flannel shirt collars, came ashore in boats, and they killed the steers, and they took off all the sheep, every sheep. They did not go in the house, because some of them with muskets and short swords stood by the door and kept others out; but somehow they got a crock of butter—nobody saw them do it. Then they all had to have dinner—the Lord knows how many of them, and one kissed the light colored girl that waits on the table. Three or four of them sung a song. It was about the White, Red and Blue. Then they asked where master was, they wanted to see him. Yes, yes. There will be a settlement one of these days, and a heavy one too. Did they look at the horses? No; they said they would come again. Ah, did they? In the morning the horses must be taken to the swamp.

He came into Maria's room with a heavy tread. His hat was in his hand, and his sword was by his side. He told her her friends had been plundering the plantation all day. He was poorer by twenty thousand dollars than he was in the morning. He supposed she was glad of it. When she got well he thought he would make a field-hand of her. She deserved it; she was fit for nothing else. She said she would go. She did not know that she was any better than the rest of the poor creatures. He doubled his fist and raised it on high as if he would strike her; he brought it down to her face and gave it a hundred quivers. She closed her eyes to hide the sight; she gave a loud cry and became senseless. Then he left her.

Some time in the night they restored her. Her first thoughts were that she would be happy if she could go out with the slave women and work in the cotton. She would welcome heat, coarse clothes and measured food. All day she would work faithfully. She could talk and sympathise with them, and they with her. They, too, were her friends.

The house was early astir, for the ships were moving up

again. With the first dawn of light the windows rattled and the house jarred with the opening guns. It was the sweetest music she ever heard. It was enough to throw a man from his feet, almost enough to raise the dead, if they could be raised, and yet at each report she smiled. Soon the air, thick and blue and smelling of powder, filled the room. It was like the choicest perfume.

Again Mr. Harper came and stood at the foot of the bed. She would not look at him, and closed her eyes. He went away. Then came into her mind some of those passages of Scripture which in all ages support those who are weary and heavy laden. "Be merciful unto me, O God, be merciful unto me, for my soul trusteth in thee. Yea, in the shadow of thy wings will I make my refuge until these calamities be overpast. I will cry unto God the most high that performeth all things for me. He shall send an angel from heaven and save me from the reproach that would swallow me up." She was comforted, and believed she would be saved. Then she thought of the days when she was at school. She thought of Oscar. "Lover and friend thou has put far from me, and my acquaintance into darkness." Meanwhile, the cannon of the fleet and the shore batteries roared. She made them roll her bed so that she could see the river. It flashed its broad waters between the masts made of New England pines. The smoke of the guns rose and became wide clouds obscuring the sun. All day the fight went on. How it was going she did not know, but she was conscious that it would continue, though there might be pauses, till the river should be free. That night Mr. Harper came to her side. He sat in a chair. They looked at each other. Neither spoke. Then he went away.

Vicksburg was in new danger. Commodore Foote and his captains had come down from above with black ironclads, and he had given a hand to Farragut. The city was between two fires. But the rebels worked night and day. They built new batteries and they fired right and left. They shall have the credit of fighting well. Up the Yazoo they had a powerful ram, the Arkansas, nearly finished. It will come down at the earliest day. The Commodore hastens to take the city. He knows their plans. He shelled all day long. In a quiet place lay thirty-four mortar boats, these, every few minutes, and all night long sent a globe of destruction weighing three hundred pounds into the devoted city. The people fled beyond the hills or dug caves in them. One day the Arkansas is seen coming out of the Yazoo. She steams straight for our vessels. Some she sinks, others she disables. Our ironclads fire on her, our balls glance harmless from her iron sides. At last, we send a ball through a port-hole; twenty men are killed, her engine is disabled. She flees, and, half a wreck, works her way to the Vicksburg landing. Once more, afterwards, she will attack us. The brave Porter is ready. He finishes what before was begun; she is blown up and burned, and her dead and dying are scattered on the waters of the great river.

We know now that when the bombardment was hottest and highest that the city could have been taken; its defenders had fled—there were none to show the white flag; we relaxed our efforts, they returned, built new works, heavier guns were sent them; at last we withdraw.

Soon, however, Sherman will attack with a large army from a base on the Yazoo. He comes to the rear; behind breastworks they are ready, the battle rages, and he retires leaving his dead and wounded. He can do no more.

A hard place to take is this Vicksburg on the Walnut Hills. During these struggles the rebels were fearful of the result. They might lose Vicksburg; and if they should be driven from place to place, what could they expect?

At last Maria was able to sit up, and she even went down and looked around, and sat in the cabins with the slaves. They came around her, and looked tenderly on her. She felt that they were not so low but they could pity her. They were deeply interested in hearing her talk about her folks and the country she came from. Surely now, some of them could visit her, and if she wanted any thing, help her.

One evening after the ships had gone, he sent up to ask if she could not walk down to supper; if she could, he would like to have her. She came down with Ellen. The table was not spread with its former magnificence, she knew that some things were got with difficulty. She sat opposite. He asked her if she would have such and such things, but he said no more. She thought she would try to eat and to appear cheerful. She looked into his face but could not catch his eyes. Her victuals almost choked her, her eyes swam, and she bit her lips.

At other times when he came home he frequently asked her to come to the table. She did not dare to come unless he did ask her. He would not converse with her, and she did not address him. When she spoke to the attendants, he could hear her sad sweet voice.

Often after such meals she would throw herself on the bed and weep. She felt that she lived in a land of darkness, the light whereof was darkness. Mentally, she would address her father. How little had he ever thought that his daughter would be cast aside as despised and worthless. Then she took refuge in the Bible, and looking beyond this life, and over the extent of the existence of the soul, she became calm, and as happy as many times she had been in her fortunate days. Her father would prepare a place for her, he would be the first to take her hand, when she should rise out of the river of death, and they would live with each other and with the saints forever more.

During a part of this time the bombardment continued, when she would fervently pray for the success of the Union army. How the cause was progressing elsewhere she knew, for papers still came into the house, though having passed through many hands, they were in tatters.

At the commencement of the year it became known that a large expedition was fitting out at Memphis, and all the boats were pressed into government service. It was clear that a grand attack was to be made on Vicksburg, and that what they already had endured was but an introduction.

They had not been idle, and now they put forth new efforts; new and long lines of defences, and strong forts were constructed, and new river batteries with heavier cannon were planted.

General Grant is their commander now. We met him at Donelson and Shiloa, and we must prepare for him, for he differs from their Macks, their Buels, and their Porters. It seems that he is much given to smoking and thinking, and cares about nothing so much as fighting; he does not even want to be President. We had rather vote for him than fight him. But we will beat him; we will bring every thing to a focus, we will drive back his armies, and hold the river; then peace will come, and we shall have our independence.

We hear of him, now, at Lake Providence; he is trying to get through the bayous into the Red River; again, he is in Yazoo Pass, hiding the water with his boats; then in the Cold Water, and he will try to get in our rear above Hayne's Bluff. We send batteries across, through swamps, by dry land and by water, and at the Tallahatchie we plant them; we tear his ironclads, riddle his transports, he cannot pass us, and he works his way slowly backwards. Now we hear of him in the Sun Flower, the Lord knows how he got there, but they say he had engineers who could do wonders, once back-wood sawyers, school teachers, merchants, farmers,—men with twisted noses and hawk eyes, but he cannot run his boats thither, and now he comes kiteing down on us, fair in front and goes to work digging a canal by which he will make our Vicksburg a town in the country where the river used to run. Why does he not fight us in front, and what does he want to get below us for? We shall be here. Do you say he will take us in the rear and cut us off from Hayne's Bluff? Truly, he might do that. Something of a wiery fellow is this man Grant—as well as the men under him. That clay is tougher than they, the river will not do their bidding, still they dig night and day, and he bombards us, he and that man Porter bombarding us, and it is a sore time for the women and their little ones. Woe to us, what is this? Last night, in the thunder, lightning and rain his vast fleet slipped past our batteries, and though we burn buildings to make the river light, and fire from all our guns, away he goes, and now what next? They say his army is on the march across the river, doubtless to appear elsewhere. Truly this man Grant is terrible. He rages like a wolf around a sheep fold; he gnaws, he digs, he tears, he makes the air hideous with noise, first on one side, then on another, now on all sides to get at us; he is remorseless, cruel, bloody, and he holds, they say 200,000 men ready to spring on us,—yes, springing on us, to wrest away our last hold on the river. That is not a human soul of his, for when darkness and despair should come over him, and when other men shrink and wither away, he launches his men on us—men brought up to labor, mere common men, and we who are gentlemen are shot down by them. He will not give up. Why will they not let us alone? We do not want war. But we will fight. There is nothing left for us if we do not fight them—if we are victors there will not be much left. Did you say we have not men enough? Truly we should have more. For these Yankees have fighting cocks among them,—yes, yes, we admit at last that they do fight. It would have been money in our pockets, and sunny days would have run on, had we known before that they would fight like this.

When the fleet had passed Vicksburg, it was in a sack, Port Hudson being below. The army marched across the country on the west side to Bruinsburg. Grand Gulf was another fortified place, and beautiful, the river being between two and three miles wide, but it was flanked by this movement, and it surrendered. On May 1st Grant fought and defeated the rebels at Port Gibson, and on the 3d at Fourteen Mile Creek. Then he rapidly pushed his army northward to throw himself between Vicksburg and the covering army of Johnston. A series of battles were then fought in rapid succession as follows: at Raymond May

12th, at Jackson the 14th, at Champion Hill the 16th, and at Big Black on the 17th. In all these he was victorious.

Notwithstanding all these successes his army was in a critical condition. He had left Bruinsburg with only a few days' rations and no transportation. The country was overrun with armies. However, he marched immediately upon Vicksburg, and drove Pemberton within the defences. As a consequence, the strongly garrisoned post at Hayne's Bluff was forced to evacuate; this opened the Yazoo for our transports from above, and supplies at once were poured into our camp. On the whole, these vast movements were wisely planned and executed with astonishing rapidity. On May 22d a direct attack was made on their works, principally by Logan's men on Fort Hill, which was unsuccessful.

After the first flank movements had commenced Mr. Harper seldom was at home. He was either in the army or the town. When they had been driven from the field at Raymond he came home to spend a few hours in looking after his affairs, and in resting from fatigue. Several gentlemen came with him, and the bustle that was made seemed to revive old times.

Maria had heard of the rebel disasters, and she knew that Mr. Harper would be more pleasant to her, for his conduct was gauged by the success or ill success of their arms. When the prospects were bright she dreaded to meet him. She was much recovered, and her cheeks glowed with red amidst the lilly white. She presided at the table, and conversed with the guests on common topics. Then she retired to her room, and saw no more of her husband till three o'clock in the morning. They had eaten breakfast and would soon start. He sat by her bed, and took her hand. She must try and pardon him for much that had passed. He had learned something since that dreadful day. He was going into the battle. Every one that could lend must encourage the soldiers by example. It was a hard condition, but it could not be helped. Her folks would fight after all. He might be struck down as so many of their best had been, and struck too perhaps by the hand of a common man. But he would do his best. Should he never come back, he knew not what to say. His affairs were embarrassed, but much would be left. Till better times come he would ask nothing of her only this; he ought to ask it considering whither he was going—would she pardon him? Oh, yes. He raised her hand to his lips, kissed it, and was gone.

Mr. Harper and his company rode fast across the country, and striking one of the Vicksburg roads, joined reinforcements going out of the city. As they approached the Big Black they heard the Union cannon.

Ah, they seek to dislodge our forces that they may cross. If we can prevent them, and for three days keep them where they are, they will perish, for they have no supplies. But there are many of them—hosts—to the last we will defend the crossing. How can they make way through our fires? Every man of them will be shot down. Indeed, they can not do it. They are fools in making the attempt. Surely they should know more. Yes, we thought so—see, they are falling back—they are ruined and we are saved. But what mean these fugitives of ours in the rear? Why, our artillery is retreating, some are cutting the traces and they mount and flee. Alas, they have crossed above us—they are coming down, wagons choke the way—let him save himself who can, for these are not our men. Still, all is not lost—for do we not hold Vicksburg?

The next day at sunrise an ambulance drove into the large gate of Mr. Harper's mansion. The people were all up, and had been for hours. During the week there had been a battle or a skirmish every day, and the news had come in the night. The jaded horses drew their load up the carriageway, and stopped at the front door. A friend of the family got out and came up the steps. Maria was told that Mr. Harper was dead, and that they had brought him home. After he was taken out and laid on some tables in the parlor, something wrapped in a cloth was brought in and laid by his side. It was his arm. There was a cloth black with blood bound over the top of his head. He had been in the thick of the fight, and would not surrender to a Union cavalry man, whose sabre finished what the cannon ball had commenced. No coffin could be had till the next day. One of the creole women, a house-servant, and who was the mother of a boy almost white, raised the cloth on his head and did not shed a tear. In the night Maria heard a terrible scream. The friend who had been watching the corpse had left the room and locked it. On going back, and as he turned the key, the scream arose. No one was there but the window was open.

And the siege of Vicksburg went on. The Union army drew nearer day by day, the ironclads dropped down, the cannons roared and the musketry rattled from right to left; from left to right, in long lines. It was boom, boom from morning to night. Maria hardly ever awoke in the night but it was boom, boom. With intense anxiety she waited from day to day, to learn the progress of the siege. Neither side was willing to give up. She knew now it would go on. Grant was receiving reinforcements, five, ten, and twenty thousand in a day. Anxiety was felt through the whole South, in Mobile, Charleston, and Richmond. It was felt in the whole North, Boston, New York, Washington, St. Louis, San Francisco. It was felt through the whole world, in London, Paris, Canton and Calcutta. It will be felt and understood through all ages of time.

Meanwhile foraging parties were sent out in all directions. Plantations were stripped of grain, cattle, and of everything that could feed or be of use to the army. Maria wrote a letter to headquarters, briefly giving her history, and asking protection. She asked to be sent North, or that a guard might be given her. The guerrillas were seizing what the army spared. No attention was paid. Everything was pressing. So small a matter was crowded away by larger matters. Oscar was in the army; she wrote to him. The next day twenty soldiers, with their own rations, came and guarded her.

When the war broke out Oscar had acquired a wide reputation. From the first, he gave all his influence and time and mind to the Government. He spoke to many, often, to vast audiences. In his State he raised one of the first regiments, and was its commander. With his firm will, with his physical and mental energy, with his ability to grasp a subject quickly and well, and with his ambition, he could not fail. Soon he commanded a brigade. He was directed to perform a difficult work. He marched with his men day and night; there were storms of snow, rain and hail; they crossed rivers and penetrated thick woods. The enemy on the point of a great work was surprised and defeated. On other occasions he was distinguished.

At last, Vicksburg fell. The strongest and most elaborate fortifications; weapons of the most improved construction, and hosts of brave veteran soldiers could not prevent its fall. They had been allowed ample time; at least two different and furious assaults continued for weeks, and much of the time by night and day, sufficiently warned them; they had gathered and combined, not only from their own country, but also from the Old World, the most powerful means of defence known to modern times, and they were animated with all the energy and desperation mortal man can feel. All was in vain, and they surrendered forever the river from Itasca to the sea.

One day Maria noticed several soldiers talking with the sentinel at the gate. They were cavalrymen, and their horses were hitched to the fence. She was wondering what was wanted when an officer came in view close to the door. She started up, for it was Oscar. She smiled and laughed, and gave him her hand—it had been so long since she had seen an old friend. They were seated, and had a long talk about Oberlin and their acquaintances.

Dinner was ready. It was neither so plentiful nor so elegant as formerly, but the people knowing the guest was from her own country, and that he was a Union officer, did the best they could and even contributed something they had saved for themselves. She was really cheerful, but she remembered nothing of the past except they had been friends.

Being again by themselves, he began to speak of himself, and gradually he revealed to her the state of his mind, the doubts he had of the Christian religion, and the immortality of the soul, and how his classmate had struggled and pleaded with him. She was deeply interested—amazed and almost held her breath. Then he showed her what he did not see at that time, but which afterwards was clear to him: that in this cold state he was unable properly to value his Maria— unfaithful to his God he was unfaithful to her. With hesitation he related to her what dreadful horrors flowed from his attentions to a most amiable lady, and the shame and disgrace which seized him when another, having through some source, learned his history, spurned him. Then he seriously reflected, and he confessed to himself what a hypocrite he had been, and how little he had understood what religion is, or how broad is the basis in the human heart on which Christianity rests. Instead of seeking support by faith, till his mind should be able to take wider views, he depended on himself alone—and the result was that he became nothing. But he was thankful that his life had been spared, that he might commence anew. Like a child he would be dependent and look upward.

Then he told her that though he had been separated from her by impassable gulfs, his heart had turned back towards her with a power he was unable to resist. That she was lost to him, plunged him into untold horrors. As he became more enlightened, his mind continued to grow more tender towards her, and finally, his wickedness was held out to him in all its enormity. Upon this he repeatedly declared to himself what he would do if an opportunity ever should offer. He vowed he would lie upon the ground at her feet, where he would confess to her how hard hearted, how blind and wickedly cruel he had been in his conduct towards her, and if, while lying prostrate, she should stamp on him and revile him, perhaps in some measure she might be avenged. The opportunity was presented. When she saw him sinking down, she seized him by the arm and said she would not permit it, and if he did not obey her she would flee from him. It was before God he was to humble himself, not before her a weak and sinful being. But it was pleasing to her to learn that the scales had dropped from his eyes.

After this he called on her again. He was able to give her great assistance in saving much property from the wreck of things, and by the help of the slaves much that was hidden was found.

They were married. He was selected to fill an important office. The splendor of his reputation could add little to her attractions; nothing to her grace and beauty. Moving in the best society, no lady in that brilliant throng was more admired.

Only a little was required to complete their happiness, and that little came. But one night, after they had removed to their Western home, Maria waited for her husband. With a staggering, heavy step he entered. Eagerly she sprang forward and asked what was the matter. One hand was on his breast, with the other he pointed to blood running on the floor. She screamed and assistance came. Minutes, hours, perhaps days, passed. She noted little else except his bloodless face and his fixed eyes.

Alas! this is not a world of rest. Continually do the bitter waters return and the hair changes to gray. Alone in the chamber one can only weep. Still, after a season, smiles will be seen through the mist of tears.

MARCHING ON.

OLD Dr. Graham came from Kentucky. He had reasons for believing that a free State would suit him best. He was the most skillful doctor in the country. When the reform in medicine commenced, he was asked why he gave so much calomel; he said he had to do it. People loaded themselves down with fat pork, in a manner made soap-tubs of themselves, and then called on him to clean out their soap-tubs. Mild medicines would have no effect; calomel alone would clean them out. He was rough but kind. He would talk to the women as though they were cattle, and they would laugh. However, he died. One of the symptoms of his disease was a red nose. He left a small farm in the village which had grown around him, a good house with things tasty about it, a snug office, and much owing to him. It was said that the reason why he had been able to save property was because he got his whiskey from Kentucky.

His only son took his place. He had finished his studies some time before, and the two had practised together. He was much like the old man, only he was temperate and dressed neatly. Most people thought he was the best doctor. It is true he lost many patients, but if their friends did not complain, why should we repine? Dr. Graham got a wife. She was a fine woman, beloved by all; she was pious, taught at Sunday-school, and grieved at nothing except that her husband would not go with her. They lived in good style, and had every comfort. The doctor was attentive to his business. He had three good horses. Usually he rode in a sulky. Every day you would see him go out of the village at a rapid pace. If you were around a good deal, you would see him on this road and that; you would see him, too, among the hills; his ride was fully five miles each way; sometimes he went twenty; and he was seen equally at the houses of the rich and the poor. Unless he really was unwell, he would go in the night as well as in the day. By night he rode horseback. When it was raining he had a fine, nice suit of India-rubber to draw over, and he came to the sick-bed fresh and dry. On the whole, he improved. He studied his cases. He began to doubt whether it was proper to run the risk of maiming and making cripples of his patients with calomel. He told people to be more temperate in their living, to take better care of themselves. He learned much. His wife taught him some things concerning which books are silent. Frequently, as he began to learn, he began to laugh. He saw so many curious things. A doctor has a better chance to study human nature than anybody else.

Then two important events occurred. One was the death of his wife. She died of consumption. Like a summer cloud, pale, wavering and spiritual, she was lost to him in heaven. Religious people did not call him a good man. How could they, when he used such language? This loss seemed to cut him down, and he went to church. He would sit on his office-steps or in the stores, saying little. When he met old friends he seemed hardly to notice them, but he gave them a low, friendly word.

The other event was the commencement of the war. At first, he thought he would try and get a commission. But he stopped. He could not sympathize with the North. For years the South had been wronged. Intermeddlers and negro-stealers had maddened them. Slavery might be right or wrong, but there was a compact: the North, by electing a president opposed to giving the South equal rights in the Territories clearly was ready to violate that compact. The spirit of disunion had its birth in the North, not in the

South. Old John Brown ought to have suffered a thousand deaths. But there was another question; he could not think of having the country divided. He had too much patriotism; he was too much of a Kentuckian to agree to that. The South should be treated kindly. If there must be war, it should be carried on for the avowed and only purpose of restoring the Union. Then he thought if he should go he might do some good. Beside this, he would forget much of his trouble.

Dr. Graham was one of the influential men of the county. In many western counties the number of these men in each does not exceed half-a-dozen, sometimes not more than three. The people waited for the doctor to make up his mind. They knew they had to fight; the question was whether they would fight Cook County with Chicago or South Carolina. The doctor and his friends met several times. Finally, they decided that the North was wrong in everything but one, and the South right in everything but one. This was regarding the Union. They could not give it up. They must support the Administration. If the South wanted war, she should have it; they would whip her, give her the slaves, give her more slave states, and tell her to behave herself.

The doctor could make a speech; for, when studying, he had hesitated whether he would be a lawyer or a physician, and he had read Blackstone and pettifogged cases. He addressed public meetings; he talked with the people, and ended by raising a regiment. Almost every man in the regiment knew him. Many were his schoolmates. The officers of his staff were some of the best men in the county. One had been a banker. The captains had families and good property; most of the privates left wives, children and snug houses. For a long time every one called him Doc, or Doc Graham. Privates gave good morning to the doc.

Then the wives, mothers, fathers, friends came to see them march. They told the doctor to take good care of the boys.

Playfully he asked, if they expected none would be hurt. Oh, no; some would be wounded, some killed. What they meant was, that he should see they were not sent to places where they could do no good, and yet would be shot down. He promised this. He felt that his responsibility was great; he was determined to be faithful.

The regiment did not reach Fort Donelson in time to engage in the fight. They went thence to Pittsburg Landing, and were in the two days' battle of Shiloh. Here they began to see what war was. Then they engaged in the long approaches to Corinth, and were at its capture. By this time Commodore Foote had taken Memphis, and they marched across to this city.

Colonel Graham became known to the leading officers of the army. He was esteemed for the care he took of his men, and for their strict discipline. In all their marches, no citizens complained of their depredations. The Colonel was known to be opposed to anything like subjugation. His men were in the habit of using the term "abolition war." When it became necessary to guard the railroads from Memphis to Florence, Corinth, Holly Springs and Jackson, to garrison the towns and to establish posts every few miles, Colonel Graham, among several, was selected, as one well fitted to do his duty, to explain to the people the object of the war and to conciliate them. In view of future operations, it was of the first importance to make West Tennessee and Northern Mississippi friendly to the Federal Army. The Colonel had his headquarters at a flourishing and handsome town. He had his own regiment and several companies of native cavalry. He had about twenty miles of railroad to guard each way, and he was to keep out cavalry and scouts, chasing guerrillas and watching rebel movements.

He ably carried out his instructions. In the town, he established wise police regulations, and the people were as undisturbed as they were before the war. When matters settled down, and each day became like another, the Colonel had time on his hands. There were four churches and he attended; he became acquainted with the leading and business men. He improved the opportunity to explain the sentiments of the Northern people. He tried to remove their prejudices. The army did not come to devastate the country and show themselves to be thieves and robbers. The time soon came when he had to prove his words true. Some slaves had run away, and were working for his officers. Their owners applied for them; he cheerfully gave them up. He ordered they should not be harbored within the lines. His men willingly obeyed, although they found the blacks useful. Some of his men, when on picket-duty, had burnt rails. He ordered them to make new ones; and not only this, but enough to pay for the timber. They were all one people: it was true they must fight in battle, but the property of all citizens must be respected. The people were pleased with this; it was a pity all Northern officers were not as patriotic.

One thing troubled Colonel Graham. The people had parties and balls. He and his officers were not always invited. It struck him that they considered there was some kind of a wall between them. The Colonel was fond of female society, and he was fitted to adorn it, and he knew it. When he met fine ladies on the street he gracefully recognized them; they would bow, often smile, pleased, but it was some time before he detected, after they had passed, contemptuous tones and gestures. Could it be they despised him because he was a Federal officer? He learned to observe more closely. When he compared the reception they gave him to that they gave outspoken rebel gentlemen, he bit his lips. His officers joked him on his want of success, and they told him if he would be more strict he would find the ladies almost in love with him. But he had his joke on them; they had no better success. They concluded that the whole subject required a little study.

Then came the rebel attack on Holly Springs. A most beautiful town was reduced to ashes, millions worth of government property was destroyed. General Grant's plan of attack on Vicksburg by land was broken up. Simultaneous attacks were made on various garrisons through to Columbus. Colonel Graham defended his post bravely, and the enemy was repulsed. Then came the pursuit of Forrest under Sullivan, and the rebels' defeat at Parker's Cross Roads. Still, the guerrillas swarmed through the country; their spies and agents were everywhere.

A complaint came from headquarters to Colonel Graham, that he was better to defeat rebels than to detect their spies. He must establish a rigorous system of passes; all trading with the county and the town must stop. It was known that the guerrillas bought supplies, revolvers and ammunition in the town. He obeyed to the letter, and was glad to do it. It made the old fellows, and the young fellows, and the girls who could not see their beaus, squirm, and they came to him. He was busy, could not talk, but he could say he was obeying orders.

Soon there was a change. There was a grand ball. The Colonel, all his officers and some of the privates were invited. Every attention was paid to them; the Colonel could dance with any lady as many times as he chose. He overheard that he was witty, that his officers were witty; all were perfect gentlemen. There were select parties, morning calls, meetings on the street; no ladies ever were more charming. The Major had been in a bank. His eyebrows hung over, his beard was bristly. He said he had a wife at home. He did not care how handsome, how free the women were. No one could tell him any thing new about a woman. He was going to keep a lookout. The Colonel told him to do so. The Colonel believed in the Major.

One night at dark the scouts brought one of these fine ladies to headquarters. They told how it was. It will be seen whether so many passes amount to any thing. She protested against being searched. The sutler's lady was a thorough-going woman. She brought out several packages of percussion caps, and about forty letters. The Major kept the lady close and read the letters. His beard bristled more than ever. The Colonel came in quite merry; when he got quiet and was ready to go to bed the Major showed him the letters. He sat up nearly all night. Once in a while he would speak out, not in an unknown tongue. A church member would have been shocked. Sometimes it was a low-toned, rapid torrent. He mentioned the animal subject to hydrophobia, and the place of darkness and despair. One letter he read several times. It was written by a lady with whom he had spent the evening. He scarcely could believe his eyes that she would wish him such awful things. But it was plain enough. Then there were letters from rich old sinners with faces of the color of a copper kettle. They wrote to their sons. The Colonel had a fair view of the inside of the rebellion. The lady was sent to Memphis, thence to St. Louis. Then the Colonel ordered that every one within his lines must take the oath of allegiance. Some flatly refused. He sent them away. The rest took the oath; he was satisfied many did it with mental reservations. By this time Colonel Graham concluded the North had a big job on hand. He began to change some of his views.

Short time after, three of his pickets were shot in one night. The next night one was shot. The regiment was aroused. Nearly a whole company went out after dark and lay in ambush. Nothing stirred. They lay out two nights more. Then they saw three men crawl through a corn-field, and coming to the road, shoot. The company arose and took them prisoners.

It was a hard case. All three belonged in the town, and were young men. Each had his protection papers in his pocket showing he had taken the oath of allegiance. They were tried without delay and found guilty. Several men came to headquarters; they hoped the Colonel would not be hasty. He came out and told them how it was. Three of his soldiers had been shot; they were his neighbors, and were as good as he could be, if he tried. Who shot them? Their friends, their sons, belonging to no army. Of course they were nothing but murderers. What could they expect? Surely the Colonel would consider. They were young men well brought up. He would not proceed to extremities, would he? Yes, he would.' But he had no right to do this. The proceedings must be submitted for General Grant's approval. General Grant was a very good man, but he knew something about military law himself; he would teach it to them too. Would he not telegraph to Memphis, or let them? No; and he would speak no more. The young men were brought out. They were shot and their bodies given to their friends.

At dress parade the Colonel made a speech to his men. He went over much ground and stated to them some things they had not heard before.

There was necessity for greater caution; they were in the country of an enemy who was deceitful and without mercy. He would take much of this advice to himself. They must look to themselves, and he hinted that there might be a change in the policy of the war. Some of his men were well posted; they were glad he was getting his eyes open. It was known through the camp what kind of game the ladies had been playing, and there was much laughing. They had a good deal to say about making rails. One of the teamsters thought he would see which way the wind was blowing, and he hauled a load of rails into camp. One time the Colonel said they had mighty good wood to make the stove so hot. Why, it was rails. About this time he was made a Brigadier. More soldiers came, mostly cavalry. His own regiment was mounted and every man had a horse to take care of. They picked up their horses. They occupied all the stable room in the town. They turned their horses into lots where there was anything to eat, and into yards. They hitched them in door-yards to evergreens; they would get loose and browse shrubbery. Fine fences would get down; things looked desolate. The soldiers made their mark. Every morning after breakfast eight or ten troopers, with haversacks well filled, and with revolvers and carbines would ride out of town by every road. They were careless till they passed the lines, then they would scan every field and tree, they would call at every house, they scoured the whole country. Often they had fights. Sometimes it went one way, sometimes another. It was dangerous for less than five well armed to go into the country. The guerrillas were active and numerous. Almost every day there was a fight. Two freight trains were burned and passenger trains robbed. Men were wounded, killed and taken prisoners. The guerrillas shot four at one time after they surrendered. General Graham had full as much as he could attend to.

The destruction of the trains made provisions and forage scarce. To supply the deficiency he was ordered to live off of the country. Trains went out and swept the country. The people of the town said they never saw a man so changed for the worse. Once in a while he talked with them. He said there would be peace when the rebels laid down their arms. They said they had heard their friends say they meant to gain their independence. He said the war would go on then. The only way to get their independence was to go to another country; they could not have it in this.

The General wanted more men. He wrote asking for five companies. None could be spared. When friends came from the North they were asked whether Lincoln was not going to make another call. Then the General said if the people made his men so much work he would keep their runaway slaves. He would have them cook and drive teams, and he told the men to help the slaves. Then the masters flocked in to get their boys. He needed all the help he could get. But did he understand that as loyal citizens who had taken the oath, they had constitutional rights? Yes, he knew all that. Did they know there was a rebellion on hand, and that it took men to put it down? For his part, he was beginning to think a black man was no better than a white man. They said they were worth a thousand dollars a piece. He was glad of it. Such men would be of use to the government. But the slaves were their property. Yes, yes, yes. When the war was over they would get pay for them. They supposed they would. There was Sam and his wife, could he not spare them? The General turned to other business.

About this time one of the Adjutant-Generals came to the command to talk with him. According to the census there were very many blacks there. What would be the chance to raise two or three regiments? It could be done. What was his opinion on the subject? It was a good plan. He believed they would fight then? This he knew nothing about; but they should be made to fight. Had he men in his regiment who would make good officers? Would he name them? Cheerfully.

There was no asking leave. Able-bodied blacks were taken wherever they could be found; they were drilled and put into companies and regiments. General Graham had a black man who took the place of a soldier and waited on him. His family lived in the country. One Sunday he went to see them. The next day the scouts found him in the road, not only murdered but cut in two pieces, as if with an ax. Only a few days before two of his men died from eating poisoned cherry pie. The leading men of the town agreed to present an address to the General on the subject of arming their slaves. Ten of their number appeared in a body and handed it to him in writing. He looked at the paper a long time. He turned it over and read it again. Then he asked them if they wanted a reply. Yes, if it would not take up too much of his time. They thought they might depend on his remonstrance, at least. He commenced, and after saying a few words stopped. Yes, they should hear what he had to say.

It was plain that the gentlemen did not value a united country except on the condition that they held their slaves. People at the North valued it so much that they had given up sons, husbands, fathers and brothers. The gentlemen valued slaves more than a united nation of educated and wealthy freemen. Their hopes were fixed on holding slaves, not on elevating posterity. The people of the North never could submit to disunion. He was convinced no union was possible while slavery remained. He was convinced that the North could not conquer, he was willing to say they did not deserve to conquer, unless they made the blacks earn their freedom. He believed if slavery was continued long it would so debase their people that they would become incapable of sustaining a free government. He would tell them why. He was going to speak the truth. It would make them bitter to hear it. He could afford to speak; he would speak from the fulness of his heart. He did not suppose it would do them any good, still, in his words would be their only salvation.

In all his reading he had seen no accounts of greater cruelty than their people had practised. They had violated the most common rules of warfare; they had committed the most atrocious crimes. Saying nothing of cases within his knowledge, their treatment of our prisoners would cover them with everlasting infamy. The accounts of their sufferings would make the blood run cold in the last age of the world. His body-servant had been murdered and horribly cut into two pieces; two of his men, within a short time, had been poisoned. A people ready to commit these deeds was travelling on the high and broad road to barbarism.

The gentlemen must know another thing. In all West Tennessee they could not point to a single farm which had been twenty years in cultivation, that was not as good as ruined. Let the slaveholders have the whole earth and they will turn it into a desert. Already slavery had made the vast majority of their people wretchedly poor. There was no time when they had a regular and full supply of food. When they could get a plenty they would eat till they could hold no more. Look at them. Small legs, big bellies and little brains. He had heard of their children eating clay. He thought it was a slander, an infamous lie. With his own eyes he had seen them eat it. Not one in a hundred ever saw an apple in winter. The flesh, the muscles, every tissue and organ of their bodies was elaborated from the coarsest food, principally from the flesh of the most filthy of all animals.

With a deathly grasp they were clinging to slavery. They were ready to commit every crime to preserve it. From the lowest to the highest they were deceitful; in the accounts of all civilized and savage nations there were none which showed greater treachery. There was no limit to their wickedness but their fear. To these infamies had they descended that they might preserve slavery. They seemed to have the idea that slavery was their salvation, their heaven and their God. It ran through all their thought, it was present when they rose and when they lay down. It colored and distorted every other object. It was in the marrow of their bones, in the breath of their nostrils. They must get rid of it or there was a power that would do it for them. No matter how stern the process, or how terribly it may tear them, it must be done. They had read of the Egyptian embalmers, how they got the brains out of their subjects by introducing a wire through the nostrils, and of the doses of aloes. The people of the North and the civilization of the age will tear slavery from them even if it require their dying agonies.

He had come among them as their best friend. He was anxious they should have their rights under the Constitution. If they had been contented to enjoy them, he would have fought on their side to the best of his ability. He respected their property, he returned their slaves, he did everything they could demand. They had plotted against him, they had deceived him and ridiculed him, both he and his officers had been subjects for their amusement; they had murdered and poisoned his men; they would be glad of his skull for a drinking cup. Why was this? For no reason except that he had been in favor of the Union as our fathers made it. Now they had come to ask more favors. He begged to be excused.

When the time of General Granger's regiment expired

they re-enlisted and went home on a furlough. There were wagons at the railroad to take the sick and their baggage to the village, where many of them and the General lived, and where the people had a grand dinner prepared for them. They came into the village in marching order. There were some sad vacancies. The people marked their tanned faces and the older look of the young men. They were just from Vicksburg. Then they began to sing; and as they passed with their heavy tread, people wondered and were awe-struck with the chorus of the song. It was about somebody's soul that was marching on.

THE WAY AND THE WILL.

LEMUEL MERRICK lived in Wisconsin. His farm was on the border of a lake with gravel shores. He was twenty-six years old and unmarried. He was from the State of New York, where, by teaching school and saving his money he made enough to come west and buy and improve a farm. His father also came and bought a farm adjoining, and Lemuel lived in the family. On his farm he built a nice house, in which a tenant lived, and a very large barn which every year he filled with hay and grain. He kept much stock. In a valley of about ten acres, looking south upon the lake, he planted an orchard. The hills and the waters afforded protection, and the trees were beginning to bear.

Across the lake, scarcely half a mile distant, but a mile and a half around, is the village of Lake View. Here is the outlet, and on it stands a grist mill, and several kinds of machine works; there is a nice meeting-house with a bell in it, a flourishing seminary, several stores; in short, Lake View is quite a town. The whole region is celebrated for raising a superior kind of wheat known as the Milwaukie Club.

People wondered why Lemuel did not marry. They supposed, of course, that he built the house to put a wife in it; but though he was attentive enough to the girls, he did not propose. He was too bashful to do so, and, besides, he was particular. Still, had one of two girls whom he liked most known this and made some advances, she would have got him. She gave him up and married somebody else.

When the war broke out Lemuel said he would go, and

he undertook to raise a company. This he found difficult because he was not popular with that class which first volunteers, and the friends of the girls who felt slighted threw obstacles in his way. Everybody said he would fail. Well, he would go as a private, but he believed he could raise a company. He had got about twenty mechanics; it seemed as if he could not get another one. Several good sort of men told him that if he would furnish liquor he would succeed. This he would not do, nor would he have men who loved whiskey, at least, who would get drunk. Then he went out among the best farmers, whose boys, as yet, had not thought of going, and talked with them. The old folks seeing how determined Lemuel was to have sober men, thought he would make a good officer, and told the boys that if they ever intended to go, this was their time. Several out of the first families volunteered; in a few days he had a full company, and they started for the wars.

The trouble with Lemuel was he did not talk enough. He scarcely ever spoke, except when he had something important to say. But he was always ready to listen—he was a listening man; even when no one was talking, he seemed to listen. He succeeded because he could smile. He seemed to be glad to see everybody; for everybody he had a smile. Such had been his careful habits of life that whatever he had in charge he watched as a mother watches her child. When his men saw this, they got through the crust of the man, and they liked him. They believed he was a model captain, and he was. In one sense the captain is the highest officer in the army. He is the same as the father to his children. The company is a family. The officers of higher grade correspond to judges and legislators. Every soldier looks to his captain; there is no one else to whom he can look. His regiment went to Cairo, and afterwards to Paducah. Then he was sent to Cairo on detached duty. While attending to it, a move was made on Belmont, and he asked and obtained leave to go along. He wanted to see what a fight was. There were several other similar volunteers; among them there was the editor of the Carbondale Times. Each had a musket.

The battle of Belmont was fought on the 7th of November, 1861. The place is nearly opposite Columbus, twenty miles below Cairo, and has only a few hovels. Our troops landed a mile or so above, and then marched down. Before they could reach the rebels, they had to work their way through a large mass of fallen timber, in which they lay shooting at us. Our boys spread out, and worked their way through, killing every one that did not run. On coming to their encampment we rushed upon them, they fled into the woods, or jumped over the bank, where some were drowned and many were taken prisoners. Their tents, stores, and the like were burned, but we lingered too long, for, before we were aware, they sent over reinforcements, attacked us fiercely, and we left on the double-quick. Things seemed not well managed. They followed us to our boats and we got aboard as quickly as we could. General Grant, in particular, led his horse down the staging in a lively manner. Then they fired on the boats; they were going to shoot every pilot, every engineer, anybody in sight, and do great things. The bank where they crowded was only about fifty feet from the boats, and only one thing prevented them from doing as they proposed. We had a gunboat there. It opened on them. A matter of fifty or sixty staid, the rest thought they would go.

Next day was a flag-of-truce; we buried our dead and brought away a few wounded, the rest had been taken to Columbus. At that time they claimed a great victory. It is singular they have not said much about it since. Afterwards, when we got possession of Memphis, we found out for a certainty that they lost in killed not far from five hundred. Our loss at the time was stated at eighty-five killed. There is little doubt but it reached nearly two hundred. On both sides there was much hushing up. Now, neither boasts. It is certain that the way our men drove them out of the fallen timber was gallantly done, and they have performed things since more heroic. In this work, Colonel Logan was conspicuous, so were Colonels Fonk, Dougherty, Buford, and others. The affair was badly planned, for at the same time we had 3,000 men fifty miles back in the country. But it was one of the first battles in the west. It had been thrown up to us that we could not fight. It never has been since the battle of Belmont.

When they commenced driving us out, they cut us partly in two, and Colonel Buford, with his regiment, was on the southern side. He could not get to the boats. He started back from the river, driving still farther the stragglers, who at first had fled. Taking a wide circuit, he was able by the next morning to reach the river, some ten miles below Cairo, where he was taken on board our boats. Still, several days passed before all got in; a party of seventeen came to Bird's Point, which is on the Missouri shore, opposite Cairo, about a week afterwards.

During the last retreat Captain Merrick was shot in the arm and leg, and he was thrown among Colonel Buford's men. There were no horses, and he had to walk. This was very painful, and after going quite a distance, he could proceed no further and stopped. The men were worn out with the heat and the fight, they could not well carry him, no one knew him, and he sat under a tree fixing his wounds, while they went by. Several humane, thoughtful men stopped to consider his case; he told them he could not walk, in fact he could do nothing just then but attend to his wounds, for there was not a surgeon with them; they lingered and pitied, then bade him good-bye.

He did not know how badly he was hurt. Much blood had run, but he had stopped it; then his leg flowed again. Tearing off another piece of cloth very quickly he stopped the bullet-holes, for they went clean through, then loading his gun he looked around.

Every thing had become still and the squirrels had begun to run. The sun was about two hours high. He thought he might have strength, by walking slowly, to reach some house. He determined to keep his musket, although he had a revolver, for he knew what kind of a country it was, and he meant to fight till he should die, rather than give up to guerrillas. It was not difficult to follow the regiment; by sun down he reached a path, and thinking he would be lost in the dark, or be picked up by those looking after stragglers, he turned into the path. Still he had his fears. He knew that many in such a wild place would be glad of the chance to kill him. It was important for him to know whether the house he should come to would be a slaveholder's. In a little time he came to a sheet of water, which was partly a cypress swamp and partly a bayou, and across was a large plantation, and a brick house with many small dwellings near by. He knew there were slaves there. The water was not very wide and there was a rude bridge made by planks laid on benches. He could see a little path running down to the water, he went thither and found a cabin where they had been making cypress shingles. There were a plenty of shavings, he went in, made him a bed, and lying down on his back began to think. He fell asleep.

In the morning he was awakened by a gun going off. The sun was shining. He saw nobody. The brick house was in sight. Birds were singing. On the water were many wild ducks and geese; some one seemed to be shooting them. These inland waters are great places for sportsmen. Sometimes they go thither from St. Louis. He needed breakfast as much as anything, unless it was a surgeon to look at his wounds. For fear some one might want to go to work, he got up, went out, and sat down in some tall rush grass, near the water, and where he could see the house. After a little, six men came along the path and crossed over to the house. They had guns, and blankets and overcoats piled up. While thinking what was best to do, he tried to dress his wounds. The blood had so dried that he could not get off the rags unless he tore them away. He concluded he had best follow the regiment and run the risk of meeting rebels. The men seemed to be eating breakfast, for he could hear the dishes rattle. Then there was much fast talking and loud laughter. After that they went away. Two came back, others went down the road. He saw the negroes going to work, some were driving cattle. There were many children about, black and white.

After a while a girl, woman grown, brought a big spinning-wheel out into the porch and went to spinning, and as she spun she sang. Her voice was pleasant, but she did not sing the old tunes correctly. He knew she was a girl because she stepped spry, and once or twice fixed up her hair with attention. He waved his handkerchief a while, hoping to catch her eye, but he stopped suddenly on thinking a man might see him, or that she might call one. As every thing had been quiet for some time, he thought he would try to get away. He found his leg very stiff, still he could walk, and he got into the path leading to the track made by the regiment. He was keeping a sharp look-out, and at a distance he saw the men with the guns on their shoulders. He got into some pawpaw bushes and lay down. He felt doubtful about being able to walk far. The men went by. They had overcoats and blankets piled on their backs. One carried in his hand something about the size of a large watermelon in a cloth stained with blood, and blood dropped upon the ground. They were rough looking fellows. He thought they would have killed him had they seen him. I have no doubt but they would have done so. I well know how the captain felt; for at this time I was out alone in similar woods, and know all about the condition of things.

For, at that time, it was thought a great thing to show Yankee bones. From Northern Virginia pieces of skulls and bones were sent in letters all through the South. Skeletons of our soldiers at that very time, as well as afterwards, were labelled and shown in shop windows in Mobile and New Orleans. The distance from modern civilization to barbarism is not so far as some may suppose. The region beyond barbarism is cannibalism. That is not far off either. We need not be shocked to learn the truth. We must take men and society as they are. Northern men, when they became slaveholders, were almost the same as Southern men. It is supposed they differed only in being worse. It was not long before this business was stopped. In most of the cases the ladies who had been receiving these Yankee relics learned that the givers had fallen by the Yankee bullets. Thousands of loved young men in families, in towns and cities sunk before Yankee musketry and cannon, and never would their friends see them again. They were buried in shallow graves. Some lay where they fell in the fight and in the flight. Birds found materials for their nests. We are often taught humanity in a roundabout, but most terrible manner.

After Captain Merrick had seen the men go across and enter the house he thought he would travel on, and he was getting out of the pawpaws, when he saw the girl coming over the bridge with a bucket on her arm. He went to the side of the path and sat on a log. He would speak to her. She seemed in a hurry, and she had a very sad look. When she saw him, she stopped short and ran back a little. He was a ghastly sight. His clothes were very bloody, his coat and pantaloons had been cut open, and the bandages were plainly seen. He was pale as a cloth, and yet showed the smoke of battle. His beard seemed too heavy for his face. She was pretty and fresh-looking, about eighteen. She had on old shoes, but no stockings. Her dress was of stripped domestic cotton, the stripes running around.

He asked her if she could not help a poor wounded man. Ah! how came he this way? Was he not a Union soldier? Yes, he was one; if he could not get help soon he must die. He had been without food since the morning before. Could she not help him? Perhaps she might get him something to eat. She did not know what else she could do; but he had better go into the bushes, he would be seen. He didn't know what was going on—he couldn't guess. He must keep out of sight. They were coming and going all the time. She was going to a field through the woods to get garden truck. She would be back soon. He went into the bushes, and she went on her way fast.

When she came back, she had cucumbers and tomatoes. Father had bought a crop, and the garden of a man who wanted to go away. He might have some of them to eat. Could he not get to his friends in the Union Army? He was afraid he could not walk. If she could send word anyway, they would come. She said she could not go herself, there were none but Confederates about. The captain was busy eating the tomatoes. Could she not bring him something else? he would pay her well. He wanted some water to drink, and some cloths to fix his wounds. She said she would come again about sundown. She would be going to the field then, and would bring him some victuals. But he must not show himself. The Northern people were very wicked to be making war on them, that she knew, and they ought to stay at home and let them alone; still, she would not let him suffer. He must get away. She knew of a Union man about three miles off, and she would try and send him word. Everybody else was for the South.

The planter was a saving, hard-working man. He had made almost all his property himself. His wife had two negroes to start with; he had run in debt for more; these paid for themselves and helped buy others. In all, he had twenty-five. He worked with them. He could read and write, but his knowledge was limited. His children were about the same that he was. At first, he had no doubt but the South would win. Latterly, the large army gathering at Cairo, and which was magnified, had made him doubt a little. He and others of the common people had thought the best policy was to kill every soldier who should come South. That would teach them a lesson. They knew little of the geography and population of the North. Their leaders were glad that they did not. The battle of Belmont showed that the North had fighting men. It might not be so easy to kill them all. Why, their own men got killed, and it was whispered that these were many.

Kate was his oldest daughter. She could read, write and cypher a little. She knew more about spinning and weaving.

She could plan and put a piece in the loom as well as her mother. A plenty of young men were after her; but she had agreed to have a lieutenant in the rebel army, whose father had a large plantation opposite Wolf Island.

About sundown she brought Captain Merrick a bottle of milk and some meat and bread. The soldiers had eaten up all the butter, but they would churn in the morning. She had a two-quart tin pail, she would bring it back full of water. There was a good well where she was going. And here were some cloths. Could he put them on? He guessed so. Had she any pins? Yes, she had brought half a row.

It was growing dusk when she came back. He had eaten, and was working at the wound on his leg. He could not get the cloth off the one on his arm, it stuck so tight. He would have to soak it till morning. The ball must be in, it hurt badly. The other ball was out. He wanted to get the bandage on tighter. It was in a bad way, he had stuffed in some cloth to keep it from bleeding. Could she contrive any way, to send word to Cairo? Surely enough he must get away. She would try. Would she help wind the bandage around, and then pin it? He did not like to ask her, but he would pay her well. He had sisters at home who would be glad to help him. Let her think while doing it that she was his brother. She did the best she could; her hands trembled. If the wound had been below the knee she would not have minded so much. But she had courage in her heart. He thanked her very much, asked her name, and told his.

While she was here, a young man by the name of Scott, who had lived in the Settlement, and who wanted to get her, came along, and hearing the talking peeped in and saw something; then he stepped back and watched till she left. Then he went and looked in again, and saw the captain lying down, and he thought he saw a musket. As he was not a soldier, and as he had no gun, he thought he would keep away from muskets. By and by he saw Kate slip back, carrying a bundle, and it looked like bed-clothes. Ah, ha!

he thought, here were fine doings. He came near enough to hear the captain say if she ever wanted anything, or ever got in trouble, she should come to him or write to him, and he would do anything he could. There was nothing he would not be willing to do to pay for her kindness. David almost knew it was loving-kindness, as the hymn says. But who could the fellow be? She soon went back. Then he waited long. The captain did not stir. Surely he had gone to sleep. He would go and get some friends of his and see about this business.

Kate had sent a negro boy whom she thought she could trust to tell the Union man to come to her as soon as he could, and to bring two horses. He could do some good. By ten o'clock the Union man came, rather suspicious, but he met Kate, and she told him what it was. The captain heard them coming. She had to go to him first. With difficulty they got him on the horse. When the negro found out it was a Union officer he was highly pleased, and he lifted with all his might. It is no small job to get a man on a horse by main strength.

The Union men of this region know all the paths as well as the Indians used to. They almost know the trees. They travel more by night than by day. It was over fifteen miles to Bird's Point. When half way, they came to another Union man, waked him up and got his buggy. He went along too, and all were well armed. It cost something to be a Union man in many places. A little after sunrise they went through our lines, for we had quite a force there. The ferry-boat soon went over, and in a short time the captain was in the brick hospital.

On dressing his wounds, the bullet was taken out of his arm. It had stopped against a bone. But the wound in his leg was highly inflamed. The surgeon said that in one day more it would have been too late. Quite a crowd came around to look at it, saying, "Oh, dear." However, there was time, and he would soon be up again. The captain had the ball, that came out of his arm, put in the chair by him, and he kept looking at it. Afterwards he sent it home to his mother. She keeps it in the bureau-drawer, and shows it to folks.

In about a month the captain was out and doing a little. He was a careful hand at his business, and he was in request. One day a young man came to him and told him that a lady at the St. Charles wanted to see him. Wondering who it could be, and whether it might not be his mother or sister, he went up stairs into the parlor and was surprised to see Kate. Well, now, if this wasn't the greatest pleasure he ever had in his life, and he shook hands with her so warmly that she thought he wanted to kiss her. If he had kissed, she would have blushed. Instead of being a sad sight, he was a healthy and well-dressed officer. She must tell him how she got along, and if anybody ever found out that she helped him.

Yes, it was all found out, and she was well-nigh ruined. He couldn't think what a dreadful time she had. David Scott found it out; he had got the quilts, and he had made up an awful story. She would not tell what. At last she had to tell her folks how it was. This made things worse, even if it was true, which some doubted. But if it was true, why did she not let him die? They would have knocked him down with a club and let the hogs eat him. Some would have been glad to get his bones; one wanted his skull. Worse than this, and she told it, the lieutenant she was going to have, got jealous and wrote her a letter that he would have nothing to do with her. Her parents looked over it, but she had done very wrong. Through the whole Settlement an outcry was raised; and when she went to meeting some smiled, some whispered, and few spoke to her. She cried herself almost to death. At last, having no peace, she determined to leave. He had parents; could she not go and live with them? She would be no trouble. She believed they would treat her well.

Certainly she could. It would be a good place. He would see that she had everything she needed. It was not far, was it? and could he not take her thither? Oh, but it. was far, and he could not go, but she would travel safely It would take two days and two nights. She could sleep. Did she ever ride on the cars? No. She would like it then.

When the lieutenant cast her off, and when every one turned against her, she remembered that she had shown pity, and by night and by day, the figure of the fainting and bloody captain was before her eyes. Where she had pitied and given comfort, she believed pity and comfort were to be found. She could not understand why others so bitterly should hate a man nearly dead. She was shocked that they should be so cruel and ferocious towards one so gentle and weak. She would go and see if she could not find the bread she had cast upon the waters.

Captain Merrick partly saw how this was, and he conversed with her long to see if he could find out more. He saw that she had good sense, he liked her looks, and at last he had the vanity, which is common in men, to suppose that in some degree she was in love with him. If this was so, Kate did not know it; however, like most women, she might be willing to be loved.

All the time, slavery is war. There is no hour of the day or night in which the slaveholder is not in arms. When the war commenced, he had no idea of there being rules of war, or that his enemy was not to be killed whenever he could get a shot at him. Even the leaders growled that there must be flags of truce. It was not long after this that some ten or fifteen of our cavalry pickets, a few miles from Bird's Point, were shot dead on their horses in one night. The historic pen is not permitted to say much more, it only adds that you must imagine all you can. General Grant waked up from his thinking, and taking the cigar from his mouth, told the clerk to write. The result was they learned some of the usages if not the rules of war.

At last Captain Merrick told Kate that she had run a great risk in leaving her parents to seek strangers. But she had not mistaken. He would care for her as if she were the apple of his eye. Her confidence in him deserved this. She should go and live with his parents. There were many advantages there for young people. Whatever other young ladies had learned and become, she could learn and become. She should go to school. Yes, she knew she would please his folks. She knew how to work, she could pay her way. Truly enough she could do that. But he was going to say something else. He wanted her to go to school and become accomplished, like other young ladies in his country. She would soon know what this meant. He wanted her to understand better the meaning of words; she pronounced as she had been taught—was she willing to learn different? Oh, yes, if he wished her to. He had not time to talk long, the cars would come early in the morning, he would get her a ticket, and write letters and directions so that she would go safely and be well received. Then he wanted to say this, if she would go to school and learn to be like the other young ladies, he would make her his wife.

She blushed all over, and scarcely could say she had not thought of such a thing—she would not think of it—but what he wanted her to do, she would do.

Some one came to the door. He said he would be along soon. Then he took her by the hand and said that in the place she was going to she would have every opportunity to become a lady. He was providing the Way, she must provide the Will. What helps folks most in this world is, *The Way and the Will.*

There was quite a sensation when Kate arrived at the far-off home. The letter she brought showed who she was, what she had done, and why she came. She was received as a sister. It was the first time any of the family had seen a native of the South, and they wondered at her strange words and ways. But soon she was seen not to differ from other human beings.

Kate became accustomed to her new home, and she liked it. She wondered at the abundance of many articles of food which in her country were considered luxuries. She took so much pains to do as she saw others do, that she had credit for having the Will. Multitudes of Southern women in those days, fled from burning or ruined homes, and saw no chance but to adopt new habits and words. It came hard, but it was not impossible, it grew easier every day. Others would not learn.

Kate went to the Lake View Seminary. New garments had been made for her, and she wore them well. When she entered the room an awful feeling came over her, but she was encouraged by repeating, *The Way and the Will.* Every where, things new and strange grew familiar and old.

The teacher was like many in those days. She was familiar with every stage of mental progress. She taught by the shortest and best methods. She knew how to inculcate and how to bring out. She studied and discovered what means and reasoning induce each to strive to excel. Kate found difficulties. The very first thing the teacher did was to bring illustrations to show how difficulties are overcome. And then she showed her, what it is so important to know, and is often seen too late, that learning comes not by lofty flights, but by weak and humble steps, and that each step becomes a part of the mind itself.

Kate was old enough, and her will was strong enough, to see this, and she found no obstacle which she did not overcome. When school was out she walked home, or, if she liked, she came and returned in a skiff. She assisted the family in their household affairs and was of service.

There is no greater mistake than the one so generally made, that labor unfits for study, or that to study with profit, one must do nothing else. The truth is, the hours in which we study with good results are limited. When the limit is reached our efforts are weak, and our ideas confused. The mind is like a spring coil, if always oppressed with weights it loses its strength. Elasticity returns only when the weights are removed. The Creator has decreed that the most wholesome relaxation is to be found in useful labor.

Her parents wondered what had become of her. They traced her to our lines, but could learn no more. She must be ruined and lost. After some months a letter came. Where was Wisconsin? Was it ten, twenty, or so much as fifty miles off? Was it in Missouri or Illinois? She forgot to write that. She says she is among Yankees, that they treat her well, and that she is going to school. It was wondered who was dressing and sending her to school. It costs a power of money, so the Judge says. Oh, she says she works mornings and nights. She must be learning right smart, for she writes powerful pretty. Read that again where she tells about going to meeting on Sunday, where the bell rings and they have cushions on the seats, and the thing plays, and all are dressed up so. Can't be there's any thing bad about going to school and meeting. It wouldn't be strange if that fellow she took victuals to was in love with her and had a hand in it. They say the Northern folks have things mighty nice at home. Don't you remember that somebody was here telling how they have houses to put their wood in to keep it dry? Well, if any body gets her, she'll make 'em happy. What a pity she didn't stay and help us in our troubles. She could have done us a heap o' good.

When the lieutenant heard there was a letter from Kate, and that she was doing well, he came up to see about it. So soon as he looked at it he gave a whistle. Why, she had got to be a right plum scholar. Wisconsin? Why, it's up somewhere towards the north pole, and the ground freezes forty feet deep, and there are only two or three weeks in the middle of the summer when it thaws out, and then the mud is as deep as it froze. They have soldiers from that place. He believed he would write to her. He wrote. He called her dearest, said he was sorry for the other letter, they had found out something new, it was all right now.

In due time Kate answered. She was short, respectful; not a bit loving. She too had found out something new; of course it was all right. She wrote to her parents occasionally. They were convinced she was in good hands, and they wrote to have her come home; things had changed for the worse, and some they thought sure of had got to be very doubtful

One who is acquainted in Northern villages, where good schools are the pride of the people, know how much society is subordinate to literary influences. It is impossible for the illiterate not to be interested while they who belong to the inner circle form a strong band, walking hand in hand. In such a band did Kate find herself, and, as she progressed, she daily found strength in thinking that when the captain should return she could show him how well by her *will* she had walked in the *way*.

In about eighteen months after her arrival, a good judge of language and western society scarcely would have suspected her to be a native of the South, and born and bred in Southeast Missouri. At this time she made a profession of religion, and understandingly united with the Congregational church. It was an affecting occasion to see a young lady of her descent, beauty and age, baptized, by sprinkling, before the pulpit and all the people, and hundreds of pious hearts leaned towards her. When meeting was over, hands crowded to greet her.

Captain Merrick went through many battles. He was promoted as a lieutenant-colonel, but in the regiment could not rise higher because it was so much reduced. One December he came home. He knew Kate had improved, for her letters showed this, but he was not prepared for a surprise so great.

It was already dark when the stage came into Lake View, and he hastened across the lake on foot. The snow was falling and it was deep. It looked strange, for he had just come from Natchez where there were roses. He was shaking off the snow in the entry way; the family were in the sitting-room; they knew by the motions that it was Lemuel. His sister opened the door, and he came into the warm carpeted room, out of the dark and cold. There was a little chorus of screams and laughter, and there were father, mother, sisters and brother to shake by the hand. From their midst stepped Kate. He took her by both hands, and shaking them warmly pulled back on them that he might look at her, and she pulled back on his, to look at him. They scarcely spoke, but how pleasantly they smiled!

The captain could see as she walked how much she had changed. She stepped gracefully, lightly, and with self possession. When she talked her eyes sparkled and shone with thought, and showed deliberation.

Officers of the army are active and prompt. In an enemy's country, where inattention and want of care lead to captures and loss of lives, they delay no duty. A furlough of thirty days soon passes. The next evening the captain and Kate were married. So many were present that they had to set the table three times.

Almost every day for a week they had a sleigh-ride. Wrapped in buffaloes and furs, and with two good horses, the bells jingling and ringing, they rode around the country. The captain had many calls to make to see his old soldiers, crippled and maimed, or to talk with parents whose sons had given their lives for their country. As they rode, Kate's cheeks glowed with a cherry red and her sparkling eyes showed that her heart was warm.

Then the snow went off, but in a few days it was cold again, and the lake was glare ice. The very first winter Kate had learned to skate. It is easier for young persons to do as the rest do than to do otherwise. All the young ladies of the Seminary could skate, and there were enough young men glad to help them.

The captain and his wife highly enjoyed themselves on the ice. Sometimes there would be as many as a hundred couple out at once, but this couple was much observed for keeping close together and often locking hands. Sometimes, on moonlight nights, they would glide together around the shore, close to the village of Lake View and disappear in the distance. They went and they came like a pair of doves. In that cold country they have many fine-wooled sheep, and so warm are the houses, and so plentiful is the covering of their high soft beds, that sleep is sweet.

At last Kate went home to see her parents. She rode over

with a neighbor from Columbus, where her husband held an important station in the Colored Brigade.

"Raily now, is that our gal? must be; but she's powerful changed; 'pears like as if she'd been a livin' among the upper crust. But she aint proud none, and almost the fust thing she done arter she tuck off her things and put 'em away, was to go out to the smoke-house and look in, and says she, 'Ye don't seem to have much meat.' 'No,' says I, and didn't say no more; then she goes to the crib, and says she, 'What's the matter, you haven't no corn, that is, none to speak on?' and says I, 'Don't ye know.' 'Know what?' says she. 'Why,' says I, 'the niggers is all gone, and we can't make no corn.' She said we might a known we'd lose 'em, a goin' to fight agin the gov'ment. She didn't seem to feel a bit sorry, and she said we could live better without 'em than we could with 'em. May be we kin; may be we kin. Then she went to the stable, and says she, 'Whar's the hosses?' only she don't say hoss—I don't know how she speaks it, but she gives it a Yankee twist; why, she's a plum Yankee. 'And ye don't know that, nother,' says I; 'why, the sojers comes over and tuck 'em away, kase they said we was a feedin' and helpin' the g'rillers who shot some o' their pickets, it seems.' And says I to her, the Unioners take on terrible, and tell how much it costs to be for the gov'ment; but says I, 'it costs a heap more to go agin it—a heap more.' Then says she, 'How curis ye do talk, mother.' 'What!' says I. 'Nothin,' says she. I'd a idy she thought I wa'n't quite perlite enough, and I tell'd her I never studied no gografy, no grummer. 'Well,' says she, 'how d' ye git along, then?' Says I, 'I aint got thro' tellin' on ye what they done, —them sojers. They come hur one mornin' with seven big wagons with U. S. marked on to the sides of 'em, and every wagon had four mules, and some six, and they had U. S. stamped on the sides of 'em, and they hauled away corn, day arter day, four days, and they tuck off all the fodder, they said they wanted it fur their calvary, but we'd git pay fur it if we was fur the Union, as we said we was; but if we wasn't, it 'd be mighty onsartin'; and oh, I tell'd her how they tuck off all the chickens, exceptin' thirty or forty, and them they couldn't ketch, and they tuck off all the bacon, exceptin' some we hid, and all the lard, but I'd buried one crock in the smoke-house; all a exceptin' them things, and I ax'd her if she'd a believe it, they tuck off two cups o' honey a sayin' they'd leave us some. She said fur sartin that was too bad, they orter'n to done it; but arter all she didn't seem to kere werry much; fur she said, that's what it was to be a makin' war when there was no war, and a havin' sich a power o' folks killed and busted up, tho' them wa'n't the words she used. But says I, 'It was the niggers we fit fur. They was our property.' Then she turned kinder white, and said there wa'n't no sich thing as property in human bein's, the Bible was agin it, and the Constitution wa'n't fur it, and we'd seen what we'd got by fightin' to make a thing so when it wa'n't so. And more'n this, says she, 'Who's tech'd yer niggers?' 'Nobody,' says I, 'but they was a goin' to.' When I seed what a abolishioner she'd got to be, I thought I'd fix 'er; and says I, 'Ye don't say nothin', Kate, about yer old man. I hope yer married.' 'Oh, yes!' says she, 'I'm married, and you'll see him 'fore long.' 'Whar is he?' says I. 'He's to Columbus,' says she. 'Then he's a sojer,' says I; 'I hope he aint none of them officers to the nigger sojers.' 'Yes, he is,' says she, 'and he's as good and as high up as the best on 'em.' In course, I couldn't go no furder; it won't do to say nothin' agin 'em; but if I wasn't beat to think a gal o' mine should be the wife o' a nigger abolishioner. Still, I hope she's married; but I want to set eyes on him afore I go to braggin'; fur ye see, I kin see.

"'Did ye see, man, what a nice shawl Kate's got, and her breastpin and finger-rings is rale bright. How they do shine. Oh, how her hoops do stick out! I wish I had a pair o' ear-bobs like her'n. And she's got the purtiest yaller gloves I ever seed. They're soft as a mole. She says she's married, and that I'll see him."

The rebel lieutenant who had been writing to Kate, having

been arrested while on a visit home, concluded he had seen enough fighting, and he took the oath of allegiance. When he heard that Kate had come home, he brushed around in hot haste, determined to go and see her. For, not having heard she was married, he was going to have her. The next morning he rode up, starched as grand as could be. The first thing he wanted to know was where Kate was, and he would not listen. Assurance will go far, and he thought he would kiss her, but she came rather slow, and he thought he wouldn't. But he shook her hand warmly and stood around her perfectly delighted. How had she been—how did the Yankees use her—were they not a queer set—and was she not glad to see all the folks and old Missouri again? He had knocked around much himself, but, as the song says, there is no place like home. After she had replied, he came to business. Well, Kate, let the past be past—they must make up—he had always thought a heap of her, and now she was more charming than ever. She was a perfect lady. She said she supposed he had understood her sentiments—what could he expect after writing such a letter? More than this, he did not seem to know who he was talking to. While she said this he did not seem to know that she was talking at all, for he was looking out of the window at an officer coming up the other side of the bayou, and a negro soldier was with him. She asked him if he saw anybody. Yes, a Union officer on a splendid bay. Was she acquainted with him. She looked and said she was acquainted with him, he was her husband. What! —had he been making a fool of himself? Why did she not tell him before? He was so fast he gave no body time to say any thing. Well, that was a pretty go. So she was married, was she? When did it take place? Last December. December? This is June, and he counted on his fingers, why that was about seven months, and he to know nothing about it!

The officer and his man rode up to the house on a canter. Captain Merrick came in looking fresh and fine. He and the lieutenant had met before at the time of a little examination. They saluted each other and were on friendly terms.

The planter and his wife came in and were introduced to their son-in-law. They were glad Kate had done so well; to be sure she had run great risks, no girl ought to do so, but she knew whither she was going, and all was well. They never would have done as they had, if they had not been lied to. They hoped peace would come soon, and some how, they did not care much how, so that it was peace. They wished there had never been a slave, then there would have been no war. If they had their land left they would get along. The captain listened and smiled, and agreed with them. He rose in their esteem. Farther acquaintance led them to believe him a worthy man.

Now the colored soldier was the one whom Kate sent in the night for the Union man, and who helped the captain to escape. He had hitched the horses and was sitting in the porch paying no attention to any one. He did, however, keep turning his eyes a little on one side. He was dressed in clean blue clothes, and he had succeeded in raising quite saucy moustaches. After a little the children came around him and were attracted by the revolvers in his belt, then they whispered, asking each other if this was not Bob. At last they went and told their parents who the negro soldier was. They came out: "Why, Bob, is this you?"

"You used to call me Bob, but that is no name. My name is Haynes, Robert Haynes."

"Ah, Haynes, is it? Well, Mr. Haynes, let us shake hands." Haynes shook hands all around, and they seemed mutually glad to see each other. Let folks say what they will, there always has been some affection between the master and slave. One need not reply that the same may be said of a horse. The truth is, people cannot live long together without forming attachments, and all know that masters have often felt keen anguish when they sold their slaves. Still, they could sell them, because, by association with a low order of minds, their mental standard was reduced so as to permit them to sell them. However, nothing so much has enabled them to overcome their feelings as the infamous doctrine taught by our preachers that slavery is a divine institution.

The old master thought he would try Haynes, and said:

"When the war is over, would you not like to come back and live with us?"

"Yes, I would; I was born here. I have no other home. But if I come, I must have land, or pay for my work. I have wife and children to take care of. I love them much. I love them more than you do yours, because they are black and have few friends. But I will fight till I die before I will let you make me a slave, and you will have to be right smart if you don't go along with me."

THE NORTHERN REFUGEE.

DR. McINTOSH is a first-rate physician. He is well informed on a great variety of subjects. He dresses neatly, has a fine taste, and takes pride in having a large garden, where are raspberries, strawberries, and all kinds of vegetables, as well as peaches and cherries. In addition, he had hot-beds covered with glass, where he started melons, cucumbers and tomatoes. This garden was the work of his own hands, during his leisure hours. His practice was extensive; he kept two fine horses and a sulky and a top buggy.

The place where he lived was in the centre of one of those thriving townships in the Ohio Western Reserve. There are schools, churches, shops, stores, mills, good society, thrifty farmers and rich land—everything which can help to educate and make families comfortable and happy.

The doctor was a democrat. He believed that the democratic party, like the righteous, is to endure forever. If it should fall from its high standard, it was to be raised up by its leaders; but it never could die out. He believed in the perseverance of the saints.

The republican party and the abolitionists were his aversion. He battled with them continually. The slavery question he would not discuss; but if the institution was wrong, his party, North and South, would attend to it. No one else had a right to say a word. That a President should be elected, as Lincoln was, on a sectional basis, was monstrous. He had no patience when he thought of it. If ever there was a wicked war, this was one. It was striking at the very foundation of our Republic. To coerce a sister State was tyranny of the worst kind. True, he blamed the South for withdrawing from the Union and for throwing away the old flag and taking up another. They made a woful mistake in not fighting under the Stars and Stripes. Had they kept the old flag they would have secured a great part of the navy. Still, he did not expect them to be wise in everything. Something must be granted to their resentments under a sense of wrong.

In the excitement of volunteering his oldest son wanted to go with his acquaintances in the army. The mention of it threw him into a rage. He could go!—could disgrace himself and the family, but he must not show himself in the house again—never write—he must cut himself off forever. His oldest daughter, a fine amiable girl, had a sweetheart among the volunteers. The business had advanced very far. She needn't think of him for a husband except at the cost of his life-long displeasure. No matter if he was as learned as Plato and as rich as Astor; she should not have him. In no shape or manner should he or his become connected with this mad warfare on the constitutional rights of the people.

The family thought he understood such things better than they. He was a good father, he indulged them in many things; none were better provided for. He was what a father should be. Though they could not understand his reasons, or see the force of all his arguments, they took it for granted that they were true, and partly were satisfied. His wife, however, had many doubts; for when she considered that the question seemed to turn upon whether slavery was to be protected or discouraged by our Government, her heart was with the Union Army. And when she read accounts of the poor slaves with their bundles of rags flocking to our ships in South Carolina, and to our army elsewhere, she secretly rejoiced, even though she read the account in a disloyal paper. Still, she loved her husband; she could not think of setting up her own notions, which, likely enough, would be her prejudices, opposed to his convictions, and she never disputed with him a word. He noticed, however, that she might mean much by her silence.

Perhaps this region of the Western Reserve had more uncompromising enemies to slavery, and more stanch friends to the Union cause, than elsewhere, in proportion to the population. They had become so established in their views as to be almost intolerant. Some noticed that when their soldiers came home, and having learned what it is to fight the rebels, did not use such sweeping terms and unsparing reproaches as they who staid at home. A public speaker was better liked the sharper and more bitter the language he used. There seems in this a lack of proper discrimination. It is the extreme. Undoubtedly the people of South Carolina show the other extreme. The merits of the two are determined by comparison—"By their fruits ye shall know them." The people of the Western Reserve, by God's blessing and their own industry and good sense, possess in more abundance, and in a higher degree, the fruits and advantages of modern civilization and of modern Christianity than almost any other people. It is well known in what comparative poverty the people of South Carolina live. Even the houses of the rich planters often are less comfortable and have less good furniture than frequently is the case in the houses of common blacksmiths on the Western Reserve.

It was not long before the doctor found his situation disagreeable in the extreme. With every quality calculated to fit him and his family to take the lead and to command universal respect, he found himself and the family looked upon with suspicion, mistrust, contempt. On public occasions, at church and elsewhere, he could see in the slurring cast of the eye, in the giving of ample room, and the cold shaking of the hand, that, to say the least, he was held in low esteem. He was deeply mortified; his family felt cut to the quick, and they had no happiness except when they shut the doors and found it with each other.

One day, when he was trying to gather comfort from the columns of his paper, he noticed an advertisement of a fruit farm for sale in Southern Illinois. There were forty acres; the soil was excellent; schools and churches were near; a choice orchard was beginning to bear; there was an acre of strawberries; the location was well suited for a physician; if a democrat; it was just the place for him.

The doctor was at once taken with the idea of buying the place and removing thither with his family. He would get rid of the abolitionists. He wrote immediately for further information, and, in particular, he inquired if there were any abolitionists near by.

The answer was satisfactory. There were only a few Union men in the county, and these were scattered here and there among the democrats. Upon this he sent his son with money enough to make the purchase if he should think best, and then to write, for, being February, it was important they should get ready for spring work. His son went on, and soon wrote. All was as represented, though things looked rather new and rough; the roads did not seem first-rate;— as for schools and churches, he had not seen them, but he presumed they were as stated; consequently, he had bought. The price of the place was $1,000, but the man wanting to sell, he had got it for $800. The family must come on as soon as they could.

The doctor having an offer for his house and the twenty acres of land, which with such improvements, are always salable, gave a deed, received the money, then leaving his accounts for collection, they packed up their things, and starting early in March, in a few days were safely set down in their new home.

The house was of logs, but neat and comfortable; there was a little log barn, a cistern, with good water, and some other conveniences, but not many. The fruit trees were exceedingly nice and thrifty. Plainly enough could they see that the last year's growth of the peach was from three to eight feet. But on many of the trees he saw very curious arrangements. Some had cloths tied around their bodies, a foot or so from the ground, and they were smeared with tar, while others had long grafts inserted near the ground and bent over scarred and cut places, then inserted above, in a manner quite ingenious. Why Hobart, what kind of work is this? Did he know anything about it? The young man had to try to laugh. Mr. Lockstock, the man we bought of, came from New York, and was a republican. He taught school when they would have him; he was quite peaceable; they had run over him; somebody had come in the night and girdled the trees; it almost broke his heart; his life and soul had been in his orchard, and he had grafted them in this way. The folks say it was the deserters who did it, and that if he had staid he would not have been troubled more, for they have all gone back. Everybody condemns such business. But no matter, we are all right.

"How is it, Hobart; have you seen much of the neighbors?"

"Well, something. They seem to be very friendly folks; they have curious ways, but they are good-hearted and accommodating. They are all glad a doctor is coming among them. They say we can make our independent fortune."

"No doubt we shall enjoy ourselves. We must expect some inconveniences in a new country. There is nothing like living in a place where we can be something. Here we can grow up with the country."

The doctor had horses, cows, and grain to buy, and he went around to get them. He had to pay fair prices, for he was supposed to be loaded with money. The cows did not look as though they would give much milk, but he bought the best he could find.

"I tell you what it is, wife, you must go out and see those folks. You will be amused; I know you will. You have no idea how few things they get along with in the house, or how funny everything looks. But they are the most friendly people in the world. It is true they are ignorant. I am reminded of our ancestors when they lived without any of the modern improvements; of the old Bible days of David, and Solomon, and Jeremiah, and Isaiah. Why, to go around is almost like reading Virgil's pastorals, or Homer's Odyssey, where the king's daughters go down to the stream to do washing."

"How is it, doctor; have they many orchards?" "I can't say as they have. There are some scattering old trees, not grafted. I was surprised at this, and asked them about it. They said they thought they had 'a heap'—'a power'—that's the way they talk. There's another thing. We have been calling this a new country. It has been settled longer than Ohio. I don't know what they've been doing. There is no use of talking about growing up with the country. The country has already grown up.

"Did you get any bees?"

"No. They wouldn't sell any. They said it was bad luck to sell bees. But one thing did me some good. They are all right in their politics. People up North, with all their schools and information, may come here and learn what the true principles of government are. I did not talk with a man but was opposed to Abe Lincoln and the war. I mistake. I saw Lockstock, the brother of the man we bought of."

"So there are some northern folks here. Did you go in and see his wife? How do things look?"

"Pretty well. I didn't get off. I was enquiring the way. Lockstock was by the side of the road preparing ground among his peach trees for planting cotton. Cotton grows here, did you know it? and they say it does well. I must plant some. He had a refugee at work with him. I shouldn't think any of the deserters would trouble Lockstock. He has an awful big beard, that curls over and makes him look as fierce as an army in battle array. He and the refugee came to the fence. The refugee looks poor enough. They say the country is filled with them. I wonder what they are doing here. When they found out my politics both of them began to grin. Lockstock didn't say much; but he said he was glad I had come, and he hoped I'd get enough of it."

"I wonder what he meant by that?"

"So do I. He can't be much."

"I don't know what he meant and I don't care; but this I know, we don't want to have anything to do with him, for they say he is the blackest kind of an abolitionist, and a desperate fellow. They say all the Union men here are desperate—always go armed, and just as lief shoot as not. Some of them swear like pirates. We'll keep clear of them. Did you get any butter?"

"No; but they said they'd have some day after to-morrow."

"I tried to get some too, but could not. It is a scarce time for butter everywhere. You know it was so in Ohio this time of the year. How long before you can make some from our cows?"

"Not very quick, unless they give more milk. The children must have some. It seems to be very good what there is of it."

"I think it ought to be, when they eat nothing but Indian meal. I can't find anybody who has hay, or who is going to have. Well, we will have grass pretty soon. They say it is good feed by the first of April."

"I'd like to know where your cows will get it, for I see none in any of the lots."

"I know that. I must sow clover and timothy. The way they do is to let the cows run in the woods and on the creek bottoms. I'll get a bell. Then we can find them. I have read how cane grows on the bottoms, and cattle live on it all winter."

"So you expect the cows will run in the woods a few years, till your grass grows?"

"Oh, we must get bran and save all the slops."

"Very well; but it don't look to me as though this were likely to amount to much. We shall see."

The Sunday after they arrived one of their nearest neighbors, with his wife and young child, came over. The style of dress amused the girls.

"We waited a good bit expectin' ye'd come over, and when we seed ye didn't, thought we'd come, and we fotch'd our young one; it cried powerful hard to come. We want to be friends. But we didn't know whether to come or not when we seed yer door was shot. We allowed yer was gone off."

No matter about the rest of the visit. When they got home a crowd of neighbors were there waiting to hear their report.

"Ye see, they've got things powerful nice. They've carpetin' on the floor and brass candlesticks, and heaps o' books, and the little gals has short dresses, and panterletts all scolloped and worked off, and they've got their har done into a net, and their shoes do shine, and she's got a nice long dress, and her har into a net, and a buzum pin, and her shoes do shine; and the big gals has nets and buzum pins, and their dresses stick out, and is starched, and all on 'em wears boughten store goods. I can't tell what sights o' things they got. Then they've got a musical thing in a chist, and a little table with a lot o' wires and fixins on top, with a spool o' thread in among 'em. Well, they treated us well; but they looked kinder solemn like, and ax'd if there wa'nt no meetin' to-day."

"I've hearn tell o' some folks as don't never go a visitin' on Sunday. May be they's this kind."

"May be; but they're powerful pretty folks. They've mighty quare ways though, and speak curis English. Corn meal, they call Ingin meal; for cheer, they says chair; and instead o' sayin' drap—she draps her hankercher, ye know—they drups or drops it, I do not know which; and a heap o' sich words."

About the first thing the doctor did was to send his children to school. Other children went with them, and there was no difficulty in finding the way. It was dark when they came back. Oh, it was a dreadful long way; they were so tired and so hungry; the school-house was down in a hollow among the trees, and there was a spring near by, or hole in the ground, where they dipped water into the pail, half a cupful at a time. There were no backs to the seats. How did they like the teacher? Oh, very well, but he didn't teach as they do in Ohio. Ah! why not? they say he is a first-rate teacher—splendid, was the word.

"Well, he didn't pronounce the same way, and he can scarcely read. Oh, dear, you never heard such a reader; Milly can beat him."

"That's bad. I remember now, they said they had got over having northern teachers; they always turned out to be abolitionists. Perhaps they make a little mistake here. There must be good teachers. There is nothing like having good schools. The winter school will be out soon. It is likely that the next teacher will be better."

In a few days the doctor told the children it was so muddy they had better not go any more at present. But it was quite dry in the woods. Is it? Well, stay at home and help mother pick up chips. They could get them all picked up in the morning. Never mind. They must do as they were bid.

When the winter school closed, the doctor made great efforts to have a good northern teacher employed, but he quickly found that their prejudices were so strong that he had to give it up. Then he proposed that his daughter should teach; she had taught three summers in Ohio. This took them by surprise. They had never heard of a woman teaching. Yes, they had, way back yonder a certain planter had one in his family; that might do, but in a regular school it wouldn't. Besides, and this was whispered, what would their women say?—they couldn't read; and to see her dressed up and getting so much money, wouldn't they be jealous? Of course. However, by coaxing and worrying he succeeded in having her try. At his own expense, he got some backs for the seats, had a blackboard made, and another window put in.

She opened her school, and being anxious to please, did her very best. The children were delighted, and well they might have been. But soon there was trouble. She was teaching them to sing. They didn't hire her for any such fol-de-rol. There was another thing—she didn't keep hours enough. Only six hours! That wouldn't answer. She must commence early and keep till sundown. If they paid a man to do a day's work, they wanted him to do it. More, the children didn't say their lessons often enough. Twice in the forenoon and twice in the afternoon was nothing but play, these long days. They must be kept at it, around and around. Things must move lively. She saw the absurdity of these things—the utter absurdity. Children will scarcely learn at all if forced in this way. Her father knew it as well as she. She quit singing; she kept all day. Is it, or is it not possible to suit them? Possibly she might do now.

This was thought to be quite a condescension. For no other Northerner would think of doing so much. But he was a powerful nice man. Perfectly splendid! He had queer notions, it was true; but he would get over them. He should have time. They did not expect it would come all at once. Then, his family was good stock. His children would marry theirs, for where else could they go? Theirs would marry his. That would make them all alike. They saw it. The country was coming up. It wanted a few more such families — of course they must be democrats. They considered their land worth three or four dollars more an acre. He would write and have others come. Only think that he should be so generous as to give them what strawberries they wanted, when he could sell them for so much money. He wanted his neighbors to have fruit. It was more fruit and less meat that people wanted. Fruit was good. How different from Lockstock. He wouldn't give them any. All he would do was to offer the plants, that they might raise them themselves. But he was not going to hoe and sweat to raise strawberries for them. A great fellow he! They did think that, may be, they would get some plants and set them out if they could find a place; but what was the use? The doctor would always have a plenty. He was the fellow for them.

Not long afterwards, some woman let out in this style:

"I seed something was the matter, and I ax'd him what it was. He said 'Nothin';' but the young uns telled it; he'd been to axin' the doctor's gal, that thar schoolmam; ax'd her something about something; young folks has feelin', and she said she wouldn't. I'd like to know if my boy John ain't as good as she ar' eny day! Han't we got land, han't we got housen and hosses as well as hern? Gettin' mighty big, mighty big. S'pose she thinks kase John can't read he ain't no 'count. My 'pinion is, readin' an't no use if it sticks 'em up this yur way. If it wan't we'd be taxed, I wouldn't send my young ones another lick."

"I wonder, now, if she sarved your boy like that! My Jake ain't much, and when she sacked him, I telled him he mought a knowed better, and I telled him afore 'twan't no use. But he thought he knowed more'n his mam, and he had to go; and he went and gone and done it. The trouble with Jake is, he han't got no git up. Still she mought a-gone furder and fared wus. Jake is nobody's fool, if I do say it. But it's a shame the young fellers should be a-runnin' atter her, and a-neglectin' the gals they knows all about and is used to. That's a bad business, and it's got to be put a stop to. It's a-makin' a fuss all through the Settlement. It's wus nor if he'd cum yur like all the rest o' the Yankees, then the fellers wouldn't a-expected nothin' o' his gals. They mought be kinder pooty for 'em to look at, and that's all the good it'd do 'em."

"Lor' me, 'pears like as if he is a thinkin' hisself better nor we is. Wonder if he don't now; a talkin' 'bout fruit and roads—seems we haint got no roads good enough for him, and about butter and cheese and grass—why he's talking half the time 'bout our not havin' no grass, and he can't git no butter. Why, that little sarpent o' hisen, Georgey, he came over here tother day to git some butter, and I hadn't got none, and he seed the churn a standin' in the harth corner, and says he, what's this? Says I 'taint butter, but may be 'twill be some day. 'Jes so,' says he, 'let's churn it,' and to get rid o' him I let him churn, and he helped me git it out, and then he weighed it just like a marchand, when he out with the money and away he went with his butter a kiten'. I believe them folks git butter enough to grease themselves all over from top to bottom. They can't eat unless they have it. Now, one day I sent for the old doctor to come and see my sick young one, and when he sot down and looked at it, he begins to talk to me 'bout keepin' clean, just as if I never seed no water. Says he to me, says he, 'it's werry 'portant, mam'—ye know how he talks, big like, ''portant, mam to keep a child clean. It saves 'em many times from bein' sick.' And when I gits some water and a cloth he said that want half enough, so I got more, and when I went to wash him he didn't seem to like my way, and he tuck the wash-basin out o' my hand, and went to washin' and scrubbin', and the boy had a high fever—then says he, git some more water, if you please; then he washed him all over agin, and I had to git a big cloth for him to rub him. Then he said I must do it just so two or three times a day. 'Well,' says I, 'but whar's the medicine?' 'Oh, yes,' says he, and he kinder smiled, and he gin some powders lookin' like flour. But I guv him the credit o' gettin' the boy well."

"Yes, that's the way he does; nobody can't suit him. 'Taint no use o' tryin' to get along with such folks. They better stay whar they come from. That's what they had. Thar's that other gal o' his. She's comin' on mighty toppin, like a young pullet. We don't want no sich folks—we han't no use for 'em. I don't want to say nothin', and I wouldn't, only you uns is friendly to we uns; but my gal Abby—I aint given to praise her up, kase she aint nobody; I know that; she now—I seed it, though mothers don't see nothin'—it was that night Griggs preached to the Baptist, and the moon was a shinin'; she was a comin' a long right past his Hobart, and she hadn't no beau, though I don't know how it happened—she ginerally has to sack a half a dozen—well, may be not so many, and he seed who it was, and said 'good evenin''—and she a lookin' up and seein' who it was, said, 'good evenin''—but more nor that he didn't say so much as boo. I don't find no fault. If they don't like me nor mine, nor any of yourn—nor yourn, nor nobody else's, and if they don't want to mix, nor to be mixed, what are they hur for? I wan't to know that. I know he said he come to git whar thar want no abolitioners, and that doctrine tuck mighty well with all on us; 'pears like there warn't nobody like him. But that ain't the thing. I'd rather he'd be the blackest kind o' an abolishioner than what he is. The fact ar, he ain't no dimocrat, no, not a bit on't; thar ain't no dimocratic blood in him; they don't make dimocrats out o' any sich kind o' stuff as he's made on."

"That's a fact, and I thought so a heap o' times. He's a rigeler old abolitioner in every thing except a sayin' he isn't. I shouldn't wonder if he'd run away. I shouldn't wonder if he was a *Northern Refugee*. Now, he said he come from Ohio. Ohio ain't no place. It's a river. We crossed it when we come from North Carolina, and we didn't see him then, nor nothin' that looked like him. Tother Sunday, school-master Crooks was to our house, and some on 'em told him to look in the spellin' book and see how this doctor spelt his name, and he looked and looked, nigh unto half a day, and it want thar. So you see it looks mighty like he ran away and took a name that ain't no name, kase it ain't in the spellin' book."

All these things came to the doctor's ears by way of the children; but being a man experienced in the world, he let them pass. One will be busy, indeed, if he permit such things to disturb him.

Not far from this time, I was hunting a mule through Williamson county, and came to the doctor's house. It was noon. I was hungry, and as things looked snug, for there were flowers, I rode up, and hearing nothing of my mule, asked if I could get dinner. The doctor ran his hands through his hair, thought a moment, and then went in to ask his wife. I knew then I should get dinner, for he would tell her it was a decent sort of a fellow, and she would accommodate me so as to gratify her curiosity. This is natural in this country. As I was going in I happened to see one of the boys streaking across the lot, carrying a two-quart tin pail. The table was set; they said dinner was not quite ready; it would be soon, and yet she and the girls sat around doing nothing.

I had spoken but a few words before she wanted to know if I was not from the east. Well, something like it. She thought she could tell a Yankee from a native very quick. Then they wanted to know my politics. Knowing how the land lay, I told them that the South ought to have her rights, and that I would be glad when the war should be over. Of course they took me to be of their school. After some time I saw a boy go round to the back door, and then we had dinner.

They wanted to know how I got along here, and what we did for milk and butter. I took the occasion to give my experience, how, at first, from two cows we could get hardly milk enough to put in tea, saying nothing about cream; how the people said clover and grass would not grow; how, after getting out of patience, I tried, failed, tried again and succeeded finely, and how, at that time, we had abundance both of milk and butter. I told them that northern men did not understand the climate; that it was necessary to get crops in early, not to be out of the way of frost, but out of the way of the hot and dry weather, hence anything that was not ready fully to mature by first of August would fail. As regards grass, I was fully convinced that it grows nearly as well there as in the North, because it has a long spring, and a hot June to grow in, and that as the soil of the southern States is similar to this, whenever the right kind of men should settle there, hay would be cut in abundance. Still it required much experience. The trouble is, that if they happen to get a little grass, they turn in the cattle as soon as it grows, and they destroy it. They are so miserably poor and behindhand as never to be able to wait, and they raise grain to have something to keep cattle through the whole year, otherwise they will starve. Such being the condition of the great majority there is no supply, as at the North, where one can purchase, and the only way for one to do is to depend upon himself. It is the same as if he were on an island. The trouble is not in the country at all. It lies in the people themselves. Here, better than elsewhere, can we see what enterprising, intelligent men do in making good society. There can be no refinement, no education, no wealth—consequently no good society, where the raising of stock and the raising of grain and grass do not go hand in hand. Grain and grass support stock—stock will renew and keep good the land. Don't you see that farms are getting poorer here every year? What will you do? Why simply nothing till the people change, or another class comes in.

"That's a fact," said the doctor.

I added: "The same condition prevails in the South. This style of farming was brought hither bodily from the South."

"Well, what do you do for schools and meetings?" said the doctor's wife. "Do you go to meeting?"

"As for schools, I or my wife teach our children; now that they are growing up, we are going to have a teacher in the house. As for meetings, we live without them."

Then she spoke up: "Never in my life, no never, did I go to such meetings. I have no desire to go. I think it is a shame that we have got into such a country as this—no schools, no ——"

"Wife, wife, let us not find too much fault. We may have more than we deserve. Possibly we may move to a better country next time, then we will know how to prize comforts and privileges."

I told him he must not think of leaving. The country stands greatly in need of such men to help redeem it from the curse of slavery-farming which the people have transported hither with their habits and prejudices.

"Oh, I see, you are on the other side of the house. I tell you what it is, you fellows have got at some truth after all, for I can't help seeing how cursed poor slavery makes a country."

I bade them good-by. I knew he could not stand it long, because, being a professional man and used to cultivated society, he would seek it, so soon as the novelty disappeared. It would have been different if he had been ambitious to make the soil yield his family a support, or if he had self-reliance and determination enough to isolate his family from others. This he was neither able nor willing to do. Lockstock had seen the same thing, and, as he predicted, the doctor got enough of it.

He had been troubled to find his cows. They would not come up half the time. Frequently all the children, as well as himself, would be out. It was like hunting for particular squirrels. One night, only one came up. She had been gone two days, and looked as though she had milk in her. The doctor opened the gate to turn her in the yard. She did not like the idea of being shut up all night with nothing to eat, and alone. She turned and ran; the doctor after her. He did not come back till dark; he lost his hat, and he was scratched and bruised. He believed he had been, at least, ten miles. It might have been twenty. Several times he got hold of her tail; she slung him away; he would get in front of her, when she knocked him down and ran over him. He followed after. She could run as fast as he could. He tried to outrun her. Her bell rattled and rattled; he could get no nearer. At last, a herd of cattle came up. They all stopped and looked at him. Then they hoisted sail, crushed through the underbrush and that was the last he saw of them. He came out to a clearing, found a house; they put him on the road home. It was three miles to travel. When he got through panting, he called for a dry shirt and a bed by himself.

His daughter had submitted to everything, and injured her health by teaching all day through the hot summer months. She had a fair attendance; they were going to have the worth of their money. Several times the directors came in with new regulations and ignorant remarks. The scholars ceased to respect her. After harvest, some large boys thought they would have some fun, and they went. In a few days they used vulgar language, even in school. When she reproved them, they looked at her with studied impudence. No matter what they said. She was afraid. She closed school early, gathered up her papers, and ran like a frightened deer through the woods. She would not teach school another day. Never would she enter that house again. They refused to pay her. The doctor applied to the State Superintendent and she got her money. That officer sharply reproved the directors.

All at once the doctor found his younger children speaking the native language. "You drap that;" "Whar's the saft soap?" "Mam, this is pretty store truck;" "Them's ingins." More than this, they used language unfit to hear or print. The doctor awoke. He was forced to remark that ignorance and impurity are inseparable. For two days he would not speak. When he was sent for, he said he would not go. An awful thunder-storm was on his face. No one dared speak to him. Only two or three times had they ever seen him thus.

When he came to, he went and sat down by his daughter and kissed her. She looked up and thought she never saw him look so pleasant. He asked her how long it had been since she had heard from her sweetheart. She blushed, stammered, and said it was some time. Well, she must write to him. He was a young man he liked. She should have him, and he would give her money. He said he had seen enough of the causes of this war; henceforth he was for the war, and he was opposed to slavery with all the strength of his soul and of his body. Hateful and accursed is slavery. It was making barbarians with railroad speed.

He thanked the Lord that the war had come to cut short its career.

There was rejoicing in the family, for it promised a change. Other men could do well in this country; when they had time, they did do well. But father could not. He came hither with wrong views to get along well. They were placed in a false position.

He sent for Lockstock, and made arrangements to have him take care of his place till it could be sold.

"Why not stay with us?" said Lockstock. "As a fruit country it cannot be excelled."

"I know that," said the doctor; "but rather than live here and bring up my family as I am situated"—he stopped, opened his mouth and shut it as if he had tar between his teeth—"well, I don't know what I'd do."

Lockstock supposed he was going back to Ohio. No, sir, not to Ohio. There are pretty good sort of folks in Ohio, but their knowledge of slavery and this rebellion is theoretical, not practical. He was going to Kansas, where they understand slavery from top to bottom, along the sides and through the middle. He wanted to go where he would find nobody that was for the Union with ifs and buts. If his son wanted to go into the army he could go. He would bid him God speed, and he would advise him to get into the Seventh Kansas Cavalry.

Lockstock says he helped haul his family and goods to the station. While they were waiting for the train, some got talking about democracy, and the doctor was drawn into the discussion. He attracted attention.

"I don't want to hurt any one's feelings, gentlemen," said he; "but when you talk about the democratic party, such as we used to have, permit me to say that it died long ago. It died as other parties died. It died the moment it attempted to make slavery a national institution. Slavery and democracy are as far apart, are as unlike, and as incapable of being brought together as heaven and hell. You have got something here you call democracy. Gentlemen, this is the slaveholder's democracy. I say this after having had an intimate acquaintance with it. It deserves to be cast out and trodden under foot by all men. Gentlemen, these are my sentiments. I reach them at as great a sacrifice of consistency as any man ever made in reaching anything, and I shall live up to them with honest intentions, and with all the vigor of body and mind which I possess."

PRAIRIE LIFE IN EARLY DAYS.

MANY would leave cities and turn farmers, if they were not afraid of seeing hard times. Formerly there were hard times; but let it not be thought that a life in any station can be one of ease. Still, there are great changes. A history of early days on the prairies, connected with the life of an individual, will show what has been and what is, and it will give some idea of that which is to come.

The tinkling of the cow-bell among the bushes, was the first sound David Ward remembers to have heard. Feed had not started on the open prairie, but down towards the Fork, protected by dwarf timber, the blue grass was growing, and there the cow picked away, and rattled her bell. The next thing he remembers was the clacking of his father's mill. A dam had been built across the Fork, a race was dug in the side of the bank, and the water came along and turned an under-shot wheel. The mill was built of logs, twenty-four feet square; there were two run of stone, the rock of which had been brought from a native quarry; one pair ground corn, and the other wheat; and there was a little bolt, six feet long, run by wooden-cog-gearing, which made the noise the miller's little boy heard. Every Saturday, through late fall and early winter months, the wheat stones were devoted to the grinding of buckwheat. There were few mills in the country, and some came with grists fifteen or twenty miles; others came thirty miles, and had to stay all night.

Generally, people think milling a good business, and it

was as good as anything else; still, neither grain nor flour would bring money unless taken to St. Louis. Once a year Mr. Ward took a load of flour, of about a thousand pounds, to that city; he was gone over a week, and he got a cent and a half a pound. He seldom brought back much money, for he had to bring a few dry-goods and groceries, and what little he did bring he had to save to pay on his place, for he had run in debt eighty dollars; then there were taxes of one dollar and fifty cents every year. Three years he had been paying the interest on this debt; one year he paid ten dollars on the principal, and things went so slow, and interest eat so fast, he thought it doubtful whether he ever would get out of debt. This troubled him, and kept him awake nights. One year, a man in St. Louis wanted him to drive in some fat steers, as he was going to take a couple of flat-boats to New Orleans, and he would pay him a big price—which was ten dollars a head. Mr. Ward thought it all over; he consulted frequently with his wife, and finally concluded he would try it. It might break him up, if it did, they would go further west, and squat on government land. Going to his neighbors, he engaged forty head, at six dollars each, to be paid for on his return. Then he hired a couple of young men at twenty-five cents a day and their board, to help in driving. They carried some victuals on their horses, and they slept at farm-houses, where they got breakfast. For this accommodation, for pasturing the cattle and a feed of five bushels of corn, he paid from one fifty to one dollar seventy-five cents. Once the herd stampeded, and ran seven miles across the prairie to a grove, but they were all found except one steer, which they looked for two days. Finally, they reached St. Louis, the cattle were sold according to agreement, and when Mr. Ward got home and paid everybody, he had forty dollars and a few cents clear. Little David was in the porch watching his father and mother as they talked over their business; and while he stood by his mother looking with wonder on the round half dollars as his father counted them into her lap, he thought them wonderful; for, though he was five years old, he had never seen money before then. She let him have one piece to hold in his hand, when it was doubtful whether his clutch was tightest or her watch closest. The same day his father got up his horse and carried off the money to pay on his land, while he took along his rifle, not knowing but he might kill a buck.

In their settlement was a log school-house, where school was kept three months in the winter and three in the summer, and where, every other Sunday, was preaching by a Presbyterian minister. When he was absent, the best scholar, who sometimes was not a church-member, read a sermon from a book with yellow-specked edges; but it was very dry. David used to get tired of sitting on the slab seats without backs, and with his feet swinging from the floor; but often his mother put her arm around him, and he fell into a warm sleep. Still, he was expected to remember the text, for, as they lived near the church, folks used to come in at noon to get water and eat their luncheon, and then it was known who had only bread and butter, and who sweet cake. Then his mother would call him to her side and ask him what the text was. Generally, he could stammer it out, and the women praised and the men smiled. But some used to say that she first took him into the buttery and repeated it to him, though he came out with his hair smoothed down and a piece of pie in his hand. After a while, a Sunday-school was established, and David had verses to learn, and the teacher gave him to take home a piece of thin, blue paper, with a few verses of Scripture printed on it. His father had got him a New England primer at St. Louis, but he was not often allowed to have it for fear he would tear it, and his mother printed his letters for him on a piece of writing paper. When he had learned them, she printed the A B Abs, and, finally, such words as baker and cider. In this way he learned to read without going to school. Very much he wanted to go to school, but he had no spelling book.

About this time a rich relative of theirs from the East,

came on horse-back and stayed all night. He owned a great deal of land on the Sangamon; he wore black clothes, and he had a long watch-chain and a seal, with a piece of milky white stone in it, which turned around. David sat on his little stool in the corner, and scarcely could keep his eyes off the fine gentleman, who was his third cousin, and his mother's second. There were chickens and slap-jacks, and his mother had gone to one of the neighbors to borrow some sugar to put in the sassafras-tea. Almost instinctively David had entered into his parents' feelings. The gentleman's name was David, for he had been named after him, and he had an idea there might be a present of some kind. The next morning, sure enough, just as he was going away, he took out a quarter of a dollar, and said it was for David. Mrs. Ward blushed, and said she could not think of taking it, but he insisted, and added that she could not complain, for this was what he would have been charged if he had stopped at a tavern, so she consented; and when he went away, they all stood a long time on the door step looking after him.

A great question now arose as to the use they would make of the twenty-five cent piece, and David heard them talking about it by themselves, sometime after all were abed. Two things were greatly needed; one was a spelling-book, the other a fine comb, and each would cost the same money. Finally, they decided in favor of the spelling-book, for the summer-school would commence soon, and learning must go before everything else. Accordingly, his father got on his horse early in the morning, and started for the county seat, for no store was nearer, and just before sun-down he returned, bringing the spelling-book, done up in brown paper. The first thing was to cover the book with a paper, but he had a chance first to look at the picture on the outside; then threads were ran across to hold the cover fast, when it was given to him. He had seen a spelling-book before, and it did not take him long to find a word he liked, which was "barbarity," and he soon spelled it. The *bs* rolled so harmoniously with the *rs*, that he thought it the prettiest word in world.

Providence seemed in their favor, for not long afterwards a peddler in a one-horse wagon wanted to stay all night, and they were glad to keep him, for they meant to have some pay. In the morning he asked them how much was his bill. They told him they would leave it entirely to him. He said he generally paid forty cents in goods, and twenty-five cents in money, though nobody expected money, it was so scarce; but as they had taken such good care of him he would pay fifty cents. Well, had he any fine combs? A plenty. One was selected. What else? She asked for jaconet muslin. He showed her some at a dollar and a half a yard. She would take the rest in that. Among the goods lying on the table was a small piece of white and pink calico. She asked the price, and found it to be sixty cents a yard. Thinking he was going to get some money out of her, and that he would make profit enough to pay twice over for the first cost of the goods given for his bill, which would give him a lucky start for the day, he opened the calico wide and praised it, though all the while she told him not to do it. No trouble at all, she must look at it. She did look at it, and sat down by the table, for she was tired getting breakfast, having cooked so many things; but giving a sigh, she said she supposed he would take nothing but money. Oh, yes! he would take pared peaches or beeswax, for he could buy goods with them in Philadelphia. She said she had some of both, and she brought them out in great haste, fearing she had not enough. She had four pounds of beeswax, and only a pound and a half of peaches, for their trees had only began to bear. Both were of the very first quality. He would give her twenty-five cents a pound for the wax, and the same for the peaches. She said she would take two yards of the calico. The peddler tore it off, giving good measure, and for what was coming, he gave her three skeins of white thread, six needles, and two rows of pins.

Mr. Ward needed a jack-knife, and he took a bushel and a half of wheat to the county seat, to a merchant who had a mill. He would have carried flour, but he knew he did not make the best kind, and thought the wheat would be most acceptable. It was a warm day, and he had to go without a saddle, because the weight of the wheat would hurt it and worry the horse, and coming to the store, he took it off and carried it to the door-step. He asked the merchant if he was buying wheat. It would depend on what he wanted for it. He wanted a jack-knife. The merchant said jack-knives were too good property to let go for wheat. That was bad, he had brought it a long way. Would he give salt? No. Or tea? No. Or Calico? No. Or pins, or needles? No. Well, what would he give? He would give tobacco, or domestic flannel, or woolen yarn, or socks, or whet-stones, or ax-helves, or brooms. Mr. Ward was a good sort of man, but then the thought rose in his mind about the labor required to raise wheat, the long way he had come, and the fine clothes the merchants, and the lawyers, and the preachers, and the doctors of the town wore, he hesitated as to whether he would take domestic flannel or pour the wheat in the street for the hogs to eat. Finally he took a yard and a half of five-quarter flannel, at the same price the merchant paid for it, which was 25 cts. a yard, and thus he got 25 cts. a bushel for his wheat. Then he wanted to get trusted for a jack-knife. The merchant did not remember him, and he did not know about it, but his clerk mentioned a circumstance, and the merchant said, Oh yes, he had a pocket-mill down on the Fork. Riding home, Mr. Ward often took the knife out of his pocket, rubbed it over, and hoped it would prove good stuff. It proved to be a little better than iron.

David went to school, and in due time learned to spell and read in the back part, but his mother showed him much, for he always took his book home, and had it out in the morning before breakfast. About this time he had a sister, and sometimes she wore the calico dress bought of the peddler. As time passed this dress grew too short, when it was worked over, having short sleeves, and the little girl wore it at meeting after she could walk. All the women took particular notice of it, for very few people were able to buy calico, and little girls dreamed about it in their sleep, thinking they had such a one. Alas, this sister of David's took sick one day; a doctor was sent for, he said she had a fever, he prescribed calomel and jalap, but it did no good; neighbors came in and were very kind; then the doctor gave other medicine, but the fever went into her head, she scarcely knew her mother, and at last the doctor said she would die. This was in the fall of the year. One day, when she was very bad, her father brought in a small red apple which was the first that had grown on the tree. Before the little girl got sick she had been watching this apple as it slowly turned red. They had seen a plenty of crab apples; there had been two apples in the house the year before, brought from Kaskaskia by a man who had been to the Land Office. She looked at the apple with her glassy, sunken eyes and almost smiled, then she took it in her hand and held it a long time against her breast. All this time she was lying in the lap of a neighbor woman. Now she looked at her mother as if she wanted her to hold her, and they carefully laid her in her mother's lap. While they were moving her one of the women held her hand over the apple. Every body said that she was going fast. Her mother looked at her a long time, then said, as calmly as she could, that she was going. "The Lord hath given, the Lord taketh away, blessed be the name of the Lord." Then the child struggled, the apple rolled on the floor, and in a few moments she breathed her last. This, and the funeral which followed, made a powerful impression on David's mind, for he never had another sister. Ten, twenty, thirty, more than forty years after, the pink and white calico dress, showing the coarse thread and cheap dye, lay in the drawer, and in a drawer it will lie till the whole family pass away. Thus, in those early days, and even long before, graves were made and covered with sod, and moss grew on the simple headstone, and the sun shone and the rain beat, gradually wearing away the letters of names.

When farm productions will not sell for money, farming will be conducted only with the view of supplying food. A part of the crop will be allowed to go to waste if that which remains will supply the family. Mr. Ward did not pay much attention to farming because the toll furnished him bread, but he had a well-kept garden, and a good sized orchard, which, being close to the timber, was sheltered and bore well. They kept cows, but if butter brought anything it did not exceed five cents a pound, and they had some sheep, but how many, they did not know till they would come back in the fall. After some years passed there was a little more money. Settlers brought some, but the first real start was when wheat began to bring forty cents. This came from a demand in the Southern States, for there they could pay for wheat because they were raising cotton, and they raised cotton because a man of the name of Whitney had invented a gin to take out the seed, and they could sell the cotton because Arkwright, Watt and some others had perfected engines, looms and spinners. So, you see, the inventors made their influence felt afar off on the prairies.

All through that section the farmers began to haul their wheat to St. Louis. It took nearly two weeks to go and come. They carried raw provisions, which they cooked by the side of a fallen tree in a valley, and they slept in their wagons. They went in companies of ten, fifteen or twenty wagons, and they chose the fall of the year, for then the roads were good. As there were no bridges over the slues it was necessary to double teams, which was the reason why they went in companies. There are two kinds of slues. One is when the prairie is nearly level, and in approaching, one has an idea that the ground is solid for miles. Such a slue is only a few rods across, and it looks like a mudhole almost dried up. The other is rather a series of slues, which extend across a bottom, generally on only one side of a stream, and it is before one comes to the timber. On reaching the timber the ground is likely to be sandy, and there is a sandy ridge bordering the water. Clumps of very high grass, and sometimes small willows grow through the slues, and they are so near together that it is easy to step from one to another. However, there are slues which differ more or less from this description, but such are common.

When a loaded team comes to a slue the horses step off and sink to their knees, and if it is not very deep or broad, the momentum of the wagon following will do much to throw the team over to the solid ground, when, dripping and pulling slowly and steadily they will bring out the load. But often the team will sink belly deep, they can hardly pull their feet out of the thick mud at the bottom, and yet they sink deeper every moment. When the team gets down, mixed up with the harness, and only the heads are out, then the men unhitch as soon as possible and get them on dry ground, then they fasten a chain to the end of the tongue. Of course one will have to wade in after the single-trees, and pick up pieces of broken harness, and get hammer and ax, and he will be muddy and wet.

Our folks going to St. Louis would put two, three, or even four span of horses to one wagon, the driver would get on the saddle horse, then gently drive to the slue. A wagon with twenty bushels will sink down directly, but if there is team enough the driver will make a rush. Just so soon as the wagon, is in he cracks his black whip with a noise resounding over the prairie, when the horses will spring altogether, while the rest of the men, standing on the hummocks, or already crossed, will cry to the horses all at one time, and making a noise equal to a general fight on election day. Being over, and while the black mud still is running down, the horses are unhitched and taken across to bring over the other wagons.

Sometimes, in crossing the bottom slues, several horses are required; they may go in at noon, and though the distance be no more than two miles, it will be so late before all the wagons come up, that they will camp for the night on the banks of the stream. If they go in late in the afternoon, it will be nine o'clock before they get through; or, possibly, a part of the wagons will be left standing till morning. But this seldom will be the case, except on account of accidents, for as they know the roads they can calculate their crossing-places before hand. Their pace is so regular and slow, that little can retard them, and they proceed as well through drenching rain and rolling thunder as amid the gentlest sunshine.

Reaching the stream, and they always like to camp near one, though a spring is preferred, they build fires, make coffee, fry bacon and eggs, and if there is a farm within three miles, boys will be started on horses with jugs to get milk, and some will be likely to get whiskey. The horses eat grain and cut-fodder from the trough fastened on the tongue, then, after every body gets tired of stories, they go to bed in the wagons. They are stirring early in the morning; the boys, who are sleepy, hear the horses champing while it is yet dark, and at sun-rise, breakfast has been eaten and the people in the farm houses hear the rolling of the wagons, the shouts of the men and the crackings of the whips as they cross the stream, while the swift water washes the mud from the the wheels. Having been swampy on one side, it is dry on the other, and the road follows a beautiful ridge through a grove of sycamores, black-walnuts and maples, and in a short time they come out on the rolling prairie with a grove ten or fifteen miles away on the horizon, and not a tree between.

At last they would come to the American Bottom; the low bad places were corduroyed in that early day, and, making the distance, either eight or twenty miles, accordingly, as they came down by Alton or from the Belleville way, to the eastern bank of the Mississippi, with St. Louis in full view. In those days, this was already a great city, and had above 3,000 inhabitants. For years, wheat had been selling from 25 to 30 cts. a bushel, cash, and sometimes it must be part trade, but now that the good times had come, it brought 40, 45, and some days 50 cts. Besides, almost every wagon brought a barrel or so of eggs, picked up in the neighborhood, which sold from 4 to 5 cts. a dozen, and if the market was bare, sometimes for as much as 7 cts. As for corn, that did not pay for hauling, for though a good deal was sold at 15 cts. a bushel, it was brought out of the Illinois river in flat boats. This condition greatly encouraged the farmers. For with twenty bushels, and in ten or twenty days time, they could return home with a barrel of salt, a paper of pins, a jug of molasses, a dozen needles, a pound of saleratus and a couple of darning needles, and yet have three or four dollars left, which was enough to pay the taxes on the best farm in the country. Nor was this all. There was a growing demand for fat cattle to send to New Orleans and the West Indies, and when a farmer could turn off fifteen or twenty head at $6 each every year, it seemed easy for him to get rich. Besides this, another bright prospect opened. As many as four different drovers had been buying cattle on the upper Sangamon, and from there through to the Rock River country, which were for the Philadelphia and New York markets, and though they did not pay over six dollars, still it looked as if there might be competition. They drove their cattle through Indiana into Ohio till they struck the new National Pike, which they followed till they reached tide water at Baltimore, or, they bore higher up, passing through Pittsburgh, thence by Strausburgh and Harrisburgh, whence they made Philadelphia; or crossing through Jersey they reached New York, which made a tolerable long trip. They began to get their droves together in May; by the first of June they were all branded, when they started, and they got through by the middle of August. After selling out, they brought their saddle bags full of dry goods and notions, and starting back they returned early in October, and were ready to make arrangements for the next year. Most of the drovers made money, and as they continued the business, the price of cattle rose to $9, then to $10, and in a few years to $11 and $11.50 a head. In addition, they bought a few horses, for all the hands rode, but this soon became a business by itself. The price of a young, well-broken horse rose from

$25 to $35 and $40. A story went the rounds of a span of well-matched, large and very beautiful horses being sold at Jacksonville for $120. They were said to be for a rich Englishman. Of course he lived in Philadelphia, for nobody in New York could be expected to have so much money.

The next improvement was in the opening of the Erie canal, and afterwards of the Ohio canal. But this could not affect the prairie region till vessels could be built on the Lakes, so as to come around into Lake Michigan and land at some port. After they were built, it was some time before any sailed past Cleveland and Detroit, though every year one went to the military post at Mackinaw and another to Green Bay and some other stations. At last a vessel loaded with immigrants for the Rock River country came down and landed at Fort Dearborn. As it sailed from Buffalo, and had a pleasant voyage, the way was open for others, and the steamer Enterprise, built at Black Rock, made a successful voyage to the Fort. About this time a few land speculators took it into their heads that they might do well in starting a village around the Fort, which they did, and they gave it the name of Chicago. The great obstacle was the bad roads leading into the country, and which required several years to overcome. When the Illinois Canal was built then you began to hear of Chicago. Meanwhile they went on in the old way in the interior, and money became more plentiful, still, it was only by slow degrees. Without making many words in telling why times were so hard, it is sufficient to say in general, that the principal cause of the scarcity of money lay in the fact that almost every kind of goods were made in England, or some part of Europe, grain was not wanted, nor could it be sent, and the only industry in demand was in some of the lowest conditions of life. It is true they were doing a little at Pittsburgh, but their glass was green, tumblers cracked if water was a little warm, and their nails snapped if they were a little cold. They made some butts and screws, a few door-latches and padlocks, but the supply was not large.

David Ward grew up while these improvements were going on. He went to school summer and winter, and as his father was one of the wealthiest men in the country, he thought he would give his son a liberal education and make a lawyer of him. The first step in this direction was in his fourteenth year, when his father got him a geography and atlas. This was of an entirely new kind, for no other geography had an atlas, and of course one with such a help would be certain to get a good education. David studied his geography thoroughly, and at the same time went a part of the way through the arithmetic; perhaps he would have gone farther had the teacher made proper efforts. One Saturday he went five miles across the prairie to borrow Riley's Shipwreck; and about this time the American Sunday School Union sent out a series of nice books, among which were Henry and his Bearer, Hedge of Thorns, and Dairyman's Daughter. All these books make life a tough matter. Sometimes David helped his father in the mill, or worked in the garden; he regularly milked the cows and churned, but as for continued work, it was not expected of him since he was to be a scholar. Nor did any of the people hurt themselves by work, for they had no inducements, and there were no such snug farms as we see in these days.

His mother cooked victuals neatly, though she had sour bread rather often; she spun flax wool and made cloth, and as she had no girls she had her boys help her, and often they washed dishes and mopped the floor.

When David was seventeen his father let him go with some neighbors on a flat-boat out of the Illinois down to New Orleans. They started in the spring, and had corn mostly for lading, but in addition they took on two hundred barrels of eggs and several hundred coops of poultry. He came back in the fall, much taller, dressed in new store-clothes of poor quality, with two dollars in money, and a swagger which he thought becoming. In addition, he had learned to smoke. He did not go quite to New Orleans, for the load was sold out to a speculator on the Coast. That winter they had a better school than common, for the teacher made his advanced scholars write compositions, which did David much good, and he wrote several descriptions which made his folks think he would make a fine writer. They had a debating school where they discussed little questions about anticipation, and great ones, about innate ideas.

Being now eighteen, he must study law. Arrangements were made with a lawyer at the county seat, who was to let him have books, and would hear him recite once a week. First he had Blackstone, which he read during the summer in the parlor; he smoked as much as he read. His mother kept him in shirts and pies, but as his mind was without training, a treatise of this kind was very dry, and he made little progress. Still, he recited, and during court had a seat inside of the bar, where he listened to the proceedings. The people thought well of him, though some doubted whether he would set the Mississippi on fire. After a little, he had a case to pettifog before a Justice of the Peace, and another law student to oppose him. Having no idea he could not do much, moreover, it was only an action for debt of less than two dollars. Then came two witnesses, who were examined, and when it came to David's turn to speak, he said some poor little things in a broken way, and with weak gestures, then sat down, while the sweat ran into his stockings. He never felt more ashamed in his life. Still, it did him some good to learn that he gained the case, but according to the testimony the Justice could not have decided otherwise. After this he had a case of some consequence, but he did so badly, and, in particular, made such blunders in reading the statute, when he mistook one word for another, making himself ridiculous, that when his folks heard of it they were mortified to death. Clearly enough their boy was not so smart as they had supposed.

David recited to the lawyer once more; the young folks at the county seat gave him some cuts, but he took home Chitty on Contracts, when finding it drier than the other books, he took it back and told the lawyer his health was so poor he would have to give up study. Then his father put him to work snugly, but let him go to school a part of the winter. He and his father talked his case over quite often, and it was finally concluded that he ought to go to some good school. At first Alton was thought of, but his mother said if he could go back East and board with her brother and attend the Academy, he would learn something. This would cost a good deal; the plan was adopted. Teams had begun to take grain to Chicago, he went in company with one of these; then took a boat to Buffalo, and thence, by canal, he reached Albany, and from this place he walked to his uncle's. Mrs. Ward was pretty sharp in getting this plan carried out, for she had learned that her son had got the mitten twice during the winter, and as much tittering was going on, she wished to have him in some place where he could take a fresh start.

David's uncle lived about a mile from a pretty village, where were some paper mills and other factories, and there were two churches and an academy. One part of the farm was in the valley, the other part ran up a high hill where the cattle were pastured in summer, and where wood was cut in the winter. In the house there was abundance, and things were convenient. After David had got through bragging about the West and running down the East, he commenced going to school. He was to pay a dollar a week for his board, and was to help do chores morning and evening. Among the studies he took up was Latin Grammar, but he found it so hard he wrote some words on his fingers. The young folks liked him very well, though they disliked his habit of smoking, and ridiculed him for it, but as his uncle's family was quite respectable, and as his father had three hundred and twenty acres of land, he took a fair stand and he improved in his behavior. He attended parties and the meetings of young people, but perhaps nothing helped him more than to go home with some of the girls. Though the society was not fashionable, still there were comfortable houses and good furniture; all the young folks were intelligent, while the religious and missionary spirit prevailed.

David took a fancy to a nice girl nearly his own age; he went home with her several times, then he fell in love with her, when he asked her to sit up with him. This she refused, because he was so young, for though she did not dislike him, she did not want him to get attached to her, for fear his uncle and parents would not like it, and for fear it might prevent her from getting somebody better. More than this, Flora did not know much about him, while there were a plenty whom she did know, and she had hopes of becoming a missionary's wife, and of going to Asia to teach the heathen. At that time the biographies of Harriet Newell and the first Mrs. Judson were in the hands of all the young people, and were read with many tears. Flora Miller's parents were in fair circumstances, they had an eighty-acre farm, a good part on the hills, but it was excellent for grass; they had a large old orchard, and currants and quinces in abundance, and lofty pear trees. While they had a plenty, they had no spare means, and all their children had to be industrious. Flora had been well educated, she had taught school one summer, and she went to the Academy in winter. Besides going home with her after evening meetings, and leaving her at the gate, he went several Saturdays to see her brothers, but they were busy or absent, and though Flora and her sisters had a fire made in the parlor and invited him in, they made no great fuss about him, and only had a boiled dinner. Seeing he could make no headway, he gave it up; though he congratulated himself on having a lock of her hair. Still she treated him kindly, and sometimes she smiled on him so sweetly he almost thought she meant something. Afterwards, when he got much better acquainted with her, she said it was a way she had.

The next fall David's father wrote to him to come home, because he could not afford to pay out so much money. It seems that David had written for three dollars extra to buy a pair of pantaloons, because those he had were too short. He had been mortified about this, and also about the shortness of his coat sleeves, but his aunt turned down the hem and put on a band of cotton velvet. He wanted to stay, but there was no help for it, and he went back through the canal and up the lakes the way he came. On leaving he did not see Flora, because she was away with some young folks on a ride, but he sent her a piece of poetry he had written, and it had the word dart in it. When he started his folks gave him a box of cake to eat on the way, which was very good; but by the time he got to Rochester it was mouldy, and when he was on the lake he threw it overboard. This, or something else, made him sea-sick. Riding in the wagons he recovered a little, and he was tolerably well a few days after he got home; but then he was taken sick, and he had a doctor several weeks, who gave him calomel and jalap, and opium, and one trash and another, till it seemed as if he certainly would die. For weeks he used to lie looking out of the open window, watching the trees on the other side of the Fork, and he thought the Hudson River ran in the bottom, and that only a day's journey beyond was the green valley, where he had friends. After the weather got quite cold he grew better, and every day he used to pull out handsful of hair, till at last he looked as if he was forty years old.

Then his father wanted him to take a school, but he said he was not competent. This put his father out of temper. To think of having been to school for years, of having studied law, and then of having attended a high school in the east, and not be able to teach a common school, was absurd. What did he expect would become of him? There were some hard words. David cried a little and his mother felt sorry for him. One day, however, he had an application, for the people concluded he had a finished education by this time, and he agreed to teach for $10 a month. His mother had a little money; she bought him a pair of store pantaloons, and made him some drawers and shirts. He got along better than he expected; he boarded around and had good victuals, and he slept in spare beds. Only two of his scholars were so advanced in arithmetic as to trouble him, for they had a taste for the business, and did not want to study anything else. For three or four winters they had been trying to go through the book, but the teachers had discouraged them, first by making them go back and commit all the rules and little quirks, then by neglecting them day after day, chiefly, as they said, for want of time to attend to them. The best that David could do was to treat them the same way, though he was forced to do some sums which put him to his wits, and he used to go to the school house early in the morning and cypher ahead of them, by which means he himself learned a great deal, and he made out to worry through the winter without actually disgracing himself.

When his school was out, he thought he would go South and get rich by teaching in planters' families. Putting his clothes in a long carpet sack, which almost touched the ground when he walked, he started for the Wabash; worked his passage on a flat-boat into the Ohio, then went up to Louisville on a steamer. After staying here until his money was nearly gone, and seeing no chance, he left the city on foot and traveled three days to the South. Here he took a school by subscription. About thirty signed at $3 a scholar, and he had to pay a dollar and a quarter for board. In a few weeks a blacksmith, who thought he did not treat his daughter well, was going to flog him; he shook his big fist in his face, then told him that as he had proved himself a coward, he might go. One night he was sitting up in the back porch with a black-eyed young lady, when a little difficulty arose, and he went off to bed. Then the white servant girl, who was quite smart, edged around him till she got him to walk out with her, and he had trouble in getting rid of her. Still, the other girl thought well of him, and wrote him a note about the scarcity of friends and the value of love, but some of the words were badly spelled, and he did not like it, for he was beginning to be a critic.

When his term was out he thought he would go still further South where the planters were richer, and he undertook to get his pay. Many paid without grumbling, but one man refused to pay anything but a fiddle, which he said David had agreed to take. The truth was David had borrowed it thinking he could play, but he could do nothing of the kind, and though he had kept it several weeks, he sent it back. Feeling pretty smart, he sued the man. The whole county came to the trial, and there was a row of horses hitched to the fence from the store clean round to the tavern. The man proved by one of his boys that David agreed to give five dollars for the fiddle, and he could be made to say nothing else, when the justice gave judgment accordingly, which, with the costs, David paid on the spot. Then there were some poor men who could pay nothing, and when he left he did not have much money. However, he paid ten dollars for a passage in the stage to Nashville, where he stayed several weeks, but finding nothing to do he started for Memphis on foot. The planters along the road never employed teachers in the house, but they told him he would get a chance in the lower country. He came pretty near getting schools several times, and he stopped a day or so and talked about it, and in one place said he could teach Hebrew, but finally he went on, till at last his money was all gone and still he was more than fifty miles from Memphis. Of course he had to beg; some would give him victuals and some not, but he always got a place to stay over night. Sometimes he could overhear the folks talk about him. Why didn't he go to work? Another would hang himself before he would beg. Another said he ought to be at home; there could not be anything bad about him, because he looked so fresh and innocent. Everywhere they noticed his fresh, blushing face. At one place he had slept on some rags with a child, whether black or white he did not know, because it was in a dark hole; the folks would give him no breakfast and he walked on. By this time he had sold some of his clothes and his carpet sack, and he carried what few things he had left tied up in a red silk pocket handkerchief. All he had in his pocket-book was a piece of writing paper, which held a small lock of hair. The morning was cold, for it was frosty, and his clothes were thin. After a little, as he was going through the woods, he found a piece of corncake that sparkled with frost. Some negro had dropped it, and though it tasted sweet, there was not enough of it. As he could get no dinner, he picked up an ear of corn that had fallen out of a wagon; it had some good but more of a raw taste, and instead of setting well, it griped him. All this time he was passing through a sandy valley; the farms were small, and the country had a poor look. Coming out of the valley about sundown, he found there was a river to cross, and as there was a house near by, he went in and wanted to stay all night. When the man found out he had no money he told a negro to take him across on a horse. Going up the hill as fast as he could, he heard the barking of dogs on the level, and finding a lane he turned in and soon reached a good farm-house. The dogs were so bad he had to get on the fence, when an old man came out with a candle in his hand. Then a girl drove off the dogs and he went in. The folks were Quakers, and when they heard he had no money, they asked him if he wanted supper, and he said he did. When supper was ready he went with eight or ten young people into the back kitchen, and they had a plenty to eat. There were sweet potatoes, corn bread, fat beef and stewed peaches, and when they got most through one of the girls brought in some warm biscuit and a plate of honey, though there was no butter. After supper David sat by the fire and talked with the old Quaker woman. She got his story out of him. They put him up in the loft to sleep, where a bed-quilt hung before the bed, and he slept till the sun came in at a little window. After he had breakfast, and while he was getting ready to start, and was thinking, the mother, who was heeling a pair of stockings, told him to wait a little, for she was going to make him a present. He wanted a pair of stockings, did he not? He said he did. When he was taking off his shoes, the woman told a girl to bring a foot tub of water, and he should wash his feet. After they were washed he was handed a towel, and the Quaker woman helped wipe his feet, and, handing him the stockings half turned, he put them on. She told him he ought to stop every day at a brook and wash his feet, and it would help the skin to grow over. She said some other things, the best of which was he ought to get back to his folks, for his mother was greatly concerned about him. They treated him better here than at any other place.

Finally, he stopped over night, where it was only eight miles from Memphis. The planter had two slaves, but he was kind-hearted, and he invited him to the table. Where he stayed the night before, his victuals were brought on a plate. At this last place they had butter. In the morning the man offered David a couple of dollars, but he thanked him, and said he had a friend in Memphis who would help him. It was Sunday, and while he was walking along he heard a sharp scream from a bird among the bushes. Turning in, he saw a young able-bodied negro holding a blue jay by its wings. They talked together, and the negro wanted to buy some clothes, but what David showed him were not good enough. David asked him if he knew where Canada was; he said he did, and he pointed to the north. About noon he got into Memphis.

This was quite a small place then, and most of the town was along the bluff in one street, facing the river. Across the river it was all woods, and the ground was low. After dinner-time, he watched the landlord, and when he was going through the hall, he asked him if he would give him something to eat. He said he would, and went back into the long dining-hall and gave orders to a black man. What he had tasted very good. There was cold fresh beef, good butter, pickles and warm hop-rising bread. The landlord kept him all night, and giving him his breakfast with the rest of the boarders, told him he had done his share. David thought he had better try and get to New Orleans, for he saw no other taverns, and his clothes were so poor he had no ambition to try to get a situation; and he stood on the bank watching for a boat. About two o'clock as he stood there, a waiter from the hotel told him to come to dinner.

Towards night a boat came down and he got aboard, and went into the steerage among as many as a hundred coarse men and women. His shoes were run down, his coat was rusty, and as he sat on some kind of a seat by the large stove warming himself, he looked bad. When the clerk came among them with his lantern, he and two or three more slipped back around the cotton bales towards the wheel-house and escaped. He slept in a berth on some greasy rags, but at midnight he was pulled out by one of the hands, when he sat by the stove a spell, feeling chilly enough, for the wind came in astern; but at last, he lay down on the floor, and, with his bundle under his head, slept.

For two days he managed to keep out of the clerk's sight, but at last he came up on a sudden and asked for his ticket. He said he had none. The clerk jerked him out into the light and looked him all over. David trembled from head to foot, for he expected to be shot. Then the clerk said he must "wood." The boat was just then rounding-to at a wood-pile, and he went out and helped get in cord-wood. A few hours after the boat came to Vicksburg, where the clerk told him to go ashore.

David sat on the stoop of a grocery with his bundle by his side. He had failed to get a place to lodge in, though he was told he could get good wages by working on the levee embankment. That night he slept on some cotton bales. Once or twice he awoke and saw the stars shining. The weather was warm, for he was getting far south.

Without supper, breakfast, or dinner; with only scraps for several days, he was hungry. He went out among the hills where there was some cultivation, and found turnips and persimmons. When he returned, a boat was taking in cotton. The bales were rolled down the hill, guided and held back by hooks in the hands of the negroes. He went up to the second mate and got permission to work his passage to New Orleans. Going into the steerage to find a corner where he could put his bundle, he did not see that the hatch was open, for it was dark in there, and he fell head foremost, as much as twelve feet, among some goods. He was picked up by some men who were there with a lamp, and hoisted out. He always wondered that he was not killed, but except bruises on his shoulder he was not much hurt. When the boat started the hands had supper, and one of them took him into his mess. The cook brought a large pot of coffee, a bucket of sugar, and several pieces of meat, beans and potatoes. In some of the pans were bits of chicken, beefsteak, pie and cake—the leavings of the cabin passengers—which the men picked out with their fingers, for they were not furnished with knife, spoon or fork, neither with plates or cups. Each man had his own cup which he kept in his chest, and he used his pocket-knife. The pans were placed on a board laid on barrels near the engine. With some difficulty David borrowed a cup of the cook to hold his coffee. The men were rough and swore dreadfully, but they treated him kindly, and one or two wanted to know what he was doing there.

After David began to work for his passage, and was not afraid of the clerk, and after he got enough to eat, he took more notice of things, and when off watch, he asked to sit on the hurricane-deck and view the scenery. The cabin passengers came there also, and there were some young ladies, dressed finely. They were all very merry, and he often heard what they said, but it amounted to little. One of these ladies was in the pilot-house, and looking down out of the window she saw David take out his pocket-book, and opening a little paper unwind a lock of black hair. She could not help feeling interested in him, and she concluded it was the hair of his girl who was living somewhere in Arkansas. Afterwards, when she could look at him in his face, she doubted about his living in Arkansas—perhaps he belonged to Kentucky. His work was not very hard, still they had some heavy freight to unload, and one night it took all hands several hours to get out some long heavy boxes, and two pair of screws, either for a cotton-press or sugar-mill, which had to be got seven or eight feet up the bank, and the sharp corners of the threads of the screws cut his fingers. These screws were turned out of iron, and were as much as eight feet long and six inches in diameter. At Grand Gulf the river opens like a lake, and when they reached the Coast the green trees and the fine plantations made a beautiful scene. At nine o'clock in the morning they passed Red Church, when David borrowed a razor, and, for the first time, shaved himself, and a little after noon the boat made her landing at New Orleans.

David had sold a few more things, and had only two shirts left, and having a little money he put up at a lodging-house on the levee. The beds were cots with canvass bottoms, straw pillows, and a woolen blanket. A couple of men sleeping close to him, for the beds were no more than three feet apart, talked scandalously about women. After he got some breakfast his money was gone. That night he sat several hours with some negro watchmen who had a fire. About midnight they gave him some fish, a part of which he ate, though it wanted salt, and the other part he threw away, because something stretched out like a string. The next day he came across an acquaintance who had come down on a flat-boat and was paid off, and he was living at what he called a first class boarding-house. At night he took David thither to sleep, but as the house was locked, they had to climb over a high board fence, when they went in the back way. There seemed to be no bed for David, and he slept on a piece of carpet while his friend slept in a room close by. Something bit him all night. In the morning he looked into the room where his friend lay, and seeing what kind of a house it was, he went off without waiting to speak to him.

After making several attempts to find employment, David thought some of going to South America, not knowing but chances would be more favorable; then, if he failed, he might go thence to Liverpool or Havre. If the captain of a vessel had agreed to take him to Jerusalem, he would have gone in a minute. He even went along side of the ships, but everybody was busy, and he concluded there was no chance. While he walked the streets he always kept his eyes on the ground, hoping to find something, and one day he did find a very ragged half dollar shin plaster on the Third Municipality. The way he lived was to slip up to the lunch tables when there was a crowd, and deliberately take a piece of bread, put some butter on it, then take a pickle or a piece of cheese, just as if he had bought a drink and paid for it. Generally the lunch is set out from 11 to 12 A.M., but in some of the French and Spanish coffee-houses it is set out at 9 o'clock. Around the outside Place d'Armes, or Jackson Square, were a great many orange stands, and the keepers were in the habit of throwing the defective ones inside, which he used to pick up, and he found them very good eating. He often wondered that in such a large city there seemed to be nobody else as hungry and as wretched as himself. David had formed the acquaintance of a shoemaker, who had a cot bed in the hall of the third story of a building on Gravior Street, and who let him sleep with him, though the cot was no more than two feet wide. He slept next the wall, nor was he able to turn over or to stir till the shoemaker got up. Sometimes he would be out all night, when David had great enjoyment in the whole bed, though it was very dirty. He always felt grateful to this man.

On first reaching the city he had written to his parents how bad off he was, and they sent him five dollars, but he never got it. Afterwards they wrote again and mentioned the money, and he made a great fuss in the post-office, but it amounted to nothing. Now there was a cotton factor who had talked about hiring him, and a day had been fixed when he was to go and see him. David went up three pair of stairs to his room, when the factor talked to him; had him tell his story and show his writing, which he said would do; then he took a bottle out of a cupboard and gave him a glass of wine. This tasted good. Then the man said if he would come in one week from that time he would employ him at ten dollars a week. David went down stairs, believing that he was only put off, and that this was the end of it; or if he should get the situation, he could not imagine how he could stand it another week, and he stopped in the middle of the stairs, where it was dark, and clutching the railing, he bit his lips, and raised up his eyes and shed some bitter tears. He wondered if he should ever see better times, if he ever should sit at a decent table and eat his fill of food. He knew that there was abundance in his father's house, and that his mother had a clean wide bed ready for him. For a moment he thought of committing suicide, then of joining counterfeiters, but he restrained himself, and believed that in some day he would look back on his distress with a smile. In the life of every human being there are times of despair, and he will be delivered if he do not give way to temptation.

Contrary to his expectations, the cotton factor employed him, and then he gave him an order for a hat and a pair of shoes. His business was to keep accounts of cotton, as the bales were received in a long low house; to build a fire in the office and to sweep out. He paid five dollars for his board and slept in the office on a mattress. He thought he was getting along well, till his employer found a mistake of a hundred bales. For several hours things looked dark, and David expected to go to jail; but as he would not be hanged, he determined to start for home as soon as he got out. Looking over the book with a confused head a long time, he calmed down at last, and then saw that he had entered the cotton as shipped when it should have been received. The man said he would try him once more; if he did not do better he must leave. Besides this he must take more pains with his writing, for some of it looked like quail tracks. This was a good lesson for him, and as he had a plenty of time, he took great pains and made everything neat and exact. Why he did not get into trouble with a certain girl astonished him afterwards. She was English, and when he came home from dinner he often met her on the stairs in a dim light; but he always passed by her without stopping. Perhaps it was because his clothes were poor. Among his acquaintances was an actor in the St. Charles Theater, who got a pass for him, and he went every night, Sunday's included. Among the actors were Forrest, Ellen Tree, and Madame Celeste, who made a new impression on his mind. Here he was thrown into more company, but he did not lead off with them, as perhaps he might have done if he had been dressed as well as they, and thus he was saved from perdition. In digging a grave there, they come to water in less than two feet, and the coffin is only slightly covered with earth. A great many coffins are laid flat on the ground, when tombs of brick are built over them. As he was not thought worth looking after, they who were seeking souls and money paid little attention to him. But he fell into the habit of occasionally drinking brandy, and he might have gone on had he not got too much one night, and feeling sick at the stomach, he went into a narrow alley paved with brick, where it was very clean, and water was running. After he got through vomiting he saw near by in the water a piece of fresh meat which looked like a man's windpipe. He went to his mattress as quick as he could, where he was sick all night, and there in the darkness he determined never to drink again, and he kept his word.

David stayed through the summer and laid up nearly $150, which he put in a bank, but once he sent home $30, which was the best thing he did in all his travels. He felt quite proud, and expected to become a rich man. If he could only stand it through the season and become acclimated, he would be sure of large wages, or he could go into business on his own account. Of course he expected to have the yellow fever, but he hoped it would be light; it was important he should have it, for it is one of the qualifications for business, at least it was at that time. For a time military regulations have made some change. In September, David had it. By this time his wages had been raised to $15 a week, and his board was $8, in a place nearly half decent, and where he had a room to himself, although the rats were noisy. He had it bad enough, and the doctor told the folks he would die because he had so much blood. He had his senses most of the time, and knew when anybody died in the house. However, he got better, for though his constitution was not strong it was wiry. In eight weeks he was back in the office. The doctor and landlady tried to find out how much money he had so as to take it all, but, not succeeding, they charged more than he had; but he kept a little by making the doctor wait. Still he was not well, for a chronic dysentery followed the fever; he could do little; day after day he dragged around miserably, and as no medicine would do him good, he determined to go home. After buying a few clothes he was obliged to take a deck passage. But the second clerk let him have a berth to himself, and hunting up some old canvass, he laid it across the boards, and had a tolerable place to sleep. After paying his passage to St. Louis he had only $15 left; a ten-dollar bill he put in his watch fob, and a five-dollar gold piece was in his pantaloon's pocket loose. During the voyage the ten-dollar bill was stolen.

Reaching St. Louis he took a deck passage up the Illinois river, and he was put off at the landing nearest home, with a little over a dollar left. All the way up his dysentery was very bad. He was poor in flesh, his eyes were sunken, and he had to walk with a cane; but he had a nice pair of boots and a good overcoat. He had the good luck to get a ride in a grain-wagon to his father's door. When the wagon stopped his mother was looking out of the window, so, when he rose up, she saw him, and she came down and helped him to the ground. He had a little trunk with several hundred brass nails scattered over it, and a carpet sack. By the time he had got into the kitchen, and while his brother was putting on the tea-kettle, his father came up from the mill, wearing the same hat and coat white with flour. Of course they were glad to see him, and they wanted to know how much money he had. He wanted to know if one could have the yellow fever and money at the same time. Well, no matter. We must all live and learn. It was a long time before he got better. He lost his hair again, and at night had dreadful nightmares. The first thing that did him any good was raw onions in vinegar. The buckwheat cakes helped him, and by midwinter he got able to haul wood.

Then the question arose, what was he going to do? He had better kept at his law books. Sometimes there were bitter words, and melancholy thoughtful hours followed. The best thing they could see about David was his constant reading. He read Hamlet and Othello, and remembered how he had seen them acted. His folks thought that surely something must come from so much learning—still nothing seemed to come. It is true he told his mother he would be something, and that in time they would be proud of him; but that was nothing. How was he to get a living? Not even a potato did all his reading produce.

His father proposed he should take the mill, do the work, and have half, for he was broken down with many years of labor and wanted to rest. David said the mill was old and ought to be rebuilt; that they might make other than black flour, for nobody came any more if they could help it. His father agreed to this, for he had laid up money. They tore down in part, made an addition, got a pair of French burrs and a new bolt. After a long time the mill was ready to run. They made good flour, they bought wheat, and kept two teams running to the river. David worked well and was making money, still he was as uneasy as a fish out of water; his eyes were never still, and, what was worse, he would not go into young company. They said he had a grudge against the girls because they had given him the mitten and had laughed about it. There seemed no prospect of his getting married and settling down, and his mother was afraid he would take another start. He frequently spoke of the beauty of the Lower Mississippi, and at night he had a light in his room to a late hour. This made him lie abed in the morning. They all said it was scandalous that men should come four or five miles with their grists while he was still abed. Sometimes his father would come and get the key out of his pantaloon's pocket, take in the grist and set the mill running. Then they had high words.

About this time the Spiritualists commenced their work, and David fell in with them. He attended their sittings, went to their meetings, and, after a while, got up and preached a little. His folks heard that it was poor preaching. They were greatly displeased; but a certain class, not belonging to the church, thought more of him, and they used to hang around the mill a half a day at a time. David invited some of the preachers to stay all night, which made it disagreeable; but the business cooled down a little when a few went crazy and were sent to the asylum. In addition, David had strange notions about food—he would eat no meat, drink neither tea nor coffee, and he made a great deal of trouble in the cooking department. He would eat unbolted bread, which had to be made in a particular way, and he began to talk about not eating butter or salt, or even drinking water.

While he was in these tantrums he heard a strange piece of news. Flora Miller's folks had moved out west and were living in the next county, and she was unmarried. The moment David heard it he determined to go and see her; perhaps she would have him yet. He hurried around, blacked his boots, brushed his clothes, and tried two shirts because they were not well ironed. His mother asked him whither he was going, but she could get nothing out of him; and he saddled his horse and rode away. Before night they heard that he stopped at the new store down the Fork and bought a new bridle with ivory martingale rings. After traveling till the middle of the afternoon he reached a tavern half a mile from Mr. Miller's place, put up his horse and walked over. They had bought an improved farm—there was an orchard in bearing, there were green blinds to the house, there were shade-trees and flowers. Flora's mother knew him, and was glad to see him; he should take a seat, and then she called her daughter. Flora did not seem in much hurry, though, to tell the truth, she never was more in a hurry, and at last she came down stairs in a nice dress, looking neat and trim, but she was older.

With a sort of eagerness she gave him her hand, and they were on good terms in a moment. David casually remarked that, travelling through the country, he heard they were living there, and had called to see them. They were very glad of that, but he must stay all night. He did not know. What time was it? Her mother thought she had no business around and went out into the back kitchen. When the miner has a blast ready at the head of the drift, he thinks it is the best way to walk off. Then David said. he had come expressly to visit her if she had no objection. Oh, certainly not, she was glad to see an old friend. Then he carried out a little plan on which he had been meditating. He kissed her. Several years before he had made out to get a chance to kiss a few third-class girls, but this was the only first-class girl he had ever kissed. He was a little awkward, but in time he learned the business thoroughly.

Flora's life had not been all floral. People had said that she was too proud, for she had refused many good chances, and some were above what she could have expected. Several times it appeared as though she would have a young fellow; she talked with her folks about him, and the match seemed certain; then she saw something she did not like—he was too coarse, too illiterate, or too bold, and she dismissed him. She had heard of David in round-about ways, from time to time—in particular about his sending home money, and that he was a great scholar, and she did not know what might happen if they should meet. While she was dressing, she determined to do her prettiest to get him. She made her brother get his horse and feed him well; then she helped her mother get a good supper. When the men folks came in, they saw what was going on, and they did the best they could to help her, for she was getting well along, and they wanted to work her off.

Now, Flora was no mean prize. She was well educated, even for one in a much higher station, and she had improved her mind by reading and reflection. Although her face was clouded with faint, creamy spots, still it had a wonderfully clear, transparent look, and her eyes were bright and quick with intelligence. Her nose was not much, because it was rather sharp, still there were lines of decision connected with the muscles of her mouth, which, though extremely feminine, indicated the enduring qualities of an intellectual and strong mind. A science is yet to be developed regarding the lines of the face, which will become the framework of mental researches in future ages. She had taught school many years, and though dressing well, she had laid up nearly two hundred dollars. By boarding around in families, she had learned much of human nature; she was patient with children, kind to her equals, and obliging to the old. She was sincerely, and even intelligently pious, and she never neglected morning and evening devotion. In particular does woman need assistance from religion, that her weakness may be strengthened by faith, and that she may see her sorrows in One gone on before. In missionary and other benevolent objects she always assisted; in the Sunday-school no teacher was more beloved; in the family she was always consulted, and no party could be complete if she was absent. With a desire to marry, with a great hope in her heart, she still had slighted one chance after another; in the West she had rejected her admirers as she had done in the East, and she was about to be left high and dry. But she had made up her mind that she would improve the first good chance, and she was every day expecting the attentions of a widower, with two children and a large property, when David knocked.

After the house was quiet, and the candles were lighted, and she was with David alone in the parlor, and after he had kissed and embraced her, and they had talked a little, she saw that he was unused to keeping company with young ladies. To satisfy herself, she asked him questions. He told her much of his history; and when she asked him about the young ladies whom he knew, he said he knew none, for he had been waiting all these long years for her. Ah, indeed, that was a pretty story. She watched him closely, and the hours passed swiftly. Still, for one who had little experience in female society, he seemed very cautious. He talked freely on all subjects, but of his intentions regarding her, of which she wished so much to know, she could learn nothing. After several hours, she smoothed his hair, and, taking hold of his shirt-collar, said he ought to have some one take care of his clothes. He said he knew he had, but he did not say he wanted her to do it. Then she was silent. She reflected on the proper course. All that was proper she had permitted and done, and he was comparatively cold. When it became so late that to retire could no longer be delayed, she opened the bed-room door leading from the parlor and told him that he was to sleep there. They separated. She fell asleep trying to guess the kind of man he was.

Late in the morning, she tapped at the door. He opened his eyes, saw her best dresses in a closet, and answered. She said breakfast was ready. They sat down together where vines shaded the window, and where through the door farm-work was seen going on. After breakfast she saw him in the porch striking a match, when she went out and asked him what he was doing. He showed his pipe, partly covered by his hand. She scarcely knew what to say; she would not marry a man who smoked, and now it seemed as if she would lose him and she would never marry. But she was determined, and she told him if he was going to expect anything from her he must stop smoking. He looked surprised, said he knew it was a bad habit, then meditated, and the match went out. Oh, yes, now, saying nothing about her, it was for his own good. He looked a moment in her face, in that moment she won, and he threw his pipe in the grass. Shortly after he got out his horse. She walked with him part way from the house to the gate, and gave him her hand. From an upper window she watched him till she could see him no longer.

In a few days she got a letter from him. He described how happy he had been in her society, and how much he wished to see her again. He had mentioned the matter to his parents; there were no objections, and they would be married in a few months. He did not know whether he would run the mill or buy some land and have a farm of his own; he knew of an eighty-acre farm where there was a water-power, and he thought strongly of buying it, for an old mill was on it, but the dam had given away, and he did not know as another would stand well. Then he went on to tell her how much he loved her; how he thought of her by night and by day, and all this, and appointed a time when he would see her again. She was perfectly surprised, for not one word had passed between them about marriage. On reflection, she concluded to let him take his own course, and she wrote him a letter thanking him for the good opinion he had of her, and added a little, falling into his way. He replied immediately. After a good deal of nonsense, some of which was that she must always wet the wafer with her own lips so that he would be certain of what he was kissing, he gave her directions about taking care of her health, that she must bathe frequently, eat little meat, and keep well informed. This made her smile, for she was familiar with all reformatory matters, and perhaps had three facts where he had one; but she answered she would do as he wished.

During his next visit, he thought they ought to be married sooner than he had mentioned, but this she would not hear of, for she had work to do first, and he submitted. As she got more acquainted with him, she began to mistrust him, for she was afraid he would be tyrannical and overbearing; but, after reflecting a long time, she concluded that whatever trouble he might give her would not continue always, for, as he was conscientious, she believed he would improve, and she thought so highly of herself that she believed she could direct him. She could see that on many subjects he was ignorant, almost bigoted, and in general society he would have passed for a raw country youth, though now and then there were flashes and ideas far above the common level. Flora had studied phrenology thoroughly, and principally that she might select a husband. After a time she was able to see that his mind was not wholly developed, and this fact encouraged her. Whatever he might become would, in a great measure, depend upon herself. She knew she was running a great risk; she foresaw precipices, and in the dim distances valleys of humiliation, but it was now too late to return; and then she saw that the beatings back and the disappointments were to prevent her from having another—that he alone might be her husband, and try her, perhaps, as if by fire. In all these considerations the future life rose before her, and connected with it were the inevitable trials of the Christian; nor was she unimpressed with the history of the human race in dark and distant ages, when woman, as a slave, lived in hovels dark and foul. Finally they were married.

David took her home to live in his father's house. He attended to the mill, she was busy with her little affairs, and she helped her mother-in-law, for they all sat at one table. Of course a separate table was soon established, but they had no trouble except now and then a little squabble about dishes, which ended in a laugh. It was not long before David showed signs of getting ripe; week after week gave evidence that sooner or later he would drop off, and at the end of three months he asked his father what he was going to do. What, was he not making money, and could he do more in any station? Yes; but he wanted something of his own. He was not going to work that way; for of two licks only one was for himself. He knew better than to play that game. His father said that of course that would not do always, but so long as he used other people's labor, which was capital, he need not expect to have it for nothing. Other people valued their licks as much as he did his. David opened his eyes, but said nothing. Still he did speak, but his father did not hear it till in bed. It seemed, then, that his father was not going to give him anything. Very well, he was going off for himself, and they might manage the mill as they could. His father tried to reason the case. He ought to stay two or three years and lay up money enough to buy a nice place. One brought up in the West gets notions about working with other people's property which in the East appear strange. Everybody seems as wild as a partridge.

About ten miles distant, on the East Fork, was an eighty-acre lot, and an old mill with the dam torn out. The stones had been set low, and in a freshet had been worked out, and they had floated twenty or thirty rods down the stream where they lay. Across the stream was a bottom-field grown up to burs, as high as a man's head, and it looked as though a part of the rails had been stolen, while on the hill were seven or eight acres in one field, with a log-house, one apple-tree, three peach-trees and a smoke-house. Part way down the hill was a large spring, to which, in a dry time, people used to come and get water in barrels.

David bought this place for $500, and paid all but a hundred dollars, which might have been paid, but Flora kept so much of her own back to buy furniture and other things. He got timber, fixed up the house, made his mother give him a cow, and then they moved in. As there was no cellar, he built a house over the spring, where they could set milk, but he had to fix it over to keep out the snakes. It was a rough place for a new wife who had been used to everything comfortable, and who had dreamed of carpets and tall looking-glasses. A peach tree shaded the door early in the morning, the rest of the day the sun shone in hot, except late in the afternoon, when the sun came in through the north window. The nearest neighbor was a quarter, the next half a mile distant. It was four miles to meeting, and a Methodist one at that. However, Flora fixed up her house neatly; it was her own, poor though it was, and she planted morning glories, pinks and roses. David built a stable where he could keep his horse, and she her hens, and then he rived pickets out of oak and built a good garden fence,

She soon began to have trouble with him. When they were buying things at the store, he would not allow her to have a tea-kettle or any tea-cups. However, he consented to have a tea-kettle, because it was of use in heating water, but not a tea-cup, for neither of them drank tea or coffee, and they never would. When she was married she had a nice filigree breast-pin, but after he got her home he talked so about it when she was putting it on to go to meeting, that she took it off and afterwards gave it to her sister. This hurt her feelings. Again, that same Sunday she went up to him, and undertaking to fix his shirt-collar, which did not fit well, for his mother made it, she happened to choke him a little, and he told her to go away. It was a long time before she made a similar attempt. She was disappointed, but said nothing, for these were little things. But one thing hurt her more. She found out that he was a Spiritualist. While he thought there were some very good things in the Bible there were so many contradictions it could scarcely be an inspired book, and he repeated some things he had heard of out of Strauss. She was so surprised that she was silent; he thought he had nearly converted her, though he could not account for her coldness. At another time, when she undertook to argue with him, he became so violent that it took a long time to hush him up; in fact, she had to let him get cool when he could. Both saw the necessity for avoiding religious subjects. That night, as on all other nights, after she blew out the candle, she kneeled down by a chair and prayed to herself. Once when the moon shone he asked her what were the subjects of her prayers. She said she mostly prayed for him, for she knew nobody who needed praying for more.

David had saved two hundred dollars to put his mill in order. He bought a yoke of oxen and went to hauling stone to rebuild the dam. Folks said the soil was so sandy it would not stand, but he would show them that stone and clay would make good work. He hauled over a month, then went to scraping and wheeling clay. Meanwhile he had a mill-wright at work putting in the stones and repairing the bolt. He did not expect to do first-rate work, for the stones were of native rock, but he was in a good neighborhood, and no mill nearer than his father's on one side, and thirty miles on the other; he could grind a plenty of corn; what he got for toll, he would haul to the river, and in time he would have French burrs. He worked early and late, and Flora believed that such an industrious man must succeed. After a long time, the mill began to run, and a plenty of grists came in. He had been obliged to go in debt, but he expected soon to pay up, and he even fixed the time; for he could grind so much a day, in so many days, the toll would be so much, and then he would be independent.

One morning Flora waited for him to come to breakfast. She had gone to the door several times and blowed the horn, but he did not come. At last she went down past the spring, and had nearly reached the mill, when she saw him sitting on a wheel-barrow. As she approached he looked up, when she asked him what was the matter—surely he had not lost all his friends. He told her that the water in the dam had run out, and they went down and saw a hole larger than a hogshead. But this was not the worst. The muskrats and craw-fish were working in the dam, and if the repair was made, there was no telling when another break would come. However, as the water was down, the dam could be strengthened with straw and brush, and he must get hands and go to work. After a week's labor with two hands and the team, the mill ran again. Gradually their fears that the dam would break passed away, and, for a little mill, it did remarkably good business. But when the June freshet came, the water rose high; all grinding was stopped with backwater, and while many were watching, the dam opened like a book, and the flood of water sank gliding down like an animal running away.

The neighbors were sorry, more on their own than on his account, and they proposed he should make a frolic. This he agreed to, and got sugar and raisins, and killed most of his roasting pigs. Flora killed her early chickens, and sending to the store she got some tea-cups, which he saw, but said nothing about, and the neighboring women came the day beforehand to help cook. Then all the men and dogs and boys and oxen in the Settlement came; they cut timber and brush, they plowed and scraped and made the dam good again. They had a grand dinner, also a supper; every boy had a piece of pie, some boys got cake, and long strings of cattle drawing chains after them were driven homeward in the evening. The next morning the mill was running; David hired a man and kept it going night and day.

But now you will scarcely believe it; in just ten days another freshet came, and it not only took off the dam but it scooped down to the hard pan. This startled some people. They never did believe the dam would stand. Others, having most milling to do, said it would stand, and some were irreverent. Then Mr. Ward made another frolic. This time he bought his chickens and pigs, and he went out on his horse and shot a sheep, though he had but six. They had such good victuals before that people came from a greater distance. David said they should make a log dam with the ends dovetailed together. They said they could not get through that day. Well, they should do what they could. They cut down some of the best timber he had, and Flora felt sorry to see the big logs snaked down the bottom, for they had intended to have them sawed for their new house. When night came they were only half done, and everybody was tired with chopping and lifting. After supper, when David was seen drinking coffee, they held a meeting to see who would come next day. Ten or twelve good men said they would come. The rest, having all they could eat, had pressing work at home. The few next day finished the work before night, and laughed among themselves. Then the mill ground again. Thus far, counting the cost of the frolics and the worth of the timber, the mill had done little more than pay its way. As to paying old debts this could not be thought of, and besides he had made a store debt.

The house still stood in the sun. In winter the wind from the prairie whistled and blew, and it roared and thundered through the timber in the bottom. When Flora went to look after her chickens, she wrapped her apron around her ears, and held her hands over it; and sometimes on going around the house the wind almost took her off her feet, and she screamed. They had only one room, where they cooked and slept, but they had a spare bed in the loft. Here Flora's sister slept when she came on a little visit, and David's mother slept with her when she came. They had a plenty of good victuals, and the doctor said he never drank better tea. Although it was March, the weather was cold, and the mill-wheel was frozen fast. David kept a good fire. He brought water, fed the chickens and hunted up the eggs. When he was not wanted he sat by the fire reading the Bible. It was about as pretty a baby as they make. Every baby is pretty. It is a good deal like corn just out of the ground, fresh and clean, and nothing sticks to it but dew. When Flora's sister went home she said David was the best husband that ever was; no, not the least cross, and so handy; but they were awful poor. It was too bad to think of the chances she had thrown away, and to come to this at last. David's mother said nothing, but she sent over a crock of butter, one of preserves, a sack of dried peaches, some calico and flannel, and a part of a paper of pins. About this time Flora's mother sent a sack full of things, some of which looked like flannel, and they were put away in the chest.

In the spring, Flora urged her husband to plant an orchard, for, having a family, trees ought to be growing. Yes, he had been thinking about it; but he had so much work to do he could not get time. Yes, yes, yes; but he had better take time; better be out all night; go without clothes. She would go without. He had other excuses. Was he a man or was he not? He got out of temper, said she knew nothing about men's troubles, and went to chopping wood. After a little he yoked the oxen in the wagon, came into the house to get some bread and butter and boiled eggs to put in his pocket, for he was going over to his father's to get some apple-trees. His father had a couple of long rows of trees raised from the seed, and grafted with Genitans, Romanites, Greenings, Spitzenbergs and Northern Spys. When David told him what he came after, the old man said he supposed he could have some, but he had been thinking of planting another orchard. The truth was, he had been waiting to see how David would turn out, and yet he had raised the trees for him. Still, he believed his son would have fruit nearly as soon if he had raised his own trees. There were two hundred—a few plums and peaches, the rest apples. They were set forty feet apart, and left with long tops, but they had good roots. The planting was not done very well. Then she wanted him to plant some evergreens, and other trees from the woods, such as maple and sassafras, and, being in good humor, he did so. If the ground had not been rich most of them would have died; some did die, but they were trees in the ground.

The mill still did good business. The dam stood the June freshet and the August flood. That summer he made not only a hundred dollars, but enough to buy several thousand feet of lumber, which was hauled and stacked up in the road to season. Some of it was black walnut and very choice, though it all cost the same. He could not build till the next year, perhaps not till the year after. The lumber lay there three years. There seemed two reasons for this; one reason certainly was a law-suit.

Some three miles distant the Spiritualists began to hold meetings on Sunday. They had what they called preaching, then a picnic, after that a dance. People going by from other meetings could hear a fiddle, and through the trees they saw young and old dancing. David attended regularly and wanted Flora to go, but she would not stir a step. He brought home their works, and he sat in the shady side of the house Sunday afternoon reading Andrew Jackson Davis. He said he was delighted. After she had listened a spell, she wanted to know what he thought of himself.

There he was in great trouble about the miracles of the Bible, and yet he could believe all those wonders. He had better read Swedenborg's works, whence all this stuff came. Perhaps that might do him some good. To please her he got Conjugal Love; she was willing to listen; but after a while he got tired of it, because there was so much. He took up Davis again, but his spiritual images had got entangled, and he was thrown off the track. He scarcely knew what to believe. This went on a long time. Meanwhile he worked very hard. His apple-trees did not grow because he raised oats in the orchard, and then he put in wheat. At times he was cross and could not hear the baby cry, and sometimes, he had the ague, which did not improve his temper.

One time a Congregational minister stayed with them all night. He had heard that Flora belonged to this church and he thought it his duty to call. She was glad to see him. For two years she had not gone to meeting, and she was glad to talk with him and to renew her spiritual strength. David treated him well, and got into a discussion on Spiritualism. After the minister was gone, he acted as if he was jealous of her talking on such friendly terms with another man. He said a little, the more and more, till she turned from him with contempt, and called him the meanest man that ever lived. The minister came again and he brought a book for David. He had talked enough with him to see where he stood, and the book he brought was Butler's Analogy. This is pretty hard to understand on account of obsolete words, but if one is a little patient he will get something out of it. That edition had an introduction by Albert Barnes, which David read first. He was reading it Sunday morning while his clean clothes lay across a chair, for he was going to the spiritual meeting. All at once he spoke out. He liked that way of taking hold of a subject. It asked no odds of any body. He read on. That he agreed to, and that, and that. Well, sir, if the preachers would only preach in that style they might do something. Since the weather was so hot, he believed he would not go to meeting, there would be enough without him, and the horse wanted a shoe. He would see what the book amounted to, and would read it to her. She made him put on his clean clothes, and then she kissed him. She was feeling humble those days. Sundays had been very sorrowful to her. For years before she married she had sung in the choir; now she saw nobody. They went around on the west side of the house, and he read to her. As he read he seemed to get new light. The baby had been asleep, but it waked up, and he saw her hurriedly wiping its face.

The law-suit was about his dam overflowing some land up the Fork. A man had entered it and wanted to put it in tame grass, but he could not do it, and he complained besides that the flowing made his family have the ague. Still he would be fair. David might either buy twenty acres or pay him damages. David urged in defence that when he bought the land it was overflowed, and he knew it, and as for the ague, everybody had it more or less. As they could not settle it, they went to law, and the case was put over from term to term; there were lawyers' fees, and witnesses' fees counting up. At last the trial came off and David got beat. His lawyers urged him to appeal, for it is a part of their business when they get a case to keep it; then there were more costs; then came an injunction, when the mill stopped; and more costs to get the injunction removed, and it took all that David could earn in the mill to keep the lawyers running. When one of David's oxen died with the murrain, Flora told him he had better settle it, but he was waspish, and she did not dare say much. He was going to law the man till he got enough of it; and he was going to do other things.

One evening a neighbor came to the gate, but he turned and went on as if he was only going by. Flora saw him, and she threw herself on the bed, and covered her face with a pillow and wept. At other times other folks overheard something. All these things went out; they traveled far, and even went down the Lake and were reported in that village of green grassy valley.

"Ah, just as we expected! We never thought he would amount to any thing. Clearly enough it is a judgment on her. A man who will not let his wife have a breast-pin, nor her way in any little thing, ought to be poor. But we are sorry for her. She was so handsome, so good and so well informed. We have no such girls now-a-days. What a nice house she might have had with Lucian; it is true he was homely, and may be a little coarse; but look at his farm, not a stone to dull a scythe; look at his cattle; and then he is such a religious man, and now a deacon. Then there were Theodore and Walter. Oh, dear! oh, dear! If girls will throw themselves away, I can't help it. I wonder if he drinks? They say she has a nice baby; that his folks and her folks had to send it clothes; but what is one? she will have her hands full the first thing she knows—it is always the way. If she wasn't such a fool she'd leave him—I would, I vow. But she's so proud she'll stay as long as she has a rag left. Never mind, that cold log-house, and the ague will finish her in a few years. If ever there was a girl who might have done well, and had her pick in all the land, it was she, and she must throw herself away on that good for nothing husband! If any body can help crying, they may, I can't."

While the law-suit was going on, another freshet came, and made awful work. The water did not stir the dam, but it cut across the bottom, ripping out the sand and showing the blue clay; it made another channel and left the mill without a drop. Judgments came so thick, that a judgment from court seemed hardly necessary. Mr. Ward came in and said he was ruined. He was head over heels in debt; his taxes were not paid; he had to go to court the next week, and he had no pantaloons; and he thought of running away. She could follow when he got a place. Flora never seemed less discouraged. She told him it would not do to give up this way, that trouble of some kind would come wherever he might go, and that the best thing he could do was to meet things bravely and to conquer on the spot. He sat listening like a willing little child; though he hardly seemed to understand. She added, that he never would have a better time to settle the law-suit than now; buy the land—for he could get it cheap—then repair the dam and go on again. He said he believed she was right. For a whole day he sat in the house, or walked out in the grove taking care of the baby. After his disaster was well talked over he went and made a bargain for the land, for which he was to pay seventy-five dollars, and twenty down.

To raise the money Flora went to her father. She got on the horse and David handed up the baby and she struck across the prairie, making for Dale's grove, which was nine miles distant, and she could just see it. Having reached the grove, she went up the long lane to Dale's house, when the women came out and helped her down. They got her some cool milk, then dinner was ready; after that they made her lie down in a quiet bed-room, while the girls took care of her baby. After she was rested she got on her horse, and Mr. Dale told her what points of groves to touch, how to turn the slues, and what roads to turn. She made no mistakes, and she got home while they were milking the cows. She ate supper at the kitchen table, while the family sat and stood around. When she told her story, and when she came to the part where she wanted money, her mother made a noise with the kettle cover, and every body seemed to stop, every thing stopped, and though nothing was said, every body seemed to say, "Oh ho!" A coldness struck her; but she was determined to keep bold, and she went on eating and talking; people had to come ten and twenty miles to the mill, new comers were moving in, the dam itself never would give way, and when they bought that little piece of land they would be independent. Her sisters thought she was mighty brazen, but her father said nothing, for he was too busy playing with her baby. At last she asked him for the money outright. He looked at his wife, then on his sons and daughters, but they gave no encouraging look; then he said he had not so much money in the house. Oh, he could get it if he wanted to—and she knew he would. The next morning when breakfast was ready she did not come down, and her father wishing to see the baby, knocked at her door. She did not answer. He slowly raised the latch, and saw her fast asleep with her mouth partly open, and she had a thin but still angelic look. He knocked loudly and she awoke with a start.

She was to stay that day. Her father was either out on the farm, or somewhere else, for he did not come in to dinner. At supper he was pleasant enough, and he talked about mills. He had been thinking it over that people find too much fault with millers, saying they take too much toll and they get rich too fast. They do not take into account how often mills break down; how often high water makes a clean sweep; and if steam is used, how constantly one sends to St. Louis for castings, or elsewhere for mechanics to mend water-pipes. As for David, he was afraid he did not manage well, but he believed he would learn. There was nothing like break-downs to make a man smart. He seemed to like her baby very much, for he held it all the evening and they had a high time together. At last she said she would go to bed. They would get along some way, for David never would give up—she would not let him. Then her father handed her the baby, and as he did so she gave him a look of wonder and inquiry. She started in the cool of the morning. A sack filled with something was thrown across the saddle, and a bundle was tied to the stirrup ring. As she passed through the shady lane the apples in the orchard on either side were dropping. Mother was asked if father gave her the money, but nobody could find out.

One of the first things Flora talked about when she got home was the way their orchard looked. The trees did not grow at all; they were spotted with moss; many had died, and more would die if he did not take better care of them. As she said this she handed him a bundle of old papers. What was it? It was the back numbers of the *Cultivator* for three years, which her father had given her. David said he had been wishing for something of the kind; may be he could get some new ideas. After a week's work the mill was set to running, and folks noticed that he did not attend court. Oh, they understood it; his wife did not strike across by Dale's grove for nothing. What a good thing it is to have rich relations! While the mill was grinding David used to sit in an old chair by his desk and read the *Cultivator*. After he had read a week or so he hired a man for a few days to take his place. Early the next morning he harnessed his horse to the plow, drove into the orchard and broke up the stubble. This took him all day. On the next day he got a pail full of strong soap suds, made a swab, and with it washed the trunks of the trees. Being among the trees he began to make discoveries. Flora saw him digging around them and kneeling down. She went out to see what was going on. He showed her a tree nearly girdled by a borer, and presently he pulled out a claw-headed worm. This was a thing that must be attended to. Some ten days afterwards he saw something of a pale green color on the tips of the limbs; perhaps it was some insect, and he went out to see. It was the starting of new leaves. In a few weeks there was quite a growth, and by fall they began to look like trees; while the trunks were of a healthy green color.

The mill ran a long time, but in March a freshet tore out the bank by the side of the dam. It seemed as though there was no end to this business. After repairing it he did what he should have done at first; that is, he planted as large willows as he could move, and set cuttings between. They all grew, and gradually he had less trouble, till, finally, when the roots had sunk deep, there were no more disasters. At last he began to pay something on his debts. For a long time it seemed as though he never would be independent; two or three times he had to borrow money of one who lived by shaving and who made him pay ruinous interest. During two years all of David's property would not have paid his debts. Even after he had got to paying and taking up notes he was really worth nothing. It seemed worse than if he was commencing new. Still, he was in a position where he made what he owed help him more than the same amount could have helped him had he not been in debt. For this there were three reasons: one because he was desperate; one because he had acquired skill; and the other because he had a regular business. One time he came home after paying a forty-dollar note. It was warm weather, the front and back doors were open, a young rooster stood in the door, while his little boy was playing in the dirt by the side of the fence. He wondered where Flora could be. Hitching his horse he went to the door and saw her asleep in the chair with the baby in her lap. Her hair had not been combed; her dress was disordered, for the baby had been nursing; and the unwashed dishes were on the table. He glanced around the room. The cupbard was opened and untidy; the bed was made, but not neatly; and the floor needed scrubbing. He made a slight movement; with a start she awoke and adjusted her dress. He spoke tenderly to her, and a faint smile lighted her care-worn face.

From that hour he began to think, and he determined that the utmost that he could accomplish should be directed to the relief of the wretchedness of his household. The first thing he did was to get his wife hired help. At once, she had the house cleaned, and she kept herself and the children neat. She wanted to go to meeting, and he took her in the ox-wagon, but whether the preaching was so poor, or she got so tired riding four miles, she did not want to go again, and she said she would stay at home.

Flora had been greatly disappointed in not being able to control her husband, except on some important occasions. In the everyday affairs of life she not only had little influence upon him, but she seemed to imitate him. This was because he did not love and respect her, at least, because he was careless and cold, sometimes unfeeling. She felt that she was losing her power. Meanwhile, poor health and many bad feelings added to her discouragements. She was unable to keep up with her work, and had she been ever so able, she could not have made things look well in only one small room, where the clay of the chinking fell down and the sun and the wind beat in. She was beginning to despair. For many years in her youth she had enjoyed much, but all enjoyment seemed over, and she looked forward to the grave as the only place where she could rest, for rest was all she now looked to enjoy. When David began to pay his debts she really became encouraged. Perhaps they might yet enjoy themselves, and their children might not be lost. A religious change seemed going on in his mind, and she noticed very particularly that, as he accepted revelation, in the same degree his attention and tenderness increased.

Up to this time, a wide body of government land, bounded on two sides by slues which had been almost impassable, was entered. Then a large number of settlers came on from the East, and building embankments and bridges across the slues, they opened farms. David had several hundred bushels of corn and wheat on hand, and he sold these people what flour and meal they needed till they could make crops, which amounted to quite a handsome sum. These soon brought other settlers, who picked up many forty and eighty-acre tracts, making little farms; then another body of land a little further off was entered, till it seemed as though the country was likely to be something after all. For more than twenty years there had been scarcely any progress, but now, settlements changed the whole of the prairie aspect and even of society itself, and as they brought money, trade and business became brisk, and all kinds of provisions were in request.

At last the time had come when Mr. Ward could build. The new house was behind the log one, and though it was not large, it was finished all off, having a kitchen in one end, a sitting-room in the other, and three good bed-rooms up stairs. It was a stormy day when they moved. They had got a little new furniture, all the bed-stands were thoroughly cleaned, and when the table was spread for supper and they sat down around it, the weather out doors looked very pleasant, although the snow came down whirling. Flora had dressed up the children, and she had her own dress starched. Now, the children were hungry and impatient, but their father told her to keep them still, just as though he was going to ask a blessing, and then he actually did so. So unprepared was she for this that she had to wipe her eyes with the back of her hand. It would take a long time to tell how he had changed his mind; but he afterwards said that it was her constantly praying at night which had undermined his infidelity.

At last those apple-trees really began to grow. In three years after he gave them fair treatment they bore some, and after that, the children had apples. He was so pleased with his success, that, having a chance to buy trees of a new nurseryman for grain, he took enough to plant ten acres. Perceiving how much he had learned from the *Cultivator*, he subscribed for other agricultural papers, when he became interested in general farming. Then he hired a young man by the year; he sowed tame grass and clover; built an addition to his house, for sleeping-rooms, and made a decided change in the appearance of his farm. When people rode by they were cheered with the flowers in the front of the house, and they kept turning back their heads; then they had to look at the orchard in full bearing, and still more at the large one which they had not seen before, growing among the corn.

It would do many men a great deal of good if they could understand that ideas grow like potatoes. One idea will produce eight or ten ideas. If it is a good strong idea, the ideas coming from it will be of the same kind. But you will get no good ideas from mean little ones, while what you do get will be so poor that even good ones coming in contact will go to decay. So it was in David Ward's case. Cultivating fruit, and getting other notions about religion, he began to turn his attention to things which interest mankind at large. Having much time in the old mill, for it ground slowly, he got hold of Blackstone again and read it carefully. He wondered why he did not see more good in it before. But the truth was, that, having seen so many disasters, he had become cautious, and he had acquired the habit of providing against contingencies, which easily prepared the way for his understanding the nature of law. In addition, he had insensibly received great benefit from the well-disciplined mind of his wife. While she imagined that she was leading an aimless life, she was nevertheless imprinting on the mind of her husband her habits of thinking, her forms of expression, and her religious feelings. A superior mind, when guided by moral sentiment, always will elevate an inferior one, providing there is no obstinate resistance; and even when there is a determination to plunge into ruin, the day of doom may be long delayed.

When it became necessary to divide the county seat, for it was sixty miles long, so much had Mr. Ward risen in public estimation, and such was the influence of his orchard and his clover, his wife's flowers and her white, clear face, that he was selected as one of the Commissioners. One of the results could not well have been avoided, for the geographical centre was scarcely more than two miles from his house, on a beautiful dry, sandy prairie, and there the county seat was located.

Time flies, and the grave waits to receive us all. Flora became a happy, even a proud wife, for her husband was kind, and she made rag carpets for every room. A schoolhouse was built near, and her children failed not to attend. After the court-house, a church was built and she could go to meeting. Each Sunday after meeting, they looked around to see the new houses that were going up, and then people inquired of each other about houses that were soon to be built. After Flora had been to meeting several Sundays and had listened to the preaching, which was acknowledged equal to any in the West, she felt that there was something lacking. She did not receive everything that was said with the same faith that she did before she was married. Perhaps she had been too long familiar with the sermons in the Independent, and perhaps she had embraced something of

Spiritualism. Without knowing it, she had accepted the leading ideas which characterize the spirit of this age, which, in some degree, she had derived from her husband. Whoever believes that the intellectual and religious world stand still, will be left behind.

To the many improvements going on, Mr. Ward added the rebuilding of his mill. It was a frame, and two and a-half stories high. He got good burrs, and, when it was finished, he had all it could do. After running five years it burned down, but, being insured, he built one four stories high, of stone. Two years after he built a nice brick house. One evening after they had moved into it, and he and Flora were looking at the flower-garden, he told her how many dollars each row of bricks cost. While she stooped down to tie up a dahlia, she said to herself that each brick had cost a tear. But when she arose she never smiled on her husband more tenderly.

A few days after David Ward was elected Probate Judge, he was met in the hall on his coming from the county seat by his eldest daughter, sixteen years old, whose face made him think he saw an image afar off, and she asked him if he had got it. He said he had, when he gave her a little paper box. Both went into the parlor where Flora sat, when her daughter took off the cover, and lifting up some cotton, there lay a beautiful breast-pin. Then she ran up to her own room. Flora turned her head and looked steadily out of the window. Slowly an arm stole around her, and her husband whispered that he owed her fifty thousand millions of dollars, and he hoped to pay a little of the interest with love for her, and with a little jewelry. Then he handed her two little boxes. She opened them quick enough.

A good deal more might be said, but some of it would be mixed with land, for it would be necessary to state that afterwards he went to the Legislature. Much more might have been told in filling the outlines of this story, if it is a story, for only a part has been told. So many lies have been written with the pretence that they are truths, that only a part of the real history of an actual living man can be told. The dose is too strong. In the future we may be able to stand more; but whether we can take the whole will depend on the way children will be managed.

Of course the outline of this history found its way to that village in the green grassy valley. "Well, if anybody deserves to be happy it's she. My husband was saying this morning that he told us at the time that when he heard David kept building up his mill-dam, there was something in him. Then he told Henry he could take a lesson; for, says he, it makes no odds whether it is mill-dams or anything else, a body never must give up; and so all through life there is something that is not willing to stay, but it must be made to stay. And now they say David is as rich as mud, for he speculated in town lots, and there is a railroad going through the town, and there is to be a switch to the mill. I dare say she feels as grand as the best with her ear-rings and breast-pins, though I think she is too old to wear such things. Yes, I know she can get her hair dyed and all this. I don't care a bit, though I know she's proud she has turned out so well after all her troubles. May be she saw what he was going to make, but I don't believe she did, and I know nobody here thought he would be much. But what are riches? we can't carry them with us. If a body has a plenty to eat and to wear, and not too much to do, all that is wanted more is a good rocking-chair and time to sit by the window."

RUNNING A MACHINE.

MR. WAY graduated at Gambier, Ohio, then studied law and removed to Illinois, that he might grow up with the country. He expected nothing less than to be sent to Congress. Things prevented. He was not a first-rate speaker; and there were others as smart and as ambitious as he. Besides, he had money left him by his father, and he was not obliged to tear himself to pieces in succeeding as a politician and a lawyer. He would turn farmer. He bought of the Government a section of land, that is, 640 acres, a mile square, a part was well timbered, the rest prairie, and there were springs and streams. The chances there to buy such land so cheap have forever past. But one may go farther west. He hired a hundred acres fenced and broken up—then he set out an orchard and built a good house.

The next thing was to get a wife. In this he was more fortunate than in the law. He married one of the most celebrated women in those parts. She was well educated, knew how to work and was handsome. Only two women ever looked better—these were your wife and mine. She weighed 155 pounds, her cheeks were rosy and white, her eyes melting and blue, the flesh around her chin and shoulders was full, and on the whole she was a charming woman.

They were well matched and loved each other dearly. They agreed in general things; they differed just enough to see something new. Both were pious, temperate and well bred. Soon they had a beautiful home. Everything was convenient. They had flowers, shrubbery, evergreen trees, all kinds of fruit, apples, pears, strawberries, raspberries, currants. It was too cold for peaches. In all their rooms were carpets, nice chairs, tables, and looking-glasses, and there was a piano. There were a plenty of bed-rooms, there was a bath-room, then an ice-house and all nice things. In addition, and valued more than all these, they had a baby.

A farm life pleased them. Both had lived in cities, and knew how much more is to be enjoyed in the country where improvements are good. Of course Mr. Way could not do all the work; to live well, to meet expenses, and to save something, the farm must produce much. Nothing remained but to hire help. There must be maid servants and men servants.

The plan was to make the most of the farm. As a first help, Mr. Way took all the agricultural papers in the country, bought the most important books on farming, and spent a whole year in reading, in looking round, in talking with the best farmers. Having in this way acquired much theoretical information, and not being without some practical knowledge, he had 400 acres of raw prairie broken up, and put in grain and grass. Of course he had the best farm machinery he could procure.

To carry on this farm, twenty and even thirty hands were constantly required, also six span of horses, four yoke of oxen and three hired girls. At first, he undertook to hire the men boarded in a family living on a part of the farm, but the hands were not suited, besides, it cost too much, and he boarded them himself.

They had stirring times. The kitchen was always lighted up and warmed at least an hour before daybreak; breakfast was eaten by candle-light, or certainly a little after, when the men started for their work. Then the women would wash the dishes, and put the house in order; when it was time to spring to and get dinner. The first year of hiring help Mr. Way thought he had a plenty of meat and vegetables, but he had to buy a supply for a quarter of the time. The next year he planted so largely that one man's time was required in the garden and in taking care of the hogs, and yet there was none too much. It is true some pork was sold, but not more than enough to pay the cost of raising the vegetables, and he thought the result bad, though he did not see how to mend it.

Mrs. Way laid out the women's work, expecting to have little to do, but she soon found that if she was not on hand, things would go badly. She even had to attend to the raising and baking of the bread, for she never had a woman who would have bread fit to eat more than half of the time. This was proved to her satisfaction. But she made them stir around and was out as soon as the rest. Her husband told her not to worry herself, that all she need do was to oversee. He knew little what was required. Besides, she was ambitious and wanted to get along. It must be they would make a vast sight of money in having so much work done.

It was the same with Mr. Way. He had to go out with the men, for, if he did not, one of them was always ready to tell a story, and the rest had to stop to hear it. Once he arranged with a careful man to take his place; at once there was trouble—they were not going to be ordered around as if they were slaves. Hence he kept with them; to get full days' work he must set the example. If he slacked, so would they.

I know very well that many large farmers have overseers, and they take their ease and ride around the country. I know too that after awhile they ride around the country to borrow money.

During the winter season there was not so much to do, and only three or four hands and two girls were needed. Still they kept busy in hauling wood, corn and hay, and in taking care of the stock. When the roads were good, corn was hauled to market, and usually the work for the day was all finished and supper eaten by seven or eight o'clock at night. This made the winter pleasant. Sometimes, however, when teams got fast in the slues, and the men came home with the horses covered with frozen mud and no wagons, sometimes at midnight, and sometimes not till break of day, and everybody had to stir to save the lives of the horses and get victuals, while perhaps the wind had shifted, it was cold and the snow burst in flying clouds over the prairie; then it was not so pleasant.

Mrs. Way, by managing her help, was enabled to get shirts for her husband, and by improving every moment when she sat down, she kept a supply of stockings. She did pretty well if she was not forced to get her own and her children's dresses made in town. I might remark that by this time they had several children, at least one baby was constantly on hand, and on a cold evening when the men sat waiting for their supper, you could hear two or three of them crying, and somebody asking what the fuss was.

Their house was not exactly suited for so many. Mr. Way intended to build a house for the hired men, but he could get no time, in fact, he did not always have money to spare, and the men sat in the sitting-rooms, often leaning back with their feet on the side rounds of the chairs as they told their stories. Perhaps it is tyrannical to attempt to keep men from spitting when they have been long in the habit of it. If you provide spit-boxes they will do the best they can. The children were not much in the way; indeed, the men liked to have them around, so that they could hear them talk, and could catch hold of them and tickle them. Most of the time Mrs. Way had a fire in the parlor and kept them there, though they turned things up side down.

It was a pleasant sight when the men were called to their meals, and a long string of them filed through the back porch into the kitchen, though they made so much noise with their boots as to seem all boots. It was a long table, and to look between them when they were seated, reminded one of some great doings, such as the Fourth of July. Large dishes of meat and potatoes quickly disappeared, and the butter vanished something as mortar does when the mason is plastering. After this came the cake, the pie, or the pudding, which amused them a few moments. A good piece of minced-pie made three, sometimes four, mouthsful. It is true Mr. Way fed his hands better than many large farmers, but he believed it profitable; besides, when busy seasons came he was sure of help, which was important.

In June, when strawberries were ripe, it was hard for Mrs. Way to supply the table with this fruit—so many quarts, and so much sugar and cream were required. Once or twice she tried to avoid it, but some of the men would find their way into the garden and help themselves; some, while at the table, would talk about strawberries, and others had jokes about the word strawberry. So it was regarding other fruit; the dwarf pears and early apples did the children very little good. One day Mrs. Way went to pick some Richmond cherries; she had watched their ripening, but they were all gone. Afterwards, she showed to a friend of hers the picture of as nice and as red a cherry as you ever saw. Mr. Way attempted to reason with the men, and told them there was not a supply for all. In a few hours he heard them inquire of each other whether we have kings and nobles in this country, and whether the laboring man is a slave, the same as in England. Being a good-natured man, and anxious to manage them, he gave up the attempt, but he could not clearly understand why they imagined the word slave applied to themselves. Mrs. Way, however, was in the habit of laying up in her closet as many boxes of cup honey as she could put her hands on, and she thought herself smart in so doing.

After some three years had passed, and the crops were marketed, and he had time, he thought he would look over his accounts and try to ascertain how he was doing. He had been having some misgivings. He had a room by himself; he would see scarcely any body, and he was nearly a week in getting everything together. One day Mrs. Way went in to see him; the table was cleared of papers, he had a balance sheet before him, he had footed it up, and he was staring on it, holding his pen over it, while his legs were under the table twisted together like a rope. At last he noticed her, he started and looked almost displeased, but seeing how pale she was, and reflecting on her care-worn looks, he smiled, and there returned some few glimmers from the old days. Then he told her what it was. So far as he could discover, his profits had been about ten cents a day, something like the wages of a laborer in the old country. This would not do. They must manage better, work more, and if possible live plainer. There was a very large crop of wheat on the ground, they had three hundred stock hogs, and other resources, certainly they would make money next year; by spring he would have every thing ready; nothing should wait.

Mrs. Way was hopeful, but her labors and cares were making her grow old. She hardly ever read anything. She had no time to hear her husband read, and important events occurred without her knowledge. The children had been sick; she spent many nights without sleep; often she only had time to eat at the second table. Surely they must do better.

When spring opened, Mr. Way was so fully prepared that work commenced with the suddenness and energy of a race. During a few favorable days in March, large breadths of spring wheat and oats were sown, and so quickly was this done that many others were only thinking about plowing. So was it with corn and other crops.

That year the wheat was good and hands were scarce, but Mr. Way had a plenty; and when the reapers with their drivers went into the grain it was a grand sight. Away they went across the ocean-like field which seemed to stretch almost to the horizon. The prairie chickens flew up before them as the sea gulls would rise before the ship bearing this same grain across the briny deep.

Besides cutting the grain, there were corn and other crops to work. For a long time more than twenty first-class hands and several boys were constantly required. Five girls were at work in the kitchen. One day, as dinner was ready, and all were collected, Mr. Way happened to ask himself the question, what portion of this help it was which did nothing else but wait upon, and labor to support, the other portion, and were of no service to him? Afterwards he made a calculation and found it fully one-half. This led him to investigate further, when he found the number where three-fourths were required, then seven-eighths, and finally, that where something less than two hundred laborers are employed on a farm managed as his was, they would produce no more than enough to pay their board and wages, and this when prices were good and seasons favorable.

Dinner eaten, and stories told, away to work again. They had commenced before the sun dried the dew; they will not return till the sun is set. And thus it was, day by day, week by week, and month by month. The grain cut, the threshing-machines were set agoing; a train of cars seems running, and the straw flies high. Then grain-buyers come around and the teams haul to the station. What do they haul? That which is to enrich the fields of Old England. Meanwhile, other teams break up stubble for fall sowing. Afterwards comes the gathering of corn. One day is like another, only work so crowds that the main object seems to be to do more to-day than was done yesterday. In the field, in the barn, in the house, up stairs and down stairs, there is no rest. All things seem to move faster and faster, as if in a dizzy and excited whirl. Comparing it to an engine, one would say the parts were getting red hot. Mr. Way was *Running a Machine.*

At the close of the year he footed his accounts. He had done better, notwithstanding low prices. His profit was a thousand dollars. He called his wife. With a bright face he told how successful he had been. She said it was good news. She appeared almost delighted. Still, he saw she was thinking of something. What was it? She asked what per cent. this was on his capital. He had not thought of this. It was only one per cent. That certainly is poor business. Then he looked at her fading and fallen cheeks; he remembered her slow step, and that she was never well.

All at once his thoughts changed and he seemed to breathe

another atmosphere. He asked himself if the thousand, if ten, twenty, or fifty thousand dollars, could compensate for the loss of her beauty, for her troubles and deprivations, and for the evident approach of premature old age?

Then, she had been wanting to say some things; he had time to listen now. He must build an addition to the house suitable for the family to live in. The walls of all the rooms, above and below, were soiled and defaced, even the thresholds of the doors were worn out with the nails of heavy boots. Almost every carpet was worn out, the bedclothes were in tatters, the bedsteads and furniture were broken and rusty, and she was ashamed to have company, for she had no decent place to receive them. As things were, she could have no comfort or peace. He would remember bringing her two boxes of grapes after theirs had disappeared, and they had so many. The girls had seen the empty boxes with the picture of grapes on them, and she had heard them talking about it, saying she was so selfish she had not offered them one; and "Oh, she was so mean."

Mr. Way decided he would run a machine no longer. He would reserve forty acres of land, the rest he would rent. His wife might have a hired girl; as for himself he would have nobody about. He carried out this plan. There were enough wanting to rent land. He dictated how they should manage it; some fields might be plowed, some must be put in grass. Those who expected to work for him were disappointed. In few places could they find as good fare.

Although they had several children, the house became remarkably still. One of their pleasures was to linger at the table and tell each other how much they enjoyed. For nearly a year Mrs. Way seemed to be drawing a long sigh. After that her health, and many of her charms returned. Some never returned.

Again, at the end of the year Mr. Way footed up his accounts. He had moderately worked his forty acres, had a a little help where men could board themselves, had spent much time in taking his wife to fairs, public meetings, and in several little journeys, and yet, from this and from the rent, he had cleared between two and three thousand dollars. He received several hundred dollars from his orchard, and they had abundance of all kinds of fruit for their own use.

The next year there were good crops and high prices. Mr. Way rented three hundred acres, which were planted in corn. His share, put in the crib, was about five thousand bushels, and for which he got a dollar a bushel. He had some wheat besides. And yet he offered all but one hundred and twenty acres of his land for sale. He wished no larger farm for himself and his two boys. Long experience led him to the conclusion that no farmer can do justice to more than forty acres. Such a farm he himself can control—it will bring him all that makes life desirable. He says that when the taxes and the repairs, added to the cares and the inevitable decay befalling rented land are considered, it is better to invest in government securities.

This result will surprise those who are proposing to farm on a large scale, but it has followed in thousands of other cases; indeed, I might say, in every case where one has a mind comprehensive enough to view the whole subject. To many, however, this conclusion comes late, and in their last hours they regret that they attempted so much, for they see that Providence has wisely limited human efforts to boundaries within which the greatest number of people can be made happy.

A FORTUNATE CALAMITY.

EVERY body thought that Deacon Miller's Rebecca was going to do well in having Mr. Quirk. He was a little old, but he had a farm and money at interest. People were glad he was going to be married at last, he had been to see so many girls, they were tired of talking about him. Perhaps the deacon was glad too; he wanted his girls to do well; but two of them besides Rebecca were women grown, another soon would be, and he had five boys, two of them young men; it is likely he thought it time for some of them to thin out.

Deacon Miller lived on the Susquehanna, in the State of New York; his farm was large enough, but only thirty acres were on the bottom, the rest was hilly, and the whole having been cultivated a long time had become thin. For the last few years crops had been short; they even had to buy some corn. This would not do. They must save manure. They saved it. They got muck out of swamps, hauled leaves, made compost, and worked hard. Surely there would be good crops now. They plowed and they hoed, and all summer long one and another guessed how much they would have. They were disappointed. They made the compost go too far. It was doubtful if all they had should not have been put on an acre. The boys grew discouraged. They said they did not mind working, but to work on such land was throwing away their time. One went to school-teaching; another hired out by the month. And yet by no means was the farm to be despised. They had sheep and sold wool; they made butter and cheese; they had eggs and honey; the house was large and every thing was comfortable.

The deacon had said the boys could do well enough with a common-school education; the girls ought to have a better chance. Rebecca went to school a year at Elmira. She came home looking like a lady; then Mr. Quirk came to see her. He was quite smitten and asked her consent. Her father seeing how well she succeeded, sent the next girl to school. In doing thus he borrowed some money; he was in debt at the stores before; in all, he owed about three hundred dollars.

Deacon Miller was a plain honest man; he was liked by all the church. Naturally he was so well disposed that he was made deacon when he was rather young. He kept well informed on various subjects. When he was convinced that his farm was run down, he went to studying agriculture; he determined to make his land good again. He and the boys studied the subject and labored together; though two of them had left, the rest worked on, and they made some headway. They took an acre at a time and put all their compost on it. The first year the result was fair; they put on more; the second year things grew wonderfully. It produced more than they had been in the habit of getting from many acres. Still their family was so large that this help was not great, and they easily saw that to make the thirty acres of bottom ground equally good would take many years. Then they talked about small farms, and ten acres being enough. They said if the farm were divided among a dozen Germans they would bring it to. Other people are talking in the same manner. Perhaps there is no other way of restoring our worn-out farms than to have the Germans take them. This is a question of the greatest national importance. Our soldiers fought for a fine country; unless farming is carried on better, the time will come when the country will not be worth fighting for. In studying the subject, the deacon and his boys concluded grass would pay best. They harrowed the old meadows, put on a mixture of seed, timothy, clover, red-top, blue-grass, and orchard-grass, and, when they could, let water over it from the hills. This was their most successful enterprise. Then they got more cows and some sheep; they thought they would succeed. Still they felt the need of good plow-land so that they could raise their bread.

The time when Rebecca was to be married had not been fixed. In fact, the family became a little uneasy. Still, Mr. Quirk came to see her every other Wednesday, for the deacon would have no courting going on Sunday night. At just such an hour he would knock and come in. All of them knew his day. The house was put in order, baking was done, and each had clean clothes. One of the boys would go out, unharness his horse, or take off the saddle, put him in the barn and feed him a peck of oats and the rack full of hay. He lived five or six miles distant, and always came before supper; the deacon's wife kept supper back so that he could sit down with the rest. The table-cloth was the whitest, the bread the lightest, the chickens and the cake the richest, and the tea the strongest. He was much at home among them. He showed the boys how to do sums, how to make traps; he told stories; the deacon told stories; the girls stepped around spruce enough; their mother spoke in her gentlest voice, and wore her sweetest smile and finest cap ribbon. Rebecca sat sewing; one only saw her eyelashes. At decent bed-time all went to bed, leaving them in the parlor to take care of themselves.

Things went on this way over six months. Mrs. Miller asked her daughter how it was. She said she did not know. "Well, what did he say about it?" "Nothing!" "Nothing?" She was not going to have this work. The next time he came she must find out. Rebecca was in great distress. How could she? Well, she could ask him herself. Oh, she must not! She could not bear it. When Mr. Quirk came again he was well received, but there were sly looks, many long pauses. He paid no attention to them. Mrs. Miller concluded she would say nothing, and another month went by.

Then people began to talk. They thought they had got

rid of him, but here he was again! What did the man mean? If they were in Rebecca's place they would sack him quick. At last it was reported that he was asked when he was going to marry her, he said he had not made up his mind whether he would marry her at all. The next time he came Rebecca had gone to see a neighbor. Could they tell when she would come back? They could not. He went off without seeing her. Rebecca got another beau. She and her mother had an idea that when he heard of it, he would come in haste to see about it. He did not come at all. He said he understood it. Then she dismissed her beau. If any one else tried he got the mitten. She had many sad and lonesome hours. She was twenty-two; what was to become of her she did not know. She would sit by the fire-place with her work in her lap and look into the fire. When she went to meeting people felt sorry for her. Mothers agreed that if he did not marry her he should fool with none of their girls.

Then came a great calamity. One night in February, about two o'clock, the deacon waked up; he could hardly breathe. Through the window he saw a bright light on the snow; then he heard some one up stairs calling to him, and saying the house was on fire. He sprang out of bed and partly dressed. He opened the sitting-room door; all was thick smoke. As he ran up stairs he met some of the children coming down; others were asleep; he tore them out of their beds; the fire was running up behind the lathing, and snapping in the garret. Getting out doors he saw the roof was on fire. The building was two stories; if they had a plenty of water they could not put it out; besides, they had no ladder long enough. Mrs. Miller got out the clothes of her own bed; she wanted to save more bedding and some dresses. It was too late. She had got her own clothes. Women have to get up nightly to see to the children; they can always lay their hands on their clothes; she reached into the buttery window and got out her silver tea-spoons, a few tumblers, and a deep dish—she was determined to have this, she did not know where to get another; it was so handy when they boiled victuals. The night was cold; the mercury down to zero. The girls cried as they huddled together on the feather bed and peeped through the quilts, looking at the fire; only those who slept in their stockings had any thing on their feet. Mr. Miller and his boys tried to save a few things; they got out some chairs, a parlor stove and some trifles. In a short time Mr. Miller told them to keep clear, for the roof was going to fall in; then it fell and the fire blazed far into the sky.

Mrs. Miller sat in her rocking-chair and was warmed by her burning house. At first she had cried bitterly with the rest; then she became more calm and thought how the labors of their whole life were burning up. There, up with the intense heat, went her feather beds, her pillows and pillow-cases and bolsters, her quilts, her blankets and sheets, her chests full of dress-patterns, patch-work, pieces of bleached and brown factory, and many things she expected to use; her bureau with its drawers of ironed pillow-cases, towels, table-cloths, fine shirts, linen and cambric handkerchiefs, silk shawls, kid and lisle-thread gloves, pretty gilt boxes, lace and worked collars, and hundreds of nice things; the clothes-press, with Mr. Miller's Sunday clothes, and the boys' Sunday clothes, the girls' nice bonnets on the shelves, the umbrellas and parasols; her stands, with the drawers of all sorts of useful things, pins, combs, needles, thread, buttons, knitting-work; the children's money; then the nice spare bed in the spare bed-room, where hung the girls' best dresses and her own, their Bay State shawls, their muffs and fur capes and wristlets; their parlor, with the nice chairs, large looking-glass, mahogany table, the carpet, the girls' melodeon, which cost so much, the pictures, the family record, the big Bible and the gilt-edged books; then all the things up-stairs in the rooms, two barrels of dried apples—she wished she had sold them—seven good bedsteads and the bed-clothes, all the boys every-day clothes, her large and little spinning-wheels, and all her rolls and flax and yarn; there were two full sets of good chairs, and a great many old clothes, good to wear in wet weather, or to piece with and make rag carpets, all burning and most gone;. then there was the kitchen and buttery burning; the place where she used to sit and sew and mend by the east window was a sheet of flame, and the old kitchen rocking-chair she used to sit in; all the knives and forks and plates and platters and tumblers and pitchers and wooden bowls, tin-ware and stove-ware; a wide shelf full of cheese, and there was the bread, and long rows of sausage links, and dried beef. Oh, dear! they had just got twenty bushels of wheat and ten of corn ground; and the cook-stove, and the iron-ware and the baking-tins would be ruined; down cellar too the fire was falling; it was rolling out of the window and melting the snow; there was their beef and pork, there was her barrel of thick soap, and the candles, the lard and the tallow, all their apples, the half-barrel of apple sauce, and every pot of her pear, her quince, her cherry and plum preserves, and their good sharp pickles, their cider and vinegar, their potatoes and ruta-bagas, beets and onions; there too was the jug of sacrament wine; more than this the pitcher and goblets up-stairs. Oh, dear! all burning into ashes. They were worse than beggars—they had not even rags to wear.

Mr. Miller and the boys had cried fire to the top of their voices, and the neighbors came. The first one, seeing how matters stood, hurried back home, hitched his oxen to the sled, and putting on bed-clothes returned with his cattle on the run. Mrs. Miller and the girls got in, Mr. Miller and the boys got in, glad to wrap themselves in blankets. A good fire, started with pickets from the garden fence, was burning; in they rushed, they filled the room; they crowded round the fire; some were crying, some chattering; it was, oh, dear! and what would they do? The whole neighborhood was aroused; young men ran from house to house telling the doleful news; others ran in with armsful of clothes; one girl sent hers to Rebecca; one hers to Emmeline;. one hers to Mary; one hers to Jane; one hers to Susan. The young men sent theirs to the brothers, and in a short time all had clothes to wear. When day broke the deacon and his neighbors went to look at the fire; they saw only blazing timbers; While they were there his two sons came; one from his school, the other from the farm where he worked. People kept coming during all this time; the deacon did·not shed a tear; he had seen some things in his day, but nothing like this. Frequently his lips moved, but he did not speak.

The first thing to do was to separate the family, Mr. Miller and his wife at one house, the children in pairs at other houses, for each farmer had a spare bed.

By nine o'clock, four men started out with ox-teams on four different roads. Of these two were deacons and one was the minister. The other was a man who had said many hard things about the deacon. They had quarrelled for years. The man thought it was a good time to make up. He was not a church-member, but afterwards he became one.

Coming to a house they would go in. What could they spare for Deacon Miller's family? They wanted everything. Certainly we will help them. Some gave bedding, some clothes, some meat, some butter, candles, pots of preserves and apple-sauce, boxes of honey, milk-pans, stoneware, pails, tubs; some money. The merchants gave whole bolts of calico, factory, and remnants, tea, coffee and sugar. They had to do it. They knew their fate if they did not. One of the deacons went a considerable out of the way to call on Mr. Quirk. He did not hesitate long, and he pulled out five dollars. Some of the women said he owed the deacon more than that for board.

Meanwhile the deacon and his boys had a crowd of men with them making the wagon-house fit to live in. It was a frame, weather-boarded building, twenty by twenty-four, with a plank floor and one window, and was painted red. One end was used for a stable, and there was a loft for hay. First, they got in a stove. One man had some mortar in his cellar; they built a flue; places were cut for windows, sashes, with glass, were ready to put in; they boarded up the sides; the girls might paper when they got time; a partition was run through the middle; on one side they built a buttery. By sundown it was finished. Then the four men with ox-teams came back loaded. The next day the family moved in. They were crowded, but they got along. Some of the girls only came to see them. Their mates wanted them to live with them so bad. Their new house was good for something beside to live in. They could meet and consider what was best to do. People had given liberally. They had provisions which would last till they could raise more. But they were destitute of a thousand things.

They had their days of council, or thought they had. The two oldest boys would meet after dark in the school-house. At last *they* decided. Then they came home and got their mother to agree to their plan. The deacon was told what it was. They had better sell the farm and move west. Their father looked around from one to another, then said he thought they were right. Afterwards they were a little mortified to learn that this had been his opinion from the very first. Yes, the land would sell any day; with the money they could get land they would be willing to work.

The deacon wrote to his friends out west. The West is like the grave. Who has not lost a friend—who has not a friend out west? New settlers know what is best for them. They cannot, and do not want to buy all the land. When speculators or those they do not like come round, the land is all entered. Sometimes on going to the land-office they find crooked work. The answer came; they knew of four eightys that could not fail to suit him. The railroad would come through next year; he had better send out one of the boys with the money. They were trying to start a church; he could do so much good. Then their land was sold for three thousand dollars. His stock and house property would sell for enough to pay their debts and to take them thither.

Then everybody knew of it. They were sorry to lose such a family, but perhaps it was for their good. Rebecca and her mother were anxious to know what Mr. Quirk would do. They expected he would show himself. He did come, riding a fat horse and wearing his best clothes. He looked around the sides of the house and overhead. He understood they were going west. Yes. He hoped they would do well. It was evident he did not mean to explain himself unless they should speak first. He came again. He seemed to want something and hung around. Rebecca put on her bonnet and that was the last he saw of her. The first thing he knew they were gone.

On reaching their new home they found their son, the school-teacher, with a house ready. The people were glad to see them. Everything was new. All the folks were encouraged; they, also, caught the spirit. The boys went to work; they were going to help the old man get a start, then they were going for themselves. Each one had a deed of forty acres; there were one hundred and sixty acres for the homestead. Here things were to be made comfortable, and put in the best condition. It is difficult to say which goes farthest, and which makes most show, a few thousand dollars to lay out in improvements, or a few able and willing young men. Both together work wonders. But there must be a head, that does not get dizzy, to guide. The boys seemed never to tire talking about the land. One thing they dwelt on and were agreed. Here was fresh land, some said it never would wear out. They did not believe it. They would save manure, sow clover, and keep it good. Those coming after them should not say they ruined the land. For a good farmer in the West, let us have the one who, by skill and labor, has given worn-out land a breath of life. He has quick, new, and true ideas.

When Mr. Miller and the girls looked around, they saw the chances were good. There were more young men in the country than there were girls. As a general thing, girls are good property out west. One hears of places east where they are called a drug, and yet they are the best kind of girls. Such girls as the deacon's were not to be found everywhere. By the run of things, they saw that they could take their choice. It was for them to hold fast or loose, just as they pleased.

The second year the deacon had some apples. He bought a hundred of the largest nursery trees; the freight was enormous; he did not care, and he scarcely missed his old orchard. He and the boys studied what crop would pay best. They decided on broom corn and castor beans. People called them sharp. The second year they made enough to build a fine house. They had the ground around it laid out on a wide scale. There was room for flowers, shade-trees, shrubbery and evergreens. The out-buildings were retired. The railroad came through and did a good business. It is called the Cedar Valley Road.

One morning after breakfast, when prayer was said, and they had begun to sing a hymn, Mrs. Miller happened to be looking out of the window and saw a stranger come through the gate. He seemed to hear the singing; he stopped and wiped his feet on the blue grass, while he looked up and down and around.

The hymn was about the designs of Providence. To perform His wonders, He moves in a mysterious way. He rides upon the storm, by land and sea. His skill is not to to be fathomed. His bright designs are treasured up. Let no saint be fearful. The cloud which seems so fearful will break in blessings. Judge Him not with weak minds. He hides a smiling face behind a frowning providence. The bud may be bitter, the flower will be sweet. In due time, He will interpret his plans.

When they had finished the stranger came in. It was Mr. Quirk. At last he had come for Rebecca. He would speak now. Every one in the family knew it. Every one uttered a pleasant cry of surprise. Mrs. Miller took the lead and most heartily shook his hand. The girls and boys, one after another, shook his hand. Rebecca freely gave her hand, but did not raise her eyes high. Mr. Miller was a little sober, but was glad to see him. He had not been to breakfast, had he? No, he just got off the train. They flew around and got him a good breakfast. He had not known how he would be received. He saw he was still their favorite; he took his comfort.

The boys did not go to work for several hours. The girls dressed themselves up and Mrs. Miller went to cooking. He heard them inquire for the receipt-book, they wanted to make turkey stuffing. He could tell by the smell that they were baking sweet-cake and pies. One of the boys went to the store for groceries, and had raisins around. Seeing how well off they were, Mr. Quirk remarked they did not lose much in having their house burnt down. The deacon said, that so far as it appeared to him, it would have been a good thing if the house had burned down ten years before. Mrs. Miller said they got rid of all their old trumpery; now, everything was new.

During the day several young people came out from the village. Mr. Quirk could not see but they looked full as well as they did elsewhere. The day passed pleasantly. Unfortunately it so happened that one of the boys was with him all the time, and he could not speak to Rebecca. He peeped into the parlor, but there was no fire. He saw wood and kindling; a match would set it in a blaze. He became the least bit suspicious, and talked about being sleepy. Yes, they had not thought he must be sleepy after his long journey. They had forgotten themselves, talking so with an old friend. They would show him the way. In the morning he peeped into the parlor. There had been no fire. Every one was so friendly, it must be all right.

One of the boys took him out to look at the farm. He must look at this and that. First-rate, first-rate. He wanted to talk with him about Rebecca. He would talk fast about something else. He tried the other boys. He saw that they knew enough to keep their mouths shut.

They had a most excellent dinner. Rebecca was charming. As on the day before, the girls dressed up. He thought they must be very rich, or, more likely, it was on his account.

He presumed it was all right. Mrs. Miller looked very spruce in a new black dress. After a while, company dropped in. Some were quite merry. They must be rich out west to dress so well. But the land was good. Then a gentleman came in a buggy. One of the boys put out his horse. He was a man rather old, and looked like a minister. More folks came. Mr. Quirk was introduced to them. He grew dizzy. The room was full. Then the deacon came out in a neat black suit. Next, he was introduced to a fine-looking gentleman who seemed to enjoy himself about something, and yet was a little embarrassed.

He soon found out what all these things meant. There was a wedding on hand. Rebecca was going to be married. He sat and saw her married. One next to him told him how well off and what a fine man her husband was. The evening train took a passenger who came up the day before.

TAKING AN APPRENTICE.

MR. KERR was a machinist. He had a shop in town where he did brass, iron and wood-work, and he made patterns. He kept busy himself and he had two journeymen the year round. His house was a mile from town; there were ten acres, a small orchard of all kinds of fruit, a good garden, the house was finished throughout, and everything was pleasant. By industry he had made this property; no one was more independent. His wife was a good housekeeper; most of the time she had a hired girl; his hired men boarded with him; they set a good table; only one thing was wanting. People wondered why they did not get it.

The reason why Mr. Kerr and his wife did not get it was because they were not ready. When they first married they read the life of Henry C. Wright, and agreed that the doctrines he teaches are true. Brother Wright says it is a cruel shame for married people just so soon as they get a roof to cover themselves to entice bits of young persons to come and live with them. They should wait till they have things comfortable; land must be paid for, debts settled; there must be apples on the trees or in the cellar, the house must be finished off, the rooms must have good furniture, drawers and chests are to be well filled, there must be a wood-house stocked with dry wood, the cow must give milk—and all these things; then mop off the floor, sweep up the hearth and send for the young folks. Mr. Kerr and his wife made these preparations.

The person who accepted their invitation was a young man about a foot tall, and he weighed eight pounds. They supposed that as everything was so favorable he would be delighted. For a few days he took things easy, but when he had looked around he became dissatisfied and made a terrible uproar. All they could do was to feed him and get him asleep. His father overlooked this on account of his youth, and expected he would become reconciled, and grow up to be a fine man; at least that he would make a good machinist. Already the young man had so much knowledge of hydraulics as to be able to pump.

Mr. Kerr and his wife were glad they had got him. They did not know that they wanted any more like him, or any more at all. They were anxious to do all they could for posterity. They wanted to make him the best and smartest man that ever lived. They would wait a few years; if they were likely to succeed, he would be enough; he would want the whole house and every opportunity; if they were likely to fail in their plans, they would send for another.

To them the doctrine of total depravity was infamous. All children are perfectly pure. Their purity is to be developed, and not soiled with the teachings of priestcraft and a contact with society. The young mind must not be shocked with harsh voices and with cross looks. Things must be pleasant to him by night and by day. His food was to be such as would not develop the animal passions, for, of course, he was born with a well balanced head. This course being pursued, he would love good things and hate bad things.

Young Mr. Henry C. W. Kerr was naturally well disposed. He had a fair intellect; he was handsome. His parents took great pains to teach him to be good. Twenty times a day he was told he must be good. If he was good, the good spirits would come around him. When he was awake he must be good, when he walked out doors he must be good; he must be good every moment of his life. Then, when he went to the spirit-land he would have good things.

They taught him to read, and they explained many things. Perhaps when he should get strong and have wisdom and know about uses, they would send him to school. They could not run the risk of his being whipped by the teacher, of his being tumbled over by the boys, or of his being hit in the back by a snow-ball.

Henry's path was pleasant. His father made him a little wagon just like a large wagon; it had springs, and was completely ironed off. He had handsome picture-books, and his clothes were neat and clean. His health was good. They watched him to see that he did not eat too much. Once, when he stole a large piece of sweet-cake and his mother caught him eating it behind the wood-shed, she took it away and wanted to know why he was so thoughtless. He would make himself sick. Cake was only for a relish, not to eat like bread. Another time she found him in the buttery drinking molasses out of the jug with his eyes on the ceiling. After that, he watched his chances better. She thought her white sugar went off too fast, and she found strings of preserve juice on the jars. Once she came upon him, and led him out of the cellar into the parlor. Why did he act so? What was the reason he would grieve the good spirits? He had often promised to be good. He said he had got tired of being good. Oh, what a wicked boy! He said he had heard enough of this; he wanted to go and see how his goat got along. She held him by the hand but he pulled away. When his father came home, both talked to him. Did he want to break their hearts? Did he want to ruin himself? He sat in his chair, crossed his feet and whistled a tune. At last he told them to stop talking. It was plain he intended to do as he pleased. They talked it over. They agreed that to whip him would degrade him and break down his ambition. It was a pity he could not see what was for his good, but they would instruct him. As he grew his mind would expand, and he would do better. Then his inborn purity would develop itself. It could not be that a son of theirs, surrounded from the first with everything so favorable, would go astray. All things bear fruit according to their kind.

One day Mrs. Kerr could not find Henry. She searched the place, then started for town. On the way she found him playing with dirty boys. He came back with her, for he was tired. The next day he slipped off again. He was not willing to come back. She led him, he pulled back; he kicked, he scratched, he bit, he raved and roared. When she got him home his face was like blubber.

He was getting hard to manage. In considering his case, they concluded they had done wrong in depriving him of society. His social faculties needed gratification. She would take him a visiting where there were good boys and girls. If they had thought of this before he might have had a playmate. Children want to play. Play is their life. They considered whether they would get him a playmate. In making him a good and great man, nothing should be spared.

Mrs. Kerr took him to many places and it seemed to do him good. At first there were outcries; the children would not play with him, but he changed his tune; he changed so much that they were glad when he came, for he brought something in his pockets—apples, nuts and candy—and they had good times. Mr. Kerr wondered how he lost so many pocket-knives, and he got tired buying them. At last, Henry's playmate arrived. He asked where she came from, she being a young lady. They said she came by express from California. He wanted to know why they lied to him; he knew all about it. They thought that he was quite knowing for one so young.

As time passed, Henry became active. He knew all the boys, and he improved every opportunity to be out with them. He excelled in slipping off after dark; and, streaking across the back lots, he found his way into town. When his father missed him he would hunt him up and lead him back. He had to hold his hand or he would be gone, and it was necessary to come on him slily, for if he saw his father he would run. Sometimes, after being brought back, he would crawl out of the window and away he would go. His mother found out that he liked ale, but whisky he did not like. To make a man of him, his father let him have some money, and his mother wondered how his strong pockets should get holes in them. He must take better care of his money or she would not ask for any.

Mr. Kerr began to notice that his son was backward in his learning; in reading he miscalled every word; he must be sent to school. This pleased him. He was so anxious to learn that he would start an hour before the hour. By this time the novelty of having such a nice boy passed away, and Mr. Kerr began to consider how he was coming out, and he inquired about him of the teacher. Oh, yes, Henry was a well meaning boy, but he seemed easily led astray, and he seldom had his lessons. About obedience? Well, he could not say he was remarkable. After a while it became necessary to take him out, there were so many against him. It was all envy.

His father sent him to live in the family of a country minister who had no other children than grown-up girls. Here he could pursue his studies in peace. He stayed several months; finally the minister said his wife did not care about having more than her own family.

Henry came back. He was getting to be quite a boy. He was shy and bashful. He seemed to have learned little, nor did he understand quickly; his father was afraid he was dull. He took him with him to help in the shop. He would teach him the business. When customers came he was as silent and as much in the way as a horse-block. His father tried to put some life in him; in the softest and most friendly way he explained things and showed him what to do. Finally, he would not have him about. But he could help his mother; he must saw and split wood, and keep the wood-box filled. He did something this way, but he threw in the wood with a great noise, he slammed to the doors, and seemed to try to wake up his sister.

Mr. Kerr had been waiting for his son's mind to develop its good qualities. There was great delay. He wondered about one thing, so did his wife. Why is it that our son has so little strength? He is weak as a cat, and he grows poor. There is scarcely any flesh on his jaws and neck. Are not his eyes rather weak and dull, and do not the corners of his mouth turn down? Certainly something must be the matter. A few years ago he was plump and rosy, and he was like the busy bee; now his feet drag. What makes him lower his eyes when anybody looks at him? He almost hates his sister.

Then Mr. Kerr sent him to a select school for boys kept by an old friend. It was far away. His father went with him to the cars. He stood on the platform looking carelessly around. On bidding good-by, Mr. Kerr had to take Henry's hand out of his pocket himself that he might shake it. People wondered; those who were envious, smiled.

Mr. Kerr and his wife were deeply mortified. It was a mystery that a son of theirs should be so lifeless—almost foolish. Their plan of making him the best and smartest man would clearly fail. They regretted they had not an assortment of children. Some of them might have ability. Still, something might be done. They sent to California after another. The express brought a young gentleman; then, thinking he might want a playmate, they sent for another still; in fact, they sent on every year.

After Henry had been to school a few months, Mr. Kerr got a letter, and he started for the school by the next train. The teacher was a good and wise man. After night he took Mr. Kerr into his room, and they talked several hours. The next day he brought Henry home; his mother was surprised at his looks; she could hardly speak; but she was very kind to him. Often she wiped away a tear.

That night Mr. Kerr had a talk with her. He said that his business had so increased he was going to take an apprentice. Ah, then, he would board with them. Yes. If he must have one, she did not object; though the washing of more greasy shirts was not pleasant. He was a boy she supposed; was he well brought up, and was he smart? He was smart enough, but he had been left to do as he pleased. What was his name? His name was Henry W. C. Kerr. What! our Henry? Yes, our Henry. Oh, dear! She might dear it as much as she pleased, the thing would be done.

The next morning Mr. Kerr got Henry out of bed by the break of day; he was going to turn over a new leaf; they walked out back near the barn. Mr. Kerr told him he must go to work in the shop. He said he would not do it. Yes, but he would. Yes, but he would *not;* he would die first. What! would he disobey his father? Yes, he would. Henry saw what would follow; he gave a spring and ran around the barn; his father ran after him and finally caught him. The young fellow was no match for the strong arm of the machinist; he was taken into the barn.

Breakfast was ready and the men were waiting to sit down. Had Mr. Kerr got up? Mrs. Kerr went out and called them in. When the rest had nearly finished, Henry sat down; his face looked very red; he ate little and said nothing. The men took their dinner pails and started. Henry got his mother aside and talked with her a few minutes; then he came out and told his father he was ready. When Louis XVI. was to be executed, he told the officers in waiting to march on. At the shop Mr. Kerr set Henry to cutting threads on bolts; he kept near him and watched him closely. In an hour or so he told him to rest a spell; he was glad to stop. Being rested he must go to work again; at noon he had a good appetite; when night came he was tired; he said he was sick. His father told him he would feel better in the morning. "Early to bed and early to rise." He gave him to understand that on no morning could he lie abed.

One night about a week after this Mr. Kerr heard his window open; he was out in time to catch him. He had a bundle of clothes. The strong arm led him into the barn. Henry knew he had a whip in his hand. His father said he would talk to him first; the time had come when he must talk plainly; he was mortified to the dust to be obliged to do so; then he told the young man what he did not dream his father knew. Henry was mortified to the dust. Then his father showed him that he was in the broad road to ruin; he said, too, that he himself had been to blame in not making him obedient when he was young; in this respect he had been a cruel father; but now, late though it was, he would do his duty. He was to decide whether he would go to work in the shop and get some manliness, and this without a murmur or a cross look. If he said he would, he would let him go this time; if not, he would thrash him till he could not stand, much less run away. Suppose he did get away, what could he do? no body would employ him; and he needn't deceive him, if he went off he would follow him and bring him back if it cost five thousand dollars, and he would make him sup sorrow. What did he say? would he live or die? The whip seemed anxious to get to work; it whizzed so. Yes, he would obey; he would do every thing he told him to if he would not whip him; he would never try to run away again; oh, he would be such a good boy! Would he go to work? Yes, he would; just as true as he lived, he would.

Mr. Kerr watched him closely; his care was over him by night and by day; he took him to meeting, the influence might be good; at least, he would have some regard for his appearance. In a month or so Henry became useful in the shop. There was much brass and iron turning to do—parts he could execute—and he stood by the lathe day after day; he did other work. "Really, our son does look better; he does not drop his eyes as he used to; and the corners of his mouth have become firm. How strong he is getting; the other day he lifted a barrel of flour out of the wagon and brought it in; but, dear, is he not likely to hurt his back by lifting so? With what a firm tread he walks; and do you notice that he is getting a taste for reading?"

In bringing up the rest of his children, Mr. Kerr changed some of his views. They had to obey; he would not suffer the least sign of disobedience. He said that when there was only one child it was almost certain to be ruined; the more one had the better would they obey; the house would not be habitable if they did not obey. Perhaps he became too inflexible; his wife would smooth things at times; but nothing could make him lose sight of the consequences of disobedience. From this his religious views began to change. Children might be all purity, or not; but if they were neglected, they would gather all kinds of impurity. He was not so certain after all but there was a devil; at any rate, it would do no harm to be on the look out for him.

On winter evenings Henry had to get regular lessons; if he wished, he could break off work at three o'clock, to study; he must read, write, and cypher—every thing would be explained. Who knew but after a while he might go to school? For three years, summer and winter, he worked with his father, and became an expert workman. When customers came, either would wait on them and explain how work was to be done—both seemed equally competent. Sometimes the young man was quite sharp and suggested new ideas.

The result of all this was, that in his twentieth year Henry was sent to the academy, and the scholars wondered because he was not backward. Among them no scholar was better behaved, and he always had his lessons. True, he had large hands, but they knew how to defend, and there was a good deal of money in them. Afterwards he went to a higher school, and he obtained a good education. On returning home he became a partner with his father. The town had grown so much that it was necessary to enlarge their establishment. At this time they have so much work that they employ over a hundred hands.

GOING TO BE A MORMON.

AT the centre of one of the townships of the Ohio Western Reserve, lived a blacksmith named Graves. He had a comfortable house, a barn, where he kept a horse and cow, and ten acres of land. His shop was large and comfortable; it was weather-boarded, painted red, and had a good plank floor. He had a full stock of tools, and he could do all kinds of work. In the midst of his business he was taken sick and he died, leaving a wife and daughter. He had been earning much, he ought to have laid up money; he was out of debt, but there was little. He had thought much of his wife and had given her a deed of the place, believing she would take good care of the daughter, whose name was Jane.

Mrs. Graves sent her daughter to the district school and had her learn all she could, and she dressed her well. Jane was a fine girl, and handsome enough. The young farmers thought she would make a good wife, and several tried to get her. But this was not the mother's plan. A young man who was a blacksmith came to see her; he ought to be the one. With him the shop could go on; but they must find out all about him. They inquired. Mr. Jarvis had no property, but he was a good workman. He could write a plain hand and he understood arithmetic. In many ways he had seen hard times, which had made him sober, and he was anxious to get along. If he could marry Jane how happy he would be. There was a shop where he could go to work; there was land where he could raise corn and cut grass; he would have no furniture to buy, everything would be ready.

Mrs. Graves and her daughter kept him back a year or so; they wanted to try him. They were ready to hear all that was said against and for him; but they were careful not to discourage him. Sometimes they would be friendly and tender, then they would be short and cold. It was nice business for them; but they kept him hopeful, and he did the best that was in him to do. Mrs. Graves gave him good advice and a pair of stockings. When he came to see Jane she would tell him whether he could stay; they must not sit up later than ten o'clock; if he stayed much after the clock struck that hour, she would rap on her bed-room wall.

At last she agreed they might be married. Jane liked him because he was honest. She wished he appeared better, but she would see to this after marriage. His clothes were plain, but he got a new suit; they made him some shirts and hemmed his handkerchiefs, and Mrs. Graves cut his hair.

The day after the wedding Mr. Jarvis opened the shop, fixed up the tools and was ready for customers. Soon he had a plenty to do. The farmers wanted to try the new shop. Mr. Jarvis might shoe their horses; they would see how long his shoes would stay on. The other blacksmiths had got too big. Sometimes their shoes would not stay on a month; and they had got to charging a shilling for setting a shoe when the price had always been ten cents. At this, even, a man could get rich. It was the price of a pound of butter or of two pounds of cheese.

Mr. Jarvis had opposition from the other shops, and they had advantages, for they had wagon-shops in connection. But he always had enough to do. He studied horse-shoeing. Somewhere he had learned that a shoe should have on its outer edge a narrow projection forming a calk clear around, in which is a groove for the nails. Such a shoe is light, it is nailed at the toe where the hoof is thickest, the foot feels more easy, the frog comes to the ground, there is less dryness, and a horse cannot slip backwards or forwards. This branch of blacksmithing is hard work; some horses are fractious, perhaps they are made so by the smith's hammer;

others are young and are afraid. Some are dangerous—strength and patience are required. Mr. Jarvis would put on four new shoes and find the iron for a dollar. Often he shod all day, and he earned his money. He got along well, everybody said he had a good chance; few poor young men could expect to be so fortunate. When farmers put in their crops, work was dull, then he planted corn and potatoes; and mornings and evenings he worked in the garden.

Naturally Mrs. Graves continued to manage in the house. Her daughter had little more to say how things should be than before. Mrs. Graves liked her son-in-law very much, and the three would talk together chipper enough. They congratulated themselves on how well they were doing. Mrs. Graves and her daughter had been obliged to live saving, there was little to go on. From their few sheep they had made some flannel, and they knit many socks, which they sold at the stores, and they could spare some butter and eggs. They made shirts and vests and pantaloons for the merchants. In this way they got sugar, tea and other goods. Now they could dress better and live better. Mr. Jarvis told them to get what they wanted and he would pay for it. He did not trouble himself about what they bought; when he got money, he went to the store, inquired how much it was, and paid it. On the little farm he raised a plenty, though he bought his flour; but he had corn to feed the horse, cow and hens. They fattened two nice hogs; had eggs and butter, and set a bountiful table.

Frequently, after dinner, Mrs. Graves and Mrs. Jarvis, all dressed up, would come to the shop-door and tell him they were going—yes, they were going, and he must keep the chickens out of the house. They would come back about sundown. Then, oh, they had such a nice time and they had so many things to tell. But they were tired. Could he not eat bread and milk for supper, and have some cold meat and potatoes, and there were butter and cheese and pickles? If he only said so, they would make him some tea and get him a good supper. Oh, no, anything would do.

In a few days, somebody would come to see them. The little parlor was opened and cheerful, and there all the ladies sat in their fine dresses, and there was no end to their talking. Mr. Jarvis felt quite proud of being the head of such a house. But when supper was ready and they called him, he would not come in. It would take too much time for him to wash. So they had their tea, their biscuit and butter and preserves and honey to themselves. When they were gone, his supper would be ready. Once he saw them taking off and bringing back some things—they seemed deliberating whether he should have this or that. If the fire was out, and no tea was to be had, he would eat anything. The ladies have fine times as they visit each other. They hear of all that is going on—sometimes they hear of many things that are not going on.

Mr. Jarvis' women soon dressed as well as the best. A few months after he was married his wife asked him if she might get a silk dress, it would cost only fifteen dollars. Yes, she might have anything she pleased. He thought it a fine sight to see them go off to meeting or visiting in nice clothes and with ribbons flying, clean and crisp as a May morning. He was willing to dress plain himself; but they made him get a fine suit, for they did not want to be ashamed of him in church.

Everything was prepared when the baby arrived. It had half-a-dozen fine dresses suitably embroidered. The young gentleman weighed above the average, and was in good health. Having a plenty of food, he grew fast. The hired girl stayed a long time, but at last she went away.

One evening Mr. Jarvis was looking very solemn. The women kept at him till they found out what it was. It seems that Mr. Jarvis had not money enough to pay the store debt. Mrs. Graves laughed heartily. Was that all? She knew all about such things. The way was to buy less and go without things till he could catch up. This lightened his face a little, but within himself he wondered what chance he had to lay up anything. He was getting a little tired of working for his board and clothes.

When the baby was old enough they took him a visiting. In his long white dress and pretty bonnet, he looked like a rosebud. If they had to go far, would it be too much trouble for Mr. Jarvis to come and bring the baby, he was too much for Jane to carry? Yes, he supposed, but he had promised a certain job; he might do it, by working very hard.

After a while Mrs. Jarvis' health failed a little. Her mother was the first to notice it. She was sure that great boy was too much for her weak back. If she should have any more children she did not know what would become of her. To make it as easy as possible for Jane she would get breakfast herself, and all Mr. Jarvis had to do would be to build a fire and put on the tea-kettle, and, if he was a mind to, he might put the potatoes to boiling, and cut off some meat and put it in the spider on the stove—she would do the rest. This Mr. Jarvis would do, and sometimes more; that is, eat his breakfast and go to work. Still, Jane did not improve much. When she got up and came to the fire, her mother would look at her with an inquiring eye; sometimes she would sigh, and say women have hard times, but when there was a child to take care of it took away all her strength.

Before Mr. Jarvis was married they had talked it over among themselves that he was to have a deed of the place, and he had been expecting it, but nothing came. At last he asked Mrs. Graves how it was. She looked at him with surprise. Did he expect she was going to give up all the property her dear husband left her? Of course she intended him to have it after she was gone. But suppose he should die first, where would she be? He asked pardon, but he had only inquired, for he felt like having a place of his own—he thought he worked hard enough. Yes, he did work hard, so did she, and so did Jane, and much more than she was able. If it were not for her mother she did not know what the poor creature would do.

Mr. Jarvis said nothing and worked away. Another baby

arrived. He was sorry for this; he knew Mrs. Graves would not like it, and he kept out of the way as much as he could. He had to work hard to pay the new store bill. By making collections he managed to pay it. As it was large he asked for a bill of the items. There was a long list; he presumed they had been bought, but there were many heavy charges for calico, nice dress patterns and bleached cambric, which, he thought, they might have done without. Then there were entries for so many pounds of dollar tea; he thought they had been getting fifty cent tea; and, looking it over, he found the average fully half a pound a week. He remembered that once in a while his tea was very strong. Still he did not see how he could help himself. To meet increased expenses he would rise earlier, and people heard his anvil ring by the break of day. Surely such an industrious man must lay up money. So faithfully had he shod horses that he had all he possibly could do. His back, too, began to give way, and he was forced to slight his work, so that the farmers would get dissatisfied, and gradually this branch of work slackened.

About this time two Mormon preachers came into the township and stopped with some old acquaintances—for it was in this region that the Mormons were first organized—and they had made proselytes in many places. These two had been sent out by the Saints at Salt Lake to convert the gentiles. They were plain men, and, to introduce their doctrines, they hired out to work by the day, and watched their chances. They got up meetings in out-of-the-way school-houses. Generally their success was poor, but now and then a man was attracted, either by their doctrines or their description of the country.

Mr. Jarvis talked with these men, and seemed to think so much of them that he shod their horses free, and once or twice he went to hear them preach. He was careful to say nothing about it to his family, but they soon found it out, though they kept silent, not wishing to have him know they were watching him.

One day Mrs. Graves came from the store, and, stopping at the shop door, told him she had brought the county paper, and there was another one, the *Deseret News*. What was that? Ah, yes, he had subscribed for it; it was printed at Salt Lake. He stopped work, and brushing off the anvil with his leather apron, sat down and began to read. What, was it a Mormon paper? Some folks called them Mormons; the proper name was Latter-day Saints. Latter-day devils, more like. She wondered now if he was not *going to be a Mormon!* He could not say, but his rule was to examine all things.

Mr. Jarvis read the paper carefully, but one day it was missing and could not be found high or low. At last they concluded the baby had got hold of it. When another paper came he took better care of it. After he was through work he would get out the stand and the Bible and go to reading, having the Bible to refer to, and often he would exclaim that it seemed to be so. At this the two women spoke their minds, and Mrs. Graves in particular. If ever there was a hellish doctrine this was one. Say, now, did he want another wife? Not in particular. She thought not, when he had as much as he could do to take care of the one he had. She wondered if things were coming to this, that a daughter of hers was to be to the wife of a big Mormon, with two, three, four, five, six wives all fighting each other, living in little huts with nothing to eat but corn-bread and grasshopper pies, and fifty-seven ragged children playing in the dirt. He was sorry she had such a poor opinion of this sect; perhaps if she would read some of the sermons she might change her mind. The Mormons had been shamefully abused. At any rate it is a good country there. Pear trees made a growth of five feet every year. She told him if he wanted to raise pear trees he might be saved the trouble, for they would grow on their own land if he would plant and take care of them. Still, Mr. Jarvis did not neglect his work, nor was he less tender to his wife; on the contrary, he seemed to like her better than ever, but this Mrs. Graves called a bad sign.

That fall, after the corn was gathered, the potatoes dug, wood hauled and put in the wood-shed, and every thing made snug for winter, he told the women he wished to lay up a little money the next few months, for he wanted to take a short trip. Ah! he was going to Salt Lake, was he? He thought not. Well, whither was he going? He could not say, exactly; he might go out West a piece, and he hoped they would buy nothing but what was necessary.

Mrs. Graves now saw that her plan of managing Mr. Jarvis had failed; she said she had erred; they ought to have been more saving. It had done Jane good to go a visiting, but she had gone, and now they would stay at home. They would go without things, for the children were growing; it costs money to raise them, and there might be more of them; but this was nothing to her, and she had no business to say a word, but she had heard Jane say she had as many as she wanted. Perhaps they had better eat less butter and fewer eggs. If they had butter only once a day they could buy their tea. Mr. Jarvis said the best way would be not to have any tea at all; in fact, he believed it hurt him; but Mrs. Graves would not consent to this.

One day Mr. Jarvis told Mrs. Graves that she looked very handsome; he had hinted the same thing two or three times before. Then he wanted to ask her a question. Suppose the Mormon religion true, which it is not, but suppose it, in this case would it be wrong for a man to have his mother-in-law for one of his wives? She gave a smart scream and asked if he wanted to insult her. However, after some words, she answered: Certainly not; if it is right to join Satan's kingdom, it cannot be wrong to fight for it. If one wrong thing is right, white is black, and two and two make sixty.

Things seemed likely to go badly. Jane had many sorrowful hours; she could not bear to think of going to Salt Lake, but she did not know how to prevent it. The trouble was she never had learned to talk to her husband. From the first, her mother had persuaded her to let her manage him, for she knew all about men. The result was her husband was not frank with her; he knew she would tell her mother every thing, and there was no confidence. Often she cried alone, and wished they could live by themselves; she would not care if it was in a hovel and they had nothing to eat but johnny-cake and milk, for they would soon have better; then she could talk to him and he would talk to her.

At last, when Mrs. Graves saw he would go, and they were getting his clothes ready, she asked him if he would not be contented if she should give him a deed of the place. He replied she ought not to part with it; he was able and strong, and could get one of his own; in fact, he thought this was not much of a country, and he made up his mind to go. More than this, every family ought to have a house for itself; he did not believe that there was room enough in another one's house for him to put in his bed. There was great talking and crying and carrying on, but it did no good; he bade them good-bye and started.

First they had a letter from him at St. Louis, then from St. Joseph. The train for Salt Lake was getting ready for a start, and would be off in a week; they need not expect to hear from him for some time. The emigration was large; there were people from all parts of the world; some were quite intelligent; all were hopeful, and there was no fear of Indians. It would take till the first of July to get through.

Spring, summer and fall passed, and they had no further word. The paper still came; it spoke of the train coming safely, and of the arrival of useful mechanics, carpenters, masons, blacksmiths and the like. The winter set in; still no letter. What a pity he should spend so many months seeking unlawful things, when he had a wife and two rosy children needing his care, and such a nice home; during this time he might have laid up a bagfull of dollars.

One stormy January night some one knocked, and a large man, wearing a buffalo overcoat, and buffalo overshoes, came in; it was Mr. Jarvis; his face was fresh, his eyes brightest, and he was fat; he kissed them all round, not omitting Mrs. Graves. Well, how had he been? First-rate. How was it that he had come across the Plains in the winter? Oh, the stage was running; but he was hungry. Yes, yes; they would get him something to eat; and they got the best they had. They were astonished to see him eat; positively, he took one egg at a mouthful; he cut right and left; he must have seen strange company. Well, now, one question—had he got another wife? No, not yet; he had seen no woman he liked so well as Jane. Once more, was he going? Yes, he was going—going in the spring.

In the morning Mrs. Graves asked Jane how it was. She said he would not tell her much, but he promised not to get another wife; she believed he would do as he agreed, and she was going with him. Ah, she did not know how deceitful men are; they would agree with a woman not to do a certain thing, and then they would do it; it was strange how women were led by the men—they would follow them even if they knew they were going to destruction.

Mr. Jarvis opened his shop again. If any body wanted work done, tell them to bring it on; he would work cheap; he wanted to do much while he stayed; his prices attracted customers; he hired a journeyman; they hammered night and day. Folks noticed that his trip to Salt Lake improved him. He worked, they said, like a horse; he had become a curious sort of man; some of his stories did not hang together very well, and in explaining them he told bigger lies than ever, and he had got in the habit of winking with one eye.

In April the roads settled and they started; every body paid him up; they had little furniture to move, but Jane insisted on having what her husband had bought; there were several little squabbles about towels, sheets, quilts, candlesticks, wooden-bowls, tubs and the like. At last the things were divided; he had bought some screw plates, bitts and hammers, and made other things for the shop, these he took, the rest were left to Mrs. Graves.

When they got to St. Jo they found the train getting ready. Looking around he bought a wagon and two yoke of cattle, then went on ahead, for he said their load was heavy, and they ought to get an early start. There seemed to be few people on the road, and the road itself looked new. In a day or so they came to a wide road filled with teams; Jane asked how it was every body was going to Santa Fé. Oh, the road forked on ahead. It did fork and was new again. On the third day, towards night, they got across a prairie and came to timber, where he said was a spring and a good place to camp. Near the timber was a new house with a young orchard around it, and some fields fenced in. Instead of going to the spring, he opened the gate that led to the house and drove up to the door and said they were to get out, for they had come to Salt Lake! What did he mean by Salt Lake? He meant that this was all the Salt Lake he was going to; this was his house, his farm; most rich and beautiful land; here he had worked all summer; he had raised good crops, and every thing was ready; come, they must get out. As he helped Jane down, she hugged and kissed him more than once. The children were put on the ground, the wagon was unloaded and a fire was built, then they had supper. There they are to this day; you may be sure they are doing well.

THE SHOEMAKER'S STRIKE.

THOMAS GALE lived with his parents in New Jersey. When eighteen he got their consent to go into New York to learn the shoemaker's trade. His acquaintances were learning the same trade in Newark; his higher ambition was to learn his in New York. His parents were willing, for the farm was small. There were boys enough left; he was tolerably well brought up. The man he was going to live with they knew. After this age it was not likely he would be led astray.

His boss lived in Spring-street: there were many apprentices; he soon became one of them. They had fun as well as work, and after Thomas considered the business, he got permission to turn his attention to fine boots. To excel, he studied the subject; and when he went into Broadway to see the well-dressed folks, he did so to take a look at the fine boots. By the time he was twenty he was considered a good hand at this branch of his trade, and still he continued to study it.

When twenty-one, he was in a hurry to marry and to become a man. A girl whom he had taken to pic-nics and theatres, he fixed upon; her name was Clara; her father had a place in the custom-house; but she was not prepared to marry a shoemaker, since there were so many standing higher whom she thought she might get. Her parents seeing that Thomas had made up his mind to get her, that he was temperate, and had a good trade, told her she was not likely to do better. Thousands in the city who were rich had commenced poor. They were young; it was important to become fixed when young. She was persuaded—and had him. They hired two rooms up-stairs in Prince-street; he worked in one, by the piece, for his old boss. They cooked and ate in the other. They had little; they wanted little. She bound shoes and made shirts. Everybody said she was handsome and smart; and they got along well.

She did all the business; she went early to market in Centre-street; she bought their dry goods in Grand-street, or wherever there were bargains. She stretched their money; with her own work she made enough to buy her clothes, and sometimes garments for him. She took the *Sun*, though he wanted the *Tribune;* and if he proposed an evening's amusement, she knew whither to go—and it was a cheap place. She was a fair type of many thousands of mechanics' wives in New York. It is a pity that so few of them have the means for doing all that their abilities fit them for. Their first dispute was about newspapers; he wanted the *Tribune*, because it advocated elevating the laborer; she wanted the *Sun* because it was only a cent, and because her mother took it. Sometimes he would jump up and leave his work, be gone an hour or so, and she found out he went to look at the *Tribune*. Then she took it, because she was afraid if he was out much he might get in the habit of drinking. A woman neglects if she does not keep watch of her husband, for if he goes astray all is lost.

When the baby came, which it did in good season, they had been so saving and so fortunate as to have fifty dollars laid by, and they had good clothes for themselves and the new comer. In one thing he was disappointed. He had expected to see a way open to become a boss. He had neither capital nor business knowledge, but he thought he would try. He bought leather and made a case of fine boots. He sold them after some running, but the profit was not great, and he had pieces of leather left which he could not use. On reflection, he went back to work for his old boss. Still, he did not believe in working always for others: some day, he would get money enough to leave the city, and start a shop in some Jersey village. This his wife would not listen to; she believed in New York; there was no other place in the world equal to it; there she would live, there she would die. So they continued to live for several years. In four years they had saved two hundred dollars, which they put in the bank and got interest on it. They would have made more, but there was a new comer every year or so, which cost money, and though Clara worked hard, still she earned less by her shoe-binding and shirt-making, because so much of her time was required for other things. When ten years had passed they had four hundred dollars in the Savings Bank. Then he was going to start a shop; and one day he brought a man who was going in with him; they would do all sorts of work; they would have journeymen and apprentices, and soon would be rich. Clara did not like the looks of the man; she told her husband aside he would not do; he was persuaded, and put him off. This was fortunate, for Mr. Gale soon found out that he was a sharper.

One morning Mr. Gale met his oldest son on the stairs, starting for school, and he saw him put something in his mouth. What was it? Nothing. He brought the young chap into the room where he worked. Clara hearing the shuffling, had come in. Now what was it? His cheek stuck out; the boy stood on one leg and looked around. At last his father forced open his mouth, and with his awl picked out a tobacco quid. Did any body ever hear of a boy of his age doing like this? he must stop it or he will be whipped. He was questioned—and told some things; the other children told more. There was quite a development regarding his companions and his habits. Some drinking had been going on. Clara opened her eyes; she had been thinking her boy the finest young chap in the city. Shortly after she found a box well filled with tobacco in his pocket; he implored her not to tell; she was deaf; his father took his strap to him—and the habit was broken up.

This, and other similar matters set Mr. Gale to thinking. The slow way he was getting along set him to thinking; so did his increasing family. Their expenses, too, were increasing; and now that there were six children they needed more room; in hot weather it was almost impossible to cook, eat and live in one room, saying nothing about places to sleep. Clara went out several times to hunt for a house with more rooms. She saw clearly that to get such would take all they had been in the habit of saving, while they needed this amount extra for clothing and food. They talked the matter over. Soon the time would come when they could lay up nothing, and they could have no more room. Henry was taken from school and was set to learning his father's trade. It was a pity to break him off—he was just beginning to learn fast; but there was no help for it. In thinking of his prospects, Mr. Gale became melancholy, almost discouraged. He lost flesh; his face became sickly and pale; he said little. Clara kept good courage. She was still fresh and rosy, for she had all the running to do. Every day she would go into Orchard street to see her mother, and to hear and tell the news. She called on others, but all her visits were short.

Every morning Mr. Gale would go to his bench and work till breakfast, then he would look over the paper and then work again; he worked all day long. He did not sing any more while at work. In the evening he would walk out in the park, often alone. I doubt not but you often saw him. Sometimes he would go with Clara to a free lecture; neither could dress as well as formerly, and they paid few visits. This was hard on Clara. To live in New York and not dress well was a real grief.

In the midst came a financial crash. Merchants were failing, and there was a run on the banks. Early in the morning Clara went to draw their money. She did not come back till five o'clock. Only by keeping in her place was she able to get to the counter late in the day. Afterwards she came near being robbed. The bank proved sound, and in a week she put it back again.

One morning Mr. Gale did not go to work; he sat in her rocking-chair reading the paper. Clara left off getting breakfast to ask if he was well. Yes, but he was thinking; he intended to spend some time in thinking. All the children came to look at him. It was strange father was not at work; they were afraid something would happen. When he got his breakfast, he took his hat and went out; his bench looked lonely enough, with the leather apron spread over it. Surely something was going to happen—he had never been this way before. But he was getting poorly; a walk down to the Battery or a stroll across the river would do him good. She got him an extra dinner; the table-cloth was as white as snow; the room was scoured and cleaned; father should see they had not been idle. He did not come back at noon. The dinner was all ready. She sent the children out to see if he was coming, and she kept looking out of the window. At last she saw him walking fast with the children holding to his fingers. He seemed quite bright. He had been over to Hoboken sitting under some trees, and he had got through thinking; he was *on a strike*. On a strike! the papers had said nothing about it. It was a curious time to go on a strike when he thought himself well off to get work at all. No matter, he was on a strike. Strike about what, pray tell? About work; he was not going to stand it; others might, he wouldn't. They talk about slaves, he was one; now he was going to be free. He would leave the city, he would buy land and turn farmer. Certainly he must be crazy; and she gave him to understand she was not going to Jersey. He said that was no place. He was going west, to Illinois. Let her look at that letter and that pamphlet. Yes, he must be crazy; and she wondered if he thought she was going to Illinois to live among the Choctaws, the Cherokees, and the Pottawattomies. He told her she was beside herself to talk about Indians in Illinois. There were none within a thousand miles. It seems he had got into correspondence with the Commissioner of the Land Department of the Illinois Central Railroad. Great inducements were held out, and the general statements were illustrated by accounts from settlers. Clara read them over, but could not bear the idea of leaving New York, and of never seeing her relations and friends again. He talked with her and showed her that they were doing little, and were likely to do less, and what they paid for meat in four years would buy them a farm, when not only would it be their own, but it would support them, and be worth more than the house and lot itself. She would not go; she knew it would make her miserable, and her children never could be any thing.

Then she went to talk with her parents. What was her surprise to hear her father say it would be a good plan; he had known many who went west do well. With common industry they could not fail; in fact, he had made up his mind that when he should lose his place in the custom-house to go himself. She knew not what to think. She said they were all against her. All she could do was to cry. Thomas had always been led by her, and she thought she could control him. This was a mistake. The first thing she knew he had the children on his side, for he told them such fine stories about the West, how the strawberries grew among the grass, how there were nuts of all kinds, and apples, peaches and pears; everywhere flowers bloomed, and milk was only a cent a quart.

Clara held out several weeks, but seeing there would be no peace, she made up her mind to go, and then went to work to get them good clothes. She visited auction-shops and other places where she could buy things cheap, then they started for Illinois.

At Chicago the Commissioner was surprised to see a man come in this way, with his goods and his family, for usually one comes and picks out a place first and then sends for his family. Fearing that, as they were used to a city life, they would become discouraged if they went on a farm entirely new, he sent along an agent to show them one of those farms which squatters abandoned when the Company took possession, for they settled intending never to buy, but to sell the improvements. They left Chicago in the night, and the next day were put off at a new station in the middle of the State. There was no place for them to stay, and a team was hired to take them to Mr. Goodman's, who lived near the farm the agent thought would suit.

Mr. Goodman lived about three miles from the railroad; he came from Kentucky twenty years before, and by industry had become wealthy.

The family arrived toward night. Mr. Goodman was willing to keep them until they could look around; he was anxious to have the country settled, and he would help them all he could. He had a good orchard; it was in the fall of the year, and there were plenty of apples. One saw a large plain house, long cribs of corn, for it was cheap and he had sold little, and hogs, horses and cattle in abundance. Supper was ready, and they sat down at a long table, and were surprised to see such large dishes of meat, potatoes, butter and the like, and they thought he must be very rich. They did not understand how plentiful food is in the interior of this State. All were glad to get to bed and have some sleep after their long journey.

After breakfast they went over to look at the farm, which was scarcely a quarter of a mile distant. It consisted of forty acres; eight or ten were partly fenced. There was a ruined log-house, and half a dozen old apple-trees as much neglected as possible. A creek was one side of the lot, and there were about five acres of timber, which the agent and Mr. Goodman spoke of as being of great value; all the rest was raw prairie, and there was scarcely a house in sight.

When Clara went into the house, which had neither window nor door, she said it was fit only for hogs; indeed, hogs had been lying in it. It was a most doleful-looking place. When they had looked around, which did not take long, Mr. Gale took his wife aside and told her he was sorry he had brought her to such a place; he confessed he was wrong, but he would take her back to New York. He would work faithfully and never complain again. He had no idea that everything was so new, so rough, and required so much work to make a beginning.

She asked him if their long journey and the spending of so much money was to go for nothing. He was sorry; he had done what he thought was best, but he saw she would not be pleased. How did he know she was not pleased? He only supposed so. He asked if they had not better go into some village or town?

Then she told him she had been talking with Mrs. Goodman; they lived three weeks at first in their wagon, but they got along well enough in a little time. Then she told him how cheap everything was, and they could buy a cow for what milk cost them in three months in New York. She was going to stay; she was going to have no such foolish business. He could work couldn't he? Oh, yes. Well, he had better buy the place. Mr. Goodman said the house could be fixed up in a few days; and more than this, he could get all the work he wanted to do at his trade, and then have men to work for him. The boys could learn to work, and it would do them good.

Accordingly the place was bought. They paid $250 down. The agent said they had better keep some money; the amount due could remain on interest, and there would be no trouble in meeting payments, for he would have six years' time. The house was made habitable and they moved into it. Some lumber was bought, and an addition was built for two bed-rooms, and they lived comfortably.

After a little they found out that they had many neighbors, though few were very near. They lived around on the edge of the timber. All these wanted shoemaking done, and to please them and get acquainted, Mr. Gale went to their houses to do it, and worked up their own leather. This was called "whipping the cat." He was not much used to general custom work, but he could do it. When the young men found out what elegant boots he could make, he had jobs enough to do. Then he bought his own leather.

Often he said to himself and to his family, "What a fool I was." He was thinking of the high prices he was getting, which was what the storekeepers charged at retail. Before, he only got wholesale prices. Now he had the profits of at least three classes of men: first, those of the wholesale merchant; second, of the freight line companies; and third, of the retailer. Much more than this, his rent cost nothing, and his provisions cost nearly nothing, for he had the same advantages here in buying of first hands that he had in working directly for his customers. Middle-men were making nothing out of him.

One evening he figured up how much better he was doing, and it was clear he was doing twice as well. The advantage on his side was fully equal to three hundred dollars a year clear money, and this while they had everything to buy.

They had schools and meetings. It is true there were deficiencies. But is was some comfort to Clara that they dressed as well as the rest, and that there were none to look down upon them. In the city, it is an immense distance to such a position. Even with old clothes, scarcely fit to wear in the city, they could stand well enough. There was much—she felt it, and it was so—that by her habit of speaking, and her acquaintance in society, she and her children could pass well in any company. She imagined she was imitated.

Mr. Gale earned enough during the winter to have rails made and laid up, and several acres of prairie broken. Then they planted corn, potatoes and the like, and had a garden. Of course they were awkward, and remarks were made; but they learned, and they did not do a thing wrong more than twice.

Mr. Goodman helped them, and they took his advice to plant an orchard. A horse was bought, and plows and other tools; so were hogs and cows, which ran on the open prairie.

Mr. Gale was not ignorant of farm work, but here they do differently from what they do in the East. The main point was whether he could work. Since he was married, he had worked hard. He knew what it was to stick to it from morning till night, month after month, always. For a mechanic to live in the city he must work much more than a farmer does in the country. He was faithful. He hoed his corn, which few did; and he had the heaviest and best crop in the Settlement. This gave him a plenty of pork, and he even sold some.

When the weather was bad he worked at his trade, and he always had a pair of fine boots on hand to make. I have noticed others out of a city besides him. They do more work than the old farmers; often they are the best farmers. Such men always read agricultural papers. They had some books, and they took the weekly edition of their old friend.

Those who do not know, will be astonished to learn that young people can become excellently well informed by reading a first-class weekly paper like this. Add common school advantages, and they will have what anywhere will pass for a good education.

Of course they met with difficulties; some things were dark; but never, never were they so dark as they always were in the city. The great consoling fact continually was before them that they had a home of their own—that every year, on the whole, they made progress. They built a new house, which was painted white, and had green blinds; and finally, the orchard was loaded with apples. When the war came the father and son volunteered. It may not be pleasant to relate—but it was so—the father was only a lieutenant, the son was a captain.

After a time, Clara's father came out west to get him a farm, having heard how well they were doing. One morning he was looking around for Clara. Going to the north side of the house, along the well-worn path, hardened with blue grass, and where fallen apples lay, he saw her down in the cellar. "What are you doing, Clara?" "Come down and see." He went down and found her taking butter out of a barrel churn. "Why, you make your own butter; what a sight of it! How much is there?" "About eight pounds." "Ah, ha! And how often do you get so much?" "Every other day—sometimes every day. We keep seven cows. We make much more since we built the ice-house." "Ice, eh? Why, you have things quite city-like. Now, Clara, what will such a lot of butter bring? It is high now, but it is good." "Well, not far from two dollars. I tell you, father, it will bring more than I used to get in binding shoes a whole week, and I do not work half as hard." "Yes, I see you are doing well. Your oldest girl, you say, is married to a rich farmer, and you are keeping your next at the Normal School at Bloomington. I see now, when Thomas struck, as you were telling me, he made a good strike; and it strikes me that a good many mechanics in our city will do well to strike in the same way."

HENRIETTA.

JULIUS CAIRD was born and brought up in one of the southern counties of the State of New York. His father was a farmer. He thought he would learn the carpenter's trade, and did so. There was not work enough; he would travel and seek it. He had been well brought up; his mother had taken trouble to teach him everything good; he had a fair common school education, and could write a good hand. His face was rather handsome; his manners were pleasing. On his departure, his parents gave him much good advice and their best wishes. The last words of his mother were that he must remember his Creator in the days of his youth.

Many were going west. He went south into Pennsylvania, and coming to the county seat of a rich county he found work. The people were Germans; everybody spoke this language; there were not more than a dozen Yankees in the town. Of course the business-men could speak English; almost every one could speak a little.

The town stood on the bank of a small but beautiful river. Above and below were green meadows; beyond were high hills, and beyond these were fine farms. The merchants had large stocks of goods; the mechanics had all they could do. The streets were paved; there was hydrant water. There were two German newspapers and one English; five churches and one English, and there were many good taverns. Two lines of stages ran through the town—one from Philadelphia and one from Harrisburg.

This is one of the many counties where the farmers have

got rich; where fortunes have been made by raising wheat after clover. It is limestone land, naturally rich, and the clover has made it richer. They have some fruit, and might have more; all crops are good; their horses are excellent. This is a country of good roads and good bridges. Here are the large stone barns, with gilt signs, on which are lettered the names of the farmer and his wife. Their houses are good, frequently two stories, of blue limestone. Very many of the farmers could not speak a word of English; usually, there was a boy or girl about who could. They dressed their clover with plaster-of-paris. Some put on lime, and had kilns of their own where they burnt it. Everywhere was high culture. This is an easy way to farm; that is, when you can get at it. Their houses were well furnished from top to bottom, and there was every comfort. It is understood that large sums in specie are hoarded in these houses. It has been estimated at thirty millions of dollars. Perhaps this is the only large section of our country where the land has constantly been kept good.

Mr. Caird had a plenty of work. For two dollars a week he got board at a tavern, and he had a room to himself. The fare was excellent. Perhaps he had too much meat and sausage. Wages were low; his duty was to save his money. He worked faithfully, and neither drank nor swore. He dressed neatly, attended church, and was respected. He was ambitious to get along. His notion was to become a boss carpenter. To succeed, he studied architecture and made himself acquainted with fine work. He was particular in doing his work well, and never to call a job finished when it was any way imperfect. Also, he was quick. To be correct and yet slow will not satisfy. One must have ready thoughts and a strong arm. To succeed in any calling, many things are required. Temperate habits underlie all. Time, too, is required. Mr. Caird strove to have every quality. The first fruit of his labor was to buy a lot and build on it a small house, which he rented. This gave him standing. He was looked upon as one of the citizens.

At first people took no particular notice of him; no one knew how long he would stay. They were suspicious of Yankees—Yankees had sold them copper for gold jewelry and clocks which would not run. Mr. Caird wanted to please them; he was going to make his home with them. He took pains to learn from the workmen how they named their tools and the parts of their work. Then he got the names of common things, after that, the words which described and expressed existence and action, thus picking up the language by piecemeal. After a while people found out it would not do to talk about him in his presence. The German spoken here is corrupted, as the scholars from the old country say, but they understand each other. Of course the language of the common people is different from the written.

Mr. Caird, instead of going to the English Church, went to the Lutheran and other churches where the German was spoken. Here were large crowds. The organ sounded; there were strange movements and ceremonies. The women were devout, and richly dressed. Sometimes, with white caps on their heads, they would walk around the centre of the church while the minister waved something over their heads, and they all sang and the organ played. On new year's eve there were great doings; all the bells rang; everybody seemed to be in the churches; it was snowing and stormy without, within, it was pleasant and bright; and with their singing and their ceremonies they waited and watched till midnight, when the old year went out and the new came in. There had been low wailing on the organ for the dying year; when the clocks in the steeples struck twelve, all the bells rang gaily, the organs piped high, and the people united in the song of welcome. Many of their usages have come down from the days when the Roman legions penetrated the forests of their Fatherland. Coming hither in a body, few things were changed. In old Germany, Frankfort, Berlin, Munich, Dresden, one will see the same things he sees here. There is more literature among the Pennsylvanian Germans than one might suppose. The works of the late classic writers—Goethe, Herder, Schiller and the like, are common.

Mr. Caird mingled with the people as a practical man. Of course he associated with the young. At first he knew not what to make of their amusements and strange plays. Soon he became almost like the rest. It is pleasant and easy to get around in these towns on winter nights. Most of the streets are lighted with gas; there is no mud; coal is cheap, and all the houses are warm. There were then but two classes, the ignorant and the poor, and the common thrifty rich people. The girls and young men of rich parents dressed no better and were no prouder than the others. Evening parties and social meetings were numerous. On cold nights it was common for a couple to go round from house to house. Some would be at home, some not. At such times they would enter quiet parlors where the family sat; next, where other couples like themselves had called and were talking; and next, where the room was crowded and there were merry plays. If the girls present did not like to play on the piano, or were too young, the mother would sit down and perform some grand march or sweet old time song. Education, even long ago, was not neglected. Many of these mothers had been to school in Philadelphia, more at Bethlehem, a Moravian institution, where the Christian doctrines of Zinzindorf were practically carried out. In many respects the Moravians here, and at Nazareth, six miles distant, come nearer to having what is agreed to be true religion than any other people. Of late, however, there are changes.

Such was the way the young people of the town passed their winter evenings. In the summer they used to walk in the meadows. At the foot of the mountains near which the river ran, were large springs, some giving water enough to carry mill-wheels. On Lord's day afternoon it was customary to walk into the beautiful grave-yard. The ground was shaded with fine trees, and the German inscriptions on the tombstones made it a strange and interesting place.

Mr. Caird used to take out different girls. At first his girl was a sort of curiosity, and privately she would be asked how he acted. Before he could speak much German they were so polite as always to speak English. But he strove to learn their tongue, and they helped him. He learned more from them than any other source. When he made mistakes, they laughed merrily. At some mistakes they would look at each other and be very grave, then they would tell him how to speak it. In a year or so he was even with them, for he could speak their language as well as they could his. Still, there were girls who had been to school abroad; they spoke very correctly, and they had every accomplishment. Such, likely enough, had friends in Philadelphia, and there they visited and mingled in the best society. Here was their home; they strove to make it pleasant. It will be many years before the German language will die out in this region. It has great vitality. The wealth and the vast number of the people using it give it dignity. But its antagonist will conquer. It is a conqueror. There is reason to believe it will conquer through the world. There are no laws and no conditions given to mankind, whether in Europe or America, in China, in India or Japan, so imperative and enforced by so much power as those written in the English language. The people who speak it gave the first—they have given the last blows to human slavery.

Among these ladies one at last attracted Mr. Caird. This was Henrietta Kaufman. She was a young widow without children. Her husband had been a county officer. He died shortly after her marriage, leaving her a fine farm a mile or so from town, a large stone residence in town, and money in the bank. He was a descendant of thrifty farmers. His brothers and sisters also had good property. Henrietta was educated at Bethlehem. She was as good looking as the best. Perhaps she was a little too fleshy. The seams of her dress around her shoulders and breast were very strong. Her cheeks were as red as if painted with cherry paint, and her eyes were as sparkling and as clear as the water of her native river. Her husband having been dead a couple of years, she became as gay as the rest and was counted as one among the young people. She had little occupation. Clearly she would marry again when the right man should come. Often Mr. Caird was her beau, so, too, were others; but it was seen he had a fancy for her, and jokes about them were common. May be they would make a match.

This pleased Mr. Caird well enough, but he was convinced she would think of nothing of the kind while he was so poor and so little known. As a companion in company he was well enough; to become the husband of such a woman was quite a different thing. He had mind enough to see that only one course was open to him. He must be successful in business and must have wealth, or at least show that he was in the way to it. He had made a good beginning in getting the lot, and building a house.

The next step was to get the contract for building a certain fine residence one of the merchants proposed to erect. He was known to be a good workman, but there were competitors. He drew a neat plan of the house, which pleased; made close calculations, and proposed to complete it for a moderate profit. He got the job. With all his energy he went to work. He had some money; some was advanced. He bought timber and hired workmen. He labored early and late; some thought he was doing too much, but they liked his spirit. He had a good lot of hands; the work progressed; in due time it was finished. The owner not only was satisfied, he was delighted, and so was his family. When he was paid off his profits were less than he expected.

Meanwhile, another, proposing to build, had been watching the work. He knew when justice was done to a job. He could see that, in this case, it was done well from the foundation. Then he wanted a similar house built. How much would he ask? Mr. Caird plainly told him he must have more. By doing jobs so cheap he might be ruined. This the man knew. He wanted faithful work done; this was of more consequence than money. Then Mr. Caird named his price. The man would give it. By the time this house was done he had more propositions. He had the credit of being an honest, first-class workman, who knew how to manage hands and to do business. He still labored himself, particularly on fine, nice work; but the many workmen he employed required much of his time to oversee. If they put up work he did not like, he would make them take it down; he would not allow them to spoil his reputation. If they complained they might go elsewhere.

Of course such a man takes a high stand. If he is moderately saving he will make money. Mr. Caird had several thousand dollars, and his business was more prosperous than ever. Then he proposed to the widow. Afterwards she told him she had been waiting for him. They had a grand wedding. All their friends were invited. Their garments were bought in Philadelphia and were very fine. The table was set with every delicacy that could be found in the two great cities.

Thus, by his faithful industry, united with a scientific knowledge of his trade, and notwithstanding great disadvantages, Mr. Caird was raised to a high position. He found his wife good-tempered and every way amiable. She loved him much. A woman's love is greatly increased if she can be proud of her husband. In that community it is an honor to be useful. Long may they retain this great idea. He was grateful for her condescension and her kindness. His love for her, his hope of getting her, had made him what he was. No man could love a woman more than did he his Henrietta.

Some time after their marriage, Mr. Caird was induced to run for an important county office. He was pleased with the notion, and there were hopes of his getting it, for the two candidates made confusion by their quarrels. He came out as an independent candidate, and constantly rode through the county talking with the farmers. He was the first Yankee who ever had offered for any office; it was a condescension that he had learned their language; they liked his broken pronunciation; they laughed and told stories together, and he pleased them. With the help of some experienced men, he managed sharply, and he was elected by a few votes. The business required much of his time, and he gave up his trade. Several times a year he had to ride over the whole county, and often was gone a week. He formed a large acquaintance; his object was to become one of the first men in the county, and he succeeded. He cultivated his manners, which were naturally pleasing; he would speak to men of all classes; no matter how humble a man might be, if he asked him a question, he got a civil answer. This is one of the surest roads to popularity. Such was his success in whatever he undertook, that he thought he could do everything. There is no doubt but his election made him dizzy.

In county seats there are men of good abilities, but of no principle; frequently they own or control much property, and because they are not well known, they are respected. The time always comes when they find their proper level. Mr. Caird had time on his hands; he cultivated his social habits. With these men he became intimate. It will take much time to tell how he was led on. To some extent they led each other. Such things grow. They used to meet late at night high up in the back room of a third story building. First, one would go up, then another, till they were all up. They had a warm comfortable room, and lights burning. The weather was always such that they ought to take something. They took it. Then they got out the table and went to playing cards. The curtains were drawn close, they kept quiet and played hour after hour. Sometimes people below would hear the sudden moving of chairs, the tramping of feet, loud angry voices, and sounds like the breaking of glass.

Mrs. Caird often sat up waiting for him. What kept him so late? He had an immense sight of business to do at the court-house. So much writing—so many long columns of figures to add up. Yes, but his breath smelt as though he had been drinking. Did it? Come to think, he had taken a glass of beer. He would sleep till after breakfast, till the clock struck twelve. He had little appetite; his eyes were glassy and strange. Such and such men had been to see him; they called several times. If that was so he must hurry to the court-house. Sometimes he would look at the baby; often, not.

Mrs. Caird said she wanted to live in the country. She persuaded him to move on the farm. Perhaps if he would let the office go and attend to farm work, he would enjoy himself better. He did not dispute it. They moved. But things went no better. He still was out nights. When his term of office expired, he ran again. To the surprise of many, he was beaten. Some who had been his best friends, and who had helped him get a start, said he could not bear prosperity. He did not care; he was rich enough. Farming was a business good enough for him.

One day an officer came to the house and took Mr. Caird in custody. He told his wife it was nothing; he would soon come back. She waited, then went into town and tried to find out what it was. Her friends knew, but would not tell her. They only said it was nothing. Some smiled a little. At last a woman was glad to tell her the nature of it. Her husband had his choice to pay $500 down or $50 dollars a year for twenty-one years. He paid the $500 down. But he said it was a lie.

This was a most terrible blow to Mrs. Caird. She uttered an exclamation in German which does not sound well translated, and fainted away. She was taken home. Then she had fits. Two women had to hold her hands, for she had got hold of one of her silk dresses, and torn it into a thousand strings. When the doctor came she was gnashing her white teeth. He put a piece of soft wood between them. There was blood on her lips. They had to watch her lest she tore out her hair. When she got better the cherry was all gone from her cheeks; her eyes were sunken; she had a frightened look, and she hugged her two children to her heart.

If you will take notice, every once in a while certain careless, gentlemanly men come out of the large cities and stop at the county seats. They want to buy stock or produce. They stay at the hotels some time and get acquainted with every body. They play checkers, are free to treat are good companions. One acquainted with human nature will see something in their eyes which is not right. Their real business is to hunt up country gamblers, such as were playing in the third story. All they want is to get hold of them. They know how to finish them. They have no more human feelings than tigers. When one gambles he defies the right of property; he strikes at the foundation of honest industry; and he prepares the way for committing every crime. The paths to intemperance, to licentiousness, to blasphemy, to hard-heartedness, dishonor, shame, to penitentiaries, to the gallows, and to yawning sepulchres, lead from the gambler's table.

At last these men got hold of Mr. Caird. He thought them honest gentlemen. He valued his knowledge of human nature, but it was confined to the art of pleasing; it did not enable him to know himself. For a week he was with them almost every night. At first he won several thousand dollars. Then they made him a poor man. His wife owned the house in town; he had a deed of the farm and he gambled it away. He drew checks on the bank and lost them. Then he made notes of hand, put them up, and lost them.

His wife knew that something dreadful was going on. She implored him to stay at home; he would not listen; she lost her temper, and asked him if he was not after more five-hundred-dollar entertainments. At last it was all over; two men came home with him; they steadied him to a chair and finally got him to bed. The next day he got up, and going into the back porch sat on a bench under a grape-vine and began to vomit. His wife came and looked at him. He was drawn into a heap, his torn and soiled clothes almost hid him. He looked like a wretch; he was a wretch.

When she got him into the house, she locked him up; then she got it all out of him. He told her everything from first to last. She was so astonished she did not faint; she did not go into fits. Then came an officer with a warrant. Some of his old cronies had got the notes and they sued on them. She kept him hid; she did not exactly know where he was. She might have said she had no husband.

He told her he would go where he was not known; he promised never to touch liquor or a card again; he promised always to be true to her. She made him swear it on the big German Bible. Mentally he took a stronger oath; it was by the memory of his mother, who was dead. She got his clothes together so that he would be decent. He ate his breakfast before daylight; then he bade her good-bye. The last thing he did was to kiss the sleeping children. No, there was another last thing. She went out and opened the large gate. Day was just beginning to break over the distant Blue Mountains and the Delaware Gap. He drove two fine horses and a buggy into the road. There was a large chest in the buggy which brought down the springs. One more last word. He drove away. Ten years passed before they met again.

She gave up the farm, though she had some interest in it, and moved into town. She had some funds, for she had not been such a fool as not to be prepared for what might happen. She sent the children to school; the boy to Nazareth, the girl to Bethlehem.

He reached Pittsburg; this was no place for him. He entered Ohio; there, many came from Pennsylvania; then he reached New England settlements, where the people struggled with the forest. Still he traveled on. He considered different locations; he inquired and talked with many, and went on. At last he was far away. There was no mail route near, but settlers were coming in from New York and New England. Here was his place. He selected a location which he knew must be valuable; the question was whether he could make it so in his time. He bought 160 acres, which included good water-power. He sold his team, and with what money he had he went into company with a man and built a saw-mill. There was a plenty of hard work, but he was rested and could do it. Soon the mill was running; they sold all the lumber they could saw.

Many of the western regions settle with great rapidity. But this depends on whether speculators get hold of much land. If small farmers fill the country, everything prospers. It was so here. Mr. Caird's plan was to build a town; but another man got the start of him and built a grist-mill higher up the stream. Then the rival town began to grow. Mr. Caird was forced to sell lumber to help build it. There was no other way, hard though it was; more than this, he even went thither and took jobs at building houses. At last he got money enough and built a grist-mill himself; next, he built a store and a man came in and sold goods. There was a great struggle between the two villages. To carry the day, he borrowed money at a frightful interest. Then he set up machine shops. To induce mechanics to come in he gave them lots and built their houses at cost. He came near breaking up by having so much interest to pay. It took him several years to get rid of this load. Then hard times would come, and nothing could be done. Often he was quite discouraged; but he believed he would succeed. What he most depended on was the fertility of the soil and the enterprise of the people. At last a man with capital came from Ohio and put up a woolen factory. This sent his town ahead and he sold his lots at good prices. He was considered one of the finest men in the country. He managed matters so that there was no liquor sold in the place. Gamblers can do nothing without a bottle.

He wrote to his wife every week. He told her how he got along; he was full of courage, and believed he would overcome all difficulties. Much of all he wrote was about love. He mailed his letters from the upper village. He had a surprise for her. At last he sent for her, and she and the two children came on.

When they left the railroad they took the stage. She was expecting all the while to go to the upper village. He was watching, and when the stage came he bid the driver stop before his house. It was a handsome building among evergreens and flowers. The branches of some pear trees bent down with fruit. They went up-stairs, each one had a room nicely furnished. Then dinner was ready. Mr. Caird looked on his children, as they sat beside him, with love and pride. He noticed how beautiful they were, how well they behaved, and how fitly they spoke; and he saw they would be an ornament to the new country. But he gazed most on his wife. So fresh and so healthful did she look that his mind went back to the days when he first saw her.

After dinner he took her into the parlor and opened the blinds. What a nice house! how large, and what good furniture! And what a pretty village!—stores, mills, churches, and the like! But how was it dear? He had been living in the town further on. How came his house to be here? To tell the truth, this was the village all the time. What, the place where his letters were dated? No. That was strange. But as this was the village, what was the name of it? It had a very pretty name; he had given it himself; he was sure she must like it. The name of it was Henrietta. She blushed finely and looked around. The young gentleman and his sister were among the flowers.

THE LITTLE TURNPIKE AND THE SEVEN GARDENS.

SOMETIMES the mind is in such a state as to be able to see the whole of life at a single view. From the door, our daughter, just in womanhood, set out on a walk, and she trod on a narrow little turnpike which runs through our county. She walked briskly, and sang in the morning air. Beyond she saw the blue landscape of distant mountains. Green grass bordered the path, and also the brightest flowers that ever bloomed. In one hand she carried a book and in the other a rose. Although she seemed to walk from us, she did not get far away, because the little turnpike bent around our farm to avoid wet ground. This turnpike was so narrow two could not walk abreast.

Beyond her path were low green fields and tall trees, and in some places a mist arose as from a lake or a wide marsh, obscuring many things. Still, one saw the sun shining on the tops of fine buildings, and, as if in a grove, voices were heard singing. Down in these fields our daughter saw, as she walked, some finely-dressed girls, attended by young men in new and good clothes. They seemed to know her, and they asked her to come down and join their company. She looked at them, but neither spoke to them nor did as they wished.

As she walked forward everything grew more pleasant, and at the end was a gate which opened into the first of the Seven Gardens, whither she was going. This gate was almost hidden by shrubbery and flowers, and was painted of the color of a bright autumn leaf, and just beyond it, we saw a summer-house, almost good enough to live in, and it was shaded with climbing June roses and cherry-trees, red with ripe fruit.

That was a curious little turnpike, for sometimes when she thought she certainly was very near to the gate it seemed farther off than ever; and then, the first thing she knew, it appeared close by again, just as though this turnpike was made of india-rubber, and somebody was stretching it and then letting go. All this time the young people in the low green valley beckoned to her, and once she thought nothing could prevent them from being happy. But then the sky clouded, the thunder rolled, the notched lightning blazed dreadfully, and the rain poured down so swiftly, as almost to take away her breath. She was not prepared for such a storm. She looked back towards us, then towards the gate and the summer-house. Why we could not go out and help her was the strangest part, for, though all of us saw her, we could not stir to help her, and we seemed to have the night-mare. Close by, and on her left, stood a fine house, with a porch in front. The young people insisted that she should come down and sit in the porch till the rain was over, and they would have some nice plays. Whether she thought she would go down or not is uncertain, but just then, a high window in the gable end, was opened, and what seemed a dead body was thrown to the ground, when she started to run. As she raised her dress to keep it out of the wet, she was startled to see a large hand reaching out to grasp it, and glancing backward she saw a tall man, dressed in a long woolen coat, reaching with his hand up to the little turnpike. His hair was long and uncombed, and his face was bloated. At the same time she was frightened to see other men along the path hiding in the bushes. Some beckoned to her, some tried to smile, some almost touched her. She went faster than ever. Nor were there any more flowers along her way, and every step was in slippery mud, while there were sharp stones, which tore her shoes and bruised her feet.

Now, over on her right, she saw another turnpike, and it was only a few steps distant, and it came from another part of the Settlement, all the while coming nearer to one she walked in, and in it came a young man who was a son of a neighbor of ours, and he had a stout stick in his hand. He, too, was taking a little walk to the turnpike-gate, and the storm had overtaken him, but he trudged along without much minding it, and when he saw our daughter he spoke pleasantly to her, and he told her if the villains troubled her again he would break their backs for them. After that she had no more fear.

Then the rain stopped, the sun shone again, and in a little time the ground was dry, when the birds sang, and once more there were flowers on either side, and the air was filled with a delightful odor, a part of which came from the garden, for they were getting close to the gate. It was a little strange that the nearer they got to the gate the more this young man had a desire to get over and walk in the path with our daughter; but she forbade it, as the path was not wide enough for two; so they both walked forward to the gate where the two paths met. When they got very near the mist rose from the fields and one could see what kind of country it was, and what was going on.

Not far off was a large, fine house, and out of the front door sprang a young woman, giving scream after scream. One side of her face seemed cut off with a sword, showing a white bone, and a man ran after her carrying a rope that had a slipping noose at one end. A little further on was a long, low house, which was dirty and mean, and into this the young woman ran, when the man stopped and seemed pleased. Old clothes were in the windows; outside, ragged children dragged kittens by their necks through pools of dirty water, and from the inside one heard the high voices of men and women, and screams and curses and prayers. A hearse stood by the door, and a drunken driver continually called for some one in the house. At last two men, bareheaded, brought out a coffin, when the driver drove off as fast as he could, but several times he stopped to mend his harness, and at last he reached a grave-yard in a grove of dead trees, when he put the coffin out on the ground, and only an old man, with a broken spade in his hand, came, when he stood a long time with one foot on the coffin. All around were old and broken coffins; by the sides of graves dug long before, but not filled, were bones and pieces of boards. On several of the trees women hung by their necks; and slowly floating down the sluggish stream were the bodies of men whose clothes floated out in strings and rags.

Even close to the gate sights were seen and sounds were heard. In front of a house that had green blinds and lace curtains, some pieces of human flesh were lying in a flower-bed. From within, one heard sobs and groans and sharp screams, and the creaking and slamming of heavy iron doors, and the drawing up of chains, and the falling of heavy weights. From a back door a man with only one boot on, went across the field carrying a little coffin under his arm, while he held out, as if he wanted everybody to see it, a printed parchment.

At the time our daughter reached the gate, the young man reached it also, and then they took hold of hands, when the gate opened, and, bowing their heads a little, they went in. There they found many young folks, the girls having flowers in their hair and the young men nosegays in their button-holes, and when the gate was shut, there were sounds of laughter and merry-making, and the clinking of dishes as if they were eating dinner. After that they had some pretty good singing.

The next thing we could see was our daughter walking with the young man through the first garden. There were no fruits yet ripe except cherries and strawberries, but the trees were in full bloom, and there was the most beautiful shrubbery, with leaves which were green on the upper side, while the under sides were of mottled gold and purple, while they had silvered edges. There were other wonderful things which they saw; and we were seeing them, though not exactly in the way they saw them. It was as if we were looking backward through an arch that was partly in ruins, and covered with vines which had leaves of the color of a red sunset.

There was one thing which did not seem plain; this was, they appeared to have a house to live in; but we could not see into it because there was a green curtain between, which hung down from the sky, and each corner was fastened to a star; but we could see them walking through the garden, swinging their hands as they were clasped together. You may be sure we spent a good deal of our time looking at them. Another thing was singular, for although what we were seeing appeared as if it were in one forenoon, still, by the changes in the leaves, as in the ripening of fruits, periods of time, such as days, months, and larger circles went by.

After awhile the walls of the garden turned round and closed before them, and in their path was another gate, over which was written a serious Scripture passage, and when they read it our daughter shed a few tears. Then they went through the gate; but instead of going on, our daughter entered a little summer house, as if to rest while her companion sat on the outside and waited. The roof and walls were covered with creeping cypress, which made a deep shade, and a large weeping willow enclosed it, so that its branches almost touched the ground. A little back of the summer-house was a high wall made of black volcanic rock, such as is quarried out of enchanted mountains, and at the foot of the wall was a grave partly dug, and the shovels and picks were lying around as if the workmen had just gone to dinner.

Our daughter's partner having waited some time, went on ahead a little, and he was picking apricots and summer-pears, when she came towards him smiling sweetly; but she was grown pale, and she held by her hand a little boy, and when they came up the three walked abreast and the little boy was between them. This was a great mystery to us, and the more we tried to understand it the less we knew, and we stopped thinking about it.

We noticed that the flowers began to lose their beauty, and to drop their leaves on the moist ground. Some of these leaves our daughter saved in her book. Now instead of there being only flowers, several kinds of fruit began to ripen, and though a good deal of it was wormy and rotten inside, there was enough which was sweet and juicy. But the most of the fruit was very small and green, and it seemed as if it would take a long time for it to get ripe.

Now it seemed to us that sometimes they got tired of the garden and saw nothing lovely in it, and when they were this way, the sky would be covered with a pall of blackness, and claps of thunder broke and leaped from one part of the sky to another. Often, at such times, our daughter opened her book and read passages which did them both good, for the effect was such that the sun shone out, and the thunder rumbled among clouds along the horizon. This was another mystery. One time our daughter and her partner got out of the path leading through this garden, and coming to the walls they looked over and saw things not good for weak eyes.

For the country was cheerless, and in no way seemed fitted to supply food to whomsoever might try to live there. Near by was an asylum for people who had lost their senses. They were chained inside to pillars and to rings in the walls, and many were seen through the iron grates with woe-begone looks, long hair, and with imperfect teeth. Some with scarcely any skin on their lips gnawed at the bars, by which means they broke their teeth, others gazed upward as if at the moon, nor did they wink with their round white eyes; while others silently sat and kneeled with their chins bending on their breasts. In some parts of the building were heard sobs and groans; in others shrieks, and jumpings, and the lashing of whips.

At a little distance, and in what seemed a decayed garden, stood a gallows and a skeleton hanging on it. Some having snapped their chains were slipping over the walls like squirrels, or were running across the lots with a few clothes on, but their keepers always overtook them. In a low marshy valley some men were digging shallow graves, and when the coffins came they stood on them to make them sink down through the mud and water.

Beyond the asylum was a penitentiary, and long lines of convicts, guarded by soldiers with shining muskets, were driven to labor in stone quarries. And still another building was near. This was a hospital in which the grievously sick were cared for and fed on gruel; and it was doubtful to the most humane whether life or death to such was most desirable, for they had but taste and sense and smell, and some parts of their features did not remain.

After seeing these things, our daughter and her partner drew back into the path of the garden, and without speaking they went on, still being in our view, seemingly happy that they were subject to none of the regulations of the public buildings. Soon after they came to the gate by the fourth garden. Here a little girl came to play with the boy, and they had pleasant society with each other.

It is enough to say that they went on till they came to the seventh garden, where there were six boys and girls. By this time the fruit on the trees was quite ripe, and there were vegetables and other products in great abundance. There were also all kinds of nuts, not excepting English walnuts and soft-shelled almonds.

Now as all things come to an end, and then take another shape, our daughter and her partner got tired with such a long walk, and they were changed so as to be very serious, and they had each other's ways and looks, when they came to a summer-house, shadier than any other, and situated in a little valley where water was running, but they only heard it sweeping by, for it was so obscure they could not see whether it was deep and broad, or only shallow. At this place her partner went in first and lay down, and as he did not come out, she went in and lay down also. The boys and girls stayed around some time, and called to them, but as there was no answer, they were taken out of the gardens by some friends with the promise that they might come back again.

Well, when our daughter and her partner awoke, they looked around for the boys and girls, but they did not see them, and the place appeared strange. It seemed as if it was about day-light, but when they tried to get out of the summer-house, they found a black stone wall, made of the rock of the enchanted mountain, across the entrance, and beyond it they heard the water running, but it was behind them, and not before them, as it was when they went to sleep. When it grew a little lighter, they saw a few stone steps, and as this was the only way, they took hold of hands and went up, when they entered into a garden which had a striking resemblance to the one they first entered. Wondering what it all signified, they went forward slowly, and looked around and soon it grew bright in the east. All at once, they perceived they had on different clothes, and then they saw persons coming to meet them. It will take a long time to tell the rest of this story, besides, it will be hard to understand, therefore we had better stop before we begin.

FARMING AND LAW.

MR. HIBBARD was a young lawyer in a county town in one of the New England States. He was quite promising, he could make a flowery little speech, and folks expected he would make a great man. Such wonderful things did he expect to do, that he quit keeping company with a young lady he had agreed to marry, and began to look around for a rich, handsome wife. He would have a woman who would honor the high station he expected to occupy. While he was making up his mind what girl he would have, for he presumed he could have any, considerable talk was going on about the way he had treated Lucy, and he could see he had made a mistake. He thought he would brave it through, but this was difficult. There were lawyers, young and old, seeking business; they were glad of a chance to say something against him.

Lucy had waited a long time; she was proud of his progress, and when he was admitted to the bar she felt equally honored. In a short time she saw his head was turned; then he ceased to visit her; at last, she felt she had lost him. She was now twenty-three; the offers she had rejected could not come again; she had little hope, and her heart was tortured with anguish and indignation. So much was she affected that her cheeks became bloodless, and her friends feared she would go into a decline.

In these communities a sense of strict justice pervades the people; they frown upon wrong doing; and Mr. Hibbard found himself speedily obliged to change his course. He was worth little and people would not employ him. After a long struggle with himself, he went back to Lucy. At first she would not see him; he persevered, and they had an interview. She spoke her mind freely, and strongly hinted that the few hundred dollars she had was an object. This he was forced to deny, not to resent; he pleaded for pardon; she finally granted it, and they were married.

Upon this, the public seemed to heave a sigh of relief. Justice had been done. People were willing to overlook, and some business came to the young lawyer. This event gave his mind a sober and practical cast. He would turn to his studies anew; he would excel. With a part of Lucy's money he bought more books. As he reflected, he saw men of experience and ability greatly in his way; for years every case of importance would be intrusted to them. To excel, to equal them, would require much study and a well-trained mind. The reading necessary to admit to the bar is general; it is not difficult; many of very slender acquirements, both in law and in general knowledge, become lawyers. Mr. Hibbard began to see that a wide understanding, not only of the law, but of whatever relates to society and civilization is indispensable. How to obtain this was not clear; study was important; but he thought there was something more. On inquiry, the answers were not satisfactory; he believed he had fair ability, but he greatly doubted whether he was the genius he had supposed himself to be. In coming in contact with eminent lawyers, he would ask himself what it is that gives broad, clear views and a power over the court and the jury. On several occasions, when he had cases of some little consequence, he found himself unable to reply to the arguments of the opposing counsel, and he was beaten. Then he became discouraged; he doubted whether he would make anything but a third-rate lawyer. By using a little art he found out that his abilities were not highly esteemed, and that people were in the habit of speaking of him as not being much. When going into public he attracted little attention; and when the judge and leading lawyers were conversing on general subjects, if he attempted to join in, no attention was paid to him. When he made mistakes he saw a smile go round; if older men made similar mistakes, it was a different kind of smile. These things were highly mortifying; he set himself to the task to discover the cause; and he concluded that he had presumed to act as if he was a good lawyer, when he was not. He could see other young lawyers of poor acquirements treated in the same way. He felt sorry for them; it struck him that he was like them. He had confidence in an old lawyer; he told him that much was expected of the young; if, when grown older, the expectation was not fulfilled, there would be a reaction.

Many young lawyers meeting similar treatment become discouraged and they abandon the profession; others sink into clerks and copyists; others are contented with what little business may come; they lose their ambition; when it is a busy time they can pick up something. Mr. Hibbard did not know what to do; he wished he was a merchant, a good mechanic, anything but a lawyer.

He kept a horse, for sometimes he had cases in the country. One day a man wanted to buy his horse; he wanted to sell him, for he needed money; but the man had no money; then he would not sell. Ah, but he would give him a deed for one hundred and sixty acres of land out West. Mr. Hibbard was struck with the proposition. In a measure, his affairs were desperate; his family was growing; Lucy had to pinch along; may be he would go West, though he did not want land; no matter, they traded.

Western land then was sold in this manner from one to another; perhaps neither knew anything about it. The property was in the deed, not in the land; it was like an uncurrent bank bill, selling for ten or twenty cents on a dollar, good to trade with. Some day the bank might come up. Mr. Hibbard felt interest enough to inquire where the land lay, and whether anybody lived near it; he learned that several families from an adjoining township had moved thither and were beginning to do well. He went to see their relations and found a man who had been out, who was pleased,

18*

and was going to move. He knew Mr. Hibbard's land; it would make a fine farm; there were neighbors near; the township was settling fast.

Mr. Hibbard reflected a long time; he talked with Lucy; she was willing to go, indeed thought it best; she could not keep up with society. At last he made up his mind to go; then his mind was all alive with the prospect; but he would do this: he would clear the land, improve it, make a good farm, and have things comfortable; this would be sure; he would not sell it; there should be his home. Meanwhile, he would study, he would go to the foundation, he would see what law is. True, it was twenty miles to the county seat; that was nothing; there might be first-rate lawyers there too; that was nothing; he would take time to make himself as good as they. If he succeeded, good; if not, he would have a farm. He believed himself capable of carrying out both plans; he knew something about work, and thought he could make himself a good farmer.

They got their little property together. Lucy had a fine outfit. He bought a yoke of oxen and a wagon. In those days the journey was as long and as hard as it is now from the Missouri river to California. The country was new for hundreds of miles, the roads bad, and it took from six to twelve weeks to get through. They started in September; they had two children and nearly a hundred dollars in money; when the roads were good, Lucy rode; when bad, she got out, carrying the baby, while the other fellow rode and clutched with his little hands on the side of the wagon box, peeping out to see how things were going; at other times he would lie down in a soft place and go to sleep. There were several other families going with them; they went about fifteen miles a day, sometimes much less; they had to go a long way around over mountains, for they could not get through certain swamps. For six weeks the weather was fine; after that, it rained frequently, and there was deep mud, except where there were rocks. In some places they had to go over ledges of rocks; the wagon was taken to pieces and carried up; the cattle made out to get along; then, in mud holes, all hands had to lift and pry and cry to the oxen. Next the nights became frosty and there was some snow. Their load was found so heavy that they had to sell some of their things; even then, they were afraid the oxen would given out.

At last, in the tenth week, they came near their destination. It was a raw, chilly day; but at times the sun shone brightly. They thought they would get through by noon, but there was a wide stream and a swamp to cross, and there were several hills. One of the oxen got down, and it was as much as Mr. Hibbard and his wife could do to make him get up. The farms were about a mile apart. Then they came to a long hill; there were so many stones in the road that Mr. Hibbard had to cut a road farther round, and they made out to get up. While the oxen were resting, Mr. Hibbard paid close attention, for by the description he knew that this was his land. Driving on thirty or forty rods, he stepped on a gentle knoll; there was heavy timber in every direction. When Lucy came along, nearly tired out, he told her that this was their land; there was to be their home. But this was no place for them to stop; there was a clearing ahead, and he would drive to the next house. Lucy sat on a log to rest, holding her baby; she looked all around; the underbrush was thick; tall maples, beeches, hickories and the like rose high in the air. She thought the prospect gloomy enough, for the trees must be cut down and a house built before they could begin to live. She did not know how it would be. Still, she knew her husband was ambitious, and wanted to get along. While she sat there several deer walked across the road.

Then she went on after the wagon; it stopped before she overtook it. The people of the house were out, and the woman came forward and took her baby. Bless the darling little soul; how pretty it was. They all went in; the people acted in the kindest manner, and were happy they had come. Lucy apologised for her looks; her feet were sopping wet, and she was muddy up to her apron. That was nothing, and they laughed. The women got into a long rapid talk, and there were inquiries about mutual acquaintances. The news that another man had moved on flew quickly, and by dark many people came to see them. From no one was anything but encouragement and praises of the country; of course they would do well.

The next day was devoted to rest; but on the day after a crowd of men and boys, with cattle, oxen and chains, came early. They were going to put up a house for Mr. Hibbard. He selected the place where he would build, and they went to work. The trees fell rapidly. The boys trimmed and piled brush, the men chopped the logs of right length, then the oxen were hitched to them and then they began to roll. To make a decent log house, sixty trees are required, this will clear half an acre of land. When the body was raised they split puncheons from large trees, smoothed them the best they could and laid a floor. The way to have a fire was to build it against the logs at one end, they would burn out, then Mr. Hibbard could build a chimney with stone or of sticks and clay. As for a door, they could hang up a bed-quilt. Meanwhile some had been riving long shingles out of oak, these were for the roof, they were laid across poles, weight-poles on top kept them in their place, and the house was done. The same day they moved into it, a fire was built, and they cooked and ate their first meal in their own house in the West.

These difficulties look great; but they do not last long. In these days one can travel to this country in twenty-four hours; in four days he can reach regions as savage and new. However rough a home at first may be, constant improvement will soon make it pleasant. A door was made first, for there were wolves about. They had a spring not far off; she told about seeing six or seven dogs running fast when she went for water. Then they had a chimney; next a stable for the oxen. Their greatest want was bread. Almost every day he could get a deer. Scarcely any body as yet had grain to sell, and there was no mill nearer than eighteen miles, where was an older settlement. Mr. Hibbard went thither; most of the way was woods. He had but little money left; corn was high, but their family was small; the cattle eat most.

During the winter Mr. Hibbard cleared land. When planting time came he had six acres fenced; five he put in corn; there were so many roots he had to do all the work with a hoe; an acre he put in spring wheat, scratching the soil with a thorn-bush. They had a garden and every thing grew finely. They bought a cow; she ran in the woods, but came home at night, and they had milk and butter; sometimes it tasted of leeks. They got pigs, which lived in the woods. New settlers want many hogs to eat up the rattle-snakes. The result of these labors was corn and wheat enough to last through the year. Then among the corn grass seed was sown; the next year he cut hay; then more land was cleared. On this fresh soil every thing grew rapidly.

Like all other settlers, Mr. Hibbard had brought out a little sack full of apple-seeds. These were planted early in the spring, so that the frost could act on them, and they grew. He gave the young trees good care; they were to be his orchard. Peach trees he bought in the old settlement. All this work Mr. Hibbard did himself; sometimes Lucy could help. Many hours, with her hand-spike, she rolled logs. She need not lift hard; he would raise one end, she put her hand-spike under it, he would go to the other end and roll it up. But she could lift too when he got more than he could manage. Besides, she piled brush and picked up chips and chunks to make the ground clean. When he tapped trees she would carry the sap and boil it into sugar. That boy of hers became very fond of warm sugar. Once he came near being scalded to death; she was just in time to jerk him out.

One might think that these labors wore them out and discouraged them; such was not the case. Providence did not intend when fixing the condition of making a home in the wilderness, that the labor required shall be more than the body can endure, or that the mind shall not be hopeful. No people are more healthful, or more cheerfully look forward to the future. Afterwards the settler will look back on these as their happiest days. When Lucy and the neighboring women were able to dress in silk and to go a visiting in nice buggies, they would say they never enjoyed so much as they did when the country was new.

There are rainy and bad days for the farmer. Long winter nights give much time. Mr. Hibbard improved every spare hour in becoming more familiar with the law. He had prepared himself by buying fundamental works on common law and the law of nations, and those in particular which related to Roman law, including the compilations of Justinian. He laid out for himself the particular study to learn how laws originate, to trace common law along with the progress of society, the development of learning, of inventions, of commerce and manufactures. As he pursued his studies, he saw how common law is the outgrowth of society; that it expresses this growth or change at every step; that habit becomes custom, customs form rules, and rules become common law; then, that it is the province of the legislature to confirm, add to, and modify this common law, but never to supersede it. Gradually his mind opened to the truth that in all new countries a common law will naturally be created which will differ from any other to the extent that the circumstances differ; that is, regarding fertility or barrenness, the scarcity or plentifulness of timber, abundance of food in common, tracts of marshy land, or regions deprived of water and other peculiarities. This led him to consider how this new common law is to be confirmed. Of course this would be by judicial decisions; the judge alone would be competent to declare what these new customs, rules and laws, growing out of new circumstances, are. On further reflection he saw that no man, however learned he may be in the laws of old settled countries, or however great his other qualifications might be, would be fit to declare the common law of the new country and to give decisions which courts and juries would reverence unless he was well acquainted with all the customs of the new country. To Mr. Hibbard this seemed a point of much importance, and the more he reflected on it the more clearly did he see a way open for a lawyer occupying the position he himself occupied. When the subject was presented to him in its full force, he could not help seeing that Providence had been preparing him by trials for some important work.

Thinking in this way, and still pursuing his studies, still never neglecting farm-work, time went by. Of course litigation arose, as it always will, but in well-ordered communities suits are brought more through misunderstanding than ill-will, and here the court and jury have simply the duty dispassionately to decide on the misunderstanding. Then the defeated party will see that his error arose from a want of clear statement on his part, and he will be thankful for the experience.

Mr. Hibbard took no pains to get business; he could well afford not to be troubled with undignified quarrels. Still, he would serve when requested. After a while he had a case of some importance, and it was one of that class which grows out of the new conditions of the country and in reference to which no laws were exactly applicable. He was scarcely known. He had taken no pains to get business or put himself forward. He was known to be a prosperous farmer. Of course he had influence, and could command votes. This gave him a consequence which surprised him. A reputation had run on ahead. He had studied his case in the light of analogous ones, with diligence, and he founded his arguments on natural justice and on what is required by good faith. For every rebutting argument and authority he was prepared with stronger ones. His speech was well arranged and convincing. It was the result of study, and he gained the suit.

From this he acquired a solid reputation. He was urged to remove to the county seat. He said that in coming west he had proposed making a comfortable home; it should be secure from all accidents; if business offered he would take it; if not, he could live well without it. To Lucy he said more. At the county seat he would be interrupted with trifles; much of what he could earn would be expended in being more fashionable; his aim was high; he could not afford to be diverted from it.

In those days money was hard to get; still, by his profession, he got several hundred dollars a year. This enabled him to get more land cleared; to stock his farm and make improvements. His orchard did well, and was grafted. They had wool and flax; Lucy spun and wove. The roads were made good. Scarcely a mile distant was a nice church, and there were stores, and mechanics, and schools were good. At an early day an academy was established to which young folks were sent from abroad. The reason why things prospered was because the people were intelligent and industrious, and the soil was good.

In a few years Mr. Hibbard had the reputation of being the safest and soundest lawyer in the country, and he was employed on every important case. By this time he understood what is meant by large powers, comprehensive views, and influence with the court and jury. Many think these must be a natural gift—such as genius or inspiration. It is industry directed by practical knowledge and good sense. Of course there are accomplishments, a flowing style, easy delivery, ready wit. But these are inborn only in part. True, the men must be given. I am talking about men.

Then he built a good house. It was on the New England plan, and of the largest size. It was finished throughout, and nice furniture was bought. Lucy had good carpets of her own making to lay down in every room. She had feather-beds and all kinds of bedding made in the family. There were four girls. At meeting they sat in a row. There were three boys. They became good scholars and had farms. One became a minister, another a lawyer, and the youngest one had the old farm.

Mr. Hibbard became County Judge, and presided several years. No one was better fitted than he. When Court adjourned he hastened back to his farm. A part of every day he labored, the other part he was in his library. He said it was necessary for him to labor if he would study with most profit.

Then the time came when he reached a high station, and this, notwithstanding his politics differed from the administration which appointed him. His district was extensive; he was away from home more than half of the year. Sometimes Lucy went along. She proved to be a lady fitted to adorn the station he occupied. The branches of study to which he had turned his attention, and his practical knowledge of the customs and pursuits of the people, fitted him to decide questions upon which statute and common law were silent. The quiet of his life had given him the habit of judging carefully and without partiality. While he was fully informed of the wants of the people, he was withdrawn from party influences. You will find a great many of his decisions in the Reports. Few have been reversed. They are more respected and more binding than many legislative enactments, because they declare what are the bonds which, in the nature and fitness of things, bind society together. There were two cases where Judge Hibbard declared laws enacted in the legislature to be void.

This account is written to point out a way for professional young men who linger in towns, repressed by rivalry, by poverty, perhaps by youthful indiscretion. Did I choose I could take you to the judge's elegant home, show you his well-cultivated acres, his red, fat steers, his sheep, his orchard and his nice large garden. Quietly sitting where wood still burns in the fire-place in the wide cheerful kitchen, is an elderly lady. For gentle behavior, kindness to all, and for true piety, few excel Lucy the judge's wife. She waits, for her husband has gone on before. Her girls have married wealthy and influential men, and are looked upon as the first ladies in the land.

Among the very eminent and useful men who have adorned our country, it will be difficult to point to many who did not have a practical knowledge of agriculture.

THE LANGUAGE OF CATTLE.

WHEN cattle talk they make use of the cattle language, which differs from ours in having the basis relative, and not vocative, and if one would understand it, he must commence by placing himself over in their line, or plane of life. It is now over seven years since I first paid attention to this subject, and at first I reached what I supposed the true secret, the outlines of which I sent to the *Prairie Farmer*, of Chicago, and it was printed; but upon further investigation, I found that it was only the elementary language I had got hold of, and not even one of the second degree. So far from this part being a help to further progress, it was a hindrance, and it seems purposely contrived to bar extended research. Although this branch is easily acquired, and I made use of it in attracting their attention, still it very much surprised them, but they were not offended. As I proceeded further, I thought it best to be cautious, which was extremely fortunate, for I will remark here, that cattle have a law to put an end to a man when they find out that he has a knowledge of the language beyond the first degree, saying nothing about the second, third, fourth, and fifth degrees, for there are all these; but I never progressed beyond the third degree, and even in this I was quite imperfect. This caution on my part seems now to me to have been in a measure prophetic, but I was guided by the consideration that possibly they might not like to have me hear them talk, and, not wishing to be out nights, hiding in fence-corners, I pretended during the long time I was going through my studies to be doctoring them for lice.

I learned the elementary branch partly by accident, and partly by induction; but finding it unsatisfactory I was put on a different track by listening to my son's description of telegraphy, which he was learning, when it occurred that cattle might have a similar method. Of course I then supposed that the inarticulate sounds they utter were the basis, but I found that these were too few in number to make sufficient combinations, and finally, I discovered that these sounds are blinds and guards to hide their real language with its complication of degrees from the knowledge of man. The next supposition was, that the secret lay in the motion of their jaws, when they chew the cud, but this would not explain how animals talk when they do not chew the cud. This naturally brought me to a stand, for I could find no other basis, till late one Saturday afternoon, having put on a clean shirt, and given the boys permission to go in swimming, I was sitting on the bars, while the cattle stood in the road, having come up from the bottom, when I got a new idea. Some time before I had noticed that they were always sure to come up on Saturday night, if they were coming at all, though they might be absent all the rest of the week. Still, instances were not rare when one or two would not get in till daylight on Sunday morning. I had also noticed, and often had been mortified, that about ten o'clock on Sunday morning, when folks were going to meeting to the campground, or to the Baptist school-house, an exhibition would be presented not seeming to me proper for the occasion.

While some were standing, and others were lying down in the road before me, it seemed to me that the only remaining method by which they talk must lie in the movement of the muscles of the gums and lips, which almost constantly was going on. To prove that this might be the case, I had to make a series of experiments on the acuteness of their hearing. The first result was the learning that their hearing is of two kinds: one of the common kind, and the other of a nature unknown; and on this last I studied about nine months, till I was able to hear the vibrations of their language in the second degree. The first clue which I obtained was a cypher which led me into a labyrinth, that for a long time seemed inextricable, by reason of the strange formulas I had to deal with, and for seven months I was nearly stationary, while at times I was almost led to believe that the cypher was an airy vision out of which nothing intelligible ever could come.

Not only a whole year, but a portion of a second year had gone by since starting from the basis of animal telegraphy, I had taken up the formula of three figures, which might be 5, 7 and 9, or 2, 4 and 6, multiplied by themselves as a basis for indefinite combinations, when one day as I was hoeing potatoes on a piece of new ground, and had stopped in a fence-corner to rest, I picked up a smooth bark which had fallen from a deadened sycamore in the potato patch; and, taking out my pencil I made some calculations by means of fluxions as to the capacity of the combinations. Seeing these to spread out with great rapidity, I shifted the answer of the 49th power from 2, 4 and 6 to the mean of 5, 7 and 9, and reversing the operation, down to the cypher previously obtained, and which I have called xy, I had a very strange result, but on looking it over, I saw I had made an error of several thousand millions, which I corrected, and then going down cautiously, I had a short sentence, which unmistakably related to a transaction in which I knew the cattle had been engaged. I was so astonished at my success, that I put down a stake to show where I left off hoeing potatoes, and started for the house. Going through a part of the corn-field, where there were too many stalks in the hill, I cut out a good armfull with my pruning-knife, and putting the hoe in among the stalks, I carried the whole on my shoulder. I had several fences to get over, and being somewhat blinded by the blades, I went a little out of my course, and came to the border of a field where the boys had been grubbing in the forepart of summer, where I saw they had planted a little patch of water-melons, and that some were very large. Not satisfied with what I was carrying, I had to go and pick out the largest water-melon I could find; and as it weighed forty or fifty pounds, and I only had the stem to carry it by—for if I undertook to carry it under my arm, it was certain to slip out and burst on falling—you may be sure I had as much as I could do to stagger under my load. It was sunset when I reached the barn-yard, where the cattle already were, and being exhausted, I put the fodder in the mangers of the two cows and shut the door, when, without thinking what I was really doing, I repeated the sentence I had mentioned with the corresponding organs of my cheeks. But in the next instant it flashed through my mind what I had done, and I threw myself into one of those coughs which always are connected with the ague in this country, but while I was coughing I heard all the cattle give an unearthly bellow, such as is common when they see blood. However, when they saw how composed I was, for it was a matter of life and death with me that I should be so, they seemed to take it for granted that my remark was purely accidental, the same as is the case when we see a letter or an indistinct landscape made by the white-wash brush on the wall.

All this is introductory to the studies which were necessary in getting into the second degree, and thence onward to the third degree. Now I could go on and divulge this whole matter so that by the help of studies the reader would have all the knowledge I possess, but this could not be commended, since young men, being guided more by curiosity than by prudence, would rush without caution into the cattle kingdom, when they would be disposed of so quickly that neither themselves or their folks would know what hurt them. The only proper way to have this knowledge imparted, that I can think of, is to have a special meeting of the Faculties of our Agricultural Colleges, when they should fully discuss the matter, and only decide after the most mature deliberation. If I were called upon to give a candid opinion on the subject, I should say it is doubtful whether it would be advisable to let it out at the present time.

In the course of three or four generations, and possibly in

two—but I could be certain on this point if I should make a few casts in fluxions—when there will be discoveries in many branches of art and in science, and particularly with regard to motive power, which will change the whole system of transit, both by sea and by land, and of course it will revolutionize the details of industry, all of which will be associated with the most frightful risks to human life, and in some cases will put the existence of whole cities in jeopardy. That time, in my opinion, will be the one to have the cattle language made a part of a college course, for by reason of the caution everywhere infused into the human mind, it can then become a part of a finished education with comparatively little danger.

Meanwhile, that this knowledge may be preserved to the world, I will endeavor to take time from other duties to write out a cattle grammar, and with a preface, including their alphabet, and what I know of their etymology, which should be deposited in the corner-stone of some agricultural college on the occasion of its being laid. But now, for fear some young man should take a crow-bar and try to pry out the corner-stone in the night, that he might get at this treatise, I will relate what took place on one occasion, which became a turning-point in my life, that he may know what to expect should he get hold of the book.

Early in the spring I had a black-and-white calf stray away, and as we were very busy for a long time we did not get it home till September, though we knew where it was all the time, which was in a range along some bluffs at the foot of which commenced a cane-brake that extended several miles along Cypress Creek. At that time we had a yoke of oxen, some young steers, two cows, another animal, a horse, and some colts big enough to work, remaining in the woodlot, a small flock of sheep, and a very few hogs—certainly not more than thirty—which lay in the fence-corners and were not permitted to go into the yard. I should remark that the cattle language is the standard, and that all others correspond to provincialisms which arise from organic differences; thus, the sheep have a Frenchy dialect, horses one partaking of the Latin, mules of the rich Irish brogue, hogs of the German, and dogs of the Greek accent. Of the bird language I know little or nothing of my own knowledge, though I got many ideas from the cattle, but as they are only second-hand I need not repeat them. From the same source I learned that the snake language lies in an interval between the second degree of the bird language, and the first degree of the fish language, which shows that the degrees of different species interlock with each other, and, when taken collectively, are complicated; but I gathered that, after seven degrees are acquired, the remaining twenty-four degrees are derivative. This includes the languages of all animals, whether wild or domestic, and all insects down as low as mosquitoes and horse-flies. At this point comes an inversion, and a scale of an ascending order commences which apparently goes downward among the animalcule, and it really spreads out among orders which are wholly invisible. With these we need not trouble ourselves, for we have enough on hand regarding things before our eyes.

I was sitting on a pile of lumber, out of which I hoped some day to be able to build a new barn, when the boys, just at dusk, came along with the calf and drove it into the yard.

"Now, where under the sun have you been?" said the white cow, the mother of the calf. "You look as though you had been through the mill, as the old man says."

"Well, mam, I've been under the bluff and in the canebrake, and I had mighty good pickin'."

"Good pickin'! Only hear him. You're as poor as a crow, and your face is scratched with briars. What's that gash in your leg? I should think the dogs had been after you."

"Dogs can't catch me," said the calf.

"Yes, I see, you're skin and bone and can run like a deer. I wonder if you think I'm going to go through the trouble of having calves and then taking care of them when they are little and then have them turn out this way. You ought to be as fat as a mule by this time. But I'll let you know

I'll have no such work. I'll break up your gadding through the country."

Then I heard quite a scuffle, and the calf made a great outcry and said:

"Oh! don't, ma, don't! don't! Oh, you hurt my side. Please, ma, don't, dont! I'll never do so agin!"

"Agin! Only listen to the language this calf uses. Bless me, if it isn't enough to loosen my horns. I've a good mind to give you another going over, and I believe I will."

"Stop," said Bright, one of the oxen, "you've punished him sufficient; but if he runs off agin, I'll take him in hand myself."

"Very well," said his mother. "I'll let him off. I really feel sorry for the poor thing. Come here, my son, your mother only did it for your good."

The calf went up to its mother, when she licked its face and sides, and put it in a little decent shape. Then the calf showed signs of repentance by shedding tears, and the mother also wept.

"I've been thinking," said Dick, the other ox, "how delightful it is for us to dwell together in sweet accord. Trouble enough inheres within our nature, and we should be on the guard against any of a self-creation."

"I don't see any trouble in this world," said the heifer, then over four years old.

"What do you know about trouble?" said the other animal. "You never had a calf, and, in my opinion, you never will have."

At this all the cattle smiled, the sheep tittered, and the horse gave one of his peculiar laughs.

"You needn't run me down," said the heifer. "I havn't said anything against you, and you ought not to hurt my feelings."

"Never mind what they say," said Bright. "You must expect some little rubs in this world. Still, it is a good thing to have self-respect and not to permit even an equal to detract from your true merits. On the other hand, you should not attach too great importance to your individuality. This is to resemble man, who has an idea he is the lord of the fowl and the brute."

"It is really amusing," said Dick, "to hear the old man talk to his boys about us. For instance, he told them to treat us kindly, because all our sources of enjoyment spring from them."

"It is characteristic," said Bright, "of every vain creature to place himself at the head of everything else, whether in small or in large communities, and without any regard to the figure he cuts. So long has man gone on in this style that he thinks he alone has a soul. However, it is extremely proper in the constitution of things that he should be self-deluded in this manner, because the relation between him and us coheres by reason of his misconception. Our philosophers have long seen that if he should discover that he is inferior to us he would at once struggle to emancipate himself. Thus, our well-being depends on his ignorance, for he will be our slave so long as he imagines that we are his slaves."

"These observations are just," said Charley. "When I carry him on my back I cannot help smiling at the importance he assumes; and yet, he is such a simpleton as not to suspect that he spends the greater part of his time in working for me, while he considers what little I do, in order to keep up the game, as of the utmost importance."

"It is impossible," said Dick, "to conceive of a more ingenious arrangement than this, which leads man to imagine himself our superior. Often have I thought of it with wonder and gratitude, and we never can be too thankful that we are born to this high estate."

This lingo was too much for me, and I made a short contemptuous reply, in their own language; but no sooner done than I realized it, and immediately turned over some boards.

"I declare," said Bright, "I thought the old man spoke to us, and my heart almost rose into my mouth to think he had got hold of our language. But it must have been the boards. It can't be that he has an understanding of his low condition."

"I hardly conceive it possible," said Dick; "but our suspicions have been aroused several times. We must be on our guard, and keep watch of each and every action as closely as a cat watches a mouse."

"What would you do, Dick," said the heifer, "if he should come out, now, and talk to us?"

"Do? I'd know what I'd do pretty quick. Only one course could lie open for me to pursue."

"Yes; but he'd run into the house."

"No matter for that. No matter for fences, gates or other obstacles. It would be a time to unmask. I would burst through doors and search him out even though he should get under the bed. Should he happen to get away or climb a tree, his life would be prolonged only a few days, for we would issue a proclamation which would travel a thousand miles a day; he would be fully described; when every animal, whether on, over, or under the earth—beast, bird, fish, insect, which no eye can see, would combine to sweep from the earth such a dangerous character. This is one of the fundamental requirements of our Constitution, and wisely is this so, that the subordinate relations which man sustains to us should remain inviolate. But there is no use in talking over these old matters—we are secreted by the most impenetrable circumvallations, and there need be no fear. Let us sink to our nightly repose—may balmy sleep be disturbed by no distorted dreams, and may there be rain soon, so as to start the grass, for it is getting to be dry picking."

Of course every young man will see the dangerous position in which I had placed myself in my thirst for a knowledge of the languages. On thinking the matter all over, I thought it best to quit the farm and engage in some business that would prevent my coming in relationship with cattle, and that my dangerous knowledge might wear away in the course of time.

THE EGYPTIAN PREACHER.

LAST year I was away from home during June; on my return certain crops which I was expected to keep clean were overrun with weeds. I went to work. Each day the sun grew hotter; it beat on my back and the sweat streamed. Under a shirt, and with no vest on, the sweat becomes scalding hot; and blisters are likely to follow. One used to it can tell when a blister commences. It is like a sharp flea-bite. If it is over an old blister, it is like a hornet's sting; if over two or more blisters, it is like the acute itching of an old sore. I think the heat there, in Southern Illinois, is as great as in North Carolina, where they have a sea-breeze. Still, for ten years I had not found it so stinging as last summer. I did not work much in the afternoon.

One day, after dinner, I was sitting in the shade of my cedars, wearing a clean dry shirt and thinking of the weeds, when our preacher, the wagon-maker, rode up to the gate and wanted to know if we had any cool water. I told him of course we had, and that he must alight and take a seat under the trees, but that he had better hitch his horse in the shady barn-yard. Besides water, we had cider three days old, made in a mill which the boys themselves had invented, and it was just about right to cut the phlegm. It seemed to do the preacher's heart good.

After we had chatted a spell, I told him about a job I had in cleaning my cuttings and vines, and wondered why weeds were so abundant. He said he would tell me why. Now the Bramins of Hindostan give the origin of many things.

Let our Egyptian, Illinois preacher, educated in Western North Carolina, have a hearing, and in his own words:

"Thar's a heap o' things in Skripter as has ter be tuck figgertive. When the devil come ter Eve in the Garding of Eding ter git 'er ter eat apples, it's said he was a sarpint. That's figgertive. Ye see, he telled 'er them apples was good, green, baked, stewed, or made inter apple-butter, and fur pies they couldn't be beat. It was kase he was so plaverin' and ily, and had so many reasons why she should eat them apples, he 'peared like he was a sarpint. That's the figger.

"I reckon now he was like some o' them chaps from the Rawchister Nurssy a peddlin' trees, and they kin lie, oh, they kin! T'other day that big fat feller come round, and gittin' on the fence with me tried more nor two hours to get me ter buy some o' his truck. At last ter git shet on him, I telled him I'd take a dozen Buckinghams, kase I wanted 'em wurst way. He said he hadn't got 'em, and never hearn on 'em, and yet he'd just been tellin' me he had all melodious keinds. That proved he was a liar. They all orter be strung up. Bym-by, my least gal come and called me ter dinner; and, sir, that feller went right in, and my old woman thinkin' I brung him in and was gwien ter sell him a hoss, was powerful perlite, and got some butter, and, sir, he sot right down without anybody a axin' him, and when he got thro' he made a low bow and said when I come ter Rawchister I must call, and he went off and didn't offer ter pay the fust red. What d'ye think o' that? But now 'bout the devil who's at the head of all fruit men.

"Them apples he wanted Eve to eat I 'spose was grafted keinds, like yer Northern frouit, meller and red on one side. You uns has 'em I see, and they've got heaps on 'em ter South Pass, and ter Rawchister, too, may be. Fust he picks one and gives ter 'er, and when he seed 'er take a bite he tells 'er ter stand one side, and he gin the tree a powerful shake which brings 'em down good. 'Them's the keind ye want,' says he; 't'others aint worth shucks.' That bein' done, he goes off thro' the garding; then he stops and looks back, when he sees 'er a eatin' on 'em and a pickin' 'em up in her apring.

"Then the devil says ter hisself, says he, 'she's gwien ter take 'em ter her old man, which 'll be the eend o' this little game; fur he.'ll eat 'em too, and then he 'll have ter pack up his duds and roll out, and go ter choppin' and grubbin' land fur hisself. Now he wont make no fuss, and he 'll go, fur he's rail clever, and don't want ter get inter no fights, but ye bet I'll fix him.

"Then he scooted across thro' the peach-orchard, and come ter a little patch o' corn planted fur roasting years, and clost ter the stable which is in front o' the house. Just as he come out o' the corn he seed Adam a workin' in his truck patch. He'd got thro' a few rows of cotting, and was a hoein' his cowcumbers, but the devil stood still, fur he 'lowed his old woman 'd be atter him. Sure 'nuff, she come round the house whar the posies was, a lookin' like a posy herself, and telled him to come inter the porch, and not be a workin' like a nigger, fur she'd got something fur him. Yes, she'd got something not quite so funny. So he followed 'er. Thar's no tellin' where he wouldn't follerd 'er.

"Then the devil goes into the stable and looks around, but didn't see what he wanted. Thar wa'nt much thar, but he seed a hen's nest and a one-hoss harness. Ye see thar wa'nt but two hosses in the world, and one was hard to ketch, so he worked t'other, and bein' fat, she made corn nuff fur his bread, and ter fat his bacon. Then he slipped inter the smoke-house whar he seed what he was atter, which was a sack that was a hangin' on a hook, clost to a couple o' hen's nests. He tuck it down, and lookin' in ter see if thar was any holes, he dusted out the meal, when he put his head inter the mouth and sayin' a few hocus pocus words, gin three or four strong blows with his breath. Immejently the sack seemed three parts full, like as if it was clover seed, but it wasn't, it was the seed o' weeds and all kind o' foul stuff. Then he fixed the sack around him, like we uns does when we're gwien to sow wheat, and he started off with a peert step, a swinging of his arm and a sowin of the seed. So, ye see, that's why all you uns, and all we uns, has ter work so hard ter keep our craps clean."

When the preacher had finished this account I saw that the boys had been holding their breath; when I asked him if he would have any more cider. He said he would. After he wiped his mouth I asked him how he learned so many things about Adam. He said he studied them out, and what he had told was only a part. Ah, perhaps he could tell how Adam got along on his new farm, and if the devil troubled him any.

"Yes, sir-e. It's nigh onto fifty mild up ter the Salines, whar onct a month I goes ter meet my 'pintments, and ridin' along I study out what I'm gwien ter preach, besides a heap I never preaches, kase I forgits it, or it don't dove-tail. Yer Northern preachers can't do much without a bureau-drawer full o' books, but I don't want ary book but the Bible; no, I don't want a dictionary."

One of the boys said he thought it was impossible for a public speaker to get along without this book.

"Now, see heer, young man, ye may write a purt hand, and may be has read books, the leaves o' which I han't looked inter, but let me ax if a dictionary aint tur learn how ter spell? Don't interrupt. Sartin 'tis. Well, how ye gwien ter find a word onless ye know how ter spell it? Why, young man, I spent most a whole day lookin' fur one lettle word, and then I gist happen'd on it. So, don't ye see, if ye've got ter spell it fust ye don't want ter look."

Here I told him that as civilization had not commenced, Adam could not have tools and a house such as we have.

"Don't ye be troubled none about that. I tell ye, I've studied this subjick a heap. Don't nobody seem ter understand the business, kase they begin at the wrong eend. Now, say, ye put a man in a garding with nothing but peaches, apples, and water-millions ter eat and he'd die with the diree, or git the ager which'd throw him inter the winter fever, and that'd fix him. Then think of his havin' a wife guv ter him, —buteous in course—and then, soon as conwenient, young uns, all a layin out doors, and nary rag ter kiver 'em, and the skeeters and ticks bitin' on 'em; why, they'd be wus off nor hogs, kase hogs has brussels and kin eat grass and waller and don't want no more. Mighty buteous, I reckon his old wooman'd be atter campin' out a spell, and nary comb for her har, nor towelin' ter wipe her face. So, ye see, he had ter have a house, and a bed, and fire whar he could cook his wittles and warm hisself, when he was likely ter have the ager. Ye may say what ye're a mind ter, he had ter have help, and I'll argy it with ary man, little or big. Them things he couldn't a got hisself, kase it takes time, and afore he'd got 'em he'd been laid out. Who 'twas helped him I don't say, kase when a feller can't swim, it's easy nuff to get inter deep water. Thar's a heap more things on this pint, but I won't dwell on 'em, fur ye see they belong ter a sarmon I preaches at camp-meetings, when I have for orditers lawyers, marchands and flossifers.

"We all know Adam had ter roll out o' the garding ter open a new plantation; I understand all 'bout that myself. Dad had a good farm in North Carolina and two niggers, but thar got ter be too many o' us young uns, and craps was mighty weak—not more nor one bale ter four acres, so I come ter the Eelinois, and when I landed in old Jonesboro, all I had was six bitts in money, a hoss and a chist o' tools, which my kin brung. I squatted on Gov'ment, and in five years I entered, but me and my old woman seed hard times afore we got a goin,' kase the range was most eat out afore we come.

"Adam didn't go no furder nor a mild or two. He tuck what plunder his hoss could pull on the slide, and his old woman tote on her head, and he fixed up a shanty of poles and green brush whar he was gwien ter clar land. In course he had a bustin' big spring, and the sile was fust best, kase the job o' startin' the human race wouldn't a ben begun whar the land was pore. Them was happy days, fur thar was a big range, thar wa'nt no land-office, and no taxes. He druv off his stock, fur he had ter have cows and hogs and hosses as well as oxens, which is mighty handy in new ground. I don't spose the trees was werry big, kase they hadn't much time ter grow.

"Onct in awhile, he tuck his hoss and slide back ter the old plantation, ter see what he could pick up, and thar didn't nobody tell him ter clar out, kase he couldn't git a start nowhar else. Fust, he had ter pick corn ter last till he could make another crap, and thar was inyuns, beets, and sweet taters and water-millions which he left a growin' and cabbage ter make his krout, and all kinds o' garding seeds; then he tuck sprouts off o' the apple trees, and there was this and that and tother thing, so he piled up his slide with all his hoss could pull.

"I know he must a had a power o' work in him, fur he was the dad of all the good workin' fellers atter him, and he put in his time airly and late, fur he had a heap ter do. Unfortunate, Caanan hadn't ben cust then, so he couldn't get no niggers, but his old woman piled brush and helped roll logs ter build his housen.

"In a few years he had a double log-house, with a chimbley at each eend, and porches on both sides, whar he kept his sacks o' small grain, and his flour and meal, and his saddles and harness, and whar he sot and smoked his pipe on a rainy day, while his old woman was a spinnin' or weaving, and his young uns was a cuttin' up. The cook-house was back; then he had a spring-house and a smoke-house, and a stable and a paleing around his garding ter keep out the chickings, and all was on the plan of the old place called paradise.

"The range was fust best, and all his stock ran out, but it came up every night, kase it wanted ter be near the only man thar was, so's ter see how he got along, and so's to get a little salt; and as nobody else kept hogs, he had a big gang which got plum fat on the mast. It must a been like the Eelinois in airly day, when the grass and pea-vines and the range were good all winter, and a fat buck could a ben killed any mornin' afore breakfast.

"Now, atter they'd got the plantation well opened, and it was a bringin' on 'em in a big pile o' money every year, the devil says ter hisself, I'll give 'em a call ter see how they git along. He comes in the fall, when peaches and water-millions was ripe, expectin' ter have a good time. When he comes to the barrs he stops and hollers, but the dogs didn't bark a hait, and they run under the house kinder yelpin'. Now Adam was a good religious man, and he tuck great kere ter bring up his chaps in nurture and admonition. So every day he had 'em knock off work airly, say a hour by sun, and gettin' 'em tergether in the room, they had a little Sunday-school and said their catecism. Them young uns was handsome, ye better believe, and they was as smart as a steel trap; and they want 'tall kentrayry, for when they got a lickin' they didn't keep on bellerin', but shet up, kase they knowed they desarved it. They was sayin' their lessons when the devil holler'd. Immejiantly they all ran out inter the porch and their pap follered 'em. Adam says ter the devil, says he, 'Howd'y?' The devil says, 'So's ter be a stirrin', how's all you uns?' 'Right purt, though some o' the chaps has the chicken-pox; but don't be feared, come in.' The devil tries ter let down the bars, but they was wedged so's to keep out the hogs; so he jumps over sprier nor a cat. A gal brings a cheer out on the porch, her pap gets one hisself, and they sot down and went ter chattin'.

"Afore the door was the cows, and Eve was a milkin' 'em in a tin cup, while a gal was keepin' watch o' the bucket fur her man ter pour in the milk; and their hosses was comin' up and layin' down, and in the fence-corners was the hogs a squeelin'. Other things was a comin' up and layin' down, sich as deer, illiphants, camels and rhinocerhosses, and on a hill clost by was the lions, bars and tigers. Their sheep was put in a pen by the stable kase some had run off in the night.

"Eve seed him jump over the bars, and she'd a ide who he was, but she kept on milkin'; and when she got through she went down to the milk-house, where she skimmed milk for supper, which a gal carried up by the back way on her head; then mam follered 'er with a little crock o' butter.

"'Peared like supper was most ready, for somebody had tuck the kiver off the baker, and the corn-bread smelled good through the house, and there was another good smell of cabbage and bacon. Adam wondered what had done and gone with his old woman; so he went atter 'er and found 'er in tother house puttin' on a clean dress. He telled 'er there was a gentleman wanted ter stay all night. She said, maybe he mought stay, but she wanted ter see him fust. Then she piled a lot o' new quilts in a cheer by the door and went inter the porch. When the devil seed 'er he gits up and makes a scrape and a bow, and she makes a little curchy. One says its a fine ev'nin', and tother says it 'pears as though it mought rain. He looked different, but she was most sartain she knowed him, and she watched him powerful sharp.

"Then supper was ready, and they went through the two housen and by the door whar the quilts was inter the cookroom. Hur was a loom with a piece in it, and a long table kivered with wittles, and all the young uns standin' round; and thar was their eldest gal, about sevingteen, who'd been a cooking, and who stood ready ter pour the coffee out o' the tea-kettles, kase coffee-pots wa'nt inwented then. The devil hadn't seed 'er afore, and she was the pootiest gal ever on this yarth afore or since, and her pap and mam thought a heap on 'er; and when the devil seed 'er, he gin a wery perlite bow. Her mam, who was on the watch of him, seed then by his eyes who he was, fur he let it out, and she fired up on a suddent. They was jist sittin' down when Eve slipped back the cheer the devil was gwien ter sit in, and he fell back in a bad shape. Then she tuck the paddle out o' the big mush-kettle over the fire, which was closet by, and gin him eight or ten licks, sayin' she knowed who he was; he'd told a big lie about them apples, and got 'em turned off their plantation; and now atter they'd got another one gwien, atter a heap of hard work and a power o' bad luck, he'd come round had he, ter cut up some more of his didos, so's ter get 'em turned off agin? She'd larn him. He was gwien ter git round her oldest gal, was he? Yes, she'd see him git around 'er.

"In course, the devil was tuck by surprise, and when he tried ter git up she slapped him in the face, which settled him a wee bit; but she seed by the red of his eyes that he was alfired mad, when she dipped the paddle in the mush and laid it on his cheeks and whiskers thick, and some she put in his har. This hurt him so bad that he crawled under the loom and got behind the treadles whar she couldn't reach him. Then the devil ax'd Adam if he allowed his old woman ter treat strangers that way, almost as soon as they landed. Adam said as 'twas a quarrel 'twixt 'em he wouldn't meddle, and he reckoned she'd take kere of herself.

"This incouraged 'er, and she tuck the pokin' stick from the corner and went at him agin. It was made o' dogwood, and, in course, burnt on the eend, and bein' long nuff fur ter reach him, she punched his ribs and head like he was a snake. It's a mighty tight place fur a feller ter git under a loom, fur there's so many cross-beams and so much gearin' he bumps his head. It's powerful tangled, and the devil couldn't do nothin' but whop over and over. All the time she kept givin' him her mind, and he must a felt awful shamed.

"At last the devil couldn't stand it no longer, and he gin a dive out o' the loom, when she fetched down the biggest kind of a pound across his back which made him scrouch and crawl under the table, when he got up on t'other side. Then, as soon as he could stretch hisself, he turned inter his own shape; his horns stuck up, and he spit fire. He ran inter the porch, and, givin' a spring, he landed in the lane, whar he gin the awfulest yell ye ever hearn, and the wind began ter blow. But in less nor two minutes it was all over, and when they went inter the porch all they seed was a black cloud over the tree tops which was a switchin' in the wind."

The boys were so pleased with the preacher's account of

Adam on a new farm, that they went up in the haymow and got him some apples. After he had chanked a spell, one of the girls in the house began to play on the melodeon. The preacher asked the boys if they ever played on the fiddle. They said not.

"That's right," said the preacher. "Fiddles is the wust thing a young man can play on. Heaps has been ruined by 'em. The fust fiddle made a power o' trouble, and it aint through yit."

"I wonder now," said one of the boys, "if the devil didn't have a hand in it."

"Sartin; and I'll tell how 'twas. Atter Eve druv him out o' the house he dussent show hisself, and he sneaked round the lots and through the corn-fields hopin' ter git a chance ter play some more tricks. Some on 'em saw him onct in a while, and he telld 'em ter stop, he wanted ter tell 'em somethin', but they wouldn't hear nary word.

"When the two oldest boys growed up, the range was most eat out, and as they'd gone inter the sheep business pretty stiff, they had ter drive 'em out on the prairie and take turns a watchin'.

"Now Abel was a good boy, and when it was his turn, he spent the time when the sheep was eatin' in reading good books and in singin' himes. But Cain was 'nother sort, and he didn't do nothin' but hunt rabbits. The devil soon larned this, so one day he comes and ax'd him if he'd seed any o' his sheep. He didn't look like he did afore, but like Cain and we uns. Then they scraped acquaintance, and it didn't tuke long fur 'em ter git pretty thick.

"One day the devil brings him a fiddle and tells him it's the best thing ever was ter kill time, and he played him a chune. Then, ye see, Cain bein' natterly bad, tuck ter the fiddle, and he didn't stop till he larned ter play hisself. When he got so's ter play quite peert he tuck it home, and they ax'd him whar he got it. He said he made it. One lie allers follers another. They looked in it and thought it was mighty funny. Then he sot down and played a lot o' dancin' chunes, which made 'em feel lively. Atter that he uster sit in the porch of an evenin', and with his hat cocked on one side, a segar in his mouth, and a beetin' time with his foot, he played the chunes the devil larned him—Opry Reel, Munny Musk, and Fisher's Hornpipe.

"In course, the young uns soon got ter dancin', but their old dad had ter stop it, fur he seed whar it was leadin' to. But Cain kept on playin', and when he went out with the sheep he had the fiddle handed up to him on the hoss, and he got in a grove, and sot on the saddle like a gal, so as to be ready when the sheep went off, and he played away. Sometimes the devil come ter give him lessons, or ter hear how well he could play, while he sot on a log and chawed tobarker, not bein' much inclined ter smoke, as he had enough of that at home.

"Sunday afternoon, them two gentlemen had high times. There was a white-oak grove whar the straw was left when they thrashed wheat, and whar the devil sometimes slept nights. Cain brung apples, peaches and water-millions, and sometimes sweet taters, which they roasted; and atter they'd stuffed theirselves, Cain tuck his fiddle out of the green bag, and the devil tuck out his'n, and they went to playin' lively as a span o' hosses in a right smart trot. Bym by a young couple was seed comin' up through the grove a dancin', and then 'nother and 'nother, till the grove was like a ball-room. The fellers wur good-lookin', and had black eyes, long har and red faces, and the gals wur the handsomest ever seed, fur they wore their aprings low. Who they was, or whar they came from, I can't tell, and when the fiddles stopped they wanished.

"Abel wouldn't have no hand in this business, and he telled his brother he ortent ter do it. Cain said if he didn't like it he might lump it. Then Abel went ter argering, till they got ter disputin'. It's allers bad ter argy. Then there was 'nother thing. We all know how it turned out. O Lord a mercy! what a heap o' trouble thar is in this yarth! The trouble about young uns turns the har grey.

Yes, sir, the har turns grey if we've got 'em, and it turns grey if we hain't got 'em. Don't nobody know nothin' 'bout it till they git thar. How kin they? But we won't talk 'bout it. No.

"So Cain had ter pack up his duds and move off west. Afore he went he had a mark put on him. My ide is, he got a tap from a cane that was blackened in the fire, and it spread all over and made a nigger of him. That's why a nigger allers likes a fiddle.

"Now, ye see, if thar hadn't been no fiddle, thar wouldn't a been no niggers; and if thar hadn't been no niggers, the North wouldn't a gone and fit the South, and then, atter that, our party wouldn't a got licked."

THE SHEPHERD OF SALISBURY PLAIN.

IMPROVED.

IN one of the most fertile regions of New England, where the farms were large and the farmers wealthy, lived Bryan Ray. He was a poor young man, his parents were dead, he worked for different farmers by the month. At the free school he got some learning, he was steady and well-behaved, he was slow to think; he was not considered smart.

When he was eighteen years old there was a revival of religion; he, among many, experienced a change of heart, and he united with the church. Then he became noted for his piety. Time strengthened his convictions, and no one more enjoyed religion.

Wages were low; he got nine dollars a month, he could not dress fine. His best garments were home-made full cloth; his handkerchief, domestic check linen. After paying for his clothes and giving to missionary charities, he had little left at the end of the year. He was a humble member of the church, but he gave so much in proportion to his means that like the widow in Scripture he was considered to give more than they who donated largely. The minister would kindly take him by the hand, and well-dressed ladies asked him how he did.

When the time came for him to marry, he selected a pious and poor young woman, also an orphan, who had been brought up in a good family to habits of industry. They had a pleasant wedding, even though some of their clothing was borrowed. The folks who brought up Ruth gave her a good bed, rather they had given her time to make it, with some few things beside; with what little money he had, more were bought, and the new family was established. Then he boarded himself and worked for the farmers by the day.

He could see no chance for rising; land and houses were very dear, land in the western country was far away; there, churches were few, and it was sickly. Among the few books he read was the "Shepherd of Salisbury Plain." He was charmed with the piety and contentment of the shepherd. That poor man owned nothing; he lived in a poor cottage on Salisbury Plain, in England, and he supported his family by taking care of a rich man's sheep. His children picked up sticks for fuel, and searched for wool which the thorns tore from the sheep; this helped to make their garments, which, though clean, were a series of patches. Bryan Ray loved to read those passages where the shepherd speaks on religious subjects, and he learned that to be wise unto salvation should be the chief object of every human being. When a poor man seeks this he becomes rich in the inheritance of an incorruptible crown. Mr. Ray seeing himself hopelessly poor, and having found peace in believing, settled within his mind that he would live like the Shepherd of Salisbury Plain. He would not be ensnared with riches; free from care, he best could serve his Maker; if a man is poor, he is honest; the sleep of the laboring man is sweet.

One cannot tell how many poor and pious men have been made contented with their lot by reading this book. Perhaps many of the children of these poor men have been tempted and lost. It would be saying what is not known to be true, that this book was written in the interest of the English nobility and the landed aristocracy. But it is known to be true that they have recommended it to the poor as a book by which they ought to be guided. Rich and pious people in other countries have done the same; its influence has been great, and it is powerful to-day. The strongest link in the chain of slavery has been the teachings of religious people. The most important of the precepts of the Apostle is, that the laborer is worthy of his hire. Human legislation approached the divine when it passed the Homestead Bill.

Mr. Ray would eat his breakfast by the break of day; then, with a light step, he hastened to the farm where he was to work. When his day's labor was done, the farmer would pay him with a piece of pork, a few pounds of flour or any thing else he might need, and tying it in a little bundle, he put his ax-helve through it and returned home. His dwelling was an old school-house, remote and cold. He had neither cow nor pig. Ruth kept three or four hens which looked pinched and pale, so few were the crumbs which fell from their table. A little garden-spot was attached to the house, but the ground was so poor scarcely any thing would grow. His first enterprise was to take corn instead of Indian-meal for his work. If it was a wet time, he got it ground near by, he could carry a bushel on his back; but if it was dry he had to hire a horse. The farmers did not like to let a horse go; often he spent a whole day in getting one; it took another day to go to mill; sometimes the delay was so great they had to borrow meal, and when it was paid there was not much left.

Had good farmers been the parents of Ruth, she would have been called handsome. She had fresh cheeks, beautiful eyes, regular features, and very long hair. She had not been certain whether she could get married at all, and she thought herself fortunate in getting such a man as Mr. Ray. It is the men who own and earn every thing. She thought it was much to be united to one of this class; perhaps, in some way, he might get a little property. She would help him with all her soul and strength.

She made, washed and mended his clothes; his meals were always ready. On cold, stormy nights, when he had to help the farmers fodder and get in wood, she had his supper waiting, a fire burning, and the room was cheerful. It was very plain food, but with a most sincere heart he would give thanks to the Divine Parent for bestowing food and health, and for the great gift of his Son, through whom every one may come into the inheritance of eternal life.

Ruth was industrious; sometimes she was lonesome and

went to see the neighbors. They always treated her well, and if they were eating dinner they would ask her to sit by. If the woman was frying nut cakes she would offer Ruth one. At other times she would sit and look all around the house, considering the bunches of skeins of yarns, and the many pieces of dried beef, and she did not fail to look into the buttery where were cheeses, pies, bread and meat and butter on the shelves. Near her house was a spring, around it grew spear mint; often she went thither and eat it as if she was hungry. One morning her husband told her to go to a certain farmer and get a pint of vinegar which he had paid for. At supper he asked for it, he would put some on his cabbage. She said, when she brought it home, she thought she would taste of it, and she liked it so well she drank it up.

The second year of their marriage, Mr. Ray rented an acre of land and planted it with corn. Ruth heard that a farmer's wife wanted to hire some spinning done, she went to see her and got it to do. She was to spin a certain number of knots, and was to have a small pig. It took her some time to do it, for she had a sick spell; then she took it to the woman and got her pig. It was a mile and a half she had to go; she ran all the way; the pig was soon caught; she put it in her apron and ran back home. Great was her joy to find that her baby had slept all the time. Her pig grew some; it ran in the road; she fed it all she could spare; in the fall there was some corn for it. The crop of corn was not large. In that country little grain will grow without manure. At killing time their hog was light and lean. Two or three times she made nut cakes, but as she had to put part Indian meal into the flour, they were hard and heavy.

In the summer time when her hens got into the oat and rye fields they laid eggs. There was a wooded hill near by; she got permission to pick up dead wood; she saved something by getting it. Mr. Ray thought he did not make any thing by raising corn, the farmers wanted him every day, his wages were sure. It was little he got—little is really required in this world; it is here we are to prepare for the next; we lose all if we are not prepared.

Sometimes Ruth would ask him if there was no better way to get along. It was hard for him to buy flax, wool, bread meat, every thing. He could think of no way; why should they complain? They ought to be thankful that their lot was cast in a Christian land where they could hear the gospel preached, where they could read the Bible and walk in the way that leads to life. She would answer; to be sure these were great privileges, but it was no sin to have comforts, and were not certain well-to-do farmers as hopeful of salvation as if they were poor? Of course they were, but the Lord had seen fit he should be a poor man; the time would come when they would see this was best; they would be tried as by fire, and if they were faithful to the end, they would walk the streets of the New Jerusalem, they would wear golden crowns glittering with precious stones; they would sing the song of deliverance; no more sighing, no more tears; they would be led by still waters, and they would eat bread from the tree life.

When there were two children, Mr. Ray saw he must earn more, and to improve the stormy days, he made ax-helves, and door-mats, and after several trials he made baskets. This was quite a help. After this there was another child, when, with the greatest reluctance, he was forced to give less to the heathen. He said he was sorry, but rich men must give more. Some of the neighboring women, when she went to get work would press her to eat, and if it was not meal time they brought her something on a plate. They gave her to take home a piece of meat, a loaf or a pie, and their nice little girls would carry the children baskets of red apples. When the cold winter was coming on, one or another would give her pieces of flannel, almost as good as new, only faded a little, to make dresses for her children, nor did they forget some wool from which she could spin stocking-yarn. Their husbands did not always know about this.

One time a cousin of Ruth's, who lived in the West, came

to Boston with some cattle, and he rode out to see the place where he lived when he was a boy. He called on Ruth. He was a large fat man, using many curious words; he was good-natured, and he gave each of the children a quarter of a dollar, every piece smelling strongly of tobacco. He said he could not stay long; he wondered how the people got a living, and he was bidding her good-bye, when she asked him what kind of a country he lived in, and whether her husband could not do better there. Best country in the world, just the place for a poor man, for he could get land. Did her husband want to go? She was afraid not; well she had better persuade him to go. Should they come, he would see they had a place. But he could not stay. They must write if they were coming.

All the rest of the day Ruth kept repeating to herself that they could get land. That was what they wanted. If they could get five or six acres, they would do well. Spinning, carding, sewing or getting supper, she said, *land, land, land.*

When Mr. Ray came home, she told him that her cousin said they could get land out west. He said he knew it, but it was sickly there. Perhaps it was a little, but had he not rather be sick once in a while and have land than always be so poor? Besides, were they not sick where they were? poor people were likely to be sick. More, her cousin looked as though he never was sick. Yes, yes, but how were they to get thither? Since he had been married he had not had money enough to take the journey. Oh, yes, they had; it was put in the contribution box. He turned sharply around, as if she was a tempter. She stopped and had him eat his supper.

A woman looks at many things. Principally, she considers what will become of her children, how they are to be fed, clothed and schooled. Will they be respected—will they be tempted and end their lives on the gallows, or in the penitentiary?

In an hour or so she commenced again. She had been thinking. Would it not be better to stop giving to the heathen a year or so, and make use of all he could save in getting land, for when he got it he could give more in one year than he could give in many years without land. It was his duty to lend to the Lord; he had done so; surely now, the Lord would be willing to lend to him. It was their duty to be comfortable. One prayed that he might neither be rich nor poor, lest he should be proud and lest he should steal. For her part she would be willing to work till she died if she was sure her children would be respected. If they did not get land, the time would soon come when they would have to put out their children, for they could not take care of them. Who could tell whether they would fare well or ill? Certainly it was better to get land so that they could have their children with them. Whithersoever they might go the Lord would hear them in mercy and look down on them.

She said more, for she knew what to say. Her words had an effect on him. He said perhaps they might go. But they must be more saving than ever. When she saw she had the advantage, she found out where her cousin lived. It was in the Kankakee country, and she wrote to him, for she could write. Yes, he could get land, the best that ever lay out doors; farm hands were scarce; he himself would hire; in a year, if they were very saving, they could get a place.

Surely they would do well, and if the land was rich, as he said, they could raise eighteen or twenty bushels of corn to the acre. If they had eight or ten acres, and five were in corn, this would give them nearly a hundred bushels, which would fatten two hogs and give them their bread. They could keep hens that would lay, and have ducks, and even geese. They would have three or four sheep. Perhaps, if they had good luck, they might keep a cow and have milk and butter, but they were not certain about this, for it might be that they would be obliged to get a horse to plow with, and he would eat all the corn-stalks. Oh, if they were going to have a horse, that would be grand for the boys; and they talked about riding it till they got into a dispute as to which should ride before and which behind.

It became known that Mr. Ray talked of moving west. He was told he would repent it. He would lose his wife and children, and be happy if he himself could get back. There were such and such men who went to the Maumee country, they had good farms when they left, they came back with nothing. This discouraged him. She said she understood it; they wanted his work; they got rich by poor men's labor. There was her cousin—what was the matter with him? Maumee might be a good or bad country—call it bad—they were not going thither. He listened to her and determined he would go.

On a cold stormy day he was making baskets, and one of the deacons came to see him. The Mission of Burmah was greatly in need of money; last Sunday it was noticed he gave nothing; it was supposed he had forgotten to bring his money; he had called that he might have the pleasure of giving to so noble a charity. Neither Mr. Ray nor his wife said a word. The deacon thought it strange, he hoped Mr. Ray was not going to faint in the midst of the harvest, while the laborers were so few. The poor man knew not what to say; with a stare he looked at his wife. Ruth had to speak, she did not know what would be the result. She told the deacon to look at her children; some of them had shoes, but none of them had clothes so that they could go to school. She had made them caps out of strips of black and red flannel, high and warm caps—she remembered when they used to be worn, but the boys called them night-caps. Her children were not heathen, but if every body was as poor as they it would make a heathen country. They had made up their minds to go west and get land. They must save their money. The deacon wished they would do well, but it was a very hazardous step. He hoped they would not gather to themselves the mammon of unrighteousness. Ruth had a sharp reply on her lips. She did not dare to utter it, for his wife had been most kind to her, and her husband worked for him.

It is hard to tell how saving Ruth was. She demanded every cent of money he got and put it away. Half a pound of tea used to last them six months—she made rye and crust coffee instead. Father must have butter, he cannot work unless he have a plenty to eat; the rest must go without. The farmers' wives let them have skimmed milk. Sometimes it had not stood long. She and the children could eat johnny-cake and milk. It was good enough; it would stay in the mouth and have a sweet taste longer than meat. No more buying any thing at the store, no laying out money for any thing—father must get what is wanted where he cannot get money. They could not even afford to be sick; if they were, they must go without a doctor. If one found fault with the victuals, he was to go without till he liked it. If their clothes were ragged, they must be patched—it was patch upon patch. Think of the poor heathen with only a cloth around the middle. If there was work to do, they must work with all their might. Think of the little slave who labors in the sun.

The time came when they were to start west. Their last Sunday at church was an affecting season. Letters were requested for Bryan Ray and his wife. All eyes were turned towards them. When meeting was out the whole congregation took them by the hand and bade them farewell. The wide benevolence of the rich farmers' wives had clothed their children in plain and good garments. They felt that it was no more than due to one who had labored on their farms so faithfully and long.

The next day they started; all their furniture had been sold; their clothing was in two dry goods' boxes. They had sixty dollars—a small sum for such a long journey. For eight dollars a man carried them to Albany. Then they took the canal, and arriving at Buffalo they went on board a steamer bound for Chicago. They were surprised, after traveling so far to find a city fully as large as any on their route. It was fortunate that their cousin found them the first day. He had come up with several wagons loaded with grain. There was no railroad then. So saving had they been that a few dollars were left.

While they were riding along, Mrs. Ray heard her husband repeating, it could not be done; not all the men in the country with all the cattle could do it. Do what? Get manure enough to make the ground black like that, and so many miles. Their cousin had a large farm and a long one-story, unpainted house, with porches on each side. The kitchen was very long and had a fire-place. There was timber near the house and a nice stream running into the Kankakee. There were two or three large fields, the rest was open prairie. Their cousin had several hundred head of cattle and fifteen hundred sheep.

He had a house ready for them; it was not much better than their old one. Things looked rough, but all was in such plenty that the place was like a fat man laughing as loud as he could. Ruth did the talking. They were here, what were they going to do? how would they live? they had no money, no property. Living was nothing. Her husband might work for him till spring; by that time he would find out what manner of man he was. If he was the right kind, he could earn enough to buy a forty. He had heard he was good to work. He knew of a forty with some timber that was number one. He would keep his eye on it, but there were plenty more. Ruth asked what he meant by a forty. Why, a lot of forty acres. But that would cost so much. What! is fifty dollars much? Maybe they could get it. They had not expected to get more than five or ten acres. Nonsense; forty acres was only a garden spot. Mr. Ray said he would do what he could; he might not understand the way they worked. Much would depend on what his wages were. The cousin would give him twenty dollars a month, he boarding himself; but that would cost little—corn was fifteen cents; wheat, forty cents; pork, two cents; beef, less. They asked if they understood him. Certainly. Then they could get a forty. They knew they could.

Ruth wanted to know who owned all that high grass with no fence around it. That was all government land; he kept his stock on it without costing a cent, and he cut a hundred tons of hay. If this was so, maybe they had better try and buy a cow if she did not cost too much. They had some money; maybe she could pay the rest herself; she could card, spin and weave. She would do most anything. They had wanted one ever since their first child was weaned. Oh, that they could get a cow! Could she milk? Oh, yes; when she was a girl she milked six cows night and morning. She always had to break the heifers. That was lucky. He had a heifer just come in; he would make her a present of it. He was so good, but she would pay for it. No, not a cent. They had cows enough; more than they made good use of.

They went to housekeeping. They borrowed some things and did without many. Ruth bought some milk-jars and set her milk in her cousin's spring-house. Every day she looked at it, to see what kind of a cow she was going to be. It was a great day when she borrowed a churn, and churned and brought butter. The children crowded around and peeped in to see it. Oh, what a noble cow, her butter is so yellow, and how much there is!

Mr. Ray showed himself a good farmer, and so faithful, so careful and so saving, that before fall his cousin, on going away, as he often did, left him in charge. In a short time he found out where the church members were. The church was very weak, and Mr. Ray was warmly welcomed. He gave them new life.

On new year's day, his cousin took him across the prairie three or four miles to where the Kankakee makes a bend, and he showed him the forty. There were nearly ten acres of heavy timber running down to the rocky bed of the Kankakee. The rest was most beautiful prairie. Then he handed him a deed for it in Mr. Ray's name. That night, first of the new year, was the most joyful in their whole lives. Struggling long, often nearly ready to sink, they had got land. Not less joyful is the shipwrecked mariner when he touches land.

I need not tell how they progressed and prospered. This

15

would require another narrative. Here, in the West, thousands, though few as poor, have made blooming homes from the wilderness and the prairie. Now, one sees the house they were at last able to build. It is two stories, with a long kitchen, and wood-shed in the rear. The green blinds, the barns, the other buildings, and the large orchard, remind one of a New England home.

When the travelling preacher or missionary comes into this section he always stops with Deacon Ray. No one gives so liberally as he to religious charities. He is convinced that he is none the poorer for these gifts, and that, if he withholds his hand, he will suffer by losses of stock or short crops.

Ruth is sure to hear of destitute families. When they call on her she presses them to eat; if it is not meal-time she brings them something on a plate, and she gives them to take home a piece of meat, a loaf or a pie, and baskets of red apples. When the cold winter is coming on she gives them pieces of flannel almost as good as new, only a little faded, to make dresses for their children, nor does she forget some wool from which they can spin stocking yarn. Mr. Ray does not always know about this.

Once a year their oldest son comes home to see them. He is a grain-merchant in Chicago. In telling how he gets along, he speaks of little things. He is liked in every respect except in one—he finds fault with the men when they waste grain, and when they see him picking up kernels of corn they smile. His father commends his saving habits, and shows him that he owes much of his success to it. Frequently the deacon speaks of himself; and gives the result of his conclusions regarding one's duties to his Creator and to his fellow-man, which is: when the power to do good, when health, education and the advancement of mankind are considered, no Christian for a moment should be contented to lead a life like that of the Shepherd of Salisbury Plain.

A DESCRIPTION

OF THE

MISSISSIPPI VALLEY.

WHEN the Mississippi Valley is mentioned, it is understood to include the whole country between the Alleghany and the Rocky Mountains, and between the greater part of the chain of great lakes and the Gulf of Mexico, making a region running 1,400 miles northwest, and from 1,000 to 1,400 miles southwest. The States and Territories lying within this valley are generally stated as follows: Western Pennsylvania, West Virginia, Ohio, Indiana, Illinois, Wisconsin, Minnesota, Iowa, Missouri, Kansas, Nebraska, Montana, Dakota, Kentucky, Tennessee, Arkansas, Mississippi and Louisiana. Not the whole of all these States lie within this valley, but there are many streams coming from several States not mentioned which flow into it. Properly, a valley has a rich, alluvial soil. The parts of this valley having such a soil are the valley of the Ohio river, and the valleys of its tributaries extending into Western Pennsylvania; the bottoms of all the streams in Ohio, except of the few flowing into Lake Erie, several small prairies in this State, the extensive river bottoms of the Wabash and White rivers in Indiana, the whole of the State of Illinois, except a fraction of hilly country in the southern part, much of Wisconsin, seven-eighths of Minnesota, almost the whole of Iowa, Nebraska and Kansas, North and West Missouri, a part of Arkansas, a tenth of Kentucky, less of Tennessee, an eighth of Mississippi, and fully three-fourths of Louisiana. Very little of the country south of the mouth of the Ohio river is prairie; very little north of it, and west of Indiana, is wooded.

The soil of the prairies is remarkably dark; when properly managed, it is as soft and productive as the very choicest garden mould, and it varies from one foot to two feet, and even to six feet in depth. Generally, in the northern section it is deeper and richer than in the southern. The extent of these prairies is about six hundred miles square. They lie a little southeast of the centre of the continent, and they are in the heart of the Mississippi Valley.

In estimating the value of a country, every important fact having universal application should be stated. I claim to have discovered, that in that part of North America, extending as far west as it is moistened by summer showers, a distance of 1,600 miles, there is a belt of limited width, better suited to the natural and tame grasses than in any part north or south of it; and that with each mile of departure from this belt, these grasses grow with greater difficulty, till at last they nearly disappear. This belt is five degrees, or 300 miles wide, and the centre of it is in $42\frac{1}{2}$ degrees of north latitude. While the region north of $42\frac{1}{2}$ degrees is much wider than on the south, there are conditions in the south which make the two equal. An elevated region will correspond to a higher degree of latitude. For this reason, West Virginia, Eastern Kentucky and the Cumberland table land, West Missouri and Kansas are suited to the grasses. A particular kind of soil is also equal to a higher latitude, as in the Blue Grass region of Central Kentucky. On the other hand, a sandy, light soil, by reason of its warmth and porous nature, will produce results corresponding to a lower latitude; and with respect to the grasses, the difference may be as great as five, or even more degrees. The best grass land has a rich clay soil, and such a soil two or three degrees south of $42\frac{1}{2}$ degrees will be equal, if not superior, to a sandy soil two or three degrees north of it. An acre of land on which grass grows naturally, is at least double the value of an acre on which it grows with difficulty; and it has the additional value of retaining its fertility, while the other is quickly impoverished. To this we must except valleys, which are sustained at the expense of the uplands.

The southern line of the region natural for grass passes through, or very near the following cities: Philadelphia, Columbus, Indianapolis, Springfield, and Atchison, Kansas, but Lawrence may be said to be on this line, owing to its elevation. The centre of the grass belt is on the line of the following cities: Boston, Albany, Rochester, Buffalo, Cleveland, Detroit, Chicago, Davenport and Rock Island, Des Moines and Omaha. Although Rochester and Buffalo are geographically north of this line, they are to be placed upon it, because, feeling the influence of the waters of Lake Ontario, which seldom freeze, they are removed a degree south by the higher temperature. The lines of traffic, the many cities and towns, and the intelligence of the people, are the natural growth of the grass belt. Incidentally, it may be mentioned that white clover, a species of grass, furnishes abundant food for bees; and it is here the largest amount of honey is produced. Whether the grass belt is more natural for fruit may be questioned. Still, orchards and vineyards are more profitable here than elsewhere. Perhaps this arises mainly from the condition of the people, for fruit is cultivated by those whose tastes are refined, and by those who gain their bread with ease; never by those who live in hovels and on poor food, uncertain in supply and difficult to obtain.

Whatever may be true as to the locality in which the potato is alleged first to have been found, it is certainly produced in large quantities and of finest quality only in a cold climate. I would therefore fix the line on which it succeeds best on the 45th parallel; that is, where grass grows finest and makes the densest sod, though not most abundantly; this will be through Maine, Northern New York, Canada, Northern Michigan, Central Wisconsin and Minnesota, and Dakota and Montana. Here snow falls early and deep, it lingers late, and the ground freezes but little. Around Mackinaw the Indian has raised the potato for an unknown period; it is still his chief food; nor does he save seed, for the root is a perennial, and like an evergreen. It is highly probable that Europeans derived the seed from the Aborigines of Nova Scotia, and not from a warm climate, where even with the culture given by the white man it is barely retained.

WESTERN PENNSYLVANIA.

The whole of Western Pennsylvania lies in the Mississippi Valley, though only small portions have the character of a valley. It is decidedly a mineral region; bituminous coal, iron and limestone abound; and many railroads converge at Pittsburgh, a city more largely engaged in staple manufactures than any other in America. North of this city and on the Alleghany and its tributaries are the oil wells, which are the wonders of our time. On the western border of this State is a level strip of country, thirty miles wide and sixty miles long, running north and south. It extends into Ohio, and stretches far westward. This is the eastern boundary of the Mississippi Valley.

WEST VIRGINIA.

This is a mountainous and mineral region; there are some oil wells, and on the Kanawha river large quantities of salt are made, and sent to many of the river States below. Much of the country is undeveloped, and in remote sections land can be had cheap. Some of the hilly region has a soil composed of decayed limestone, giving it remarkable strength, and frequently it produces crops of grain superior to the valley of the Ohio. Owing to this fact, and to the elevation above the sea, West Virginia is a favored grass region. In the settlement of any country, the quality in which it is superior is sure to be developed first. Hence this State has long been noted for fine-wooled sheep. This State extends through the latitude of Central and Southern Ohio and almost the whole of Kentucky. They who would be pioneers in a rough country, who have self-reliance, and who value majestic scenes and solitude, where bread and health will be sure, can find beautiful rural homes for little money in this new and rising State.

OHIO.

Square miles, 39,964, or 25,576,900 acres. Population about 2,500,000.

This is one of the choicest States in the Union. Except in a limited region on its northwestern border, it is mostly under cultivation, and farms are valued at from $25 to $150 an acre. The length of the Lake Erie shore is 236 miles, of the Ohio River shore, 672 miles. Along the Lake shore for eighty miles are two tiers of counties, some ten in number, known as the Connecticut Western Reserve, which, being within the grass region, have been noted from the first settlement for dairy products. A strip along the Lake shore, about three miles wide, is favorable for all kinds of grapes, particularly for the Catawba, and this, in connection with the islands, is, as far as now known, the best grape region in America; though perhaps parts of California may be excepted. The Western Reserve is about forty miles wide from north to south, and across it run several small rivers, which empty into the lake. Interlocking with the heads of these, are a great many small streams forming the headwaters of the Muskingum, the Scioto, and the Little and Big Miamis, which empty into the Ohio river. These streams arise from beautiful springs, and the country through which they run is in places undulating, and in others level. Here is a part of the northern boundary of the Mississippi Valley. The soil is of sand, gravel and loam, rich and easy to till; it is especially adapted to wheat, and to most kinds of fruit; it is a fair grazing region, and during thirty years the farms have paid for themselves many times in various productions. There are mines of coal and iron, and wood is abundant.

Taking into account these things, as well as the health of the country and accessibility by railroads, this must be considered the most favored region on this continent. When the prairie States shall be planted with groves, they will be superior.

Further south, the country is more diversified; in the neighborhood of the Ohio river it becomes hilly, and is similar to West Virginia; but in the vicinity of the interior rivers, the land declines into broad and extremely fertile valleys. Here is the centre of the corn region, and large numbers of hogs and cattle are fattened for the Eastern markets. In the southwest corner of the State is the flourishing city of Cincinnati, largely interested in commerce, merchandise, and almost every variety of manufactures. This State is not excelled in the extent and number of its railroads. The northwestern part is level and inclined to be swampy, and there are large districts, so to speak, where the original forest remains, and the few settlers are struggling with the difficulties common to pioneer life.

INDIANA.

Square miles, 33,809, or 20,673,760 acres. Population over 1,500,000.

Here, as in Ohio, is the same interlocking of streams which run into the lake and into the Ohio. The State is rather more level than Ohio. A large part of the State is drained through broad and exceedingly rich valleys of the Wabash and White rivers. Beyond Fort Wayne one will find much of the primeval forest, among which are new farms, while, in localities remote from lines of transportation, new land can be purchased from eight to ten dollars an acre, but such will have few or no improvements. Many of the forests are rich in black-walnut timber; saw-mills are frequent, and immense quantities of this lumber are shipped to New York, Boston and Europe, selling at from $25 to $35 per thousand on the railroad or Wabash and Erie Canal. Dealers go thither from the East to buy this lumber the same as others go to buy wool or wheat. The northern part, from Fort Wayne to Chicago, requires more settlers, and when developed it cannot fail to have immense resources. The central portion is better settled. On a line west from Central Ohio the improvements are good, and there are many flourishing towns. The capital (Indianapolis) is active with business, and there is no interior town in our country to which so many railroads converge. In wide sections the land is so level as to be monotonous, even where remote from streams, and there is much of what may be termed a white-oak or wheat soil. In the southern part are many hills and knolls, alternating with level stretches, even near to the Ohio river, and all this section is well adapted to particular varieties of fruit. There are some prairies in this State, and on the northern borders some are very beautiful, well tilled, and highly valued, but none are very large, and for this reason they are very desirable. The far greater part of the State is level like a prairie, and presents all the characteristics of a valley.

ILLINOIS.

Square miles, 55,405, or 35,459,200 acres. Population over 2,500,000.

After one crosses the rich valley of the Wabash, and rising, generally, a slight eminence, the prairies break into view. Even if one crosses so low down as Vincennes, the prairie will stretch, with here and there a few belts and groves, to the streets of Chicago, and to the north and east across the Mississippi, the Missouri, through Iowa, North Missouri, Nebraska, Kansas, Colorado and Dakota, till at last the pine forests of the Rocky Mountains appear. Of the appearance of these prairies little more can be said than that they present a vast expanse of gently rolling country, entirely destitute of trees, with streams from five to twenty miles apart, having a fringe of timber along their banks, and an occasional grove, generally on ground considerably above the general level. The prairies of Illinois are of two distinct kinds. One kind is similar to black muck, with more or less admixture of sand. The black color seems to be derived from soot of burned grass; the sand is more manifest on ridges, and when there is drainage by which the black has leached out, and the color inclines to red or purple. This of the two is most desirable. The line of black prairie commences at about $39\frac{1}{2}$ degrees, or on the line of Terre Haute, and thence westward, including all of Illinois, most of Wisconsin, Minnesota, Iowa, North Missouri, Kansas, etc. North of this line, commences the corn region, and it extends to forty-one degrees, being about one hundred miles wide. Although good corn is raised both north and south of this line, still here this grain uniformly yields well, while on either side, north and south, the production diminishes with each mile till at last, in a hot climate, and in a cold one, it ceases to be grown. Still, some corn is raised within the tropics, for it requires heat, and its culture is extended southward beyond its true region, the same as grass extends northward, each unequally spreading from the centre, but unless in elevated localities, the amount of corn produced within the tropics is insignificant. Even no further south than the cotton States, it does not yield more than one-third of a full crop.

Upon the southern boundary of the corn region, and of the black prairie, commences another kind of prairie. This is of a light, almost chalky color, with an inconsiderable depth, often near a hard pan, while in places there are patches of "scalds," of small extent, which are utterly barren. Even in the black prairie these scalds are sometimes found, and they are indicated by a growth of thin fine grass. This prairie extends southward about one hundred miles, when the ground rises into ridges divided by small streams, with a large portion of tillable land, all originally wooded with a heavy growth of oak, tulip, hickory, gum, cypress, etc. It is a theory that the black prairie was formed by a drift from a limestone region far to the north, and that it subsided from a still lake on the line of $39\frac{1}{2}$ degrees; and that the light colored prairie was formed by a deposit of sand and clay held in a solution by the waters of the Missouri river, which crossed the Mississippi and lapped evenly upon the black prairie. The line of separation is so distinct, as in places to be marked by the eye, and in plowing a field across the line the plowman feels the difference in the draught, for the light soil has greater resistance. This light prairie is natural for winter wheat, and as St. Louis lies in the centre of a very large region of this description, it has become celebrated for its superior flour. All kinds of fruit do well, and Southern Illinois is marked upon maps as the "Fruit Region."

Where such a vast body of land is without timber, there would be great obstacles as to its settlement if there was no compensation. It is estimated that the coal field underlying three-fourths of the prairie, and ceasing to be found where the timber grows, is the largest bed of the bituminous variety in the world; that is, 35,000 square miles, and averaging in the thickness of the deposit fifteen feet.

At Galena are lead mines of great richness, which, so far as yet discovered, contain better defined and permanent leads than exist anywhere else in America. Some have asserted that they have been mostly exhausted, but it is doubtful whether they are more than fairly opened, for the deepest shafts do not exceed one hundred and twenty feet, while English mines in the same kind of rock have been worked a thousand feet, and, in one case, under the bed of the ocean itself. A considerable part of these mines lie in Wisconsin. There are inconsiderable lead mines in the southern part of the State along the Ohio river, found in the lower magnesia lime-stone, while the Galena mines are in the upper.

Unimproved land can be had in Illinois as low as five dollars an acre, which will be remote from railroads, though not distant from prospective ones, mostly in the southern part. Near railroads it is from ten to forty dollars, and improved farms vary from twelve to one hundred and fifty dollars an acre. The higher prices are in the central and northern part. Well improved farms with orchards, good buildings, near towns, schools and stations can be had from half to two-thirds less than farms of the same class can be purchased in the Eastern States, while the soil is far superior. The renting of land is practised by enterprising young men, and by men who have little energy. It is a disgrace there not to own land.

WISCONSIN.

Square miles, 53,924, or 34,511,360 acres. Population about 1,000,000.

Nearly two hundred miles of this State form the western shore of Lake Michigan, and a much greater line is on the Mississippi river. The lake shore is sandy and monotonous; the river scenery is beautiful and sublime. In the interior, and north, are many lakes from one mile to thirty miles in extent, abounding with fish. There is supposed to be no coal, as the limestone which lies below it comes to the surface; but there is a plenty of peat. The lead mines are in the southwest corner of the State, and are four hundred square miles in extent. In addition, some are recently reported in the central part of the State. These mines have been very productive, and still are worked with profit, while new leads are frequently announced; but in most of these water is an obstruction, and heavy outlays are required to remove it.

From the southern part of Green Bay a line may be drawn directly southwest to the Mississippi river, and a triangle will be formed, within which the greater part of the population of the State is to be found, though there is a tier of counties up the river well settled. The remainder of the State, or fully one-half, lying in the interior, and a considerable portion of it wooded, is new, and though the climate is cold, there are sufficient resources to sustain more people than many sections with a milder climate.

MINNESOTA.

Square miles, 83,531, or 53,491,840. Population in 1850, 6,037; 1860, 172,000.

This is the most northern of our States, and it reaches as high as forty-eight degrees. It joins Penembra, in British America, and on the east, lies north of the western arm of Lake Superior. The Mississippi runs through a large portion, so also the Minnesota river, and a considerable part of its western boundary is the Red river of the North, which is the only water in the United States that runs into the frigid zone, for this river empties into Lake Winnepeg, thence into

Hudson Bay, the outlet of which is by the Arctic ocean. Minnesota has a dry and steady climate, supposed to be favorable to consumptives; and though in so high a latitude, the rigors of winter are tempered by warm airs from the southwest, which extend far across the vast plains of Central British America and are peculiar to that region. This State has vast prairies through the southern and central part, and thence they extend, with some variation, by elevated and wooded ground, far towards Oregon. Perhaps the region between these two distant points is less explored than any in our domain, and a large part of it is overrun by savage tribes. There is said to be no coal, but this is uncertain. Peat is known to abound. In the northeast is much valuable timber. Beautiful lakes are scattered through the interior, and there are innumerable streams in which speckled trout are plentiful. In fully half of the counties land can be entered under the Homestead Act, and in many places immigrants from the East are settling on such land in colonies with encouraging prospects. The prairie soil is probably unexcelled in the world, and from its depth on the high swells and plateaus the theory of drift from the north seems to be sustained. Minnesota is taking a front rank among the wheat-producing States. A particular variety of corn does well, and potatoes should be unexcelled. There are certain apples, among which are the Red Astracken and Dutchess of Oldenburg, which are hardy and mature their fruit, and as these are natives of Russia and Sweden there is little doubt but other sorts from those countries will yet be introduced, and give to the country abundance of fruit. There are large districts of country settled by Swedes and Norwegians who find a congenial climate, and who will add much to the wealth of our country and to the physical constitution of our people. The school fund is very large. Such a State must contain within itself great power, and it is not improbable, nay, it is certain, that in the future it will furnish a strong and healthful race who by intelligence and native vigor will form an important if not a controlling element.

IOWA.

Square miles, 55,045, or 35,238,800 acres. Population, 1,000,000.

The eastern boundary is the Mississippi, the western the Missouri. This State has extensive coal beds, and around Dubuque are lead mines belonging to the Galena District. Lying between $40\frac{1}{4}$ and $42\frac{3}{4}$ degrees of latitude, it is wholly within the grass belt, while the southern part, having a quick warm soil, is equivalent to being within the corn belt. The surface is undulating; the interior is an elevated plateau, and perhaps there is no commonwealth or kingdom on the earth which contains so much good land. As a State, it is far inferior to Illinois for variety of climate and productions; but for special crops it is unexcelled, and, with such a large extent every way suited to staple productions, they are destined to give unparalleled intensity and power. The southeastern portion early attracted attention by its marvelous beauty, and large breadths were brought into cultivation at the time the Grand Prairie of Illinois was without inhabitants. The northern and western portions are more destitute of timber, but the scenery is bold and striking; many streams cut through the limestone bluffs, which form the breastworks of the table lands, and often the streams are precipitated in cataracts. Some sections are in a state of nature and await immigrants; while prices are low, not because the land is of little value, but because there is more land than there are people. In a few years there will be great changes, and places which now are thought remote will be in the midst of wealth and activity. Already this State is on the great highway between the Atlantic and the Pacific; and as the line of greatest wealth and population is directly east, its extension hither is unavoidable.

MISSOURI.

Square miles, 65,350, or 41,834,000 acres. Population, 1,182,000, and rapidly increasing, as are also Iowa, Minnesota, Nebraska and Kansas.

Missouri must be considered in at least two parts. That

north of the Missouri will divide it diagonally into two unequal sections, each quite dissimilar. The two kinds of prairie soil, dark and light, are as marked here as in Illinois, hence only a portion, or a strip about one hundred miles wide of the superior soil, lies within this State. However, as the elevation westward above the sea increases, this strip widens, and it deflects so far southward as to be one hundred and fifty miles wide on the western border, where it coalesces with the Missouri bottom and forms what is known as the Platte Purchase, a mixture of prairie and groves, forming a limited timbered region, the most fruitful of any between the Mississippi and the Rocky Mountains. In the southeastern part, and far inland, the country is almost mountainous, and here is the richest mineral region, so far as is now known, within our dominion. Iron exists in such enormous quantities, and over an extent so great, that hills of hematite ore, in localities now remote, have no particular value, and they are passed by with scarcely a remark. Lead has been mined for many years with great success, though without much system or capital. Still, nowhere do the mines cross each other at right angles, forming "EASTS" and "WESTS" as in the Galena region. There are also zinc and copper, and recently tin has been discovered, and the first pig of this metal made in America has been exhibited. It is safe to say that the mineral wealth of Missouri is beyond human estimate, nor is it confined to a limited region, but, with some exceptions, it extends to the western border. Land can be had very cheap, also large quantities, under the Homestead Act, and though the soil is not deep, it is quick, and in parts of the mining region has a vitality which is scarcely suspected. Here grows the best wheat in the world, and the capacity to do so for an indefinite period could be secured if clover were early and persistently sown. The old cultivators have been so shamefully improvident that many of their farms are not worth having. Several of the counties along the Arkansas line are level, low, and surprisingly rich, and there are some small prairies. There the inhabitants have been without industry or enterprise; labor has been compulsory; and although society is improving, it is still with few attractions. A few years must witness a great revolution; the idle, ignorant, worthless and shameless must die or emigrate, and their places will be filled by men who will cover the land with beautiful homes.

When we consider, first, the vast country to be supplied with the mineral products of this State, without the least burden of inter-State taxation; second, the knowledge of agriculture now sufficiently prevailing to prevent further exhaustion of soil, and sufficient to bring the larger portion, now in a fresh state, to one of high fertility; and, third, that Missouri has 7,000 more square miles, or 4,480,000 more acres than England and Wales combined, we may safely predict that the future destiny of this State is to rise to a position as commanding as that which England now occupies. There are several other States of which a similar prediction may be made. England has 50,922 and Wales 7,389 square miles, total, 58,311. Ireland has about 30,000 square miles. Scotland, including all its islands, 29,000 square miles.

KANSAS.

Square miles, 81,318, or 52,043,120 acres. Population, 250,000.

The eastern part of this State contains the principal settlements, it is about two hundred miles square, and it is similar in many respects to the western half of Northern Missouri. There are many streams with wooded bottoms, but the prairies are so large that timber is not plentiful, and there are coal, marble and gypsum, and salt springs so valuable as to be reserved by the State, as is the case in New York. The Kaw river comes from the west; in four hundred miles it has a heavy fall, and the whole country generally slopes to the Missouri river. The idea a stranger will have is of great elevation. None of the rest of the prairie States has so much stone, it crops out in innumerable places; it is easily worked, and is largely used for fencing. Only in low or wet ground is the soil black, elsewhere it has the reddish purple hue; much of it, evidently, is composed of decayed limestone, and it is from two to four feet deep. The surface presents a succession of long majestic swells, or lofty mounds, singly, in pairs or groups, every part of which is covered with grass, even upon the rounded summit. On the high Missouri hills, the soil is frequently very fertile. So many and so commanding are the views, that Kansas seems to look out upon the world, and the imaginative traveler will fancy that the country has a vast and unknown antiquity. When the humble home of the pioneer is built of stone from an adjacent ledge, one might think it a locality where long ago a city had turned to dust. It has been objected that Kansas is subject to terrible droughts, but during the last few years it seems most afflicted with descending rains and sweeping floods. The plague of grasshoppers is more serious, but they have left abundant harvests. The State was born amidst skirmish and the terrors of war. These are past; emigration is at a flood tide, and improvements are on every hand.

The western part, also about two hundred miles square, has not been supposed favorable for agriculture, owing to a want of rain and an alleged infertility of the soil. It is acknowledged that the rain-fall is small, but grass is abundant, and is as fattening as grain. Even now, while excavation is going on for the Union Pacific Railroad, three hundred miles from the Missouri, the soil exceeds two feet in depth, and this is on the border of what has been called the American Desert. When a people below the average of the inhabitants of the North settle and develop any country, they add twenty per cent. to its supposed value. When an average people settle it, they add one hundred per cent. The greatest obstacle in settling a new country lies in a want of intelligence and enterprise in the first proprietors of the soil.

NEBRASKA.

Square miles, 75,795, or 48,508,800 acres. Population, 150,000.

This is one of the newest of the States. To some extent it

is a continuation of Iowa, but the prairies soon merge more positively into the great plains, and two hundred miles west the climate begins to assume an oriental character. In the vicinity of Omaha, improvements are rapid, as well as in many of the valleys. There are many choice localities. At present the soil is said to excel Iowa for wheat, while it must be equally good for other products, that is, as far west as the 98th meridian. Beyond that a new system of farming must arise, when experiments will give more knowledge of what shall be required.

ARKANSAS.

Square miles, 52,198, or 38,407,720 acres. Population, 500,000.

About fifteen miles above the mouth of the Ohio, stretches from east to west a ridge of high land with a limestone base. It is to be traced across the Ohio, thence across the Mississippi, very near the towns of Caledonia and Commerce. It is called the Grand Chain. Geologists suppose that in a former condition of the world a tremendous cataract poured over this ledge into an arm of the sea, which has gradually filled up and now forms the valley of the Lower Mississippi. This arm of the sea was confined by bluffs, either on the present bank of the river or a few miles east of it, and by hills from fifteen to one hundred miles to the west. The States lying east of the Lower Mississippi cannot be said to lie in the Mississippi Valley, except so far as their tributaries are concerned, nor do they present any character of an alluvial country. The eastern part of Arkansas, occupying the supposed arm of the sea, is decidedly alluvial, and it may be said to be a region not yet made, for it is composed either of vast swamps or of bottoms subject to overflow. These swamps vary from cane-brakes and cypress swamps to stagnant bayous. It is considered that in some seasons of high floods the backwater of the Mississippi and of its tributaries finds its way across the country and even across Red river into the Gulf of Mexico by interior bayous. Beyond this the high land commences, and there is a gradual elevation terminating in the Ozark mountains, and beyond these commence the broad plains which extend into Kansas and New Mexico. Large portions of the mountain or hilly regions of Arkansas are rich in lead, iron and gypsum, but at present very little is known, and it may be said to be less critically explored than Montana and Idaho. The climate is mild, though the southwest part is subject to those terrible winds, the northerners. Every variety of fruit grows with great luxuriance, and the first that was heard of the celebrated Catawba grape was that it grew here in wild luxuriance. The soil is sufficiently rich, and when industry shall be reorganized and natural advantages are improved, it will afford all the comforts that men can desire. The first settlers in a warm climate labor under great disadvantages. It is possible to live in houses which imperfectly keep out the wind and cold; what is possible, and what shall bring temporary ease, man always will adopt. The development of countries where the hidden energies of man are not aroused by frost and snows is reserved for the last and the highest triumphs of the human race.

KENTUCKY.

Square miles, 37,680, or 24,105,200 acres. Population, 1,300,000.

The alluvial or bottom lands bordering on the tributaries of the several rivers which run eastward into the Mississippi, must comprise many millions of acres. As a general thing a bluff, or at least a hill, comes close to the stream on one side, while the bottom is opposite. A few miles above and below, the bluffs and bottoms change places. Still there are exceptions, for sometimes high ground recedes to quite a distance on each side, presenting a beautiful and rich country. From February to June these bottoms are subject to overflow, and immense damage has often followed; still, this is by no means the case every year. These valleys often branch out along small streams and extend up into the country, sometimes spreading into magnificent stretches; and if there is a limestone base, as there frequently is, the value of the land can be scarcely over estimated. In the valleys of the larger rivers, such as the Cumberland and the Tennessee, the farms are generally laid out so as to front the river, and they run back and include more or less rough and unproductive land.

The Kentucky river runs through the centre of the State, mostly a limestone region, and often between high rocky bluffs. On the upper waters is the Blue Grass region, which is due to a naturally fertile soil and to care and attention; and, as a consequence, some of the finest stock, both of cattle and horses, has been produced, giving the people great prosperity. The Green river, flowing through the southern portion, is navigable a portion of the year; but since the day of railroads only rivers affording a plenty of water are valued for this purpose. This is the Green River country, also very fertile, but a portion of it, some twenty years ago, was supposed to be so very poor as to be worthless. It had the general name of "barrens." In many respects it resembled the barrens of South Jersey, particularly the Vineland tract. But after awhile the soil grew better, more through cultivation than the application of manure, for it was scarcely ever used, and it became highly fertile. This uncommon circumstance was undoubtedly owing to some latent fertilizer, perhaps partly decayed limestone which was decomposed by cultivation. I have seen another similar region, though more limited, in Northern Ohio, which was thought entirely barren, but which has now become extremely rich. Kentucky is an old State, and some of the farms are held at very high prices. The land yet unimproved is either subject to overflow or is of inferior quality.

The Cumberland river passes through Kentucky into Tennessee, and, making a great bend, returns again to the State and has its head in the Cumberland mountains. Its length is about six hundred miles, and it is navigable to Nashville, three hundred and fifty miles, for first-class steamers. The mineral wealth along this river and elsewhere in Middle Tennessee is considerable, and along both the Cumberland and Tennessee are many iron works. The scenery of these rivers is of the most pleasing and majestic character; sometimes improvements are good, but often they are indifferent. The width and depth of these streams remain undiminished for hundreds of miles. Unless colored during a freshet, the water is as clear as a mountain spring.

The Cumberland flows down out of Kentucky into Tennessee, Mississippi, Alabama and Georgia, then back into Tennessee, forming an outer circle to itself, so that its length is double, or 1,200 miles; and for the volume of water it is by far the largest navigable river in America. Rising among the mountains of East Tennessee and Western North Carolina, it presents all the characteristics of a river flowing from a high latitude to a low one, although its mouth is considerably north of its source.

TENNESSEE.

Square miles, 45,600, or 29,184,000 acres. Population, 1,115,000.

Most of the tillable land of West Tennessee is under cultivation, and a part is exhausted. Still, there are large tracts, inclining to be wet, lying in valleys along the various streams which are almost swamps, sometimes overflowed, of great extent and of unsurpassed fertility, which can be bought cheap, but one must be prepared to meet malarious attacks, producing "chills," or a species of the fever and ague. The people here are not remarkable for intelligence or enterprise, and their influence would not be great in refined society, though there are exceptions. Middle Tennessee has a more enduring soil, and near Nashville are some rural scenes, in which green meadows remind one of favored regions of the North. All this part has been settled many years. East Tennessee is noticeable for an elevated plateau in the midst of the Cumberland mountains, about thirty miles wide, and extending across the State into Georgia. The height is about two thousand feet, giving an average temperature in summer of sixty-five degrees, and in winter of forty-five. The air is dry and balmy, entirely free from malaria, and it is perhaps the most healthful region in the United States. Although the people live in a manner not supposed most favorable to health, and in houses excessively ventilated, still many live to an extreme age. With a soil of moderate fertility, grass grows well, and timothy is an important crop, while wheat of superior quality is produced. Fruit does remarkably well, and the pest of the fruit-grower, the curculio, is as yet unknown. Large tracts of the best land can be bought at a low price, and improved farms at from eight to fifteen dollars an acre. Men from the North with money and intelligence will be heartily welcomed, in provincial accents, and a little money will go far. There is one railroad connecting with the world. Still, this table land is isolated, and those who depend upon the refinement and intelligence of their neighbors for their happiness, will feel ill at ease among these unaffected people. And yet, surrounded by the honest and loyal, by the most sublime scenery, and where mountain streams are so common that they can be used to churn the butter or to rock the cradle, a man who feels himself as good as, or even better than anbody else, and who delights in developing the gifts nature gave him by his own efforts, will enjoy himself and will grow in intellect and grace in this far-off region of East Tennessee.

MISSISSIPPI.

Square miles, 47,156, or 30,179,840 acres. Population. 800,000.

The western part of this State is low, and a portion between the Yazoo and the Mississippi, one hundred and seventy miles long and fifty wide, is more or less subject to overflow. The southern region, along the Gulf, one hundred miles wide, is sandy and low, and interspersed with cypress swamps and cane-brakes, with some hills. There are a vast number of fine plantations along the Pearl and Big Black rivers. The northeastern part, called the Tombigbee country, is prairie, with a few stagnant pools and sluggish streams, but it is a very productive region. This State has immense resources; corn is produced at little cost, and cotton has yielded in enormous quantities. Much land is in a state of nature, but many first-class plantations can be bought for nearly what the improvements cost. At present some things would not be agreeable to a certain class of immigrants, but the time cannot be remote when Mississippi and all the rest of the Southern States will enter upon a career of unexampled prosperity.

LOUISIANA.

Square miles, 41,346, or 26,461,440 acres. Population, 720,000.

A large part of Louisiana is composed of the Delta of the great river, which commences with the outlet of Atchafalaya, nearly opposite a corner of the State of Mississippi, and more than two hundred miles from the Gulf. Within this delta is considerable tillable land, but naturally it is subject to overflow, to prevent which, levees have been built. Still, large areas are covered with lakes, cane-brakes or bayous. New Orleans is one hundred and five miles from the Gulf. Below the city are extensive orange orchards. The coast westward to the Sabine or State line is marshy, and overflowed by high tides, and northward and adjoining are vast plains with a slight elevation above the sea. The other half of the State, to the northwest, is considerably broken, but the hills do not extend to a hight of two hundred feet, and it is covered with vast forests of pitch-pine. The soil is not fertile. On the Red river and its bayous the soil is very rich, and here vast quantities of cotton have been produced, while on the banks of the Mississippi, which go by the general name of "coast," vast plantations before the war were exclusively devoted to the production of sugar, the quality of which has never been excelled. Generally, at no great distance in the rear of these river plantations, are extensive swamps and cane-brakes. Wherever this alluvial soil is cultivated it is highly productive, and it may be said that it will retain its fertility forever. Except when the yellow fever visits the country, the people have excellent health; but it is argued, with some reason, that this scourge can be averted by proper measures. The scenery from Grand Gulf to New Orleans, a distance of three hundred miles, is the most beautiful and imposing in North America.

LAND OFFICES.

To get correct information regarding Government lands, application should be made to the Land Offices, and for a small sum plots of unentered lots should be obtained. In addition, at the several county seats are land agents well posted. The location of the Land Offices is as follows: In *Ohio*, Chillicothe; *Indiana*, Indianapolis; *Illinois*, Springfield; *Michigan*, Detroit, East Saginaw, Ionia, Marquette, Traverse City; *Iowa*, Des Moines, Council Bluffs, Ft. Dodge, Sioux City; *Wisconsin*, Menesha, Falls St. Croix, Steven's Point, La Crosse, Bayfield, Eau Claire; *Minnesota*, Taylor's Falls, St. Cloud, Winnebago, Greenleaf, St. Peters, Du Luth; *Nebraska*, Omaha, Brownville, Nebraska City, Dakota City; *Kansas*, Topeka, Humboldt, Junction City; *Missouri*, Boonville, Ireton; *Arkansas*, Little Rock, Clarksville, Washington; *Mississippi*, Jackson; *Louisiana*, New Orleans, Natchitoches and Monroe.

NEW PHYSIOGNOMY.

KNOW THYSELF

BY S. R. WELLS, 389 B'WAY, N. Y.

SELECTIONS FROM NEW PHYSIOGNOMY.

"O wad some power the giftie gie us,
To see oursels as ithers see us!
It wad frae mony a blunder free us,
An' foolish notion."—BURNS.

Fig. 976.—HENRY W. LONGFELLOW.

Fig. 982.—ROSA BONHEUR.

THE following selections and specimen pages from "New Physiognomy," are intended as an exposition of the general tenor of this admirable work; which has received so warm a welcome from the press all over the country. In his preface, the author says:

"We know how widely mankind differ in looks, in opinion, and in character, and it has been our study to discover the *causes* of these differences. We find them in organization. As we look, so we feel, so we act, and so we are. But we may *direct* and *control* even our *thoughts*, our *feelings*, and our *acts*, and thus, to some extent—by the aid of grace—become what we will. We can be temperate or intemperate; virtuous or vicious; hopeful or desponding; generous or selfish; believing or skeptical; prayerful or profane. We are free to choose what course we will pursue, and our bodies, our brains, and our features, readily adapt themselves, and clearly indicate the lives we lead and the characters we form.

"It has been our aim to present this subject in a practical manner, basing all our inferences on well-established principles, claiming nothing but what is clearly within the lines of probability, and illustrating, when possible, every statement. Previous authors have been carefully studied, and whatever of value could be gleaned we have systematized and incorporated, adding our own recent discoveries. For more than twenty years we have been engaged in the study of man, and in "character-reading" among the people of various races, tribes and nations, enabling us to classify the different forms of body, brain, and face, and reduce to METHOD the processes by which character may be determined. Hitherto, but partial observations have been made, and of course only partial results obtained. We look on man as a whole—made up of parts, and to be studied as a whole, *with all the parts combined*."

Fig. 749.—A MISER.

Fig. 750.—A LIBERAL.

PHYSIOGNOMY OF INSANITY AND IDIOCY.

Fig. 434.—DESERTED.

Fig. 435.—MALICE.

The chapters on insanity and idiocy, are two of the most interesting in the work. Not only are the symptoms and outward appearances analyzed, but Mr. Wells endeavors to trace these abnormal conditions to their sources. He treats of the varieties, the causes, the treatment, the prevention, and the physiognomical signs of insanity, illustrated amply by portraits and accounts of celebrated maniacs and idiots. Idiocy — to which chapter twenty-one is wholly devoted —gives the causes, the education and the signs of idiocy; and is one of the best practical treatises on that subject in the language. The brain being a subject to which the author has devoted his attention for a lifetime, stamp these chapters as pre-eminently valuable and reliable.

Fig. 434, which represents a woman who became insane on account of the unfaithfulness of her lover, who deserted her, shows the lively, brilliant eyes mentioned by Dr. Laurent. She still loves; and in her mental aberration adorns her disheveled hair with flowers, and with parted lips and "hungry devouring glances" awaits the coming of her heart's idol, whom she never ceases to expect.

"Intense thought, habitual reflection, and searching inquiry of any kind cause a drawing down of the eyebrows, as shown in Chapter XIII. (p. 249). Persons who have become insane through hard study or the too close application of the mind to a particular subject will exhibit this characteristic.

Fig. 436—RAVING.

Fig. 440.—LOVE-SICK.

"In Fig. 435 the eyes gleam with some relentless purpose of vengeance. Such a character as the one here represented is dangerous in his alienation; for he combines the cunning of the fox with the ferocity of the tiger. Fig. 436 is a woman of the Cassandra order. The eyes, abandoned to the action of the involuntary muscles (see Chapter XIII., p. 233), are rolled upward with a wild look which is indescribable. She is giving utterance to what she deems prophetic warnings of the most solemn and awful character."

ETHNOLOGY, OR TYPES OF MANKIND.

Fig. 476.—THE CAUCASIAN RACE.

ETHNOLOGY is a subject upon which has been comparatively little studied. The field is a wide one for inquiry and research, and chapters on "The Races Classified," "The Caucasian, Mongolian, Malayan, American and Ethiopian Races," "National Types," "Ancient Types," are invaluable. No where else can there be found such a complete digest of the subject. In his Introduction to these chapters the author says:

"The question of race will be found to resolve itself into that of *organization*, and this determines and is indicated by *configuration*. If we desire to ascertain to what race an individual, a tribe, or a nation may belong, we must study the character of that individual, tribe, or nation through its signs in the physical system. Would we determine the status of a race or a nation, we shall find the measure of its mental power in the size and quality of its average brain, and the index of its civilization and culture in its prevailing style of face and figure.

"In so new a field of inquiry as the one which we are now entering, we can not hope to push our explorations into every part, or to investigate thoroughly every point that we may touch upon. We are, to some extent, pioneers, and as such shall do as well as we can the work assigned to us, trusting that those who follow will find their progress facilitated by our labors."

Then follows an agreeable essay on "National Types." The principal nations and tribes composed in the various races, are described in detail, with a "view to show how, in each, the common type is modified without being lost, and how, in all, configuration and character correspond."

"We shall adopt here, as best known and most generally received, though not perhaps most scientific, the classification of Blumenbach. This arrangement will serve the purposes we have in view as well as any other yet proposed, and whether it be accepted by the reader or set aside in favor of a more recent one, the value of the facts we shall here throw together will not be lessened.

Fig. 499.—THE AMERICAN RACE.

PHYSIOGNOMY OF CLASSES.

Figs. 716 to 725.

NOT only does the author divide the human family into the five great races and "National types," but he sub-divides them into "classes," presenting us with groups of distinguished Divines, Pugilists, Warriors, Surgeons, Inventors, Philosophers, Statesmen, Orators, Actors, Poets, Musicians and Artists, etc. Of the poets, he says:
"One of the essential physical qualities of a poet is a susceptible mental temperament. This must be of a clear and fine—even of an exquisite—tone, to insure perfection in the art. There are all degrees of poets, from the lowest to the highest, just as there are different classes of musicians, painters, sculptors, etc.; but to excel, and to inscribe one's name on the roll of great bards, one must be not only every inch a man, but must have 'genius' as well. It has been said by an ancient author, *poeta nascitur, non fit* '—the poet is born, not made; yet we maintain that every well-organized human being should be able to write poetry, just as he should be able to make music, or invent and use tools; for has not nature given to each a like number of faculties, the same in function, and differing only in degree and combination?"

THE TWO PATHS.

The following contrasts, illustrative of the effects of a right or a wrong course of life upon an individual, are submitted to our readers. They tell their own story. In the one case we see a child, as it were, develop into true manhood; in the other, into the miserable inebriate or the raving maniac.

Fig. 761. Fig. 762.

Two boys (figs. 761 and 762) start out in life with fair advantages and buoyant hopes. With them it remains to choose in what direction they shall steer their barks. Fig. 763 represents the first as having chosen the way of righteousness,

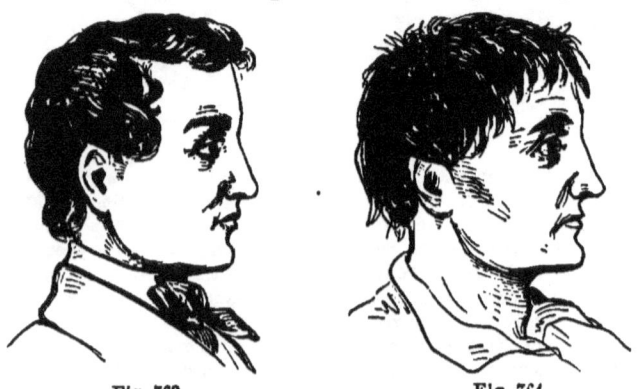

Fig. 763. Fig. 764.

the upward path. He lives temperately, forms worthy associations, attends the Sunday-school, strives to improve his mind with useful knowledge, and is regarded in the community as a young man of excellent character and promise.

CONTRASTED FACES.

In fig. 764, on the contrary, the other boy is represented as having unwisely chosen the downward course, thinking he will enjoy himself and not submit to what he considers the strait jacket of moral discipline. He becomes coarse and

Fig. 765.　　　　　　　　Fig. 766.

rough in feature, slovenly in his dress; he smokes and chews, drinks, gambles, attends the race-course, spends his nights at the play-house or the tavern, disregards all parental authority and admonition, and develops into the full-grown rowdy,

Fig. 767.　　　　　　　　Fig. 768.

and as such he sets at naught all domestic ties and obligations, leaving his wife and children to beg, starve, or eke out a wretched subsistence by the most exhausting and inadequately

CHARACTER-READING.

THE ARTIST AND THE WOMAN OF THE WORLD.

In Rosa Bonheur we see a child of inborn genius, inherited from an artist-parent, developed by necessity, and perfected by persevering exertion. From a love of them, her artistic

Fig. 982.—ROSA BONHEUR.*

Fig. 983.—THEODOSIA BURR.†

sympathies seem to fix upon horses, cattle, sheep, etc., and if she does not take on their natures, she portrayed them on can-

---

* Rosa Bonheur was born at Bordeaux, France, May 22, 1822; her father, Raymond Bonheur, an artist by profession, and in humble circumstances. In 1829 he removed to Paris, where he put Rosa in a boarding-school. There her poverty, however, was a constant source of annoyance to her very sensitive nature, as it provoked the sneers of her wealthier school associates. On that account she did not remain long at school, but being taken home was instructed by her father in drawing. From childhood she exhibited an intuitive love of art, her inclinations tending toward the representation of domestic animals. Making these her special study, she soon excelled in their portraiture. The picture which has obtained for Miss Bonheur a world-wide reputation is "Le Marché aux Chevaux," otherwise known as the "Horse Fair." It is now in the hands of a gentleman residing in New Jersey. Miss Bonheur at present resides in Paris, industriously pursuing her art. The great feature of her works is faithfulness to nature and boldness of design.

† Theodosia Burr Allston, the daughter and only child of Aaron Burr, was born at Albany, N. Y., in 1783. Her father tenderly loved her and spared no pains in her education. It is said that "in solid and elegant accomplishments she was very far superior to the ladies of her time." She married Joseph Allston, who was in 1812 Governor of South Carolina. She was lost in the schooner Patriot, on the voyage from Charleston to New York, January, 1813.

was to the life. One almost fancies he can hear her pictured beasts breathe, so naturally are they drawn. Hers is a beautiful face, if somewhat masculine; it is not coarse; if strongly marked, it is still womanly. The forehead is beautifully shaped, the eyes well placed and expressive, the nose handsome, and the lips exquisite. The chin shows chaste affection, with nothing of the sensual or voluptuous; indeed, it is rarely we meet with more natural feminine attractiveness than in this artist-woman, and we dismiss her from our considerations with the happiest impressions.

There is character in the head and face of Theodosia Burr. See how high the brain is in the crown! She was emphatically her father's daughter. There is great dignity, pride, will, and sense of character indicated in her physiognomy. Nothing but religious influences could subdue such a nature. There is something voluptuous in the lip, cheek, and chin. The affections were evidently ardent and strong. Such a woman would scarcely be content in private and domestic life, but would crave a high and even stately position where her pride and love of display could be gratified. There was nothing of "your humble servant" in this person. Educated as she was, she could be lady-like and refined. Had she been uneducated, there would have been much willfulness, obstinacy, and perhaps sensuality exhibited. Analyzed, her head and face exhibit the following organs conspicuously developed—Firmness, Approbativeness, Caution, Ideality, Sublimity, Conscientiousness, Language, Agreeableness, and those of the back-head generally.

Rosa Bonheur shows a higher forehead, a more meditative disposition of mind than her associate; her head is broader in Constructiveness, Sublimity, Ideality, and the crown, and more prominent in the region of Benevolence, Veneration, and Spirituality than that of the latter. In a social point of view, Theodosia shows more ardent feeling, more intensity of emotion. The latter had more sympathy for general society, entered enthusiastically into its enjoyments; the former finds her highest enjoyment in a life of serene retirement with a limited circle of friends and at her easel.

COMPARATIVE PHYSIOGNOMY—PORTRAITS OF A LION AND MAN.

"What They Say."—Notices of the Press.

Everybody is influenced in forming opinions by what others say. And it requires everybody to know everything and to do everything. A great book, like a great public work, is, or should be, the culmination of all past knowledge in that interest. Webster's Dictionary contains the gist of all preceding dictionaries. The electric telegraph was suggested centuries ago, and all mankind, dead and living, have contributed to its establishment. So the newspaper press throughout the world may be said to echo the voice of the people. The *Philadelphia Press* says:

Mr. Wells has put the thought, the practical experience, the close observation, and the professional collection of a life-time into this important physiological work. He treats, as Lavater did, of Physiognomy, shows its harmony with Phrenology, and explains, to elucidate both sciences, the whole structure of the human body. He treats of temperaments, and contrasts the separate features of various human races, showing also how character is affected by climate. Very curious, too, are his illustrations of comparative Physiognomy, showing the animal types of the human race. The price of the work is $5.

A familiar chapter on Phrenology is introduced, and then follows one on the anatomy of the face, with a close analysis of each feature. First, the chin. No one will dispute Mr. Wells as to the infinite variety of chins; but we are sure many will be startled to hear that this unpretending terminus of the face has been quietly telling their love secrets. The jaws and teeth also tell their own tales of character. "The closest mouth can hide no secrets from the physiognomist."—*The Anti-Slavery Standard.*

The treatise of Mr. Wells, which is admirably printed and profusely illustrated, is probably the most complete hand-book upon the subject in the language. It contains a synopsis of the history of Physiognomy, with notices of all the different systems which have been promulgated, and critical examinations of the eyes, the noses, the mouths, the ears, and the brows of many distinguished and notorious characters.—*New York Tribune.*

It contains a treatise on every feature and whatever indicates peculiarity of character, the knowledge of which requires appropriate education to bring into subjugation and be made to answer a good end, without which it would mar and injure the pleasures of life. All who can afford to possess this compendium will have value received for the expense.—*New York Christian Intelligencer.*

It is a digest of Ethnology, it gives us the symptomatology of insanity, it treats of Physiology and Hygiene, and, incidentally, of Zoology. The chapter on the grades of intelligence is instructive, and that on comparative Physiognomy is exceedingly entertaining.—*American Educational Monthly.*

There are very few men or women who do not, consciously or unconsciously, practice Physiognomy every day of their lives. They may ridicule the idea that the shape of a man's head, the configuration of his nose, or the appearance of his eyes, furnish any guide to an estimate of his character or disposition, and yet the man of business will refuse an applicant employment because his glance is restless and uneasy instead of firm and decided; and every lady will quietly but quickly form her judgment regarding the gentleman who may be presented to her at an evening party.—*New York Times.*

RESEMBLANCE BETWEEN THE FOX AND MAN ILLUSTRATED.

However some may be disposed to sneer at the claims of Physiognomy to rank among sciences, the most persistent of them will guage much of his action in his intercourse with his fellow-men by facial signs. That certain facial signs indicate peculiarities of character can scarcely be doubted. Mr. Wells records the result of observations of others as well as his own; does full justice, even where he differs from them, to the views of his predecessors, and with great industry and faithfulness to facts, builds up his system. He exhausts the subject and its cognate branches, and displays a masterly power of analysis and generalization. It is an important volume, and deserving of careful study.—*New York Courier.*

The work is thorough, practical, and comprehensive. All that is known on the subject is systematized, explained, illustrated, and applied. A chapter is devoted to Graphomancy, or character as revealed in handwriting. Taken as a whole, it is the most complete and reliable work on the subject we have ever examined, notwithstanding that we claim an intimate acquaintance with Lavater's work on the same subject.—*The Northwest.*

It is a voluminous and very comprehensive work, taking the student by a thousand paths to a conclusion as to its entire correctness of theory, demonstrated by multitudes of the aptest illustrations. It is very entertaining and instructive, telling the reader in little of great things he should further investigate.—*Boston Gazette.*

As far as the study of the face can be reduced to a science, Mr. Wells has succeeded beyond any other writer or delineator of character. His analysis of the different forms of faces, as indicating character, in the expression of the eyes, ears, nose, lips, mouth, head, hair, eyebrows, hands, feet, chin, neck, teeth, jaws, cheeks, skin, complexion, the laugh, the walk, the shaking of hands, dress, is fully illustrated by living and dead characters, besides numerous outlines to guide and instruct the reader. Ethnology is fully treated by illustrations of the different types of the human race, and presented in a pleasing and instructive form.—*Milledgeville (Georgia) Recorder.*

It seems quite natural to expect that the various features of our bodies should express the qualities and powers of which we are possessed. In all ages the eye has been regarded as an index to the soul, consequently it is a popular mode of expressing the qualities of another to say that such a one has the eye of an eagle, a lion, or a cat. When we think of a people of one country as distinguished by its high cheek-bones, and another by its lengthened nose, and another by its thin or thick lips, and how each country as a whole has a mental constitution corresponding to its physical development, we see reason for believing in the science of Physiognomy, and how that which is true of nations must be more or less true of individuals. Price $5, $8, or $10.—*Scottish American.*

The illustrations constitute the most essential part of a work like this. This is especially evident in the chapter on "Comparative Physiognomy," in which the resemblance between certain classes of men and corresponding animals is strikingly exhibited in the cuts.—*Methodist.*

The author properly considers Physiognomy as the outward expression of the inner man; it shows race, class, original inclinations, temperament, and also the effects of association and education. Close observation and long practice have given him accuracy in drawing conclusions from the peculiarities of the human countenance, and he has reduced his experience to a system, which is amply set forth in this volume.—*Philadelphia Times.*

Among those who have contributed to it in this country, the author of this book is honorably distinguished, and we feel pleasure in bearing testimony to the conscientiousness and ability with which he has executed the laborious task he imposed upon himself.—*N. Y. Herald.*

The principles sought to be laid down in this work are made sufficiently plain to the dullest comprehension, while they are elucidated still more clearly by the aid of over one thousand fine illustrations. The work is got up in the elegant style peculiar to this house, and we regard it as a valuable contribution to a science that is yet is but in its infancy.—*Jersey C. Times.*

"NEW PHYSIOGNOMY" TESTIMONIALS.

THE most complete hand-book of Physiognomy in the language.—*N. Y. Tribune.*

It is really a complete encyclopædia of the subject.—*N. Y. Gospel of Health.*

It will form a text-book for Physiognomists and Phrenologists; and serves to mark the progress these studies have made.—*N. Y. Herald.*

By far the best work ever written on this subject. It cannot be read without instruction and profit, and its suggestions are of great value.—*Chr. Inquirer.*

It is worthy of very high praise. To read such a kindly book, puts one in a good humor.—*New York Independent.*

Is a work of science, art and literature, whose purity of tone will commend it to all classes of readers.—*Wide World.*

All who can afford to possess this compendium, will have value received for the expense.—*N. Y. Christian Intelligencer.*

Our extracts last week from this popular work, proved so acceptable that we have been induced to extend our approbation to some kindred topics.—*Home Journal.*

This exhaustive and admirable work defines Physiognomy and shows its benefits. It ought to find its way to every private and public library in the land.—*Herald of Health.*

Take such a volume as this, and every one must acknowledge that Physiognomy opens a wide field for interesting investigation.—*New York Daily Times.*

A work of great value. We particularly recommend it to artists.—*Philadelph. Press.*

We view it as a worthy addition to our library.—*American Educational Monthly.*

We cannot help treasuring the book as a highly valuable repository of practical wisdom, and of vast use to us in our course of life and action.—*N. Y. Jewish Messenger.*

The best work now extant upon the subject of Physiognomy, and that it is the most interesting one of the kind ever published, cannot be questioned.—*Chicago Even. Jour.*

It will take a place among the curiosities of literature and science.—*Palladium.*

This work is well worthy of a lengthened notice; but our space enables us to do little more than to commend it to the careful perusal of our readers.—*Scottish American.*

This the largest, and undoubtedly by far the best and most comprehensive work upon the subject of Physiognomy ever published.—*Chicago Prairie Farmer.*

No one can read the book with any degree of attention, without deriving much benefit from it, and its thorough study would furnish one with a knowledge of the signs of character indispensable to success in any walk of life.—*New Jerusalem Messenger.*

NEW PHYSIOGNOMY is a voluminous and very comprehensive work, taking the student by a thousand paths to a conclusion as to its entire correctness of theory, demonstrated by multitudes of the aptest illustrations.—*Boston Gazette.*

Those who already love to study character, will find this work a delightful companion; those who desire to acquire an insight into humanity by its outward signs, cannot find a better guide than in the illustrated NEW PHYSIOGNOMY.—*Phil. Sunday Times.*

It covers the whole ground more thoroughly than any book before issued.—*The Field.*

The author has thoroughly popularized his language, and is at home in his subject. The volume is full of materials from which thoughts are generated.—*Cin. Inquirer.*

In this volume, Mr. Wells, with a very full mastery of his subject, and in very pleasant style, takes in all the methods of conjecturing character from external signs. The work abounds with suggestive and often very instructive statements. Its tendency is decidedly in favor of moral right. In its department, NEW PHYSIOGNOMY is, of course, a standard, coming from the standard quarter.—*Methodist Quarterly Review.*

PRICE, MUSLIN, $5; HEAVY CALF, $8; TURKEY MOROCCO, GILT, ELEGANT, $10.

Sent Prepaid by Post at Prices Annexed.

A LIST OF WORKS

PUBLISHED BY

SAMUEL R. WELLS, No. 389 BROADWAY, NEW YORK.

STANDARD WORKS ON PHRENOLOGY.

American Phrenological Journal and Life Illustrated.—Devoted to Ethnology, Physiology, Phrenology, Physiognomy, Psychology, Sociology, Biography, Education, Art, Literature, with Measures to Reform, Elevate and Improve Mankind Physically, Mentally and Spiritually. Edited by S. R. WELLS. Published monthly, in quarto form, at $3 a year, or 30 cents a number. It may be termed the standard authority in all matters pertaining to Phrenology and the Science of Man. It is beautifully illustrated. See Prospectus.

Constitution of Man; Considered in Relation to External Objects. By GEORGE COMBE. The only authorized American Edition. With Twenty Engravings, and a Portrait of the Author. 12mo. 436 pp. Muslin. Price, $1 75.

The "Constitution of Man" is a work with which every teacher and every pupil should be acquainted. It contains a perfect mine of sound wisdom and enlightened philosophy; and a faithful study of its invaluable lessons would save many a promising youth from a premature grave.—*Journal of Education, Albany, N. Y.*

Defence of Phrenology; Containing an Essay on the Nature and Value of Phrenological Evidence: A Vindication of Phrenology against the Attack of its opponents, and a View of the Facts relied on by Phrenologists as proof that the Cerebellum is the seat of the reproductive instinct. By ANDREW BOARDMAN, M. D. 12mo, 222 pp. Muslin. Price, $1 50.

These Essays are a refutation of attacks on Phrenology, including "Select Discourses on the Functions of the Nervous System, in Opposition to Phrenology, Materialism and Atheism. One of the best defences of Phrenology ever written.

Education: Its Elementary Principles founded on the Nature of Man. By J. G. SPURZHEIM, M. D. With an Appendix by S. R. WELLS, containing a Description of the Temperaments, and a Brief Analysis of the Phrenological Faculties. Twelfth American Edition. 1 vol. 12mo, 334 pp. Illustrated. Price, $1 50.

It is full of sound doctrine and practical wisdom. Every page is pregnant with instruction of solemn import; and we would that it were the text-book, the great and sovereign guide, of every male and female in the country with whom rests the responsibility of rearing or educating a child.—*Boston Medical and Surgical Journal.*

Education and Self-Improvement Complete; Comprising "Physiology—Animal and Mental"—"Self-Culture and Perfection of Character," "Memory and Intellectual Improvement." One large vol. Illus. Muslin, $4.

This book comprises the whole of Mr. Fowler's series of popular works on the application of Phrenology to "Education and Self-Improvement."

Lectures on Phrenology.—By GEORGE COMBE. With Notes. An Essay on the Phrenological Mode of Investigation, and an Historical Sketch. By ANDREW BOARDMAN, M. D. 1 vol. 12mo, 391 pages. Muslin, $1 75.

These are the reported lectures on Phrenology delivered by George Combe in America in 1839, and have been approved as to their essential correctness by the author. The work includes the application of Phrenology to the present and prospective condition of the United States, and constitutes a course of Phrenological instruction.

Matrimony; Or, Phrenology and Physiology applied to the Selection of Congenial Companions for Life, including Directions to the Married for living together Affectionately and Happily. Thirty-Fourth Edition. Price, 50 cents.

A scientific expositor of the laws of man's social and matrimonial constitution; exposing the evils of their violation, showing what organizations and phrenological developments naturally assimilate and harmonize.

Memory and Intellectual Improvement, applied to Self-Educational and Juvenile Instruction. Twenty-Fifth Edition. 12mo. Muslin, $1 50.

This is the third and last of Mr. Fowler's series of popular works on the application of Phrenology to "Education and Self-Improvement." This volume is devoted to the education and development of the Intellect; how to cultivate the Memory; the education of the young; and embodies directions as to how we may educate OURSELVES.

Mental Science. Lectures on, according to the Philosophy of Phrenology. Delivered before the Anthropological Society of the Western Liberal Institute of Marietta, Ohio. By Rev. G. S. WEAVER. 12mo, 225 pp. Illustrated, $1 50.

This is a most valuable acquisition to phrenological literature. It is instructive and beneficial, and should be made accessible to all youth. Its philosophy is the precept of the human soul's wisdom. Its morality is obedience to all divine law, written or unwritten. Its religion is the spirit-utterings of devout and faithful love. It aims at and contemplates humanity's good—the union of the human with the divine.

Phrenology Proved, Illustrated and Applied; Embracing an analysis of the Primary Mental Powers in their Various Degrees of Development, and location of the Phrenological Organs. Presenting some new and important remarks on the Temperaments, describing the Organs in Seven Different Degrees of Development: the mental phenomena produced by their combined action, and the location of the faculties, amply illustrated. By the Brothers FOWLER. Sixty-Second Edition. Enlarged and Improved. 12mo, 492 pp. Muslin, $1 75.

Self-Culture and Perfection of Character; Including the Management of Children and Youth. 1 vol. 12mo, 312 pp. Muslin, $1 75.

This is the second work in the series of Mr. Fowler's "Education and Self-Improvement Complete." "Self-made or never made," is the motto of the work which is devoted to moral improvement, or the proper cultivation and regulation of the affections and moral sentiments.

Self-Instructor in Phrenology and Physiology. New Illustrated. With over One Hundred Engravings, together with a Chart for the Recording of Phrenological Developments, for the use of Phrenologists. By the Brothers FOWLER. Muslin, 75 cents; Paper, 50 cents.

This is intended as a text-book, and is especially adapted to phrenological examiners, to be used as a chart, and for learners, in connection with the "Phrenological Bust."

Moral Philosophy. By GEORGE COMBE. Or, the Duties of Man considered in his Individual, Domestic and Social Capacities. Reprinted from the Edinburgh Edition. With the Author's latest corrections. 1 vol. 12mo, 334 pp. Muslin, $1 75.

This work appears in the form of Lectures delivered by the Author to an association formed by the industrious classes of Edinburgh; they created at the time considerable excitement. The course consisted of twenty consecutive lectures on Moral Philosophy, and are invaluable to students of Phrenology. Lecturers on Morality and the Natural Laws of Man. Address, SAMUEL R. WELLS, No. 389 Broadway, New York.

Miscellaneous Works on Phrenology.

Annuals of Phrenology and Physiognomy.—By S. R. Wells, Editor of the Phrenological Journal. One small yearly 12mo volume. For 1865, '66 and 1867. The three, containing over 150 illustrations, for 40 cents. For 1867, one small 12mo vol., 58 pp. Containing many portraits and biographies of distinguished personages, together with articles on "How to Study Phrenology," "Bashfulness, Diffidence, Stammering," etc., 20 cents. For 1868, 12mo, 70 pp. Containing an elaborate article on "The Marriage of Cousins," etc., etc., 25 cents.

Charts for Recording the Various Phrenological Developments. Designed for Phrenologists. By the Brothers Fowler. Price, only 10 cents.

Chart of Physiognomy Illustrated.—Designed for Framing, and for Lecturers. By S. R. Wells, Author of New Physiognomy. In map Form. Printed on fine paper. A good thing for learners. Price, 25 cents.

Domestic Life, Thoughts On; Or, Marriage Vindicated and Free Love Exposed. By Nelson Sizer. 12mo, 72 pp. Paper, 25 cents.

This is a work consisting of three valuable lectures, part of an extended course delivered in the city of Washington. The favor with which they were received, and the numerous requests for their publication, resulted in the present work.

Phrenology and the Scriptures.—Showing the Harmony existing between Phrenology and the Bible. By Rev. John Pierpont. Price 25 cents. "A full explanation of many passages of Scripture."—*New York Mirror.*

Phrenological Guide.—Designed for Students of their own Character. Twenty-Fifth Edition. Illustrated. 12mo, 54 pp. Paper, 25 cents.

Phrenological Specimens; For Societies and Private Cabinets. For Lecturers; including Casts of the Heads of most remarkable men of history. See our Descriptive Catalogue. Forty casts, not mailable, $35.

Phrenological Bust.—Showing the latest classification, and exact location of the Organs of the Brain, fully developed, designed for Learners. In this Bust, all the newly-discovered Organs are given. It is divided so as to show each individual Organ on one side; and all the groups—Social, Executive, Intellectual, and moral—properly classified, on the other side. It is now extensively used in England, Scotland and Ireland, and on the Continent of Europe, and is almost the only one in use here. There are two sizes—the largest near the size of life—is sold in Box, at $1 75. The smaller, which is not more than six inches high, and may be carried in the pocket, is only 75 cents. Not mailable.

Phrenology at Home.—How can I learn Phrenology? What books are best for me to read? Is it possible to acquire a knowledge of it without a teacher? These are questions put to us daily; and we may say in reply, that we have arranged a series of the best works, with a Bust, showing the exact location of all the Phrenological Organs, with such Illustrations and Definitions as to make the study simple and plain without the aid of a teacher. The cost for this "Student's Set," which embraces all that is requisite, is only $10. It may be sent by express, or as freight, safely boxed—not by mail—to any part of the world.

"Mirror of the Mind;" Or, Your Character from your Likeness. For particulars how to have pictures taken, inclose a prepaid envelope, directed to yourself, for answer. Address, Samuel R. Wells, No. 389 Broadway, New York.

Standard Work on Physiognomy.

New Physiognomy; Or, Signs of Character, as manifested through Temperament and External Forms, and especially in the "Human Face Divine." With more than One Thousand Illustrations. By S. R. WELLS. In three styles of binding. Price, in one 12mo volume, 768 pp., handsomely bound in muslin, $5; in heavy calf, marbled edges, $8; Turkey morocco, full gilt, $10.

This work systematizes and shows the scientific basis on which each claim rests. The "Signs of Character" are minutely elucidated, and so plainly stated as to render them available. The scope of the work is very broad, and the treatment of the subject thorough, and, so far as possible, exhaustive. Among the topics discussed are—"General Principles of Physiognomy;" "the Temperaments;" "General Forms" as Indicative of Character; "Signs of Character in the Features"—the Chin, the Lips, the Nose, the Eyes, the Cheeks, the Ears, the Neck, etc.; "The Hands and Feet;" "Signs of Character in Action,"—the Walk, the Voice, the Laugh, Shaking Hands, the Style of Dress, etc.; "Insanity;" "Idiocy;" "Effects of Climate;" "Ethnology;" "National Types;" "Physiognomy of Classes," with grouped portraits, including Divines, Orators, Statesmen, Warriors, Artists, Poets, Philosophers, Inventors, Pugilists, Surgeons, Discoverers, Actors, Musicians; "Transmitted Physiognomies;" "Love Signs;" "Grades of Intelligence;" "Comparative Physiognomy;" "Personal Improvement; or, How to be Beautiful;" "Handwriting;" "Studies from Lavater;" "Physiognomy Applied;" "Physiognomical Anecdotes," etc.

It is an Encyclopædia of biography, acquainting the reader with the career and character, in brief, of many great men and women of the past one thousand years, and of the present—such, for instance, as Aristotle, Julius Cæsar, Shakspeare, Washington, Napoleon, Franklin, Bancroft, Bryant, Longfellow, Barnes, Irving, Rosa Bonheur, Theodosia Burr, Cobden, Bright, Lawrence, Whately, Thackeray, Knox, Richelieu, Dickens, Victoria, Wesley, Carlyle, Motley, Mill, Spencer, Thompson, Alexander, etc.

Apparatus for Phrenological Lectures,

Phrenological Specimens, for the use of Lecturers, Societies, or for Private Cabinets. Forty Casts, not mailable. May be sent as freight. Price, $35.

These specimens were cast from living heads, and from skulls. They afford an excellent contrast, showing the organs of the brain, both large and small. Lecturers may here obtain a collection which affords the necessary means of illustration and comparison. This select cabinet is composed, in part, of the following:

John Quincy Adams, Aaron Burr, George Combe, Elihu Burritt, Col. Thomas H. Benton, Black Hawk, Henry Clay, Rev. Dr. Dodd, Thomas Addis Emmet, Clara Fisher, Dr. Gall, Rev. Sylvester Graham, M. D., Gosse, Gottfried, Harrawaukay, Joseph C. Neal, Napoleon Bonaparte, Sir Walter Scott, Voltaire, Hon. Silas Wright, Water-Brain, Idiot, etc. MASKS of Brunell, Benjamin Franklin, Haydn, etc. CASTS FROM THE SKULLS of King Robert Bruce, Patty Cannon, Carib, Tardy, Diana Waters. A Cast from the Human Brain. A Human Head, divided, showing the naked Brain on one side, and the Skull on the other, and the Phrenological Bust.

The entire list, numbering Forty of our best phrenological specimens, may be packed and sent as freight by railroad, ship, or stage, to any place desired, with perfect safety.

Human Skulls, from $5 to $10, or $15. Articulated, $25 to $60.

Human Skeletons, from $35 to $75. **French Manikins,** to order.

Sets of Forty India Ink Drawings, of noted Characters, suitable for Lecturers. Price, $30. On Canvass, in sets, $40.

Oil Paintings—Portraits,—can be had to order, from $5 each, upwards.

Anatomical and Physiological Plates Mounted.—WEBER'S, 11 in number, $50. TRALL'S, 6 in number, $20. LAMBERT'S, 6 in number, $20. KELLOGG'S, from the French of Bourgeoise and Jacobs. Very fine. 20 in number, $45.

We can supply all Works on Phrenology, Physiology, Anatomy, Hydropathy, etc., Maps, Charts, Manikins, Skulls, Skeletons, and Apparatus, for the use of Lecturers.

Works on Physiology.

Food and Diet, A Treatise.—With observations on the Dietetical Regimen, suited for Disordered States of the Digestive Organs, and an account of the Dietaries of some of the Principal Metropolitan and other Establishments for Paupers, Lunatics, Criminals, Children, the Sick, etc. By JONATHAN PEREIRA. M. D., F. R. S. and L. S. Edited by CHARLES A. LEE, M. D. Octavo, 318 pp Muslin, $1 75.

An important physiological work. Considerable pains have been taken in the preparation of tables representing the proportion of some of the chemical elements, and of the alimentary principles contained in different foods. The work is accurate and complete.

Fruits and Farinacea the Proper Food of Man.—Being an attempt to Prove by History, Anatomy, Physiology and Chemistry, that the Original, Natural and Best Diet of Man, is derived from the Vegetable Kingdom. By JOHN SMITH. With Notes and Illustrations. By R. T. TRALL, M. D. From the Second London Edition. 12mo, 314 pp. Muslin $1 75.

This is a text-book of facts and principles connected with the vegetarian question, and is a very desirable work.

Hereditary Descent: Its Laws and Facts applied to Human Improvement. Physiological. By Mr. FOWLER. 12mo, 288 pp. Muslin, $1 50.

Human Voice, The.—Its Right Management in Speaking, Reading and Debating. Including the Principles of True Eloquence, together with the Functions of the Vocal Organs, the Motion of the Letters of the Alphabet, the Cultivation of the Ear, the Disorders of the Vocal and Articulating Organs, Origin and Construction of the English Language, Proper Methods of Delivery, Remedial Effects of Reading and Speaking, etc. By the Rev. W. W. EAZALET, A. M. 12mo, 46 pp. Muslin Flex., 50 cents.

This work contains many suggestions of great value to those who desire to speak and read well. Regarding the right management of the voice as intimately connected with health, as well as one of the noblest and most useful accomplishments; the work should be read by all.

Illustrated Family Gymnasium.—Containing the most improved methods of applying Gymnastic, Calisthenic, Kinesipathic and Vocal Exercises to the Development of the Bodily Organs, the invigoration of their functions, the preservation of Health, and the Cure of Disease and Deformities. With numerous illustrations. By R. T. TRALL, M. D. 12mo, 215 pp. Muslin, $1 75.

In this excellent work, the author has aimed to select the very best materials from all accessible sources, and to present a sufficient variety of examples to meet all the demands of human infirmity, so far as exercise is to be regarded as the remedial agency.

Management of Infancy, Physiological and Moral Treatment on the. By ANDREW COMBE, M. D. With Notes and a Supplementary Chapter. By JOHN BELL, M. D. 12mo, 307 pp. Muslin, $1 50.

This is one of the best treatises on the management of infancy extant. Few others are so well calculated to supply mothers with the kind of information which, in their circumstances, is especially needed.

Philosophy of Sacred History, Considered in Relation to Human Aliment and the Wines of Scripture. By GRAHAM. 12mo, 580 pp. Cloth, $3 50.

A work highly useful, both for study and reference, to all who are interested in the great question of Biblical History in relation to the great moral reforms, which are acknowledged as among the most prominent features of the nineteenth century. It is among the most valuable contributions to Biblical and reformatory literature.

Physiology, Animal and Mental: Applied to the Preservation and Restoration of Health of Body and Power of Mind. Sixth Edition. 12mo, 312 pp. Illustrated. Muslin, $1 50.

The title of this work indicates the character of this admirable physiological work. Its aim is to preserve and restore health of body and power of mind. The motto is, "A sound mind in a sound body."

Physiology of Digestion.—Considered with relation to the Principles of Dietetics. By ANDREW COMBE, M. D. Fellow of the Royal College of Physicians of Edinburgh. Tenth Edition. Illustrated. 18mo, 310 pp. Price, 50 cents.

The object of this work is to lay before the public a plain and intelligent description of the structure and uses of the most important organs of the body, and to show how information of this kind may be usefully applied in practical life.

Practical Family Dentist.—A Popular Treatise on the Teeth. Exhibiting the means necessary and efficient to secure their health and preservation. Also, the various errors and pernicious practices which prevail in relation to Dental Treatment. With a variety of useful Receipts for Remedial Compounds. Designed for Diseases of the Teeth and Gums. By D. C. WERNER, M. D. $1 50.

This is a work which should be in the hands of all who wish to keep their teeth in a good and healthy condition. The author treats on the subject in a practical manner.

Principles of Physiology applied to the Preservation of Health and to the Improvement of Physical and Mental Education. By ANDREW COMBE, M. D., Physician Extraordinary to the Queen of England, and Consulting Physician to the King and Queen of the Belgians. Illustrated with Wood Cuts. To which are added Notes and Observations. By Mr. FOWLER. Printed from the Seventh Edinburgh Edition. Enlarged and Improved. Octavo, 320 pp. Muslin, $1 75.

"One of the best *practical* works on Physiology extant."

Science of Human Life, Lectures on the.—By SYLVESTER GRAHAM. With a copious Index and Biographical Sketch of the Author. 12mo, 651 pp. Illustrated. Muslin, $3 50.

We have met with few treatises on the Science of Human Life, especially among those addressed to the general reader, of equal merit with this one. The subject is treated, in all its details, with uncommon ability. . . . These lectures will afford the unprofessional reader a fund of curious and useful information in relation to the organization of his frame, the laws by which it is governed, and the several causes which tend to derange the regularity of its functions, which he would find it difficult to obtain from any other source.—*Eclectic Journal of Medical Science.*

Sober and Temperate Life.—The Discourses and Letters of Louis Cornado, on a Sober and Temperate Life. With a Biography of the Author, who died at 150 years of age. By PIERO MARONCELLI, and Notes and Appendix by JOHN BURDELL. Twenty-Fifth Thousand. 16mo, 228 pp. Paper, 50 cents.

This work is a great favorite with the reading public, as evinced by the number of editions already sold. The sound principles and maxims of temperance of the "old man eloquent," are, though centuries have elapsed since his decease, still efficient in turning men to a sober and temperate life.

ANATOMICAL AND PHYSIOLOGICAL PLATES.

New Anatomical and Physiological Plates for Lecturers, Physicians, and Others. By R. T, TRALL, M. D., author of various works.

These plates represent all the organs and principal structures of the human body *in situ*, and of the size of life. There are six in the set, backed and on rollers, as follows:

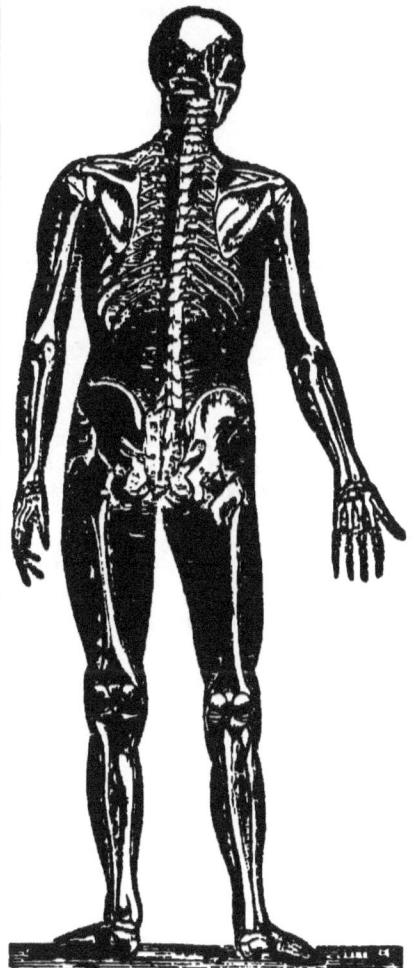

The Heart and Lungs.—No. 1 presents a front view of the lungs, heart, stomach, liver, gall-bladder, larynx, thymus, and parotid glands, common carotid arteries, and jugular vein. Colored as in life.

Dissections.—No. 2 is a complete dissection of the heart, exhibiting its valves and cavities, and the course of the blood. The large arteries and the veins of the heart, lungs, and neck are displayed, with the windpipe and its bronchial ramifications; also the liver with its gall-bladder and ducts; the pancreas; the kidneys with their ureters and blood vessels; the descending aorta, or large artery of the chest and abdomen; ovaries, fallopian tubes, round and broad ligaments, etc.

Nervous System.—No. 3. Side view of the brain, heart, lungs, liver, bowels, uterus, and bladder. Also the various subdivisions of the base of the brain, with the whole length of the spinal cord, showing the origin of all the cerebro-spinal nerves.

The Eye and the Ear.—No. 4. The anatomy of the eye and ear, representing the arrangements of the minute blood-vessels, nerves, and other structures concerned in the functions of seeing and hearing.

Digestion.—No. 5. The alimentary canal, exhibiting the exact size, shape, and arrangements of structures especially concerned in digestion, viz.: the mouth, throat, tongue, esophagus, stomach, small and large intestines, with the liver, gall-bladder, and the biliary ducts; also the internal structure of the kidneys, and a beautiful representation of the lacteal absorbents and glands, thoracic duct, and their connections with the thoracic arteries and veins.

Circulation — Skin.— No. 6. The lobes of the lungs and cavities of the heart, valves, etc., with the large vessels of the circulation; also a minute dissection of the structures of the skin—the sebaceous follicles, sweat glands, etc.; exhibiting the extent and importance of the great depurating functions of the surface.

Every lecturer, teacher, and physician should have a set. Price for the whole, beautifully colored and mounted, $20. We do not sell single plates. May be sent by Express. Address SAMUEL R. WELLS, No. 389 Broadway, New York.

Works on Hydropathy, or Water Cure.

Children, their Hydropathic Management in Health and Disease. A Descriptive and Practical Work, designed as a Guide for Families and Physicians. Illustrated with numerous cases. By Joel Shew, M. D. 12mo, 430 pp. $1 75.

Consumption, its Prevention and Cure by the Water Treatment. With advice concerning Hemorrhage from the Lungs, Coughs, Colds, Asthma, Bronchitis, and Sore Throat. Same Author. 12mo, 286 pp. Muslin, $1 50.

Hydropathic Cook Book; With Recipes for Cooking on Hygienic Principles. Containing also, a Philosophical Exposition of the Relations of Food to Health; the Chemical Elements and Proximate Constitution of Alimentary Principles; the Nutritive Properties of all kinds of Aliments; the Relative Value of Vegetable and Animal Substances; the Selection and Preservation of Dietetic Material, etc. By R. T. Trall, M. D. 12mo, 226 pp. Muslin, $1 50.

Diseases of the Throat and Lungs, including Diphtheria, and their Proper Treatment. By R. T. Trall, M. D. 12mo, 39 pp. Paper, 25 cents.

Domestic Practice of Hydropathy, with Fifteen Engraved Illustrations of important subjects, from Drawings by Dr. Howard Johnson, with a form of a Report for the assistance of Patients in consulting their Physician by correspondence. By Edward Johnson, M. D. 12mo, 467 pp. Muslin, $2.

Hydropathy for the People. With observations on Drugs, Diet, Water, Air, and Exercise. By William Horsell, of London. With Notes and Observations, by R. T. Trall, M. D. 12mo, 246 pp. Cloth, $1 50.

Hydropathic Encyclopedia.—A System of Hydropathy and Hygiene. In One Large Octavo Volume. Embracing Outlines of Anatomy, Illustrated; Physiology of the Human Body; Hygienic Agencies, and the Preservation of Health; Dietetics and Hydropathic Cookery; Theory and Practice of Water-Treatment; Special Pathology and Hydro-Therapeutics, including the Nature, Causes, Symptoms, and Treatment of all known Diseases; Application of Hydropathy to Midwifery and the Nursery; with nearly One Thousand Pages, including a Glossary, Table of Contents, and a complete Index. Designed as a Guide to Families and Students, and a Text-Book for Physicians. With numerous Engraved Illustrations. By R. T. Trall, M. D. Large 12mo, 964 pp. Muslin, $4 50.

In the general plan and arrangement of the work, the wants and necessities of the people have been steadily kept in view. Whilst almost every topic of interest in the departments of Anatomy, Physiology, Pathology, Hygiene and Therapeutics, is briefly presented, those of practical utility are always put prominently forward. The prevailing conceits and whims of the day and age are exposed and refuted; the theories and hypotheses upon which the popular drug-practice is predicated are controverted, and the why and wherefore of their fallacy clearly demonstrated.

It is a rich, comprehensive, and well-arranged encyclopedia.—*New York Tribune.*

Hydropathic Family Physician.—A Ready Prescriber and Hygienic Adviser. With Reference to the Nature, Causes, Prevention, and Treatment of Diseases, Accidents, and casualties of every kind. With a Glossary and copious Index. By JOEL SHEW, M. D. Illustrated with nearly Three Hundred Engravings. One large volume, intended for use in the Family. 12mo, 816 pp. Muslin, $4.

It possesses the most practical utility of any of the author's contributions to popular medicine, and is well adapted to give the reader an accurate idea of the organization and functions of the human frame.—*New York Tribune.*

Midwifery and the Diseases of Women.—A Descriptive and Practical Work. With the general management of Child-Birth, Nursery, etc. Illustrated with numerous cases of Treatment. Same Author. 12mo, 430 pp. Muslin, $1 75.

Philosophy of the Water-Cure.—A Development of the true Principles of Health and Longevity. By JOHN BALBIRNIE, M. D. Illustrated, with the Confessions and Observations of Sir EDWAD LYTTON BULWER. 12mo, 50 cents.

Practice of the Water-Cure.—With Authenticated Evidence of its Efficacy and Safety. Containing a Detailed Account of the various processes used in the Water Treatment; A Sketch of the History and Progress of the Water-Cure; well authenticated cases of Cure, etc. By JAMES WILSON, and JAMES MANBY GULLY, M. D. 12mo, 144 pp. Paper, 50 cents.

Water-Cure in Chronic Diseases; An Exposition of the Causes, Progress, and Terminations of various Chronic Diseases of the Digestive Organs, Lungs, Nerves, Limbs and Skin, and of their Treatment by Water and other Hygienic means. Illustrated with an Engraved View of the Nerves of the Lungs, Heart, Stomach and Bowels. By J. M. GULLY, M. D. 12mo, 405 pp. Muslin, $2.

Water and Vegetable Diet in Consumption, Scrofula, Cancer, Asthma, and other Chronic Diseases. By WILLIAM LAMBE, M. D. With Notes and Additions, by JOEL SHEW, M. D. 12mo, 258 pp. Muslin, $1 50.

Water-Cure Manual.—A Popular Work. Embracing Descriptions of the various modes of Bathing, the Hygienic and Curative Effects of Air, Exercise, Clothing, Occupation, Diet, Water-Drinking, etc., together with Descriptions of Diseases, and the Hydropathic means to be employed therein. Illustrated with cases of Treatment and Cure. Containing also, a fine engraving of Priessnitz. By JOEL SHEW, M. D. Tenth Thousand. Improved. 12mo, 282 pp. Muslin, $1 50.

Special List.—We have, in addition to the above, Private Medical Works and Treatises which, although not adapted to general circulation, are invaluable to those who need them. This Special List will be sent on *receipt of stamp.* Address S. R. WELLS, 389 Broadway, New York.

Miscellaneous Works.

Æsop's Fables.—The People's Edition. Beautifully Illustrated, with nearly Sixty Engravings. 1 vol. 12mo, 72 pp. Cloth, gilt, beveled boards, $1.
It is gotten up in sumptuous style, and illustrated with great beauty of design. It will conduce to educate the eye and elevate the taste of the young to the appreciation of the highest and most perfect forms of grace and beauty.—*Mount Holly Herald.*

Chemistry, and its application to Physiology, Agriculture and Commerce. By JUSTUS LIEBIG, M.D., F.R.S., Professor of Chemistry. Edited by JOHN GARDNER, M.D. Twelfth Thousand. Octavo, 54 pp. Paper, 50 cents.

Essays on Human Rights and their Political Guarantees.—By E. P. HURLBUT, Counselor-at-Law in the City of New York—now Judge. With Notes, by GEORGE COMBE. Sixth Thousand. 1 vol. 12mo, 249 pp. Muslin, $1 50.

Fruit Culture for the Million.—A Hand-Book. Being a Guide to the Cultivation and Management of Fruit Trees. With Descriptions of the Best Varieties in the United States. Illustrated with Ninety Engravings. With an Appendix containing a variety of useful memoranda on the subject, valuable receipts, etc. By THOMAS GREGG. 12mo, 163 pp. Muslin, $1.

Gospel Among the Animals; Or, Christ with the Cattle.—By Rev. SAMUEL OSGOOD, D.D. One small 12mo vol., 24 pp. Price, 25 cents.

Home for All; Or, the Gravel Wall. A New, Cheap, and Superior Mode of Building, adapted to Rich and Poor. Showing the Superiority of this Gravel Concrete over Brick, Stone and Frame Houses; Manner of Making and Depositing it. With numerous Illustrations. 1 vol. 12mo, 192 pp. Muslin, $1 50.
"There's no place like Home." To cheapen and improve human homes, and especially to bring comfortable dwellings within the reach of the poor classes, is the object of this volume—an object of the highest practical utility to man.

How to Live: Saving and Wasting, or Domestic Economy Illustrated, by the Life of Two Families of Opposite Character, Habits and Practices, in a Pleasant Tale of Real Life, full of Useful Lessons in Housekeeping, and Hints How to Live, How to Have, How to Gain, and How to be Happy; including the Story of "A Dime a Day." By SOLON ROBINSON. 1 vol. 12mo, 343 pp. $1 50.

Immortality Triumphant.—The Existence of a God, and Human Immortality Practically Considered, and the Truth of Divine Revelation Substantiated. By Rev. JOHN BOVEE DODS. 1 vol. 12mo, 216 pp. Muslin, $1 50.

Movement-Cure.—An Exposition of the Swedish Movement-Cure. Embracing the History and Philosophy of this System of Medical Treatment, with Examples of Single Movements, and Directions for their Use in Various Forms of Chronic Diseases; forming a Complete Manual of Exercises, together with a Summary of the Principles of General Hygiene. By GEORGE H. TAYLOR, A.M., M.D. 1 vol. 12mo, 408 pp. Muslin, $1 75.

Natural Laws of Man.—A Philosophical Catechism. By J. G. SPURZHEIM, M.D. Sixth Edition. Enlarged and Improved. One small 16mo vol., 171 pp. Muslin, 75 cents.
George Combe, in that great work "The Constitution of Man," acknowledges that he derived his first ideas of the "Natural Laws," from Spurzheim.

An Essay on Man.—By ALEXANDER POPE. With Notes by S. R. WELLS. Beautifully Illustrated. 1 vol. 12mo, 50 pp. Cloth, gilt, beveled boards, $1.

Three Hours' School a Day.—A Talk with Parents. By WILLIAM L. CRANDAL. Intended to aid in the Emancipation of Children and Youth from School Slavery. 1 vol. 12mo, 264 pp. Muslin, $1 50.

The Christian Household.—Embracing the Christian Home, Husband, Wife, Father, Mother, Child, Brother and Sister. By Rev. G. S. WEAVER. 1 vol. 12mo, 160 pp. Muslin, $1.
This little volume is designed as a partial answer to one of the most solicitous wants of Christian families. I have for years seen and sorrowed over the absence of Christ in our households. Among the Christian people of every sect, there is a sad deficiency of Christian principle and practice at home. . . . Why is it so?—*Preface.*

Weaver's Works for the Young.—Comprising "Hopes and Helps for the Young of both Sexes," "Aims and Aids for Girls and Young Women," "Ways of Life; Or, the Right Way and the Wrong Way." By Rev. G. S. WEAVER. One large vol. 12mo, 626 pp. Muslin, $3.
The three volumes of which this work is comprised, may also be had in separate form.

Hopes and Helps for the Young of both Sexes.—Relating to the Formation of Character, Choice of Avocation, Health, Amusement, Music, Conversation, Cultivation of Intellect, Moral Sentiment, Social Affection, Courtship and Marriage. Same Author. 1 vol. 12mo, 246 pp. Muslin, $1 50.

Aims and Aids for Girls and Young Women, on the various Duties of Life. Including, Physical, Intellectual and Moral Development, Self-Culture, Improvement, Dress, Beauty, Fashion, Employment, Education, the Home Relations, their Duties to Young Men, Marriage, Womanhood and Happiness. Same Author. 12mo, 224 pp. Muslin, $1 50.

Ways of Life, showing the Right Way and the Wrong Way. Contrasting the High Way and the Low Way; the True Way and the False Way; the Upward Way and the Downward Way; the Way of Honor and the Way of Dishonor. Same Author. 1 vol. 12mo, 157 pp. Muslin, $1.

Notes on Beauty, Vigor and Development; Or, How to Acquire Plumpness of Form, Strength of Life and Beauty of Complexion; with Rules for Diet and Bathing, and a Series of improved Physical Exercises. By WILLIAM MILO, of London. Illustrated. 12mo, 24 pp. Paper, 12 cents.

Father Matthew, the Temperance Apostle.—His Portrait, Character, and Biography. By S. R. WELLS, Editor of the Phrenological Journal. 12c.

Temperance in Congress.—Speeches delivered in the House of Representatives on the occasion of the First Meeting of the Congressional Temperance Society. One small 12mo vol. 25 cents.

A Library for Lecturers, Speakers and Others.—Every Lawyer, Clergyman, Senator, Congressman, Teacher, Debater, Student, etc., who desires to be informed and posted on the Rules and Regulations which govern Public Bodies, as well as those who desire the best books on Oratory, and the Art of Public Speaking, should provide himself with the following small and carefully selected Library:

The Indispensable Hand-Book . . $2 25	The Exhibition Speaker . . .	$1 50
Oratory, Sacred and Secular . . 1 50	Cushing's Manual of Parlia. Practice	75
The Right Word in the Right Place, 75	The Culture of the Voice and Action	1 75
The American Debater . . . 2 00	Treatise on Punctuation . . .	1 75

One copy of each sent by Express, on receipt of $10, or by mail, post-paid, at the prices affixed. Address, SAMUEL R. WELLS, 389 Broadway, New York.

EDUCATIONAL HAND-BOOKS.

Hand-books for Home Improvement (Educational); comprising, "How to Write," "How to Talk," "How to Behave," and "How to do Business," in one large volume. Indispensable. One large 12mo vol., 647 pp. Muslin, $2 25. More than 100,000 copies of this work have been sold. A capital book for agents. These works may also be had in separate form as follows:

How to Write, A Pocket Manual of Composition and Letter-Writing. Invaluable to the Young. 1 vol. 12mo, 156 pp. Muslin, 75 cents.

How to Talk, A Pocket Manual of Conversation and Debate, with more than Five Hundred Common Mistakes in Speaking Corrected. 1 vol. 12mo, 156 pp. Muslin, 75 cents.

How to Behave, A Pocket Manual of Republican Etiquette and Guide to Correct Personal Habits, with Rules for Debating Societies and Deliberative Assemblies. 1 vol. 12mo, 149 pp. Muslin, 75 cents.

How to do Business, A Pocket Manual of Practical Affairs, and a Guide to Success in Life, with a Collection of Legal and Commercial Forms. Suitable for all. 1 vol. 12mo, 156 pp. Muslin, 75 cents.

The Right Word in the Right Place.—A New Pocket Dictionary and Reference Book. Embracing extensive Collections of Synonyms, Technical Terms, Abbreviations, Foreign Phrases, Chapters on Writing for the Press, Punctuation, Proof-Reading, and other Interesting and Valuable Information. By the Author of "How to Write," etc. 1 vol. 16mo, 214 pp. Cloth, 75 cts.

In this little volume is condensed into a small space, and made available to every writer, speaker and reader, what can be found elsewhere only by consulting heavy volumes which few private libraries contain. The collection of synonyms contained therein, is alone well worth the cost of the whole volume. It is adapted particularly to the wants of writers for the press, and those in whom the faculty of original language is deficient.

Rural Manuals, comprising "The House," "The Farm," "The Garden," and "Domestic Animals." In one large 12mo vol., 655 pp. Muslin, $2 25.

Library of Mesmerism and Psychology. Comprising the Philosophy of Mesmerism, Clairvoyance, and Mental Electricity; Fascination, or the Power of Charming; The Macrocosm, or the World of Sense; Electrical Psychology, the Doctrine of Impressions; The Science of the Soul, treated Physiologically and Philosophically. Two volumes in one. Handsome 12mo, 880 pp. Illustrated. Muslin, $4.

The Emphatic Diaglott; Or, the New Testament in Greek and English. Containing the Original Greek Text of what is commonly called The New Testament, with an Interlineary Word-for-word English Translation; a New Emphatic Version based on the Interlineary Translation, on the Readings of Eminent Critics, and on the various Readings of the Vatican Manuscript (No. 1,209 in the Vatican Library); together with Illustrative and Explanatory Foot Notes, and a copious Selection of References; to the whole of which is added a valuable Alphabetical Index. By BENJAMIN WILSON. One vol., 12mo, 884 pp. Price, $4; extra fine binding, $5. Address, SAMUEL R. WELLS, 389 Broadway, New York.

"EDUCATION COMPLETE,"

Education and Self-Improvement Complete.—Comprising Physiology—Animal and Mental; Self-Culture and Perfection of Character; including the Management of Youth; Memory and Intellectual Improvement. Complete in one large, well-bound 12mo volume, with 855 pp., and upward of Seventy Engravings. Price, pre-paid, by mail, $4. Address SAMUEL R. WELLS, 389 Broadway, N. Y.

This work is, in all respects, one of the best educational hand-books in the English language. Any system of education that neglects the training and developing all that goes to make up a MAN, must necessarily be incomplete. The mind and body are so intimately related and connected, that it is impossible to cultivate the former without it is properly supplemented by the latter. The work is subdivided into three departments—the first, devoted to the preservation and restoration of health and the improvement of mentality; the second, to the regulation of the feelings and perfection of the moral character; and the third, to intellectual cultivation. "EDUCATION COMPLETE" is a library in itself, and covers the ENTIRE NATURE OF MAN. We append below a synopsis of the table of contents:

HEALTH OF BODY AND POWER OF MIND.

PHYSIOLOGY — ANIMAL AND MENTAL HEALTH — ITS LAWS AND PRESERVATION. Happiness constitutional; Pain not necessary; Object of all Education; Reciprocation existing between Body and Mind; Health Defined; Sickness—not providential.

FOOD—ITS NECESSITY AND SELECTION.—Unperverted Appetite an Infallible Directory; Different Diets Feed Different Powers; How to Eat—or Mastication, Quantity, Time, etc.; How Appetite can be Restrained; The Digestive Process; Exercise after Meals.

CIRCULATION, RESPIRATION. PERSPIRATION, SLEEP.—The Heart, its Structure and Office; The Circulatory System; The Lungs, their Structure and Functions; Respiration, and its importance; Perspiration; Prevention and Cure of Colds, and their consequences; Regulation of Temperature by Fire and Clothing; Sleep.

THE BRAIN AND NERVOUS SYSTEM.—Position, Function, and Structure of the Brain; Consciousness, or the seat of the soul; Function of the Nerves; How to keep the Nervous System in Health; The Remedy of Diseases; Observance of the Laws of Health Effectual; The Drink of Dyspeptics—its kind, time and quantity; Promotion of Circulation; Consumption—its Prevention and Cure; Preventives of Insanity, etc.

SELF-CULTURE AND PERFECTION OF CHARACTER.

CONSTITUENT ELEMENTS OR CONDITIONS OF PERFECTION OF CHARACTER.—Progression a Law of Things—its application to human improvement; Human perfectibility,—the harmonious action of all the faculties; Governing the propensities by the intellectual and moral faculties; Proof that the organs can be enlarged and diminished; The proper management of Youth, etc.

ANALYSIS AND MEANS OF STRENGTHENING OF THE FACULTIES.—Amativeness; Philoprogenitiveness; Adhesiveness; Union for Life; Inhabitiveness; Continuity; Vitativeness; Combativeness; Destructiveness, or Executiveness; Alimentiveness; Aquativeness, or Bibativeness; Acquisitiveness; Secretiveness; Cautiousness; Approbativeness; Self-Esteem; Firmness; Conscientiousness; Hope; Spirituality—Marvelousness; Veneration; Benevolence; Constructiveness; Ideality; Sublimity; Imitation; Mirthfulness; Agreeableness—with engraved illustrations.

MEMORY AND INTELLECTUAL IMPROVEMENT APPLIED TO SELF-EDUCATION.

CLASSIFICATION AND FUNCTIONS OF THE FACULTIES.—Man's superiority; Intellect his crowning endowment; How to strengthen and improve the Memory; Definition, location, analysis and means of strengthening the intellectual faculties. INDIVIDUALITY. FORM. SIZE. WEIGHT. COLOR. ORDER. CALCULATION. LOCALITY. EVENTUALITY. TIME. TUNE: Influence of music. LANGUAGE: Power of Eloquence; Good language. PHONOGRAPHY: its advantages. CAUSALITY: Teaching others to think; Astronomy; Anatomy and Physiology; Study of Nature. COMPARISON: Inductive reasoning. HUMAN NATURE: Adaptation.

DEVELOPMENTS REQUIRING FOR PARTICULAR AVOCATIONS.—Good Teachers; Clergymen; Physicians; Lawyers; Statesmen; Editors; Authors; Public Speakers; Poets; Lecturers; Merchants; Mechanics; Artists; Painters; Farmers; Engineers; Landlords; Printers; Milliners; Seamstressess; Fancy Workers, and the like.

Full and explicit directions are given for the cultivation and direction of all the powers of the mind. Instruction for finding the exact location of each organ, and its relative size compared with others. A new edition of this great work has been recently printed, and may now be had in one volume. Agents in every neighborhood will be supplied in packages of a dozen or more copies by Express, or as Freight, at a discount. Single copies by mail. Address, SAMUEL R. WELLS, 389 Broadway, N. Y.

ORATORY—SACRED AND SECULAR;

Or, the EXTEMPORANEOUS SPEAKER. Including a Chairman's Guide. By Rev. WM. PITTENGER, with an Introduction by Hon. JOHN A. BINGHAM. A clear and succinct Exposition of the Rules and Methods or practice by which Readiness in the Expression of Thought may be acquired, and an acceptable style, both in composition and gesture. One handsome 12mo vol. of 220 pages, tinted paper, post-paid, $1.50.

To give the reader a more complete view of the matter in this excellent work—the best of its class—we condense the following from the

TABLE OF CONTENTS.

PREFACE. Objects of the Work stated. INTRODUCTION. By Hon. JOHN A. BINGHAM, Member of Congress.

Part I.—THE WRITTEN AND EXTEMPORE DISCOURSE COMPARED—Illustrative Examples. PREREQUISITES — Intellectual Competency; Strength of Body; Command of Language; Courage; Firmness; Self-reliance. BASIS OF SPEECH—Thought and Emotion; Heart Cultivation; Earnestness. ACQUIREMENTS—General Knowledge; of Bible; of Theology; of Men; Method by which such Knowledge may be obtained. CULTIVATION — Imagination; Language; Voice; Gesture, how acquired; Distinguished Orators and Writers.

Part II.—A SERMON. THE FOUNDATION FOR A PREACHER—Subject: Object; Text; Hints to Young Preachers. THE PLAN — Gathering Thought; Arranging; Committing; Practical Suggestions; Use of Notes. PRELIMINARIES FOR PREACHING—Fear; Vigor; Opening Exercises; Requisites for a Successful Discourse. THE DIVISIONS—Introduction, Difficulties in Opening; Discussion, Simplicity and Directness. AFTER CONSIDERATIONS—Success; Rest; Improvement; Practical Suggestions.

Part III.—SECULAR ORATORY. INSTRUCTIVE ADDRESS—Fields of Oratory; Oral Teaching; Lecturing. MISCELLANEOUS ADDRESS — Deliberative; Legal; Popular; Controversial; the Statesman; the Lawyer; the Lecturer; the Orator.

Part IV. — EMINENT SPEAKERS DESCRIBED — St. Augustin; Luther; Lord Chatham; William Pitt; Edmund Burke; Mirabeau; Patrick Henry; Whitefield; Wesley; Sidney Smith; F. W. Robertson; Clay; Bascom; Summerfield; Spurgeon; Beecher; Anna E. Dickinson; John A. Bingham; W. E. Gladstone; Mathew Simpson; Wendell Phillips; John P. Durbin; Newman Hall, and others.

Appendix. — THE CHAIRMAN'S GUIDE. HOW TO ORGANISE AND CONDUCT PUBLIC MEETINGS and DEBATING CLUBS, in a parlimentary manner.

While other authors have tended to excessive elaboration, the writer of this work has striven to condense as much as possible, and present the subject as succinctly as clearness of statement will permit. He brings to his work a mind matured by years of experience in the very field of which he treats. He is also known in the literary world, as the author of "Daring and Suffering." The book is published in first-class style, well and clearly printed, and handsomely bound. A capital work for Agents.

Address S. R. WELLS Publisher 389 Broadway, N. Y.

Aesop's Fables.

Style of Engraving—THE FROG AND THE OX.

Æsop's Fables Illustrated.—The People's Pictorial Edition. With Seventy Splendid Illustrations. Complete in one vol., 12mo, 72 pp. Beautifully printed on tinted paper, bound in cloth, gilt edges, beveled boards, $1.

The following brief selections, from a very numerous collection of notices of the Press, show with what favor this beautiful edition has been received.

The New York *Daily Times* says: "This attractive volume is very appropriately styled 'The People's Edition.' The illustrations are numerous, spirited, and well engraved."

The *Christian Intelligencer* says: "The designs are new, apt, and form a decided feature of this work. The artist has put wit into his delineations, and the fables may be read *in their pictorial representatives.*"

The Cincinnati *Journal of Commerce* says: "It is an exceedingly beautiful little volume, and is well worthy of having a place in every house with the family Bible."

The Brooklyn *Union* says: "It is one of the best gift-books of the season."

The *American Baptist* says: "It is a neat volume, beautifully illustrated. It contains a larger number of fables than we have before seen grouped together under the name of that great master."

The *Rural New Yorker* says: "The form, appearance and general style of the book make it truly 'The People's Edition,' as the publishers announce."

The *Mount Holly Herald* says: "It is gotten up in sumptuous style, and illustrated with great beauty of design. It will conduce to educate the eye and elevate the taste of the young to the appreciation of the highest and most perfect forms of grace and beauty."

The *Phrenological Journal* says: "This is a beautiful edition of the sayings of the slave of Athens. The volume is complete, containing over TWO HUNDRED FABLES and upward of SIXTY FINE-LINED WOOD ENGRAVINGS, NEARLY EVERY PAGE BEING CHARMINGLY ILLUSTRATED. IT IS BEAUTIFULLY PRINTED ON TINTED PAPER, BOUND IN CLOTH, WITH GILT EDGES, AND WELL CALCULATED FOR A POPULAR GIFT TO OLD AND YOUNG."

WORKS ON PHONOGRAPHY,

OR

SHORT-HAND WRITING.

"Had Phonography been known forty years ago, it would have saved me twenty years of hard labor."—Benton.

THE GREATEST ACCOMPLISHMENT OF THE AGE,

To any youth who may possess the art, it is capital of itself, upon which he may confidently rely for support. It leads to immediate, permanent, and respectable employment. To the professional man, and indeed to every one whose pursuits in life call upon him to record incidents and thoughts, it is one of the great labor-saving devices of the age. Mailed from this office on receipt of price.

The Complete Phonographer: Being an Inductive Exposition of Phonography, with its application to all Branches of Reporting, and affording the fullest Instruction to those who have not the assistance of an Oral Teacher; also intended as a School Book. By JAMES E. MUNSON. Price, $2 25.

Graham's Hand-Book of Standard or American Phonography.—Presenting the Principles of all Styles of the Art, commencing with the analysis of words, and proceeding to the most rapid reporting style. Price, $2 25.

Graham's First Standard Phonographic Reader.—Written in the Corresponding Style, with Key. Price, $1 75.

Graham's Second Standard Phonographic Reader.—Written in the Reporting Style. Price, $2.

Graham's Reporter's Manual.—A complete Exposition of the Reporting Style of Phonography. Price, $1 25.

Graham's Synopsis of Standard or American Phonography, printed in Pronouncing Style. Price, 50 cents.

Graham's Standard Phonographic Dictionary; Containing the Pronunciation and the best Corresponding and Reporting Outlines of many Thousand Words and Phrases. Invaluable to the Student and Practical Reporter. Price, $5.

Pitman's (Benn) Manual of Phonography.—A new and comprehensive Exposition of Phonography, with copious Illustrations and Exercises. Designed for schools and private students. New edition. Price, $1 25.

Pitman's (Benn) Reporter's Companion.—A complete Guide to the Art of Verbatim Reporting, designed to follow Pittman's Manual of Phonography. Price, $1 50.

Pitman's (Benn) Phrase Book, a Vocabulary of Phraseology. $1 25.

Pitman's (Benn) Phonographic Reader.—A Progressive series of reading exercises. A useful work for every Phonographic student. Price 40 cts.

Longely's American Manual of Phonography.—Being a complete Guide to the Acquisition of Pitman's Phonetic Short-hand. Price, $1.

The History of Short-Hand, from the system of Cicero down to the Invention of Phonography. Edited and engraved on Stone by BENN PITMAN. $1 25.

Handsome Reporting Cases for Phonographic Copy-Books. $1.

Phonographic Copy-Books.—Double or Single ruled. Price, 15 cts.

The American Phonetic Dictionary, with Pronouncing Vocabularies of Classical, Scriptural, and Geographical Names. By DANIEL S. SMALLEY. $4 50.

Sent, prepaid, by return of the FIRST MAIL, on receipt of prices annexed. All letters should be addressed to SAMUEL R. WELLS, 389 Broadway, New York.

The Indispensable Hand-Book.

How to Write—How to Talk—How to Behave, and How to do Business.

COMPLETE IN ONE LARGE VOLUME.

This new work—in four Parts—embraces just that practical matter of fact information which every one, old and young, ought to have. It will aid in attaining, if it does not insure, "success in life." It contains some 600 pages, elegantly bound, and is divided into four parts, as follows:

How to Write:

As a Manual of Letter-Writing and Composition, is far superior to the common "Letter-Writers." It teaches the inexperienced how to write Business Letters, Family Letters, Friendly Letters, Love Letters, Notes and Cards, and Newspaper Articles, and how to Correct Proof for the Press. The newspapers have pronounced it "Indispensable."

How to Talk:

No other Book contains so much useful instruction on the Subject as this. It teaches how to speak Correctly, Clearly, Fluently, Forcibly, Eloquently, and Effectively, in the Shop, in the Drawing-Room; a Chairman's Guide, to conduct Debating Societies and Public Meetings; how to Spell, and how to Pronounce all sorts of Words; with Exercises for Declamation. The chapter on "Errors Corrected" is worth the price of the volume to every young man. "Worth a dozen grammars."

How to Behave:

This is a Manual of Etiquette and it is believed to be the best "Manners Book" ever written. If you desire to know what good manners require, at Home, on the Street, at a Party, at Church, at Table, in Conversation, at Places of Amusement, in Travelling, in the Company of Ladies, in Courtship, this book will inform you. It is a standard work on Good Behavior.

How to do Business:

Indispensable in the Counting-Room, in the Store, in the Shop, on the Farm, for the Clerk, the Apprentice, the Book Agent, and for Business Men. It teaches how to choose a pursuit, and how to follow it with success. "It teaches how to get rich honestly," and how to use your riches wisely.

How to Write—How to Talk—How to Behave—How to do Business, bound in one large handsome volume, post-paid, for $2.25.

Address   S. R. WELLS, 389 Broadway, N. Y.

THE
NEW TESTAMENT
IN GREEK AND ENGLISH,
ENTITLED
THE EMPHATIC DIAGLOTT,

Containing the Original Greek Text of what is commonly called THE NEW TESTAMENT, with an Interlineary Word-for-word English Translation ; a New Emphatic Version based on the Interlineary Translation, on the Readings of Eminent Critics, and on the various Readings of the Vatican Manuscript (No. 1,209 in the Vatican Library) ; together with Illustrative and Explanatory Foot Notes, and a copious Selection of References ; to the whole of which is added a valuable Alphabetical Index By Benjamin Wilson. One vol., 12mo, pp. 884. Price, $4 ; extra fine binding, $5. SAMUEL R. WELLS, Publishers, 389 Broadway, New York.

This valuable work is now complete. The different renderings of various passages in the New Testament are the foundations on which most of the sects of Christians have been built up. Without claiming absolute correctness for our author's new and elaborate version, we present his work so that each reader may judge for himself whether the words there literally translated are so arranged in the common version as to express the exact meaning of the New Testament writers.

In regard to Mr. Wilson's translation there will doubtless be differences of opinion among Greek scholars, but having submitted it to several for examination, their virdict has been so generally in its favor that we have no hesitation in presenting it to the public.

We have no desire for sectarian controversy, and believe that it is consequent chiefly upon misinterpretation, or upon variations in the formal presentation of the truths of *Christianity* as taught in the New Testament; and it is with the earnest desire that what appears crooked shall be made straight, that we present this volume to the careful consideration of an intelligent people.

OPINIONS OF THE CLERGY.

The following extracts from letters just received by the publishers from some of our most eminent divines will go far to show in what light the new "Emphatic Diaglott" is regarded by the clergy in general:

From THOMAS ARMITAGE, D.D., *Pastor of the Fifth Avenue Baptist Church.*—"GENTLEMEN: I have examined with much care and great interest the specimen sheets sent me of 'The Emphatic Diaglott.' * * * I believe that the book furnishes evidences of purposed faithfulness, more than usual scholarship, and remarkable literary industry. It can not fail to be an important help to those who wish to become better acquainted with the revealed will of God. For these reasons I wish the enterprise of publishing the work great success."

From REV. JAMES L. HODGE, *Pastor of the First Mariner's Baptist Church, N. Y.*—"I have examined these sheets which you design to be a specimen of the work, and have to confess myself much pleased with the arrangement and ability of Mr. Wilson. * * * I can most cordially thank Mr. Wilson for his noble work, and you, gentlemen, for your Christian enterprise in bringing the work before the public. I believe the work will do good, and aid in the better understanding of the New Testament."

From SAMUEL OSGOOD, D.D., *New York City.*—"I have looked over the specimen of the new and curious edition of the New Testament which you propose publishing, and think that it will be a valuable addition to our Christian literature. It is a work of great labor and careful study, and without being sure of agreeing with the author in all his views, I can commend his book to all lovers of Biblical research."

LIBRARY
OF
MESMERISM AND PSYCHOLOGY.

COMPLETE IN ONE LARGE VOLUME.

"All are but parts of one stupendous whole,
Whose body nature is, and God the soul."

Comprising the PHILOSOPHY OF MESMERISM, CLAIRVOYANCE, MENTAL ELECTRICITY.—FASCINATION, or the Power of Charming: Illustrating the Principles of Life in connection with Spirit and Matter.—THE MACROCOSM AND MICROCOSM, or the Universe Without and Universe Within: being an unfolding of the plan of Creation, and the Correspondence of Truths, both in the World of Sense and the World of Soul.—THE PHILOSOPHY OF ELECTRICAL PSYCHOLOGY; the Doctrine of Impressions; including the connection between Mind and Matter; also, the Treatment of Disease.—PSYCHOLOGY, or the Science of the Soul, considered Physiologically and Philosophically; with an appendix containing notes of Mesmeric and Psychical experience, and illustrations of the Brain and Nervous System.

In this LIBRARY is embraced all the most practical matter yet written on these deeply interesting, though somewhat mysterious, subjects. Having these works at hand, the reader may learn all there is known of MESMERISM, CLAIRVOYANCE, BIOLOGY, and PSYCHOLOGY. He may also learn how to produce results which the most scientific men have not yet been able to explain. The *facts* are here recorded, and the practice or *modus operandi* given. In order to give an idea of the scope of the work, we append a brief synopsis of the table of contents:

Charming—How to Charm; Fascination; Double Life of Man; Spiritual States; Stages in Dying; Operation of Medicine; What is Prevision, or Second Sight? Philosophy of Somnambulism; History of Fascination; Beecher on Magnetism; Electrical Psychology—its Definition and Importance in Curing Disease; Mind and Matter; The Existence of a Deity Proved; Subject of Creation Considered; The Doctrine of Impressions; The Secret Revealed, so that all may know how to Experiment without an Instructor; Electro-Biology; Genetology, or Human Beauty Philosophically Considered; Philosophy of Mesmerism; Animal Magnetism; Mental Electricity, or Spiritualism; The Philosophy of Clairvoyance; Degrees in Mesmerism; Psychology; Origin, Phenomena, Physiology, Philosophy and Psychology of Mesmerism; Mesmeric and Physical Experience; Clairvoyance as applied to Physiology and Medicine; Trance, or Spontaneous Ecstasies; The Practice and Use of Mesmerism and Circles; The Doctrine of Degrees; Doctrine of Correspondences; Doctrine of Progressive Development; Law Agency and Divine Agency; Providences, etc., etc., with other interesting matter.

The LIBRARY contains several works by different authors, making some Nine Hundred pages, nicely printed and substantially and handsomely bound in one portly 12mo volume. Price for the work, complete, pre-paid by return of post, $4.

Address, SAMUEL R. WELLS, 389 Broadway, New York.

Apparatus for Physical Training.

BACON'S PATENT HOME GYMNASIUM.

The only complete portable Gymnasium ever invented. Invaluable to those of sedentary occupations. No home should be without one. Put up in any room, and removed in a minute.

All complete Gymnasiums that have been previously constructed, have been too cumbrous or too expensive; and those of a cheap and simple character have been lacking in the necessary scope and variety, not being adapted to swinging or somersault exercises. Many attempts have been made to construct one which would overcome these difficulties, and this we now claim to have accomplished in our PATENT HOME GYMNASIUM. It is based on the principles devised and taught by Ling, Schreber, and Dio Lewis, and is a combination of these systems brought into a small compass. While the first exercises are simple enough for children, the last are such as only can be accomplished by the most athletic. It is believed that this apparatus—being cheap, portable, and adapted to all—will be the means through which Gymnastics will become universal.

This apparatus is supported by two strong hooks in the ceiling, eighteen inches apart, and screwed into the joist five inches, leaving only the small hooks visible. It can also be used in a yard, by the erection of a framework such as is used for swings. The straps are of the strongest linen, handsomely colored, and by an ingenious device, the rings and stirrups can be instantly raised or lowered to any desired height. A space six or eight feet wide is ample for any of the exercises. The apparatus can also be converted into a Trapeze for the athlete, or a swing for the juvenile. Price of the complete Gymnasium, with four large sheets of illustrations (100 cuts), and Hand-book explaining how each is performed $10 00
The Trapeze adjustment, with thirty-two illustrations 3 50
The Swing adjustment 1 50

Sent by Express to any part of the United States or Canada, on receipt of price.

Kehoe's Improved Indian Clubs.—Used by the Principal Gymnasts in the United States. Weights, from six to fifty pounds each. The best in use.

6, 7 and 8 lbs. each, per pair . . $5 50 | 15 lbs. each, per pair . . . $10 00
10 lbs. "   "   "   . . 6 50 | 20 "   "   "   . . . 14 00
12 "   "   "   "   . . 7 00 | 25 "   "   "   . . . 16 00

SIZES FOR LADIES AND CHILDREN.

2 lbs. each, per pair . . . . $2 00 | 4 lbs. each, per pair . . . $3 50
3 "   "   "   . . . . 3 00 | 5 "   "   "   . . . 5 00

Dumb Bells, Rings, Wands, etc., for Light Gymnastics; Croquet—parlor and lawn.

Books on Physical Development.

Trall's Family Gymnasium. Illustrated $1 75
Dio Lewis's Light Gymnastics. Adapted to all . . 1 75
Physical Perfection; Or, How to be Beautiful . . . 1 75
Watson's Hand-Book of Calisthenics. Illustrated . . 2 25
Watson's Manual of Calisthenics. Illustrated. . . 1 25
Kehoe's Indian Club Exercise. (Illustrated Hand-Book) . 2 50
Taylor's Movement-Cure; Or, The Treatment of Disease . 1 75
Dio Lewis's Weak Lungs, and How to Make them Strong . 1 75
Wood's Physical Exercises. Illustrated. . . . 1 50

Supplied by SAMUEL R. WELLS, 389 Broadway, New York.

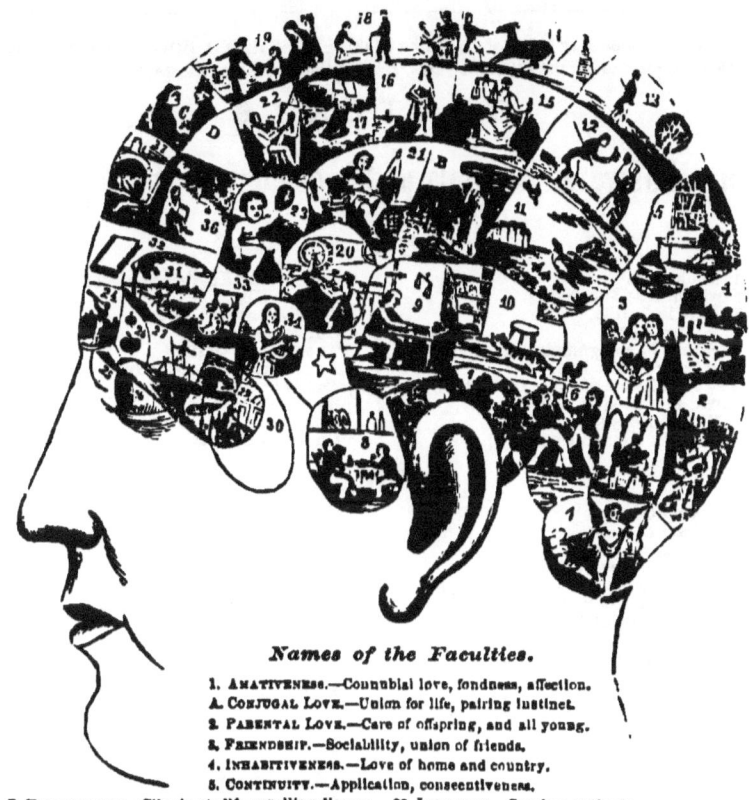

Names of the Faculties.

1. AMATIVENESS.—Connubial love, fondness, affection.
A. CONJUGAL LOVE.—Union for life, pairing instinct.
2. PARENTAL LOVE.—Care of offspring, and all young.
3. FRIENDSHIP.—Sociability, union of friends.
4. INHABITIVENESS.—Love of home and country.
5. CONTINUITY.—Application, consecutiveness.

E. VITATIVENESS.—Clinging to life, repelling disease.	22. IMITATION.—Copying, aptitude.
6. COMBATIVENESS.—Defense, resolution, courage.	23. MIRTH.—Fun, wit, ridicule, facetiousness.
7. DESTRUCTIVENESS.—Executiveness, severity.	24. INDIVIDUALITY.—Observation, desire to see.
8. ALIMENTIVENESS.—Appetite, relish, feeding, greed.	25. FORM.—Memory, shape, looks, persons.
9. ACQUISITIVENESS.—Frugality, saving, thrift.	26. SIZE.—Measurement of quantity, distance.
10. SECRETIVENESS.—Self-control, policy.	27. WEIGHT.—Control of motion, balancing.
11. CAUTIOUSNESS.—Guardedness, safety.	28. COLOR.—Discernment, and love of color.
12. APPROBATIVENESS.—Love of applause.	29. ORDER.—*Method*, system, going by *rule*.
13. SELF-ESTEEM.—Self-respect, dignity.	30. CALCULATION.—Mental arithmetic.
14. FIRMNESS.—Stability, perseverance.	31. LOCALITY.—Memory of place, position.
15. CONSCIENTIOUSNESS.—Sense of right.	32. EVENTUALITY.—Memory of facts, events.
16. HOPE.—Expectation, anticipation.	33. TIME.—Telling *when*, time of day, dates.
17. SPIRITUALITY.—Intuition, prescience.	34. TUNE.—Love of music, singing.
18. VENERATION.—Worship, adoration.	35. LANGUAGE.—*Expression* by words, acts.
19. BENEVOLENCE.—Sympathy, kindness.	36. CAUSALITY.—*Planning*, thinking.
20. CONSTRUCTIVENESS.—Ingenuity, invention.	37. COMPARISON.—Analysis, inferring.
21. IDEALITY.—*Taste*, love of beauty, poetry.	C. HUMAN NATURE.—Perception of character.
B. SUBLIMITY.—Love of the grand, vast.	D. SUAVITY.—*Pleasantness*, blandness.

EXPLANATION.—No. 1. Amativeness is represented by Cupid, with his bow and arrow. No. 3. Adhesiveness, by two sisters embracing. No. 6. Combativeness—perverted—by two boys contending. No. 9. Acquisitiveness, a miser counting his gold. No. 10. Secretiveness, by a cat watching for a mouse. B. Sublimity, Niagara Falls. 24. Individuality, a boy with a telescope. 31. Locality, by a traveler consulting a guide-board. 36. Causality, Newton studying the laws of gravity by the falling of an apple. 18. Veneration, devotion, and deference, respect, and prayer. 19. Benevolence, the Good Samaritan bestowing charity. No. 17. Spirituality, Moses, on Mount Sinai, receiving the tablets from Heaven on which were engraved the Ten Commandments. 16. Hope, the anchor, and a ship at sea. 15. Conscientiousness, Figure of Justice, with the scales in one hand and the sword in the other, and so forth. Each organ is represented by a symbol, which in some cases may show the appropriate, and in others the perverted action. The latter is shown in the case of the miser, the gluttons, and the fighting boys. It is used as a means of indicating both the location of the organs and to show their natural action as frequently exhibited in life.

[That the reader may judge of the value of this capital HAND BOOK, we append the Table of Contents for the different years, *from number one*, as follows:]

CONTENTS
OF
The Illustrated Annuals of Phrenology & Physiognomy,
FOR
1865

Introduction.
Physiognomy Illustrated.
Debate in Crania.
A Young Hero.
Fighting Physiognomies Illustrated.
The Color of the Eye.
The Five Races of Man Illustrated.
Great Men used to Weigh More.
A Word to Boys.
Lines on a Human Skull.
Palmer, the English Poisoner.
A Good Hint.
Self-Reliance—A Poem.
Our Museum.
The Bliss of Giving.
An Almanac for a Hundred Years.
The World to Come.
Signs of Character in the Eyes.
Where to Find a Wife.
General Information.

1866.

Andrew Johnson.
Abraham Lincoln.
Julius Cæsar.
Character in the Walk.
The Mother of Rev. John Wesley.
Character in the Eyes.
Practical Uses of Phrenology.
Stammering and Stuttering—A Cure.
Lieut.-Gen. Ulysses S. Grant.
The Red Man and the Black Man.
Heads of the Leading Clergy.
Heads of the Most Notorious Boxers.
Fate of the Twelve Apostles.
Two Qualities of Men.
Home Courtesies.
Cornelius Vanderbilt.
Language of the Eyes.
Phrenology and Physiology.
Brigham Young.
Richard Cobden.
Phrenology at Home.
Major-Gen. Wm. T. Sherman.
John Bright—With Portraits.

1867.

Names of the Faculties.
Hindoo Heads and Characters.
About Fat Folks and Lean Folks.
Immortality—Scientific Proofs.
Thos. Carlyle, the Author.
How to Study Phrenology.
The Jew—Racial Peculiarities.
Civilization and Beauty.
The Hottentot or Bushman.
Nursing Troubles.
A Bad Head—Antoine Probst.
Forming Societies—How to Proceed.
Matrimonial Mistakes.
Something About Handwriting.
How to Conduct Public Meetings.
Author of the " Old Arm Chair."
Rev. James Martineau, the Unitarian.
Dr. Pusey, the " High-Churchman."
Froude, the Historian.
Thiers, the French Statesman.
John Ruskin, the Art-Writer.
Rev. Charles Kingsley.
A Chartered Institution.
Significance of Shaking Hands.
Wanted—Competent Phrenologists.
Bashfulness — Diffidence — Timidity.
Cause and Cure.
Eminent American Clergymen.
The Spiritual and Physical.
Large Eyes.
Ira Aldridge, the Colored Tragedian.
Influence of Marriage on Morals.
The Bones of Milton.
New York Society Classified.
To-Day—A Poem.

1868.

A Brief Glossary of Phrenological Terms.
Advancement of Phrenology.
Circassia, and the Circassians.
Jealousy—Its Cause and Cure.
Temperament and Natural Languages.
Voices—What they Indicate.
The Two Rulers of Sweden.
Marriage of Cousins—Its Effects.
George Peabody, the Banker.
What Makes a Man?
Senator Wilson, American Statesman.
Bad Heads and Good Characters.
D'Israeli, the English Statesman.
Young Men.
Rev. Peter Cartwright, the Pioneer Preacher.
Victor Hugo, the Romancist.
Miss Braddon, the Sensational Novelist.
How to Become a Phrenologist.
Monsieur Tonson Come Again.
Mind Limited by Matter.
The Two Paths of Womanhood.
Cause of Ill Health.
Bismarck, the Prussian Premier.
To Phrenological Students.
General Business Matters.
New Books from our Press.
Phrenology and Its Uses.
Testimonials from Distinguished Men.

www.ingramcontent.com/pod-product-compliance
Lightning Source LLC
Chambersburg PA
CBHW031412230426
43668CB00007B/285